GENESIS

A Devotional Commentary

Books by

W. H. GRIFFITH THOMAS

GENESIS: A DEVOTIONAL COMMENTARY
THROUGH THE PENTATEUCH CHAPTER BY CHAPTER
OUTLINE STUDIES IN THE GOSPEL OF MATTHEW
OUTLINE STUDIES IN THE GOSPEL OF LUKE
OUTLINE STUDIES IN THE ACTS OF THE APOSTLES
ST. PAUL'S EPISTLE TO THE ROMANS:
A DEVOTIONAL COMMENTARY
HEBREWS: A DEVOTIONAL COMMENTARY
THE APOSTLE JOHN
THE APOSTLE PETER
THE HOLY SPIRIT OF GOD

GENESIS

A Devotional Commentary

By

W. H. Griffith Thomas, D.D.

WM. B. EERDMANS PUBLISHING CO.
Grand Rapids   Michigan

GENESIS

by W. H. GRIFFITH THOMAS, D.D.

ISBN 0-8028-1633-9

First printing, November 1953
Reprinted, February 1983

CONTENTS

CONTENTS — Continued 7

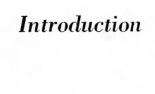

Introduction

INTRODUCTION

THE first book of the Bible is for several reasons one of the most interesting and fascinating portions of Scripture. Its place in the Canon, its relation to the rest of the Bible, and the varied and striking character of its contents combine to make it one of the most prominent in Holy Writ. It is with a real spiritual insight, therefore, that the people of God in all ages have fastened upon this book, and given it their earnest attention. It is also a testimony to its value and importance that criticism of various kinds and degrees has also concentrated itself upon this first book of the Bible. Its substance and claim are far too important to be overlooked.

In the Hebrew the title of the book is taken from its first words, *Bereshith* ("In the beginning"). The title of the Authorized Version, following the Septuagint, refers to the contents of the book. It is a book of "beginnings," and is true to this idea throughout.

I. *Its Purpose.*—As the purpose is not definitely stated in any part of the book, it is, of course, necessary to read it through in order to gain an idea of the author's meaning and object. It should therefore be read through at one time, so as to gain an adequate idea both of its contents and proportion. Indeed, the oftener it can be read right through at once with this aim the better, more particularly as we are accustomed to read it merely in chapters or sections. It is only as the book is carefully read and pondered that its purpose becomes manifest.

The first thing that strikes us is the summary and fragmentary character of the first eleven chapters, and the fullness of detail in the remainder of the book, the latter chapters (xii. to l.) dealing practically with only four men. Eleven chapters are thus concerned with the affairs of the human race, and thirty-nine chapters with one family. This, ordinarily, would seem very disproportionate, but in fact it is really an indication of the specific purpose of the book. The first eleven chapters are evidently introductory to the rest. Abraham is clearly the central figure of the book, chapters xii. 1 to xxv. 10 being devoted to him; and all that follows is seen to be closely connected with, and to arise out of, the record of his life. If then, we take our stand, as it were, at the beginning of chapter xii. and look backwards and forwards we can see (1) the descent of Abraham from Adam, and (2) the descendants of Abraham.

It must be evident from these simple facts that there was no intention of writing an universal history of man, but only of recording the development of the Divine will and purpose for and through Abraham. It is history written with a special purpose. The book might easily have begun with Abraham if the purpose had been to record the ordinary history of an ordinary people; yet inasmuch as Israel was not an ordinary people, but charged with God's purposes for the whole of mankind, it was necessary to show—at least in brief form—the connection between the progenitor of the human race and Abraham, in whom and in whose descendants the Divine purpose was to be realized.

The two main divisions, therefore, are chapters i. to xi. and chapters xii to l. The former section can be divided by the Flood, and the two parts referred respectively to Adam as the head of the original race, and to Noah as the head of the new race. Then follows the record of Abraham, the head of the family through which God's purposes for the race were to be fulfilled, and the story of his three great descendants—Isaac, Jacob, and Joseph. Before proceeding to a more detailed consideration of the book it is essential that these main outlines should be clearly in view.

II. *Its Plan.*—Taking up the book again for the purpose of fuller study, as we look at it more closely we become conscious of the recurrence of a phrase, "These are the generations," or "The book of the generations," and we observe that it occurs no fewer than ten times. Inasmuch as nine of these are without doubt superscriptions, and are therefore closely connected with what follows, it is a strong argument in favor of the view that the first of these occurrences is to be interpreted in the same way: "These are the generations of the heaven and the earth" (chap. ii. 4). It refers, not to what precedes, but to what follows. This view is clearly borne out by the meaning of the word translated "generations" (*Toledoth*), which comes from the Hebrew *Yalad* ("to beget"), and invariably refers to results, not causes; not to ancestry, but to descendants; not to origin, but to effects.

The book should therefore be analyzed as follows:—

1. Introduction.—The Creation. (Chap. i. 1 to ii. 3.)
2. The Generations of the Heaven and the Earth. (Chap. ii. 4 to iv. 26.)
3. The Generations of Adam. (Chap. v. 1 to vi. 8.)
4. The Generations of Noah. (chap. vi. 9 to ix. 29.)
5. The Generations of the Sons of Noah. (Chap. x. 1 to xi. 9.)
6. The Generations of Shem. (Chap. xi. 10-26.)
7. The Generations of Terah. (Chap. xi. 27 to xxv. 11.)
8. The Generations of Ishmael. (Chap. xxv. 12-18.)
9. The Generations of Isaac. (Chap. xxv. 19 to xxxv. 29.)
10. The Generations of Esau. (Chap. xxxvi. 1 to xxxvii. 1.)
11. The Generations of Jacob. (Chap. xxxvii. 2 to l. 26.)

All thorough study of the Book of Genesis in the light of its structure, purpose, and plan should proceed along these lines. The book is thus seen to be in great measure a compilation of family documents; the author, whoever he was and whenever he wrote, made use of pre-existing materials, as was the case in the composition of the Gospels (Luke i. 1-4), and welded together the whole into a striking and beautiful unity. The record is thereby shown to partake of a genealogical character, and this is due to the author's purpose of tracing fulfilments of God's purposes of redemption through the line of the chosen people. These genealogies are consequently an essential part of the book, and form a consecutive series from Adam to Jacob. Although, as it has been often pointed out, they are occasionally interrupted for the purpose of introducing collateral and connected facts, the thread is soon resumed and the main purpose never allowed to go out of sight.

We may therefore describe the present Book of Genesis as consisting of an introduction, and ten books representing ten sections or stages of history, each complete in itself. It is worth while noticing once again, that in the course of bringing forward these successive genealogies the plan is to deal with collateral branches first, before dwelling upon the main line of descent in regard to the purpose of redemption. Thus the genealogy of Cain comes before that of Seth, those of Ham and Canaan before Shem, that of Terah before Abraham, those of Ishmael and Esau before Isaac and Jacob. All the apparent deviations are strictly according to the idea of the book as a book of *beginnings*. As it has been well said, "Genesis is full of geneses."[1]

III. *Its Unity.*—It is generally admitted, even by men of very different schools, that our present Book of Genesis is a unity, however that unity has been brought about. For this reason it should be studied as a whole, and allowed to make its own definite and deep impression upon the reader. As Dr. Whitelaw (*Pulpit Commentary*, p. viii.) truly says, there is a chronological thread running through the entire book, and all its parts are so interdependent that if one were omitted it would create a gap, and entirely rob the book of its unity. There are few facts more certain than that of the literary unity of Genesis as it has come down to us, and no study of the book will arrive at right conclusions unless this fact is kept well in view.

IV. *Its Value.*—As the title clearly indicates, it is essentially and pre-eminently a book of origins; it deals with a number of characteristic "beginnings." It records the beginning of creation, of man, of woman, of the Sabbath, of marriage, of home, of childhood, of sin, of murder, of sacrifice, of grace, of trade, of agriculture, of city life, of races, of languages, and of the chosen people.

In the light of its title and evident purpose it is worthy of notice that there are in particular seven important "beginnings" recorded and dealt with in this book:—

1. The beginning of the material universe, or the Sphere of the Divine revelation of grace.

2. The beginning of the human race, or the Subject of the Divine revelation of grace.

---

[1] *Cf.* Green's *Unity of the Book of Genesis.*

3. The beginning of human sin, of the Cause of the Divine revelation of grace.

4. The beginning of divine redemption, or the Character of the Divine revelation of grace.

5. The beginning of the nations of the earth, or the Scope of the Divine revelation of grace.

6. The beginning of the Hebrew nation, or the Channel of the Divine revelation of grace.

7. The beginning of the life of faith and consecration, or the Outcome of the Divine revelation of grace.

The first four words form the keynote of the book, which is struck again and again throughout the record—"In the beginning God." It is essentially a book where God is prominent and predominant, notwithstanding human wilfulness, wandering, and wretchedness through sin.

God in Creation.—The outstanding impression derived from the story in chapter i. is that the universe is not self-originated, but is the result of the Creator's handiwork. "God saw," "God said," "God made," are the prominent teachings.

God in History.—In this book we have the dawn of history and the earliest years of the life and progress of the human race; and although the narrative of the first eleven chapters takes various literary forms, and is only brought before us in very summary fashion, there is no doubt of the essential historical character of the events underlying the record. And when we come to the fuller details of the patriarchal narratives we can readily appreciate the truth of Dr. Driver's *dictum* with reference to the parts of 2 Samuel: "The abundance and particularity of detail show that the narratives must date from a period very little later than that of the events related" (*Intro. O. T.*, p. 173). No student of history can afford to overlook the instructive and fascinating record contained in the first book of the Bible.

God in Providence.—No book in the world shows so clearly the truth that "There's a Divinity that shapes our ends, rough hew them how we will." From the time that man was created, God's providence is seen watching over him, warning him, checking him, overruling his mistakes, and, in spite of his wilfulness, carrying out the Divine purpose. In the record of the ages before the Flood and of the time of the Deluge, in the stories of Abraham, Isaac, Jacob, and Joseph, we see step by step the working of that "never-failing providence that ordereth all things in heaven and earth."

God in Redemption.—This is the most important, even though it is not the most prominent, feature on the surface of the book. Genesis has been well summed up in three words—generation, degeneration, regeneration. The great promise of redemption recorded in chapter iii. is taken up and gradually prepared for through a long line from Seth through Noah, Abraham, Isaac, and Jacob. In this connection, too, we must not overlook the typological value of Genesis, for it is a book of type as well as of prophecy, of picture as well as of promise. From the sacrifice of Abel straight onward to the sacrifice of Isaac, the vision of Jacob at Bethel, and the story of Joseph, we have picture after picture of redemption, which find their full meaning, vividness, and glory, in the New Testament revelation, until at length in Jacob's benediction we have a striking reference to the primeval fact of sin and the primeval promise of salvation (chap. xlix. 17, 18). The red thread of redemption binds every chapter together, and gives the book one of its essential marks of unity.

God in Human Life.—Not the least interesting and valuable feature of this most remarkable book is its record of human life in relation to God. As we read the stories from Adam to Joseph, we see various aspects of the Divine revelation in regard to personal life, and the various attitudes of human response to that revelation. The book is of preeminent value, because it has to do with the essential and abiding elements of God's relation to man, and man's relation to God. As we study point after point in individual history and character, we see abundant proofs of spiritual guidance, warning, encouragement, and cheer, and we become more and more convinced of the truth of the Apostolic word, that "Whatsoever things were written aforetime were written for our learning."

In the foregoing remarks critical questions have been deliberately avoided, in order to concentrate attention on the importance of a study of the book itself. It is to be feared that there is often a good deal of knowledge *about* Genesis without too much knowledge of the book itself. If only we would allow it to make its own impression by direct and prolonged study, apart from all authorities, it would go far to instruct us as to its own real character. Even so extreme a critic as Kuenen bears witness to the value of direct Bible study when he says:—

> "The Bible is in every one's hand. The critic has no other Bible than the public. He does not profess to have any other documents inaccessible to the laity, nor does he profess to see anything in the Bible that the ordinary reader cannot see. It is true that here and there he improves the common translation, but this is the exception, and not the rule."

And that great scholar, Dr. M'Caul, gives a very valuable reminder to all Bible readers in the following words:—

> "No reader of the Authorized Version ought to allow himself to be mystified or silenced by an appeal to foreign critics, much less to be disturbed in his faith, as if he could not apprehend the general teaching of the Bible without profound knowledge of the Semitic dialects and the latest results of German criticism."

We cannot do better than close with a striking testimony to the value of Genesis from a scholar whose books on the Old Testament have proved so valuable and convincing during recent years, Professor James Robertson, of Glasgow:—

> "It may be a matter of criticism to discover the joinings of the narratives, and to trace the literary process by which the book took its present shape; but it is of far deeper interest to note the existence of a pure light in the midst of the world's darkness. It is our familiarity with it that makes us overlook the significance of the early testimony of the Hebrew people to the truth of the one God. But when we reflect that, at a time when the great nations of antiquity were stumbling in the dark on this subject, or groping their way towards it, the Hebrew race had it as their oldest tradition, we cannot but acknowledge that they received it from God Himself. And of far higher importance it is to our faith than the anticipation of the results of modern science would have been, to be assured that from hoary antiquity the God and Father of our Lord Jesus Christ has been guiding our race and preparing it for the fulness of the times."

For the purpose of general study as distinct from critical questions two works may be mentioned: *How to Read the Bible*, vols.

i. and ii., by the Rev. J. Urquhart, and *Genesis,* in the *Pulpit Commentary,* by Dr. Whitelaw. Critical questions can be most conveniently studied in the following works: (1) From the standpoint of modern criticism, in Dr. Driver's *Commentary.* (2) From the conservative side, in Green's *Unity of the Book of Genesis,* Dr. Redpath's *Modern Criticism and Genesis* (a criticism of Dr. Driver), and Dr. Orr's *Problem of the Old Testament* (see Index S. V. Genesis).

II

THE CREATION

GEN. *i.*

In the beginning God created the heaven and the earth.

And the earth was without form, and void; and darkness *was* upon the face of the deep: and the Spirit of God moved upon the face of the waters.

And God said, Let there be light: and there was light.

And God saw the light, that *it was* good; and God divided the light from the darkness.

And God called the light Day, and the darkness he called Night. And the evening and the morning were the first day.

And God said, Let there be a firmament in the midst of the waters, and let it divide the waters from the waters.

And God made the firmament, and divided the waters which *were* under the firmament, from the waters which *were* above the firmament: and it was so.

And God called the firmament Heaven. And the evening and the morning were the second day.

And God said, Let the waters under the heaven be gathered together unto one place, and let the dry *land* appear: and it was so.

And God called the dry *land* Earth; and the gathering together of the waters called He Seas: and God saw that *it was* good.

And God said, Let the earth bring forth grass, the herb yielding seed, *and* the fruit-tree yielding fruit after his kind, whose seed *is* in itself, upon the earth: and it was so.

And the earth brought forth grass, *and* herb yielding seed after his kind, and the tree yielding fruit, whose seed *was* in itself, after his kind: and God saw that *it was* good.

And the evening and the morning were the third day.

And God said, Let there be lights in the firmament of the heaven, to divide the day from the night; and let them be for signs, and for seasons, and for days, and years.

And let them be for lights in the firmament of the heaven, to give light upon the earth: and it was so.

And God made two great lights; the greater light to rule the day, and the lesser light to rule the night: *He made* the stars also.

And God set them in the firmament of the heaven, to give light upon the earth.

And to rule over the day and over the night, and to divide the light from the darkness: and God saw that *it was* good.

And the evening and the morning were the fourth day.

And God said, Let the waters bring forth abundantly the moving creature that hath life, and fowl *that* may fly above the earth in the open firmament of heaven.

And God created great whales, and every living creature that moveth, which the waters brought forth abundantly, after their kind, and every winged fowl after his kind: and God saw that *it was* good.

And God blessed them, saying, Be fruitful, and multiply, and fill the waters in the seas, and let fowl multiply in the earth.

And the evening and the morning were the fifth day.

And God said, Let the earth bring forth the living creature after his kind, cattle, and creeping thing, and beast of the earth after his kind: and it was so.

And God made the beast of the earth after his kind, and cattle after their kind, and every thing that creepeth upon the earth after his kind: and God saw that *it was* good.

And God said, Let us make man in our image, after our likeness; and let them have dominion over the fish of the sea, and over the fowl of the air, and over the cattle, and over all the earth, and over every creeping thing that creepeth upon the earth.

So God created man in his *own* image, in the image of God created He him: male and female created He them.

And God blessed them, and God said unto them, Be fruitful, and multiply, and replenish the earth, and subdue it; and have dominion over the fish of the sea, and over the fowl of the air, and over every living thing that moveth upon the earth.

And God said, Behold, I have given you every herb bearing seed, which *is* upon the face of all the earth, and every tree, in the which *is* the fruit of a tree yielding seed; to you it shall be for meat.

And to every beast of the earth, and to every fowl of the air, and to every thing that creepeth upon the earth, wherein *there is* life, *I have given* every green herb for meat: and it was so.

And God saw every thing that He had made, and, behold, *it was* very good. And the evening and the morning were the sixth day.

OF all the chapters of this remarkable book the first has probably given rise to more thought, discussion, and controversy than any other. Nor is this surprising, remembering its contents and the place it occupies at the beginning of the Book of God. And assuredly it will repay the fullest and minutest attention, study, and meditation. In order to arrive at a right conclusion as to its meaning and object, it will be necessary to bring into view several considerations.

I. *What is its Character?*—The first essential is that we try to discover what the chapter really is.

Is it history? This were obviously impossible, since no one was present to observe and record for posterity the events here stated. The contents clearly refer to prehistoric events and time.

Is it science? This at any rate can hardly be the primary purpose of the writer, for the Bible is a book of religion, and this is its introductory chapter. Besides, science is continuous and incomplete, and we are learning more and more of its secrets every day. In any case this chapter could only be scientific in the broadest and most summary meaning of the term.

Is it myth? If by this is meant that which is inaccurate, untrustworthy, legendary, and, in modern phraseology, "mythical," we naturally ask whether such inaccuracy and untrustworthiness are likely to be found in a book of religion. But if by myth is meant a form of picturesque teaching suited to the childhood of the world, it may be said that even if it be a myth in *form*, its underlying teaching and details must be true to *fact*. Even parabolic teaching presupposes facts which correspond to the symbol used.

When we compare other cosmogonies, such as the Babylonian, we notice at once some remarkable agreements and some equally remarkable contrasts. All cosmogonies, for instance, have traces of a primeval chaos, yet their moral atmosphere is entirely different from that of Genesis, and they have nothing corresponding to the great statement of verse 1: "In the beginning God created the heaven and the earth." Moreover, the Babylonian cosmogony is, as is well known, religiously impure, with materialistic and polytheistic elements.

Is it invention? By this is meant, Is it the work of man's imagination, the record of what some early writer thought *must* have happened or did happen? If so, we naturally ask why it appears in a book purporting to be the Word of God.

Is it revelation? That is, is it to be regarded as an integral part of the Book which has come down to us as (in whatever sense) the inspired Scriptures of God? The precise *method* of revelation we know not, and it does not concern us to know; but the *fact* of revelation, and the place of this chapter in the book and in the Bible generally, seems to compel the inquiry, Is it invention or revelation?

Is it in any sense trustworthy in what it says? Can we use it in confidence in reading and teaching? Its place in Scripture must be accounted for as also its position in a book whose characteristic is truth, and whose purpose is to reveal the God of truth.

There are two usual explanations of the points of contact between the Hebrew and Babylonian cosmogonies. (1) Some urge that Genesis is to be traced from Babylonia, but was afterwards purified, the Hebrew writer using the best of sources available, and making them the vehicle of religious teaching. Apart from the likelihood or unlikelihood of any direct borrowing from so impure a source, we may fairly inquire whether this view is adequate in the light of any true theory of Divine inspiration. And even though we limit the idea of inspiration to the arrangement and use of materials, to what has been called the "inspiration of selection," the prior question still remains as to the source of those materials, and also their reliableness and accuracy. Surely we need some guarantee at this initial point. (2) Others say that the Babylonian cosmogony is the corrupt version of which Genesis is the pure record received from primal revelation. Is not this view much more likely to be true, and also much more in keeping with the idea of a Divine inspiration? When we remember the longevity of the human race up to the time of Abraham, there is nothing insuperably difficult in the view that this pure cosmogony may have been preserved among the antediluvians, and brought from Mesopotamia by Abraham without any corruption. At any rate, we have to account for the fact that this pure cosmogony is found among the Hebrews, while an impure cosmogony is found in Babylonia. Surely Divine inspiration is the only adequate solution of the problem. If the substance of this chapter is not revelation it must be, in whatever sense, invention or fiction; and in the latter case it really matters not whence it came or by what process it has arrived at its present state. In view, therefore, of the uniqueness of the Hebrew race, the place of this chapter in the Bible, and the general idea of Divine inspiration associated with the Old Testament, it seems much easier and truer to believe that we have in this chapter the record of a primeval revelation.

The following remarks from Lange's *Commentary on Genesis* (p. 147) seem to sum up the truth on this subject:—

"Holiness, sublimity, truthfulness—these are the impressions left upon the mind of the thoughtful reader of the First of Genesis. There is meant by this its subjective truthfulness. It is no invention. The one who first wrote it down, or first spoke it to human ears, had a perfect conscious conviction of the presence to his mind of the scenes so vividly described— whether given to him in vision or otherwise—and a firm belief in a great objective reality represented by them. It is equally evident, too, that it is the offspring of one conceiving mind. It never grew like a myth or legend. It is one total conception, perfect and consistent in all its parts. It bears no evidence of being a story artificially made to represent an idea, or a system of ideas. There is, in truth, nothing ideal about it. It presents on its very face the serious impression of *fact* believed, and given forth as thus believed, however the original representation may have been made to the first human soul that received it. Myths and legends are the products of time; they have a growth; we can, in general, tell how and whence they came, and after what manner they have received their mythical form. Thus other ancient cosmogonies, though bearing evidence of derivation from the one in Genesis, have had their successive accretions and deposits of physical, legendary, and mythological strata. This stands alone in the world, like the primeval granite of the Himalaya among the later geological formations. It has nothing national about it. It is no more Jewish than it is Assyrian, Chaldaean, Indian, Persian, or Egyptian. It is found among the preserved Jewish writings, but there is nothing, except its pure monotheistic aspect, which would assign it to that people rather than to any other. If the Jews derived it from others, as is often affirmed, then is it something very wonderful, something utterly the reverse of the usual process, that they should have so stripped it of all national or sect features, and given it such a sublime aspect of universalism, so transcending, apparently, all local or partial history."

II. *What is its Purpose?*—We must never forget that a chapter like this, as indeed every chapter of the Bible, must be judged primarily from the standpoint of those for whom it was originally intended. What did the first readers understand by it? Still more, what were they intended to understand by it? It must have had an intelligible message for them, however imperfectly and incompletely they grasped it. If, therefore, this chapter had been written in scientific language it would have been almost entirely unintelligible until the nineteenth century of our present era. Indeed, we may go very much further and say that many of the scientific books in our own language written a century ago are not only superseded, but practically unintelligible in the light of modern research. We are, therefore, justified in regarding this chapter as giving a simple, popular account of creation from the religious standpoint, and intended to be understood by people who lived in the time of the world's childhood. Its elementary character and religious purpose are the twofold key to its true meaning, and if this is continually borne in mind it will not be difficult to see its continued value up to the present day. The great fundamental yet elementary principles connected with the creation need to be taught to succeeding generations of people of various ages and capacities, and it is one of the most remarkable features in the experience of Christian teaching that this chapter is found to be adapted to intellectual and moral childhood in all ages and countries, and at the same time not inappropriate to mature minds and fuller knowledge.

III. *What is its Plan?*—There are those who think that verse 1 refers to the original creation, and that then between verses 1 and 2 room is left for the vast geological ages with their catastrophes which are thought to be described by the phrase "the earth was without form and void." This is urged more particularly because we read in Is. xlx. 18 that God did not create "without form" (same word in Hebrew). According to this view, verse 2 to the end of the chapter gives the story of the earth being fashioned for man's life and habitation just prior to the historic period. This view, though not generally accepted, is interesting and suggestive, and has not a little to recommend it, even though it does not solve every problem.

Taking the chapter, however, just as it stands, without any such break, we read it through, and are at once impressed with two things: (1) There is only one species mentioned in the entire chapter, "And God created great whales" (ver. 21). Everything else is generic. Why this exceptional reference? Why are these "water monsters" singled out in this way? Is it possible that we have here a hint of the writer's purpose? Was he striking at the root of some ancient worship of sacred animals? Is it impossible that if the materials for the composition of Genesis were associated with Egypt this has reference to the worship of some sacred animal like the crocodile? (See *Miracles*, by Dr. S. Cox.) (2) Then in verse 16 special reference is made to the creation of the sun and moon. Is it possible that we have here another blow to a prevalent form of Eastern worship of the heavenly bodies? These two hints at any rate possibly suggest the religious purpose of the writer.

It is noteworthy that in the Hebrew of verse 2 the adjectives "formless" and "empty" seem to be the key to the literary structure of the chapter. The record of the first three days refers to the heaven and earth receiving their "form," and the record of the last three days to the filling-up of their "emptiness." An outline will show this clearly:—

"FORMLESS"			"EMPTY"	
First Day.	Light.		Fourth Day.	Lights.
Second Day.	Air. Water.		Fifth Day.	Fowls. Fish.
Third Day.	Land. Plants.		Sixth Day.	Animals. Man.

Thus, the first and fourth days correspond, the second and fifth, and the third and sixth. First comes "form," and then "fulness." The literary structure of the chapter is clear, and is one of many proofs of Hebrew parallelism and love of parallelistic structure.

Above all, the keynote of the chapter is "In the beginning God." The word "God" occurs no fewer than thirty-two times; "God created" four times; "God said" eight times; "God saw" seven times; "God made" three times; "It was so" (God's purpose) six times. So also we find "God called," "God set," "God blessed," "God divided."

Are we not right, then, in thinking that this chapter was intended as an account of creation from the religious point of view, and written for the instruction of mankind in all ages?

IV. *What is its Relation to Science?*—It is inevitable that this question should be asked, since on the assumption that religion and science both come from God there should be at least some general agreement or points of contact between them. At the same time the truest method of comparison is not between this chapter and the results of modern science, but rather between this chapter and all other ancient cosmogonies. It is when Genesis is compared with such other ancient accounts of creation that its immeasurable superiority is seen (Waggett, *The Scientific Temper in Religion*, pp. 160 ff). Nevertheless, in view of natural questionings, and bearing in mind the evident purpose of the chapter as an account of creation from the religious standpoint, the following inquiries with reference to its relation to science may rightly be made.

Does the chapter contain any scientific error? On the authority of the greatest masters of geological and biological science we may say that this has not yet been proved. There was a time when the statement of the creation of light before the sun was regarded as a scientific inaccuracy, but this charge has long been dropped, for modern science has shown that light existed before and independent of our present sun. In entire keeping with this the Hebrew distinguishes between light (ver. 3) and luminaries, or light-bearers (ver. 15).

Is the chapter written in sufficiently elastic and pliant language to admit of the inclusion of continuous scientific discoveries? It must be obvious to every thoughtful reader that this early chapter could not be expected to be in exact agreement with the latest details of scientific research, since science is continually changing and is ever incomplete. If it had been written in strict scientific language it would, of course, have been unintelligible for centuries. As the *Speaker's Commentary* rightly says:—

> "If the wisest geologist of our days could show that there was an exact agreement between geology and the Bible, it would rather disprove than prove its truth. For, as geology is a growing science, it would prove the agreement of the Bible with that which is receiving daily additions, and is constantly undergoing modification: and ten years hence the two would be at hopeless variance."

Yet there are indications that the very language of Genesis is pliant enough to allow of not a little scientific discovery being inserted. Thus there are two words used for creation. One, *Bara*, is used three times only in the chapter—(1) at the beginning (ver. 1); (2) at the commencement of life (ver. 21); (3) at the creation of man (ver. 27). *"Bara* is thus reserved for marking the first introduction of each of the three great spheres of creation—the world of matter, the world of life, and the spiritual world represented by man" (Green). The other word, *Asah,* is found throughout the rest of the chapter, and is used of God making or moulding from already created materials. Surely in this we have at least a hint of the modern scientific ideas of primal creation and mediate creation.

In a fascinating book, *The Conflict of Truth* (by Mr. F. H. Capron), the author refers to the five factors which Mr. Herbert Spencer regards as "the most general forms into which the manifestations of the Unknowable are re-divisible." These forms are said to be: Space, time, matter, motion, force. Mr. Capron calls attention to the suggestive and even remarkable analogy between these forms and the early verses of Genesis i.

(*a*) Time="In the beginning."

(*b*) Space="The heavens."

(*c*) Matter="The earth."

(*d*) Force="The Spirit of God."

(*e*) Motion="Moved."

Even though we may think it too ingenious to be true, there is ample proof, apart from this, to lead to the conclusion that there is—at any rate, up to the present—nothing in the chapter which conflicts with any assured results of science.

Has the chapter any anticipations of science as revealed by modern research? We may reply by calling attention to the fact that there is the same general order of events. The steps of the creation of vegetation, reptiles, mammals, and man are essentially true to modern science. Professor Romanes admitted that—

> "The order in which the flora and fauna are said by the Mosaic account to have appeared upon the earth corresponds with that which the theory of evolution requires and the evidence of geology proves" (quoted in M'Cosh, *The Religious Aspect of Evolution,* p. 99).

And Sir William Dawson, whose scientific eminence and authority no one can question, states still more definitely that—

> "The *order* of that vision of the creative work with which the Bible begins its history is so closely in harmony with the results worked out by

geological investigations that the correspondences have excited marked
attention, and have been justly regarded as establishing the common
authorship of nature and revelation."

Has the chapter any indications of development and progress
answering to the great modern theory of evolution? A very superficial reading of the chapter shows that development, progress, and
change are among its leading ideas. The term "day" is regarded
by some high authorities as expressive of the ages or epochs of
science. They urge that the term "day" does not, and was not
intended to mean a period of twenty-four hours, since it is applied
to the first three days before the sun and moon—our present means
of measurement—are introduced into the narrative. And, further,
that in chapter ii. 4 the term "day" is used for the whole period of
creation. There are certainly many places in Scripture where the
word "day" refers to other periods than that of the rotation of the
earth.[1]

Has the chapter any points of contact with modern biological and
anthropological teaching about man's nature? The answer is plain.
On the one hand the chapter teaches clearly an essential unity of
man with animate and inanimate nature, and at the same time it
teaches with equal clearness man's separateness from nature and his
transcendence in view of his creation in the image of God. Thus
modern science and ancient Genesis are at one as to the complexity
of man's nature, and also as to its unity at once with earth and
heaven.

Reviewing the relations of this chapter to modern science, we
again call attention to the definitely religious aim and object of
Genesis, and may say that while the chapter is scientifically incom-

---

[1] Another view which has much to recommend it is that "in the six days
God *pronounced* all the laws upon which the production of phenomena depends," that those laws thus pronounced were "the only operative agencies
of production," and that nothing remained to be *done* but to "allow the laws
to take effect and bring into existence the various phenomena which they
have produced and are still producing today." On this interpretation an
interval is to be understood between "God said" and "it was so," an interval
as to which the Bible is silent, but which may have extended for ages. (For a
full statement of this view see Capron. *Conflict of Truth*, chap. xi. and xii.,
especially p. 193.)

plete it is not scientifically inaccurate. On the other hand, religiously, it is both accurate and complete.

Nor can we fail to ask how this correspondence between Genesis and science is to be explained. How are we to account for such anticipations of modern science in this early book? Even Haeckel admits that

> "two great and fundamental ideas, common also to the non-miraculous, meet us in the Mosaic hypothesis of creation with surprising clearness and simplicity—the idea of separation or differentiation and the idea of progressive development or perfecting . . . . In this theory there lies hidden the ruling idea of a progressive development and differentiation of the originally simple matter. We can therefore bestow our just and sincere admiration of the Jewish law-giver's grand insight into nature" (quoted by M'Cosh, *The Religious Aspect of Evolution*, pp. 99, 100).

May we not rightly see in this record a clear proof of Divine inspiration? There is surely nothing in all these correspondences which could have come into the ken of Moses by purely natural means.

To quote Sir William Dawson again:—

> "All these coincidences cannot be accidental. They are the more remarkable when we consider the primitive and child-like character of the notices in Genesis, making no scientific pretensions, and introducing what they tell us of primitive man merely to explain and illustrate the highest moral and religious teachings. Truth and divinity are stamped on every line of the early chapters of Genesis, alike in their archaic simplicity, and in that accuracy as to facts which enables them not only to stand unharmed amid the discoveries of modern science, but to display new beauties as we are able more and more fully to compare them with the records stored up from old in the recesses of the earth. Those who base their hopes for the future on the glorious revelations of the Bible need not be ashamed of its story of the past."

V. *What is its Religious Teaching?* The primary and fundamental truth of this chapter is, "In the beginning God created." It teaches that the world is not self-originated, and thereby declares, what science compels us to demand, the fact of a First Cause. The nebular hypothesis of Laplace is the best scientific account of the solar system, and yet it is obvious that this hypothesis only accounts for the second verse of Genesis i., not the first. Laplace's theory presupposes a central sun and an atmospheric envelope, but Genesis

i. 1 goes behind this nebular hypothesis and gives the explanation
of its revolution in the creative *fiat* of God. This simple thought of
creation is very familiar to us today, but, as is well known, it was
not so evident to all the thinkers and all the nations of the old
world. Some of the earliest peoples had no idea of absolute creation, and most assuredly it never was so clear and unmistakable in
any part of the world as it was among the Hebrews. In view of the
fact that "the notion of creation is one which had not dawned on
the ancient Greek mind," and was "never securely attained in the
thought of Greece," we can perhaps realize a little of the immense
benefit the world has derived from this chapter (Waggett, *The
Scientific Temper in Religion*, pp. 165 f.).

The chapter also teaches us that man is the crown and culmination of creation, that he is the earthly end for which creation has
been made and developed, and that in his life there is the promise
and potency of God-likeness. Nothing could be clearer than the
teaching of this chapter as to the spiritual nature of man and the
spiritual purpose for which he was made. Again to quote Sir
William Dawson:—

> "In man there are other and higher powers, determining his conscious
> personality, his formation of general principles, his rational and moral
> volitions and self-restraints. These are manifestations of a higher spiritual
> nature, which constitute in man the image and shadow of God."

The chapter also declares that matter is not eternal; it teaches
clearly that absolute dualism, that refuge of many ancient Eastern
thinkers, is entirely impossible and foreign to the whole idea of
true religion.

Not least significant is the simple but conclusive way in which
this chapter deals with some of the most characteristic errors of
ancient and modern thought. In opposition to Atheism it proclaims
God; in opposition to Polytheism it emphasizes one God; in opposition to Pantheism it declares the separateness of God and the
world; in opposition to Materialism it reveals the spirituality of
God and man.

And thus we find ourselves coming back again and again to the
first verse, "In the beginning God," and we rest both mind and

heart on the familiar words. "Through faith we understand that the worlds were framed by the Word of God." Let us mark this expression with great care. "Through faith we understand." Faith is the great secret of true perception. Never do we find any opposition in Holy Scripture between faith and understanding, between faith and reason, but only between faith and sight. Faith is the greatest perceptive power in the world. Through faith we *see*. And as we contemplate God's creation in the light of this early chapter as well as in the later chapters of modern science, we come back to the old word which declares that "Thou hast created all things, and for Thy pleasure they are and were created" (Rev. iv. 11).

In the study of this chapter with special reference to modern science the following authorities will be found of service: M'Cosh, *The Religious Aspect of Evolution; The Scientific Temper in Religion* (chapter vii.), by Waggett; *The Conflict of Truth,* by F. H. Capron; *The Impregnable Rock of Holy Scripture,* by W. E. Gladstone; article by Sir J. William Dawson, *Expositor,* third series, vol. iii. p. 284.

III

THE FOUNDATIONS OF HUMAN LIFE

Gen. ii.

Thus the heavens and the earth were finished, and all the host of them.

And on the seventh day God ended His work which He had made; and He rested on the seventh day from all His work which He had made.

And God blessed the seventh day, and sanctified it; because that in it He had rested from all His work which God created and made.

These *are* the generations of the heavens and of the earth when they were created, in the day that the Lord God made the earth and the heavens.

And every plant of the field before it was in the earth, and every herb of the field before it grew: for the Lord God had not caused it to rain upon the earth, and *there was* not a man to till the ground.

But there went up a mist from the earth, and watered the whole face of the ground.

And the Lord God formed man *of* the dust of the ground, and breathed into his nostrils the breath of life; and man became a living soul.

And the Lord God planted a garden eastward in Eden; and there He put the man whom He had formed.

And out of the ground made the Lord God to grow every tree that is pleasant to the sight, and good for food; the tree of life also in the midst of the garden, and the tree of knowledge of good and evil.

And a river went out of Eden to water the garden: and from thence it was parted, and became into four heads.

The name of the first *is* Pison; that *is* it which compasseth the whole land of Havilah, where *there is* gold.

And the gold of that land *is* good: there *is* bdellium and the onyx stone.

And the name of the second river *is* Gihon: the same *is* it that compasseth the whole land of Ethiopia.

And the name of the third river *is* Hiddekel: that *is* it which goeth toward the east of Assyria. And the fourth river *is* Euphrates.

And the Lord God took the man, and put him into the garden of Eden to dress it, and to keep it.

And the Lord God commanded the man, saying, Of every tree of the garden thou mayest freely eat;

But of the tree of the knowledge of good and evil, thou shalt not eat of it: for in the day that thou eatest thereof thou shalt surely die.

And the Lord God said, *It is* not good that the man should be alone; I will make him an help meet for him.

And out of the ground the Lord God formed every beast of the field, and every fowl of the air, and brought *them* unto Adam, to see what he would call them: and whatsoever Adam called every living creature, that *was* the name thereof.

And Adam gave names to all cattle, and to the fowl of the air, and to every beast of the field: but for Adam there was not found an help meet for him.

And the Lord God caused a deep sleep to fall upon Adam, and he slept: and He took one of his ribs, and closed up the flesh instead thereof.

And the rib, which the Lord God had taken from man, made He a woman, and brought her unto the man.

And Adam said, This *is* now bone of my bones, and flesh of my flesh: she shall be called Woman, because she was taken out of Man.

Therefore shall a man leave his father and his mother, and shall cleave unto his wife; and they shall be one flesh.

And they were both naked, the man and his wife, and were not ashamed.

THE second chapter of Genesis is the natural sequel of the first, and nowhere is the purpose of the book more clearly seen. After the consideration of creation as a whole our attention is concentrated on man—his formation, his relation to God, and his earthly life.

The introductory purpose of chapter i. is thus evident, and we now proceed to that which is the predominant purpose of the book —the record of human life in relation to God and religion. The thought of creation is now no longer dominant. In the first chapter man comes at the end as the crown of creation; here he comes at the commencement as the starting-point of human history.

At the same time this chapter is preparatory to the next, for it deals with some of the fundamental facts and experiences of human life which find their expression and development along the lines recorded in later chapters. We are again reminded that Genesis is a book of beginnings, for this chapter is essentially a chapter of "geneses," and is best looked at from this point of view, since it deals with some of the primary essentials of human life on earth. It is hardly too much to say that there is a great law connected with the first mention of anything in Scripture which is afterwards treated or recorded in other parts. It will frequently, if not always, be found that "the very first words on any subject on which the Holy Spirit is going to treat are the keystone of the whole matter"

(B. W. Newton. Quoted in *The Bible and Spiritual Criticism*, by Dr. Pierson, p. 41). There are several things mentioned for the first time in this chapter, and they deserve the closest possible attention.

I. *The Sabbath for Man* (vers. 1-3).—Strictly, this section should be placed in close connection with chapter i. as the crowning point of the record of the days of creation. As the Sabbath is mentioned here for the first time we are justified in inquiring as to its fundamental purpose and principles.

The Sabbath should first be considered in its primary meaning. In the light of God's creative work the fundamental and primary idea of the Sabbath is twofold: cessation from work, and satisfaction after work.

The Sabbath should then be noticed as a divine institution. The first use of "sanctify" is here, and we are enabled to see that its root idea is "separation" or "consecration." God separated — *i.e.* set apart — the Sabbath to be consecrated to a special purpose.

The Sabbath should be emphasized as of permanent obligation. The institution of the Sabbath is evidently grounded in creation, and is therefore pre-Mosaic, and not at all to be limited to the Jews. It is noteworthy that the fourth Commandment calls attention to the Sabbath as an already existing fact ("Remember the Sabbath day." Exod. xx. 8). There are many indications, both in Genesis and in Babylonian records, that the Sabbath was part of the primeval revelation which received fresh sanction under Moses. Only in his way can the universality of the tradition and the precise wording of the fourth Commandment be explained.

The Sabbath should be carefully understood as to its essential elements. God's rest after creation is put forth as the reason and model of man's weekly rest. It involves the special consecration to God of a portion of our time. While it affords physical rest and recreation of energies, it also calls for the worship of God. Nor are we to lay any stress on the day, since no one can now say for certain that any particular day of the week is, literally, the seventh day from the close of creation. It is the institution, not the day, that must be emphasized. Whether we think of the physical, or the mental, or the spiritual results of the observance of the Sabbath Day, we are face to face with one of the fundamental facts of human life. The law of God and the needs of man combine to make the observance of the Sabbath an absolute necessity.

II. *The Formation of Man* (vers. 4-7).—At this point a new section of Genesis commences extending to chapter iv. 26, and described as "these are the generations of the heavens and of the earth." This phrase, as we have already noticed, is always at the beginning of a section, and has a prospective view, not a retrospective. It is a superscription, not a subscription, and deals with some new unfolding of the record. It suitably describes the section that follows, for it describes the offspring or "generations" of the heavens and of the earth in the person of man. Man is at once the offspring of earth and heaven. It would be impossible to regard this phrase as suited either to the end of chapter i. or as introductory to it, since that chapter deals with the heavens and the earth themselves, not with their "generations" or offspring.

It is sometimes urged that this section introduces a new and second account of creation, but this is only true in the sense that we have here a more circumstantial account of what is given in summary form in chapter i. The differences are not contradictory, but complementary, and are explained by the different standpoint. The second account presupposes the first in several particulars. Thus in chapter i. 27, we have both male and female referred to as created (*cf.* chap. v. 1, 2), which prepares the way for the detailed statement of chapter ii. So also the "herb" of chapter iii. 18 implies chapter i. 29. Chapter ii. says nothing as to the relative priority of man or plants, and only refers to the trees of Eden (vers. 8, 9). Plants and man are necessarily associated here in connection with husbandry and tillage, and the association is one of thought, not of chronology. Man could hardly have been created before there was a home and provision for him (Green, *Unity of the Book of Genesis, in loc.*).

The change in the Divine Name ("Lord God" instead of "God") is also very noteworthy. "Elohim" is the God of Creation, with special reference to His power and might. "Jehovah" is the God of Revelation and Redemption, with special reference to human life and the Divine covenant. The combination of the two names ("Lord God" "Jehovah Elohim") shows the association of the God of Revelation with the God of Creation, and the discrimination of the usage of these two Divine Names in the whole section (chaps. ii. 4, iv. 26) is very striking and suggestive. So far from this usage being a proof of different documents, there are, on the contrary, clear indications that they are used with precision and spiritual meaning.

These verses (4-7) tell us of the special preparation made for man's life, and they describe the appearance of the earth at the time of man's formation.

The terms descriptive of man's physical creation need careful attention. The word "formed" is the Hebrew *Asah*, not *Bara*, and refers to molding or fashioning out of already existing materials. As these existing materials are described as "the dust of the ground," we see at once how true to scientific fact the statement is in man's point of contact with material creation. If, therefore, we are inclined to hold that so far as man's bodily structure is concerned he is a product of evolution, having come upwards from below, we may find in the story in Genesis a possible suggestion of this point.

Equally clear and definite is the statement as to man's spiritual nature—"breathed into his nostrils the breath of life; and man became a living soul." Thus, whatever may be true of man's bodily frame, there was a point of departure from material creation in regard to man's moral being which is characterized in this verse as a Divine act differentiating man from nature. Once again we are in the region of scientific fact, for, in spite of arguments to the contrary, there is—at any rate up to the present—no real proof of the evolution of man's moral and spiritual nature. Personality has never yet been expressed in terms of evolution, and requires a Divine creation to account for it. Three great facts stand outside the realm of evolution as it is now understood—human speech, human conscience, and human individuality.

III. *The Home of Man* (vers. 8-14).—Human life requires a locality, a home for its proper expression and development and consequently we read of God's provision for this great necessity. As is well known, the exact locality of man's first home has been a subject of great discussion, and the result is as uncertain today as ever. Three solutions of the problem practically sum up the known conditions—(1) At the head of the Persian Gulf; (2) Armenia; (3) Babylonia. The weightiest authorities seem to favor the last-named locality.

The two elements of man's home call for our attention—the characteristics of beauty ("pleasant to the sight"), and utility ("good for food"). As it was with the first home, so should it ever be, in the possession and proportion of these two requirements. The beautiful without the useful, or the useful without the beautiful, will fail in that which is essential to a true home.

The tree of life and the tree of knowledge of good and evil seem to be symbols of spiritual realities. We may set aside the unworthy and unnecessary literalism which thinks of the fruit of these trees as capable of conveying life and knowledge. They are in keeping with the pictorial and symbolical character of the narrative as expressive of great spiritual realities.

IV. *The Service of Man* (ver. 15).—From the very first man was intended for work, and the necessity of service is one of the fundamental principles of man's existence. Moreover, this necessity will be realized in enjoyment under normal conditions, for there is nothing which is so full of genuine satisfaction as the performance of the work which God has given us to do. Work which is not toil and trouble always gives pleasure. In the Garden of Eden man was to "dress it and to keep it." May not this latter phrase give us some hint of already-existing danger? May not defence as well as preservation be included? If so, man was not only to do the work of the gardener in dressing it, he had also to safeguard it, presumably from foes. Again we seem to be in the realm of spiritual realities in this hint of the existence of evil on the earth.

V. *The Probation of Man* (vers. 16, 17).—For the first time we are reminded of the possibility of human understanding, human speech, and human language in this communication from God to man. Man had this primeval revelation from God, giving full permission of freedom in the garden with one simple, but significant, limitation. There was one thing, and one only, that he was not to do. Again we notice the underlying spiritual reality involved. The narrative gives in a pictorial form the concrete fact of human responsibility and probation. Man's life was to be limited by obedience, God's law being the standard of his life. There is nothing unworthy in the form of the probation. The principle of obedience can be emphasized as easily one way as another. The result of disobedience is stated to be death, and the precise meaning of this term will come before us later. Suffice it to say, as we have it here for the first time in Scripture, the root idea of death seems to be that of separation, not annihilation.

VI. *The Authority of Man* (vers. 18-20).—We are here taught in detail what is mentioned briefly in chapter i. 26—man's original dominion and lordship over nature. In a very true sense God intended man to be the crown of creation, and this naming of the creatures of the earth and sky is the Scripture method of emphasizing a fact which all scientific research during the centuries has gone to confirm more and more. Man was intended to be supreme, the culminating point of God's creation. Hints of this are found in various parts of Holy Scripture (*cf*. Ps. viii.), and it is not altogether speculative to attempt to imagine the precise forms that this dominion would have taken had sin not come into the world. In any case that lordship will one day be resumed (Isa. xi. 6; Heb. ii. 6-10).

VII. *The Companion for Man* (vers. 21-25).—We are now to read the detail of that creation of the female already barely mentioned in chapter i. 27. The words of verse 18 express a profound truth which can be proved from various points of view. "It is not good that man should be alone; I will make him an help meet for him." "It is not good" whether we consider man's character and its development, or his need of fellowship, or his position as head of the race. It is curious that from this verse, by an error of reading, the English language has been supplied with the term "helpmeet." The Hebrew phrase is "a helper suited for him," or, quite literally. "a helper as his counterpart." This is the true idea of woman's relation to man, his counterpart, his complement, and whenever this is realized in marriage, God's purpose is being fulfilled.

"For woman is not undevelopt man,
But diverse:

Not like to like, but like in difference.
Yet in the long years liker must they grow;

Till at the last she set herself to man,
Like perfect music unto noble words;

Distinct in individualities,
But like each other ev'n as those who love."

The narrative continues to be pictorial and picturesque, though we must ever take care to avoid the idea that it is purely allegorical. The pictures have distinct realities corresponding to them, and are expressive of actual facts. The question of sex is one of the problems still unsolved (and perhaps insoluble) by the science of today, and it may perhaps be asked whether science could ever have given a more religiously fitting and helpful account of the physiological facts as they are now known to us.

Matthew Henry quaintly says that woman was taken out of man's side to suggest her equality with him; not out of his feet to imply inferiority, or out of his head to suggest superiority, but out of his side, implying companionship and equality.

Not only the formation of woman, but the great primary ordinance of marriage, is brought before us in this section, and so the chapter ends with this account of one of the essential facts and factors in human life and history.

Once more let us call attention to the real value of this record both as to its pictorial form and the underlying facts suggested and implied. As the Editor of Lange's *Commentary*, referring to these early chapters, says:—

"Great truths, great facts, ineffable truths, ineffable facts, are doubtless set forth. We do not abate one iota of their greatness, their wonderfulness, by supposing such a mode of representation. It is not an accommodation to a rude and early age, but the best language for every age. How trifling the conceit that our science could have furnished any better!

. . . Her language will ever be more or less incorrect; and therefore, a Divine revelation cannot use it, since such use would be an endorsement of its absolute verity. The simpler and more universal language of the Scripture may be inadequate, as all language must be; it may fall short; but it points in the right direction. Though giving us only the great steps in the process, it secures that essential faith in the transcendent Divine working, which science—our science, or the science of ages hence—might only be in danger, to say the least, of darkening. It saves us from those trifling things commonly called reconciliations of revelation with science, and which the next science is almost sure to unreconcile. It does so by placing the mind on a wholly different plane, giving us simple, though grand, conceptions as the vehicle of great ideas and great facts of origin in themselves no more accessible to the most cultivated than to the lowliest minds. There is an awful sublimity in this Mosaic account of the origin of the world and man, and that, too, whether we regard it as inspired Scripture or the grandest picture ever conceived by human genius. To those who cannot, or who do not, thus appreciate it, it matters little what mode of interpretation is adopted—whether it be one of the so-called reconciliations, or the crude dogmatism that calls itself literal because it chooses to take on the narrowest scale a language so suggestive of vast times and ineffable causalities" (p. 211).

We see in this chapter some of the essential elements of human life. They call for earnest thought and definite personal application. They cover almost everything of importance in life and experience, and are a constant reminder of God's purpose for humanity and for each individual.

(1) Man's kinship with God (ver. 7).
(2) Man's worship of God (ver. 3).
(3) Man's fellowship with God (ver. 16).
(4) Man's service for God (ver. 18).
(5) Man's loyalty to God (ver. 17).
(6) Man's authority from God (ver. 19).
(7) Man's social life from and for God (ver. 24).

When these ideas are realized in personal experience, God's purpose in creating man and man's perfect life are being fulfilled.

IV

THE FALL

GEN. iii.

Now the serpent was more subtil than any beast of the field which the Lord God had made. And he said unto the woman, Yea, hath God said, Ye shall not eat of every tree of the garden?

And the woman said unto the serpent, We may eat of the fruit of the trees of the garden:

But of the fruit of the tree which *is* in the midst of the garden, God hath said, Ye shall not eat of it, neither shall ye touch it, lest ye die.

And the serpent said unto the woman, Ye shall not surely die:

For God doth know that in the day ye eat thereof, then your eyes shall be opened, and ye shall be as gods, knowing good and evil.

And when the woman saw that the tree *was* good for food, and that it *was* pleasant to the eyes, and a tree to be desired to make *one* wise, she took of the fruit thereof, and did eat, and gave also unto her husband with her; and he did eat.

And the eyes of them both were opened, and they knew that they *were* naked; and they sewed fig leaves together, and made themselves aprons.

And they heard the voice of the Lord God walking in the garden in the cool of the day: and Adam and his wife hid themselves from the presence of the Lord God amongst the trees of the garden.

And the Lord God called unto Adam, and said unto him, Where *art* thou?

And he said, I heard Thy voice in the garden, and I was afraid, because I *was* naked; and I hid myself.

And He said, Who told thee that thou *wast* naked? Hast thou eaten of the tree, whereof I commanded thee that thou shouldest not eat?

And the man said, The woman whom Thou gavest *to be* with me, she gave me of the tree, and I did eat.

And the Lord God said unto the woman, What *is* this *that* thou hast done? And the woman said, The serpent beguiled me, and I did eat.

And the Lord God said unto the serpent, Because thou hast done this, thou *art* cursed above all cattle, and above every beast of the field, upon thy belly shalt thou go, and dust shalt thou eat all the days of thy life:

And I will put enmity between thee and the woman, and between thy seed and her seed; it shall bruise thy head, and thou shalt bruise his heel.

Unto the woman he said, I will greatly multiply thy sorrow and thy conception; in sorrow thou shalt bring forth children; and thy desire *shall be* to thy husband, and he shall rule over thee.

And unto Adam he said, Because thou hast hearkened unto the voice of thy wife, and hast eaten of the tree, of which I commanded thee, saying, Thou shalt not eat of it: cursed *is* the ground for thy sake; in sorrow shalt thou eat *of* it all the days of thy life;

Thorns also and thistles shall it bring forth to thee; and thou shalt eat of the herb of the field;

In the sweat of thy face shalt thou eat bread, till thou return unto the ground; for out of it wast thou taken: for dust thou *art,* and unto dust shalt thou return.

And Adam called his wife's name Eve; because she was the mother of all living.

Unto Adam also and to his wife did the Lord God make coats of skins, and clothed them.

And the Lord God said, Behold, the man is become as one of us, to know good and evil: and now, lest he put forth his hand, and take also of the tree of life, and eat, and live for ever:

Therefore the Lord God sent him forth from the garden of Eden, to till the ground from whence he was taken.

So He drove out the man; and He placed at the east of the garden of Eden cherubim, and a flaming sword which turned every way, to keep the way of the tree of life.

IT is hardly too much to say that this chapter is the pivot of the Bible, for if we take it away the rest of Scripture becomes meaningless. With the exception of the fact of Creation, we have here the record of the most important and far-reaching event in the world's history—the entrance of sin.

The record in this chapter, like that of the Creation, is variously interpreted. Many speak of it as "mythical," by which is often meant that which is unreal, untrue, and impossible. Others use the term "myth" as indicating an elementary method of conveying moral and spiritual truth, even though the narrative itself is not historical in form. The former view is naturally to be set aside by all who believe in the fact and veracity of a Divine revelation. The latter interpretation of "myth" does not seem to be quite satisfactory on any intelligible principle of Divine inspiration. The truest method of interpretation is that which regards these narratives as pictorial records of actual fact; solid history in pictorial form. It is inadequate to speak of the narrative as poetic or merely symbolical, lest we should give the impression that the story is not concerned with actual fact. Allegory, too, is identical with the truth illustrated, and does not necessarily presuppose any historical basis. What we must insist upon and ever keep in view is that, whether allegorical or pictorial, the narrative is expressive of actual fact.

The chapter is so full of spiritual truths that it is impossible to deal with everything in detail. It must suffice to call attention to four great realities of the spiritual life which are here brought before us for the first time in the Word of God.

I. *Temptation.*—Consider its source. The practical character of the narrative is clearly seen in the reference to the serpent as the immediate cause of human sin. Inasmuch as Satan is not actually mentioned in the chapter, we are surely right in regarding this reference to the serpent as a pictorial and symbolical reference to Satan himself, a view which is confirmed by later passages of Scripture, such as 2 Cor. xi. 14; Rev. xii. 9. and xx. 2. There is no reference to the problem of how and when Satan sinned. The one point of stress is laid upon sin in relation to man, and we are taught very unmistakably two great truths: (1) That God is not the author of sin, and (2) that sin came to man from without, and was due to a power of evil suggestion and influence other than that which came from man's own nature. Even though we fall short of identifying the serpent of this chapter with the personal Satan of later Scripture, we may still regard the teaching of the Fall story as suggesting the personification of an evil principle from without, which in later times is seen to be more than a personification and nothing less than an actual being (Orr, *Image of God in Man*, pp. 219 ff.).

Mark its subtilty. The stages of the temptation should be carefully noticed: (a) The serpent first of all excites the woman's curiosity by speaking to her; (b) then he raises a suspicion of God by the question that he puts to her (ver. 1); (c) then he proceeds to inject a threefold doubt of God—of His *goodness*, by reason of the restriction (ver. 1); of His *righteousness*, in the assurance that they shall not die (ver. 4); and of His *holiness*, in the assurance that, so far from dying, they "shall be as gods" (ver. 5). (See Candlish's *Lectures on Genesis, in loc.*) (d) Thus he incites the woman to unbelief, and (e) leads her eventually to disobedience. It is very

noteworthy that the temptation is associated entirely with doubt
of God's Word: "Hath God said?" This is characteristic of sin
at all times; the doubt, the denial, and the disbelief of God's Word.
First Satan *distorts* the Word, then he leads the woman to *doubt* it,
and last of all he *denies* it. It is also significant that Satan and the
woman in their conversation use the term "God," and not "Lord
God." This inadequate and defective reference to God was doubtless part of the explanation of the temptation and the Fall. It
would not have served Satan's purposes to have introduced the
specific covenant term "Jehovah" when raising questions about the
veracity and faithfulness of God's Word.

Observe its success. The stages of the woman's attitude have
often been pointed out: (*a*) She heeded the temptation, and listened
to Satan's questioning of God's Word and his new interpretation
of that Divine utterance. In her reply to his question, she perverted
and misquoted *three times* the divine law to which she and Adam
were subject: (1) She disparaged her privileges by misquoting
the terms of the Divine *permission* as to the other trees. (2) She
overstated the restrictions by misquoting the Divine *prohibition*.
(3) She underrated her obligations by misquoting the Divine
penalty. And thus she was easily exposed to the temptation to question, doubt, and deny God. (*b*) Her curiosity was roused, perhaps,
by Satan demonstrating before her the apparent futility of heeding
God, for we are told that she *saw* that the tree was *good* for *food* as
well as pleasant to the eyes. (*c*) Then sprang up physical craving,
and she desired to disobey, with the result that (*d*) she took and
ate, and "gave also unto her husband and he did eat." Her fall
was consequently due to dalliance with temptation. She did not
repel, but yielded to it. Had she resisted at the very outset she
would not have fallen; for it is a universal law that if we resist the
devil, he will flee from us. Nothing is more remarkable in the
whole history of man's moral life than the powerlessness of the
devil to overcome us apart from our own assent and consent. If
we resist, he flees; if we yield, he wins. It is this simple fact that
constitutes man's ultimate responsibility for his actions. He never

can say, "I was overpowered in spite of myself." All that he can say is, "I was overpowered because of myself."

II. *Sin*.—The reality of sin is undoubted. The chapter is clear as to the fact of a Fall. There is such a thing as moral evil in the world. Human nature, with its constant tendency to retrogression and degeneration, clearly proves this. However and whenever it has come about, we know the universality and persistence of evil today, and the world has never had any other adequate explanation than that which is afforded by this chapter. Traditions of the Fall are almost as numerous as those of creation (*Pulpit Commentary*, p. 59). There is scarcely any part of God's Word which is more in accord with the known facts of history and science than the story of this chapter. We have recently been told that the doctrine of a Fall from original righteousness is only found in this chapter and in the theology of St. Paul, and yet it is surely obvious that the facts of sin and its universality are pre-supposed in every part of the Old Testament.

"If a Fall were not narrated in the opening chapters of Genesis, we should still have to postulate something of the kind for the Bible's own representations of the state of man" (Orr, *ut supra*, p. 201).

We may also add that the same postulate is necessary to account for the tendencies to evil seen in the natures of little children throughout the whole world.

The root of sin should be understood. The foundation of all sin lies in man's desire of self-assertion and his determination to be independent of God. Adam and Eve chafed under the restriction laid upon them by the command of God, and it was in opposition to this that they asserted themselves, and thereby fell. Man does not like to be dependent upon another, and subject to commands upon another, and subject to commands from without. He desires to go his own way, to be his own master; and as a consequence he sins, and becomes "lord of himself, that heritage of woe."

The responsibility of sin needs constant emphasis. The possibility of sin is involved in the fact of personality. Unless man was to be an automaton, with no opportunity for character, there must be granted the possibility of sin. It is at this point we realize the solemn fact of personal accountability. Whatever may be true of environment and heredity, they never can blot out the distinction between right and wrong, or rob man of his responsibility. Nor must we for a moment suppose that sin was any inherent tendency or primal necessity of human life. Adam had liability, but not a tendency, to sin. Our Lord had neither liability nor tendency, though of course His temptation was real, all the more so because of His sinless nature (Heb. iv. 15 R. V., not A. V.). We today, as fallen, have both liability and tendency. And modern theories of evolution which make sin a necessity of human development tend thereby to blot out the eternal distinction between good and evil. In view of certain aspects of modern evolutionary thought, man had no alternative but to fall; and to add to the confusion of thought and morals, we are also told that this failure was not a fall, but a rise —a fall upwards—so that we must now, it is said, speak of the ascent, not of the fall, of man. In opposition to all this the Bible teaches us that sin was not a necessity, and there never will be any clear Christian thinking until this necessitarian theory is entirely banished from our minds (Orr, *ut supra*, pp. 158 and 298).

III. *Punishment.*—"Be sure your sin will find you out" is the great principle written clearly and deeply on this record of the first sin, as, indeed, of every other since that time. What was the punishment associated with the sin of Adam and Eve? The narrative shows this plainly.

They soon had a sense of guilt. At once their eyes were opened, and they became conscious of the shame associated with their wrong-doing. The reference to nakedness and clothing indicates the profound shame that actuated them, and at once they hid themselves from the presence of the Lord. Fear was the result of their guilt; the old experiences of innocence and fellowship were at an end, and now they were guilty before God. Conscience, that element of the Divine image and likeness, was already at work, and their sin was indeed finding them out.

Then followed a sentence of condemnation. God soon dealt with this wrong-doing, and there was a threefold condemnation. All subterfuges (ver. 10) and all cowardly attempts to blame others (vers. 12, 13) were unavailing, and man stood face to face with the holy God, conscious of guilt and unspeakable shame. (*a*) The serpent was first dealt with, and judgment passed upon him (vers. 14, 15); (*b*) the woman was next judged, and condemned to sorrow and subjection (ver. 16); (*c*) the man last of all was dealt with, and sorrow. hardship, toil, and death were made his portion (vers. 17-19).

Last of all came an act of separation. It was impossible for man to remain in the garden, and in a state of fellowship with God. Sin and Paradise were incompatible, and so the Lord sent them forth, driving them out, and placing the guard with the sword that turned every way. Mark the significance of this phrase. There was no possibility of a return to the old life. Paradise was lost, and by no human effort could it ever be regained. Separation is always the result of sin. "Your iniquities have separated between you and your God" (Isa. lix. 2). And thus the threefold punishment of guilt, condemnation, and separation accrued to man because of his sin.

The chapter, however, does not end with sin and its punishment, and we pass on to consider the fourth great reality.

IV. *Redemption*.—The announcement of enmity between the serpent and the woman, and between her seed and his seed, is the first message of Divine redemption in its antagonism to, and victory over, sin. This is indeed the *Protevangelium,* and is the primeval promise which is taken up again and again henceforward in Scripture, until He comes Who destroys him that has the power of death, and casts him into the lake of fire.

Redemption is not only promised in word, it is also pictured in deed. Man attempted to cover his shame by the leaves of the fig-tree, but this was far too slight a covering for so deep a shame. No human covering could suffice, and so we are told with profound significance that the "Lord God made coats of skins and clothed them." This Divine clothing took the place of their own self-made clothing, and now they are clothed indeed. The mention of skins suggests the fact and necessity of death of the animal before they could be used as clothing, and it is more than probable that in this fact we have the primal revelation of sacrifice, and of the way in which the robe of righteousness was to be provided for them.

> "Jesu, Thy blood and righteousness
> My beauty are, my glorious dress."

Looking on to the New Testament, we cannot but associate with this chapter the great Pauline chapter, Romans viii., which ends very significantly with three questions triumphantly asked by the Apostle, and it should be carefully noticed that these questions exactly correspond to the three aspects of punishment mentioned above.

(a) "Who shall lay anything to the charge of God's elect?" (ver. 33). That is, "There is no *guilt*."

(b) "Who is he that condemneth?" (ver. 34). That is, "There is no *condemnation*."

(c) "Who shall separate us from the love of Christ?" (ver. 35). That is, "There is no *separation*."

Thus, where sin abounded grace did super-abound, and "as by one man sin entered into the world and death by sin, so now grace reigns through righteousness unto eternal life by Jesus Christ our Lord."

God's question to Adam still sounds in the ear of every sinner, "Where art thou?" It is the call of Divine *justice*, which cannot overlook sin. It is the call of Divine *sorrow*, which grieves over the sinner. It is the call of Divine *love*, which offers redemption for sin. To each and to every one of us the call is reiterated, "Where art *thou?*"

The answer to the question must be either: "in Adam" or "in Christ." These are the only two places where we can be. If we are still "in Adam," we are still in sin, and therefore in guilt, condemnation, and in danger of eternal separation. If we are "in Christ," we are already pardoned, accounted righteous, subjects of His grace, and heirs of eternal glory.

Note.—For all modern evolutionary and philosophical questions connected with this chapter attention is earnestly called to the very able and scholarly book by Dr. Orr, already quoted and referred to.

V

CAIN AND ABEL

GEN. iv. 1-15

AND Adam knew Eve his wife; and she conceived, and bare Cain, and said, I have gotten a man from the Lord.

And she again bare his brother Abel. And Abel was a keeper of sheep, but Cain was a tiller of the ground.

And in process of time it came to pass, that Cain brought of the fruit of the ground an offering unto the Lord.

And Abel, he also brought of the firstlings of his flock, and of the fat thereof. And the Lord had respect unto Abel, and to his offering:

But unto Cain, and to his offering, He had not respect. And Cain was very wroth, and his countenance fell.

And the Lord said unto Cain, Why art thou wroth? and why is thy countenance fallen?

If thou doest well, shalt thou not be accepted? and if thou doest not well, sin lieth at the door. And unto thee *shall be* his desire, and thou shalt rule over him.

And Cain talked with Abel his brother: and it came to pass, when they were in the field, that Cain rose up against Abel his brother and slew him.

And the Lord said unto Cain, Where *is* Abel thy brother? And he said, I know not: *Am* I my brother's keeper?

And He said, What hast thou done? the voice of thy brother's blood crieth unto Me from the ground.

And now *art* thou cursed from the earth, which hath opened her mouth to receive thy brother's blood from thy hand.

When thou tillest the ground, it shall not henceforth yield unto thee her strength: a fugitive and a vagabond shalt thou be in the earth.

And Cain said unto the Lord, My punishment *is* greater than I can bear.

Behold, Thou hast driven me out this day from the face of the earth; and from Thy face shall I be hid; and I shall be a fugitive and a vagabond in the earth; and it shall come to pass, *that* every one that findeth me shall slay me.

And the Lord said unto him, Therefore whosoever slayeth Cain, vengeance shall be taken on him sevenfold. And the Lord set a mark upon Cain, lest any finding him should kill him.

FROM the origin of sin (chap. iii.) we pass to the consideration of its progress. Sin in the individual is now seen to develop and express itself in the family. This chapter, like the three preceding it, is full of "geneses," for we have brought before us the first motherhood, the first birth, the first family, the first murder, the first martyrdom, the first indications of human development. Not least of all we have in it the record of the first conflict between the two seeds (chap. iii. 15), and this in connection with religious worship.

It is a necessary and useful reminder that only a few things are touched upon in this chapter, and that many things are left unexplained. The writer calls attention to the mountain peaks only of human history and experience as he passes from one fact to another. Thus there is no statement of the time that elapsed between chapter iii. 24 and chapter iv. 3; no explanation of the origin of sacrifice, of blood revenge (ver. 14), of the method of Divine acceptance of sacrifice, of the sign appointed for Cain, and of the growth of the population implied (vers. 15-19). Whatever views we may hold upon these subjects must necessarily be problematical in the absence of clear teaching. Turning now to the record of the two brothers and all that the story implies, we notice:—

I. *The First Home.*—We have here brought before us those home relationships, conjugal, parental, brotherly, that constitute the foundation of all social life. The parents, although expelled from Eden, are evidently still influenced by the consciousness of their relation to God, and by the thought of a Divine promise of a seed (chap. iii. 15). The words of Eve at the birth of her first-born son are to be noted. She called the child "Cain"—*i.e.* "possession"—evidently thinking that in him would be fulfilled the promise to her seed. It is possible that the literal rendering of her words, "I have gotten a man, even Jehovah," suggests a more definite belief and knowledge than are warranted. At the same time, to render the words, "I have gotten a man with the help of the Lord," seems unduly to weaken the Hebrew phrase. Probably we are to understand some such rendering as "I have gotten a man in relation to Jehovah," pointing definitely to a conviction that somehow or other this new-born son was related to the Divine promise and purpose. Eve must have been quickly undeceived in this respect, for when her second child was born there was no reference whatever to any relation to the Lord, and the fact of his name meaning "vanity" seems to show clearly that the mother had already become disappointed in her hopes of her first-born son.

II. *The Two Brothers.*—Their work is first of all brought before us—the one being a shepherd, the other an agriculturist. Thus early in the history of the world are we reminded of the necessity and dignity of work as one of the essentials of human life and progress.

They not only worked, however, but they also worshipped. "To labor" is *not* "to pray" in the literal meaning of the phrase. Man must pray as well as labor. Their worship took the form of offerings, and this must always be the case. Worship is giving, not getting; ascribing, not appropriating. It is evident from the phrase, "in process of time," that this worship was regularly rendered as something habitual in their life. Man is never more truly man than when he is worshipping God; for it is only then that he finds, realizes, and expresses his true relationship of dependence.

III. *The Divine Response.*—One offering was accepted, the other was not. It is noteworthy that the Divine "respect" is stated in both cases, not merely with reference to the offerings, but primarily with reference to the offerer. "Unto Abel and to his offering; unto Cain and to his offering." The value of the offering is seen to depend upon the character of the offer. Not costliness, but character, constitutes true worship. We naturally ask why it was that God had respect to Abel and to his offering, and not to Cain and his. According to Heb. xi. 4, the explanation is to be found in the words, "By faith Abel offered a more excellent sacrifice than Cain." Faith always presupposes a Divine revelation to which it is the response, and in the light of the New Testament interpretation it would seem clear that one was an offering of faith, and the other an offering without faith. Why should faith be emphasized by the Epistle to the Hebrews more than gratitude or prayer? May it not be because of a prior revelation from God as to how He was to be approached? We must never forget that while death is very familiar to us now, it was not so in those early days, and it might well have been asked why it was necessary to destroy the life of a lamb when it was not needed for food. In what respects are we to think of death as making a sacrifice acceptable to the Creator? Is it not possible, and even probable, that Abel's sacrifice, involving death, was his response to an already existing revelation of God as to this method of sacrifice? May we not see in the coats of skins (Chap. iii. 21) a hint of the revelation of sacrifice through death as the way of approach to God? This view at any rate makes it intelligible why Abel can be said to have offered "by faith," while Cain offered a sacrifice which did not involve death, and which was therefore, on this interpretation, not in accordance with the Divine revelation. At any rate we may fairly say that these two aspects represent two attitudes today—the attitude of the man who responds to God's revelation and submits to His will, and the attitude of the man who will only come to God on his own terms, refusing to do what does not suit him or commend itself to his judgment. It does not seem unjust to Cain to say that his was a sacrifice which, however good in itself, was not prompted by a faith that rested in and responded to God's revelation of His will. In this connection the works of Professor Curtis (*Primitive Semitic Sacrifices*, and *Expositor*, 1904, 1905) on the primitive Semitic ideas of sacrifice should be carefully studied, since they indicate very clearly that the root idea of sacrifice among the Bedouin tribes is propitiation rather than communion.

IV. *The Divine Expostulation.*—Cain's anger clearly shows that his worship was only a form of godliness without the power. If his offering had been made in the right spirit, there would have been no anger and no lowering of the countenance. The Lord meets this wrath with a very definite inquiry and an equally definite reminder. Verse 7 has long been a *crux interpretum*. The following rendering seems worthy of attention: "If thou doest well, will there not be acceptance for thee? And if thou doest not well, sin is lying at the door like a crouching beast, ready to spring upon thee, and unto thee is sin's desire, but thou shouldest rule over it." (See R. V.

Margin.) It is very evident from these words that Cain had not been "doing well" previously to this, and hence the necessity of this solemn warning of the bitter consequences of continued sin. Sin is personified as a lurking beast of prey ready to spring upon its victim, and against this enemy Cain is warned, and commanded to rule over it. (See Murphy, Conant, and Lange *in loc.*) For another view see Note, p. 58.

V. *The First Murder.*—The warning went unheeded, and the jealousy and hatred found expression in anger and murder. Thus, in connection with religious worship, the first murder was committed. Could anything be more tragic?

> "If you want to find out Cain's condition of heart you will find it after the service which he pretended to render; you know a man best *out* of church; the minister sees the best side of a man, the lawyer the worst, and the physician the real. If you want to know what a man's religious worship is worth, see him *out* of church. Cain killed his brother when church was over, and that is the exact measure of Cain's piety. And so, when you went home the other day, you charged five shillings for a three-shilling article, and told the buyer it was too cheap: and that is exactly the value of your psalm-singing and sermon-hearing. You said you enjoyed the discourse exceedingly last Thursday; then you filled up the income-tax paper falsely; and you will be judged by the schedule, not by the sentiment" (Parker's *People's Bible,* Genesis, p. 147).

VI. *The Divine Condemnation.*—Very soon comes God's inquiry, "Where is Abel thy brother?" for sin cannot possibly be hid. There is a solemn significance in the repetition of "his brother" and "thy brother" in these verses. The Divine rebuke immediately follows (ver. 10), which in turn is succeeded by the Divine sentence of unrequited toil and wandering. Thus once again we are taught in most unmistakable terms of the Divine holiness and righteousness, which will not for an instant tolerate human sin.

VII. *The Divine Judgment.*—Cain now realizes something of what he has done, though it would seem that his thought is more of his punishment than of the sin that led to it. In mitigation of the results of his sin the Lord gives him a pledge of protection from vengeance. The phrase "set a mark upon Cain" should be rendered "appointed a sign for Cain," the same word being used as in chapter i. 14, ix. 12, and elsewhere. There seems no reason to think of a mark or brand upon his body, but some pledge or sign in regard to the question of vengeance. Then the judgment was executed, and Cain "went out from the presence of the Lord," realizing now to the full the separating character of sin, and the fact that when a man does despite to the Spirit of grace in rejecting God's will there can be only spiritual solitariness and misery.

The two men, Cain and Abel, are brought before us in several passages in the New Testament. They were both worshippers, for Cain was not a profane man; and yet how different was their worship, by reason of the difference of their lives! Two New Testament phrases sum up the practical lessons:—

1. "Righteous Abel." Abel teaches us very clearly that—

(1) God is to be worshipped.

(2) God is to be worshipped through sacrifice.

(3) God is to be worshipped through atoning sacrifice.

(4) God is to be worshipped through an atoning sacrifice responded to by faith.

(5) God is to be glorified by a life of faith.

(6) God is to be glorified by a life of faith which expresses itself in righteousness. (Cf. 1 John iii. 12; Heb. xi. 4, xii. 24.)

2. "The way of Cain." In the life of Cain we see

(1) Human thought as opposed to Divine revelation.

(2) Human wilfulness as opposed to the Divine will.

(3) Human pride as opposed to Divine humility.

(4) Human hatred as opposed to Divine love.

(5) Human hostility as opposed to Divine favor.

(6) Human loneliness as opposed to Divine fellowship.

NOTE ON VERSE 7.

Another interpretation which has much to recommend it is: "But if thou doest (or offerest) not well, even then there is a sin-offering ready at hand for use as a propitiation. And not only so, but Abel, thy brother, will submit himself to thee as the first-born, and thou shalt exercise thy right of authority over him" (cf. iii. 16). The word rendered "sin" is translated "sin-offering" a large number of times in the Old Testament. This view regards the verse as at once a divine expostulation and an offer of grace. It is further argued that as the word for "sin" in the Hebrew is feminine, and the verb and pronouns in the last clause are masculine, the "desire" must refer to Abel and not to sin,

VI

HUMAN PROGRESS

GEN. iv. 16—vi. 8

AND Cain went out from the presence of the Lord, and dwelt in the land of Nod, on the east of Eden.

And Cain knew his wife; and she conceived, and bare Enoch: and he builded a city, and called the name of the city, after the name of his son Enoch.

And unto Enoch was born Irad: and Irad begat Mehujael: and Mehujael begat Methusael: and Methusael begat Lamech.

And Lamech took unto him two wives: the name of the one *was* Adah, and the name of the other Zillah.

And Adah bare Jabal: he was the father of such as dwell in tents, and *of such as have* cattle.

And his brother's name *was* Jubal: he was the father of all such as handle the harp and organ.

And Zillah, she also bare Tubal-cain, an instructor of every artificer in brass and iron; and the sister of Tubal-cain *was* Naamah.

And Lamech said unto his wives, Adah and Zillah, hear my voice; ye wives of Lamech, hearken unto my speech: for I have slain a man to my wounding, and a young man to my hurt:

If Cain shall be avenged sevenfold, truly Lamech seventy and sevenfold.

And Adam knew his wife again; and she bare a son, and called his name Seth: For God, *said she,* hath appointed me another seed instead of Abel, whom Cain slew.

And to Seth, to him also there was born a son; and he called his name Enos: then began men to call upon the name of the Lord.

This *is* the book of the generations of Adam. In the day that God created man, in the likeness of God made He him;

Male and female created He them; and blessed them, and called their name Adam, in the day when they were created.

And Adam lived an hundred and thirty years, and begat *a son* in his own likeness, after his image; and called his name Seth:

And the days of Adam after he had begotten Seth were eight hundred years: and he begat sons and daughters:

And all the days that Adam lived were nine hundred and thirty years: and he died.

And Seth lived an hundred and five years, and begat Enos:

And Seth lived after he begat Enos eight hundred and seven years, and begat sons and daughters:

And all the days of Seth were nine hundred and twelve years: and he died.

And Enos lived ninety years, and begat Cainan:

And Enos lived after he begat Cainan eight hundred and fifteen years, and begat sons and daughters:

And all the days of Enos were nine hundred and five years: and he died.

And Cainan lived seventy years, and begat Mahalaleel:

And Cainan lived after he begat Mahalaleel eight hundred and forty years, and begat sons and daughters:

And all the days of Cainan were nine hundred and ten years: and he died.

And Mahalaleel lived sixty and five years, and begat Jared:

And Mahalaleel lived after he begat Jared eight hundred and thirty years, and begat sons and daughters:

And all the days of Mahalaleel were eight hundred ninety and five years: and he died.

And Jared lived an hundred sixty and two years, and he begat Enoch:

And Jared lived after he begat Enoch eight hundred years, and begat sons and daughters:

And all the days of Jared were nine hundred sixty and two years: and he died.

And Enoch lived sixty and five years, and begat Methuselah:

And Enoch walked with God after he begat Methuselah three hundred years, and begat sons and daughters:

And all the days of Enoch were three hundred sixty and five years:

And Enoch walked with God: and he *was* not; for God took him.

And Methuselah lived an hundred eighty and seven years, and begat Lamech:

And Methuselah lived after he begat Lamech seven hundred eighty and two years, and begat sons and daughters:

And all the days fo Methuselah were nine hundred sixty and nine years: and he died.

And Lamech lived an hundred eighty and two years, and begat a son:

And he called his name Noah, saying, This *same* shall comfort us concerning our work and toil of our hands, because of the ground which the Lord hath cursed.

And Lamech lived after he begat Noah five hundred ninety and five years, and begat sons and daughters:

And all the days of Methuselah were nine hundred sixty and nine years: and he died.

And Noah was five hundred years old: and Noah begat Shem, Ham, and Japheth.

And it came to pass, when men began to multiply on the face of the earth, and daughters were born unto them.

That the sons of God saw the daughters of men that they *were* fair; and they took them wives of all which they chose.

And the Lord said, My Spirit shall not always strive with man, for that he also *is* flesh: yet his days shall be an hundred and twenty years.

There were giants in the earth in those days; and also after that, when the sons of God came in unto the daughters of men, and they bare *children* to them, the same *became* mighty men which *were* of old, men of renown.

And God saw that the wickedness of man *was* great in the earth, and *that* every imagination of the thoughts of his heart *was* only evil continually.

And it repented the Lord that He had made man on the earth, and it grieved Him at His heart.

And the Lord said, I will destroy man whom I have created from the face of the earth; both man, and beast, and the creeping thing, and the fowls of the air; for it repenteth me that I have made them.

But Noah found grace in the eyes of the Lord.

WE have now to follow the development of humanity along two lines—that of Cain and that of Seth. This progress is first seen in the family, and then it extends to society in general. The entire section now before us has a completeness all its own, even though it forms parts of two of the original sections of Genesis. Thus (*a*) iv. 16-24 gives the line of Cain; (*b*) iv. 25 to v. 32 the line of Seth; and then (*c*) vi. 1-8 the blending of these two lines, culminating in the Flood on the one hand and the preservation of Noah on the other. The entire section thus calls for careful study, both in connection with what precedes and with what follows. "The section chapter ii. 4 to chapter iv. had recorded a constant descent from bad to worse—the sin of our first parents, their expulsion from Paradise, the murder of Abel, Cain's descendants reaching in Lamech the climax of boastful and unrestrained violence. That the section might not be suffered to end in unrelieved gloom a brighter outlook is added at the close, precisely as is done at the end of the next section in vi. 8. Seth is substituted for Abel, whom Cain slew; and instead of piety perishing with murdered Abel, it reaches a new development in the days of Enos. The whole arrangement bears evidence of adaptation and careful thought, and is suggestive of one author, not the combination of separate compositions prepared with no reference to each other" (Green, *The Unity of the Book of Genesis*, p. 48).

The characteristics of Cain and his line must be carefully followed.

I. *The First Stream—Irreligion* (iv. 16-24).—Cain went forth from the immediate neighborhood of Eden and dwelt "in the land of Nod." The precise locality is, of course, unknown, though it is probable that it was the country of Elam. As to the perennial question of Cain's wife, it is sufficient to say that she was either his sister or some other relative. In the absence of any law there would, of course, have been no sin in the marriage of a sister, and it is worthy of mention that within historic times the marriage of brother and sister was in practice in the royal family of Egypt, in order to secure unquestioned royalty of blood in the descent; and this was the case when the civilization of Egypt was at its highest. The suggestions of the narrative with regard to Cain show no trace of the influence of God's mercy upon him, and no indication of penitence on his part. He is still godless and reckless. His sacrifice showed that while he was prepared to recognize God as the God of providence, he had no conception of Him as the God of grace. There was no trace of real homage of heart; and as there had been no thought of sin and salvation in his offering, so now there is no indication of real devotion to God.

One characteristic of the line of Cain was the settled life they lived. The birth of a son was followed by the building of a city, to which Cain gave the name of his son, Enoch. This indication of a settled abode and a new line of descent seems to show that Cain was now going his own way, regardless of everything else. Nothing more is said of his line until the fifth generation.

It was in the line of Cain that the terrible evil of polygamy was first experienced, and the way that it is mentioned in the narrative by contrast with chapter ii. 24 shows the impression that it was intended to convey.

From the sons of Lamech come the founders of agriculture (ver. 20), music (ver. 21), and manufacture (ver. 22). This development of earthly civilization in connection with Cain's line is very suggestive and significant.

In Lamech we have the culmination of Cainite irreligion. Whatever his song may mean, it seems on the face of it to suggest the glorification of two great evils—polygamy and murder. If heredity accounts for anything, we may see in Lamech the intensified form of those evil tendencies which were evident in Cain.

Thus we have the Cainite race in six generations, and with an entire absence of all indications of religion, unless we interpret the name of Cain's son to mean "Consecrated." This line was devoted to things earthly and lived absolutely apart from God. Natural ingenuity characterized the race. There was art and civilization, but no religion. Not that they were all necessarily flagrantly sinful, but just living without God (Eph. ii. 12). Is it not suggestive that the first time art, trade, and manufactures are mentioned they are associated with godlessness? Is it, or is it not, an accident that art has often flourished most when religion has been at its lowest? Is it not a fact that there is that in music, art, and civilization which easily panders to the very lowest in man? And while these things should be, and can be, devoted to the highest interests of human life and the glory of God, the possibilities of evil which they contain must never be overlooked. As for regarding them as substitutes for God, this is utterly impossible. This vivid picture of human society without God should be carefully pondered, and the message for society today clearly understood and proclaimed.

II. *The Second Stream—Godliness* (iv. 25-v. 32).—By contrast with the line of Cain we are now introduced to the new line of Seth, his brother. The points of contrast are many and significant.

The first is the birth of Seth. The death of Abel had left an indelible mark on the soul of Eve, and now with the birth of her third son her hopes of the fulfilment of the primeval promise again spring up, and she calls him Seth, and recognizes in his birth a Divine appointment and providence. It is noteworthy that when Cain was born she associated his birth with the Covenant God of Grace (Jehovah). With Seth's birth she associates the God of Creation and Power (Elohim). This distinctness of usage of the Divine names should be carefully noted at each stage of the narrative, for it is full of spiritual significance and cannot be satisfactorily accounted for in any other way.

Another point of emphasis is associated with the son of Seth. It is interesting that in the same chapter we have the record of the birth of Cain's son and also the son of Seth. Still more interesting is the fact that with the birth of Seth's son there came what may very fairly be called a revival of true religion, for "then began men to call upon the Name of Jehovah." This may mean, as in our A.V., a revival of prayer; or it may mean still more than this (see margin), and indicate consecration to Jehovah, "calling themselves by His Name," and thereby separating themselves from all those who were not prepared to take the same action. They realized that they were in covenant with the God of their father, Who had promised victory over sin.

Then follows the record of the line of Seth. Once again we have a reference to Adam which comes in naturally at the head of the line of Seth. Ten generations are given, and the monotony of the chapter has often been remarked. It is a simple record of living and dying, only broken by the references to Enoch and Noah. We know nothing more of the names here mentioned—a reminder, however, that human history is not necessarily to be judged by the outstanding names that every one knows:

> "The best part of human history is never written at all. Family life, patient service, quiet endurance, the training of children, the resistance of temptation; these things are never mentioned by the historian" (Parker, *People's Bible, Genesis*, p. 155).

The three breaks in the whole narrative from Seth are associated with Enos, Enoch, and Noah, and they seem to represent three typical aspects of religious life. (1) Separation (iv. 26, margin); (2) fellowship (v. 22); (3) service (v. 29). No inventions, art, or civilization are connected with the line of Seth. There is a simplicity about the record, perhaps indicative of the quiet, simple religion that characterized most, if not all, of them.

The witness of Enoch is given to us as an oasis in the chapter, and he is one of only two men of whom it is recorded in the Old Testament that they "walked with God" (vi. 9).

(a) The fact of fellowship with God is suggested by this phrase. Several aspects of our "walk" are emphasized in Scripture. "Walk before Me" (Gen. xvii. 1), implying sincerity; "Walk after the Lord your God" (Deut. xiii. 4), suggesting obedience; "Walk in Him" (Col. ii. 6), telling of union; "Walking with God," meaning fellowship. This is life's ideal and the culmination of God's purpose for man.

(b) The commencement of this fellowship is suggested (ver. 22). Enoch is not said to have walked with God until the birth of his son. May it not have been the coming into his life of that little life, God's gift to him, that led to this close fellowship?

(c) The continuance of fellowship. It lasted three hundred years. This was not easy. Enoch was no dreamy sentimental idealist. His life had in it the real difficulty of testimony against evil (Jude 14, 15). The judgment on the line of the Cainites had to be proclaimed, and this is never anything but an irksome and trying task. Like the rest of mankind in later days, Enoch did not find it easy to walk with God.

(d) The culmination of fellowship. "He was not, for God took him." The life of faith was thus crowned by entrance upon the life of perfect fellowship above. "They shall walk with Me in white."

The chapter suitably closes with a reference to Noah. Lamech showed his faith in connection with the naming of his son, and all through the story of Noah we see the secret of a living faith in God (Heb. xi. 7).

III. *The Streams Blended* (vi. 1-8).—This section is closely connected with the preceding and following sections as their necessary and adequate explanation.

We observe the sad marks of human apostasy. Verse 1 takes up the story laid down in chapter iv. 24, and deals with the growth of the Cainites. Verse 2 speaks of the union of the two lines by inter-marriage. Some writers regard the phrase "sons of God" as referring to the angels, and it is urged that in other passages— *e.g.* Job i. 6; Ps. xxix. 1; Dan. iii. 25—and, indeed, always elsewhere in Scripture, the phrase invariably means angels. According to this view, we have here what has recently been called an "ætiological myth," though the same view is held by those who regard the story not as mythical, but as absolutely historical, seeing in it a reference to the sin of the angels mentioned in Jude 6, 7 and 2 Pet. ii. 4-6. The former view, which makes it mythological, is clearly to be set aside, since on this interpretation it is difficult, if not impossible, to understand the value of the story as part of the Word of God. The latter interpretation is also unnecessary on other grounds; and the view that regards the passage as the union of the Cainites and the Sethites is at once the most natural and the most Scriptural. The idea of the phrase "sons of God" was used in connection with Israel (Deut. xiv. 1; Hos. i. 10; xi. 1), and the teaching of subsequent Scripture is perfectly clear against the inter-marriage of Israel with the Canaanites. Besides, this verse accounts for the universality of the sin which led to the catastrophe of the Flood, and verse 3 declares God's sentence upon man only for the sin recorded in verse 2. Surely angels would have been included in the judgment and in the record if they had been involved in this sin. Further, the "Nephilim" of verse 4 are not said to be due to what is recorded in verse 2, but are spoken of as existing previously and subsequently. It is therefore in every way better and truer to the context to explain the passage of the two lines of Seth and of Cain, and as giving the explanation of the judgment and the flood (Green and Lange *in loc.*)

As a natural result comes the Divine warning (ver. 3). The interpretation of this verse is difficult. Probably the Hebrew word rendered "strive" would be better expressed by "dwell." In either case it is a warning of the limitation of mercy, and it is generally thought that the term of 120 years refers to the time yet to be given to mankind before the Flood should come upon the earth. Thus God in mercy warns while declaring His certain judgment upon evil.

Nothing could well be more pitiable than this delineation of human sin (ver 5). What a contrast we have here to the "God saw" of chapter i. 31! Instead of everything being very good, all things were now evil. Mark carefully the phrases "every imagination," "only evil continually." Could anything be more solemn in its unrelieved gloom? No redeeming feature appears. Everything is evil in human life. It is also a solemn fact that most of the unholiness in human history has been due to the same cause as is mentioned here, the relations of men and women (vers, 2. 4),

We are now bidden to note the Divine Sorrow (vers. 6, 7). The statements here are startling in their directness and definiteness. We are accustomed to speak of them as anthropomorphic; but so far from this being an objection, anthropomorphic language is our highest and best method of expression concerning God. It is no disrespect or derogation from infinite holiness to speak of God in this way. A very great deal of the objection to anthropomorphism really involves utter agnosticism and the impossibility of finding any expression for God at all (Dods, *Genesis*, pp. 60-62).

There was one exception to the universal prevalence of sin. "Noah found grace in the eyes of the Lord" (ver. 8). He and his alone were to be preserved amidst surrounding destruction.

Three subjects seem to call for particular attention from students.

1. *The Longevity of the Antediluvians.*—"The longevity attributed to the antediluvians has been declared to be inconsistent with physiological laws; but in our ignorance of the extent to which the conditions affecting human life may have been modified, such an assertion is unwarranted" (Green, *Unity of the Book of Genesis*, p. 43).

2. *The Authenticity of the Chronology.*—"It should be remarked that no computation of time is ever built in the Bible upon this or any other genealogy . . . . This genealogy could only afford a safe estimate of time on the assumption that no links are missing, and that every name in the line of descent has been recorded. But this we have no right to take for granted. The analogy of other Biblical genealogies is decidedly against it. Very commonly unimportant names are omitted; sometimes several consecutive names are dropped together. No one has a right, therefore, to denominate a primeval chronology and set it in opposition to the deductions of science, and thence conclude that there is a conflict between the Bible and science" (Green, *Unity*, pp. 49f.)

3. *The Two Genealogies.*—It is sometimes urged that there has been a confusion between the genealogy of the Cainites and that of the Sethites, owing to a certain similarity of names, six of them being nearly identical; yet the distinctness of the two genealogies is clearly stated, and in reality only two names are exactly the same

in both. If it be said that the editor of Genesis evidently intended the Lamech of chapter iv. to be regarded as the Lamech of chapter v., it may perhaps be replied that centuries of readers have clearly recognized the distinction between them (Green, p. 45; Redpath *in loc.*)

In this section we have in sharp contrast two classes of men who are still to be found upon earth, and whose characteristics take pretty much the same form as in those early days.

Man living without God.—In the line of Cain we have cleverness, culture, and civilization; and yet with all these manifest advantages everything was purely earthly, selfish, and sensual. God was ignored, and they lived their life entirely apart from Him. Self-contained, occupied with their own intellectual and social pursuits, they simply ignored the claims of God, and lived and died without Him. Today the same spirit is abroad in many quarters. Men have everything that this world can give of education, refinement, culture, pleasure, art, civilization, and yet there is nothing of God or His Christ in their lives.

Man walking with God.—The elements of true living in relation to God are evident in the line of Seth.

(1) Devotion to God (iv. 25).
(2) Consecration to God (iv. 26).
(3) Fellowship with God (v. 22).
(4) Testimony for God (Heb. ix. 5).
(5) Service for God (v. 29).
(6) Grace from God (vi. 8).

Let us therefore keep the avenues open towards God and a constant communication between us and the sky. The house of life assuredly needs its kitchen (physical), its library (intellectual), its parlor (social); but it also needs, above all, its drawing-room— that is, its *withdrawing* room— where the soul retires from all else to seek and meet with God. Only then do we come to our true life and realize the Divine end of existence. Our cleverness becomes devoted to the highest objects, our culture becomes transformed into a true *cultus* or worship, our civilization is fraught with blessing to those around, and God is in all things glorified.

VII

BEFORE THE FLOOD

Gen. vi. 9-22

THESE *are* the generations of Noah: Noah was a just man *and* perfect in his generations, *and* Noah walked with God.

And Noah begat three sons, Shem, Ham, and Japheth.

The earth also was corrupt before God, and the earth was filled with violence.

And God looked upon the earth, and, behold, it was corrupt: for all flesh had corrupted his way upon the earth.

And God said unto Noah, The end of all flesh is come before Me; for the earth is filled with violence through them; and, behold, I will destroy them with the earth.

Make thee an ark of gopher wood; rooms shalt thou make in the ark, and shalt pitch it within and without with pitch.

And this *is the fashion* which thou shalt make it *of*: The length of the ark *shall* be three hundred cubits, the breadth of it fifty cubits, and the height of it thirty cubits.

A window shalt thou make to the ark, and in a cubit shalt thou finish it above; and the door of the ark shalt thou set in the side thereof; *with* lower, second, and third *stories* shalt thou make it.

And, behold, I even I, do bring a flood of waters upon the earth, to destroy all flesh, wherein *is* the breath of life, from under heaven; *and* every thing that *is* in the earth shall die.

But with thee will I establish My covenant; and thou shalt come into the ark, thou, and thy sons, and thy wife, and thy sons' wives with thee.

And of every living thing of all flesh, two of every *sort* shalt thou bring into the ark, to keep *them* alive with thee; they shall be male and female.

Of fowls after their kind, and of cattle after their kind, of every creeping thing of the earth after his kind, two of every *sort* shall come unto thee, to keep *them* alive.

And take thou unto thee of all food that is eaten, and thou shalt gather *it* to thee; and it shall be for food for thee, and for them.

Thus did Noah; according to all that God commanded him, so did he.

A NEW section of Genesis commences here. The period from Adam to Noah is almost entirely passed over, probably because there was nothing to record as to the progress of the Kingdom of God. Instead of such a record we have, by contrast, only the

solemn and significant summary of the awful progress of sin.
We have already seen the development of wickedness which cul-
minated in the awful sins referred to in the previous verses. There
is no indication in the Bible of man's steady rise from a lower
to a higher level, developing out of barbarism into holiness. On
the contrary, the race is seen to tend downward in proportion as it
is left to follow its own way. This view of man's proneness to evil,
with the consequent results, is in exact keeping with the facts of
history, and with all the best and most accurate anthropological
knowledge of the present day (Orr, *Image of God, passim*).

The entire section dealing with "the generations of Noah' (chap.
vi. 9 to ix. 29) should be looked at as a whole, and its completeness noted:—

1. Noah and his Sons (chap. vi. 9, 10).

2. The Sinfulness and Condemnation of the World (chap. vi.
11-13).

3. The Divine Command (chap. vi. 14-21).

4. The Obedience of Noah (chap. vi. 22 to vii. 9).

5. The Flood (chap. vii. 10-24).

6. The Divine Preservation of the Ark (chap. viii. 1-22).

7. The New Covenant (chap. ix. 1-17).

8. The New Start (chap. ix. 18-29).

In studying this material in detail it is important to notice the
combination of formal phraseology with the vividness and detail—
e.g., chapter vi. 17-20 and chapter viii. 20-22. The dignity of the
narrative is also noteworthy. There is nothing grotesque or unworthy, everything is sober and in keeping with the solemn realities
involved. The simplicity and genuineness of Noah's character, the
simple and righteous motives ascribed to God, the sobriety and
purity of the promise made to Noah, should all be observed. Not
least of all it will be noticed that the story of the Flood. as such,
is quite incidental to the spiritual realities that arise out of the
events. The narrative leads up to the covenant in chapter ix., which
carries with it the new start of the human race after the failure
between Adam and Noah.

It is impossible to dwell in detail on the entire narrative of the Flood: it must suffice to follow mainly the pages of our English Bible, and look at the spiritual truths associated with (1) the period immediately preceding the Flood, (2) the time of the Flood itself, and (3) the early days of the new era after the Flood. We now dwell first of all upon the verses at the head of this section.

The contrast between the sin recorded in verse 7 and the character of Noah in verses 8-10 is very striking, especially as it is followed by another contrast in the verses now before us.

I. *The Divine Purpose* (vers. 9-13) is now clearly stated to be a judgment upon sin. Its cause is due to the awful character of mankind (ver. 11). The two words, "corrupt" and "violence," give us respectively the character and expression of the sin, the cause and the effect. The corruption has led to violence, for badness always leads to cruelty in one form or another. A life that is wrong with God necessarily becomes wrong with its fellows.

The Divine Scrutiny is also stated in simple but solemn terms (ver. 12). "God looked upon the earth, and, behold, it was corrupt." How great is the contrast here with a former occasion: "God saw everything that He had made, and, behold, it was very good" (chap. i. 31). God is not indifferent to human life, and the fact of sin necessarily compelled Him to take action. His decision to destroy the earth was at once an expression of His justice and His mercy; the end had come, and there was no alternative. Moral putridity can only be destroyed by a Divine judgment.

II. *The Divine Plan* (vers. 14-17).—The method of deliverance was the Ark of Safety about which God now proceeds to speak. The instructions are given in full detail. The ark is to be made of gopher wood, by which is probably to be understood some resinous wood like that of the fir or cypress tree. The vessel was in no sense a ship intended for a voyage, but a kind of covered raft or floating house, sufficient for buoyancy and protection during the flood. Into the details of shape and space it is unnecessary to enter, except to notice the minute care shown by these details and the indications they afford of the Divine thought for the inmates of the ark.

With great solemnity God announces his intention of bringing a flood upon the earth to destroy all life. "Behold, I, even I do bring a flood of waters upon the earth." Thus solemnly does God call His servant's attention to what is to happen and also to the fact that the flood is His own divine act.

III. *The Divine Provision* (vers. 18-22).—In contrast with the announcement of the flood comes this declaration of the divine covenant. It is noteworthy that we have the word "establish" in connection ·with the covenant. Noah was already in covenant with God (ver. 8), but in view of the special need of assurance of divine protection God now declares that He will establish His covenant. This is the first occasion on which we have this word "covenant," one of the great outstanding expressions of Holy Scripture as indicative of God's relations with man. It is particularly interesting to notice that the covenant was with Noah only, his family being included because of their connection with him. It is worth while observing that in Holy Scripture the family rather than the individual constitutes the true unity. The race, as we well know, fell in Adam, and here in like manner Noah's family was saved for his sake. Other instances like those of Abraham and Cain confirm this view of what is now usually described as the solidarity of mankind. The Apostle Peter, on the Day of Pentecost, seems to recognize the same principle when he says, "The promise is to you, and to your children." What a responsibility this places upon parentage and guardianship and every other position involving the lives of others!

God's care of the animals is not to be overlooked in the study of these verses. "Two of every sort shall come unto thee, to keep them alive " (ver. 20).

To all this Noah made a fitting response (ver. 22). Twice over we are told simply and suggestively that he did "according to all that God commanded him."

In these verses we have some of the essential elements in the life of a true believer as illustrated by Noah.

1. *His Position* (ver. 8). "Noah found grace in the eyes of the Lord." This was the foundation of his life as it is the foundation of every true life today. "By grace are ye saved." Grace, in the

Bible sense of the word, means God's unmerited favor, and it was this alone that gave Noah his spiritual position before God. He was "saved by grace alone."

2. *His Attitude* (ver. 9). "Noah was a righteous man." From grace comes righteousness, and whether we think of its Old Testament meaning of genuineness and sincerity, or of its New Testament fuller meaning of being right with God, we can see its necessity and importance for every one of us."

3. *His Character* (ver. 9). "Noah was . . . perfect." The original word means upright, genuine, and has no reference to the absence of sin. Uprightness in turn is the result of being righteous before God through grace. Our personal character must necessarily be the proof of our true position in the sight of God.

4. *His Testimony* (ver. 9). "In his generations." Here we have brought before us the thought of Noah's life in relation to his contemporaries. He lived a life of witness to God among those with whom he was associated. As the Apostle Peter tells us, he was "a preacher of righteousness" (2 Pet. ii. 5). His life as well as his words bore testimony to God and thus "condemned the world" of his day (Heb. xi. 7).

5. *His Fellowship* (ver. 9). "Noah walked with God." He is one of two men of whom this is recorded (chap. v. 22). The idea is that of friendship and fellowship with God, and it is noteworthy that such a position was possible amidst the very difficult, practical, every-day life that Noah had to lead. It meant courage and independence, for no one else was walking in that way. When a man walks with God it necessarily means that he cannot walk with any of his fellows who are going in the opposite direction.

6. *His Conduct* (ver. 22). "Thus did Noah." His spiritual position, attitude, character and fellowship were expressed and proved in practical obedience. Nothing can make up for this. All our privileges and opportunities of grace are intended to be manifested in daily obedience. "Conduct is three-fourths of life."

7. *His Thoroughness* (ver. 22). "According to all that God commanded him." This was the standard by which Noah lived, the Word of God and everything that that Word had declared. He did

not pick and choose among God's commands but did "according to all" that God had said. It was this Word of God that led him to prepare the ark, "being warned of God of things not seen as yet" (Heb. xi. 7).

What a splendid figure this man makes, a picture of solitary goodness! He was the one saint of that day. It *is* possible, therefore, to be good even though we have to stand alone. It is possible to be right with God even amidst surrounding iniquity. God is the same today as He was to Noah, and if only we are willing to fulfil the conditions we too shall walk with God and please Him.

VIII

AT THE FLOOD

GEN. vii.

AND the Lord said unto Noah, Come thou and all thy house into the ark; for thee have I seen righteous before Me in this generation.

Of every clean beast thou shalt take to thee by sevens, the male and his female: and of beasts that *are* not clean by two, the male and his female.

Of fowls also of the air by sevens, the male and the female; to keep seed alive upon the face of all the earth.

For yet seven days, and I will cause it to rain upon the earth forty days and forty nights; and every living substance that I have made will I destroy from off the face of the earth.

And Noah did according unto all that the Lord commanded him.

And Noah *was* six hundred years old when the flood of waters was upon the earth.

And Noah went in, and his sons, and his wife, and his sons' wives with him, into the ark, because of the waters of the flood.

Of clean beasts, and of beasts that *are* not clean, and of fowls, and of every thing that creepeth upon the earth.

There went in two and two unto Noah into the ark, the male and the female, as God had commanded Noah.

And it came to pass, after seven days, that the waters of the flood were upon the earth.

In the six hundredth year of Noah's life, in the second month, the seventeenth day of the month, the same day were all the fountains of the great deep broken up, and the windows of heaven were opened.

And the rain was upon the earth forty days and forty nights.

In the self-same day entered Noah, and Shem, and Ham, and Japheth, the sons of Noah, and Noah's wife, and the three wives of his sons with them, into the ark;

They, and every beast after his kind, and all the cattle after their kind, and every creeping thing that creepeth upon the earth after his kind, and every fowl after his kind, every bird of every sort.

And they went in unto Noah into the ark, two and two of all flesh, wherein *is* the breath of life.

And they that went in, went in male and female of all flesh, as God had commanded him: and the Lord shut him in.

And the flood was forty days upon the earth; and the waters increased, and bare up the ark, and it was lift up above the earth.

And the waters prevailed, and were increased greatly upon the earth; and the ark went upon the face of the waters.

And the waters prevailed exceedingly upon the earth; and all the high hills that *were* under the whole heaven *were* covered.

And all flesh died that moved upon the earth, both of fowl, and of cattle, and of beast, and of every creeping thing that creepeth upon the earth, and every man:

All in whose nostrils *was* the breath of life, of all that *was* in the dry *land,* died.

And every living substance was destroyed which was upon the face of the ground, both man, and cattle, and the creeping things, and the fowl of the heaven; and they were destroyed from the earth: and Noah only remained *alive,* and they that *were* with him in the ark.

And the waters prevailed upon the earth an hundred and fifty days.

IN view of the brief and summary character of the first five chapters of Genesis it cannot but be noticed how full of details these chapters are in their record of the Flood. Bearing in mind the constant spiritual purpose of the book it would seem as though we are intended to study as carefully as possible every detail in order to learn the lessons God would teach us.

I. *The Record of the Events.*—This chapter is noteworthy for the points of time mentioned. The details can best be studied along these lines.

First, we have the last week preceding the flood (vers. 1-6). During this time God gave the final invitation to Noah, and announced to him the coming of the flood within seven days.

Then we have the day on which Noah entered into the ark (vers. 7-10). It requires very little imagination to realize the solemnity of the occasion, and the procession and the entrance of all those who were to be preserved from the Flood.

Next comes a record of the forty days of rain (vers. 11-17). Together with the rain we are told of the movements of the great deep, both combining to bring about the Divine judgment.

The chapter closes with the statement of the one hundred and fifty days during which "the waters prevailed upon the earth" (vers. 18-24). The word "prevailed" is the keynote of this section, and may suggest not merely a physical prevalence of the Flood, but a spiritual prevalence of Divine judgment, irresistible, irretrievable, irrevocable.

II. *The Facts of the Flood.*—The evidence for the destruction of the human race except one family is very strong apart from Genesis. It seems impossible that so widespread and persistent a tradition can be regarded as an invention or myth. There is nothing mythical or unworthy about the Bible account, and it is perhaps worthwhile observing that the proportions of the ark are not essentially different from those of ships of corresponding size now sailing between here and England. It is scarcely likely that the proportions given in Genesis could be mere guess work.

Further, the tendency of recent geological discoveries is to render the account in Genesis more credible than it was even twenty-five years ago. There are clear proofs of a widespread catastrophe to animals and plants immediately preceding the period of man's appearance on the earth, and it is urged by some geologists that these changes suggest that man was introduced into the world before the instability of the glacial period had given way to the apparent stability of the present order of affairs. All this, while it is, of course, no proof of the genuineness of Genesis, is distinctly in keeping with the narrative there given (*Geology's Witness to the Flood, by* Dr. G. F. Wright, *American Sunday School Times,* July 6, 1901).

III. *Was the Flood Universal?*—It is essential, in considering this question, to view it from the standpoint of the writer of Genesis. Then we at once realize that to an eye-witness, or to one dealing with the subject from the standpoint of human sin and Divine judgment, the universality of the Flood would be certain, even though the area was quite local. The description of the Flood, so far as the destruction of human life is concerned, would be much the same, whether local or literally universal. The one and only purpose of the writer seems to be the record of the destruction of man.

The universal tradition of the Flood is no necessary proof of its universality. since the tradition, as handed down, would be necessarily carried wherever men went. At the same time there are geological facts in different parts of the world which seem to suggest something more than a local flood in Western Asia. The narrative in Genesis has been aptly likened to a sea captain's log-book (Wright, *ut supra*), and certainly all the universality demanded is that which was necessary for the destruction of the human race. The spiritual purpose of the narrative, which is, of course, the predominant factor, would be perfectly realized by supposing that the Flood was confined to the locality then inhabited by the human race (*Pulpit Commentary, Genesis*, pp. 119 f.; Urquhart, *New Biblical Guide*, vol. i., chapters xi., xii., xiii., Howorth's *Mammoth and the Flood*).

IV. *The Flood in Tradition.*—According to Lenormant the story of the Flood is a "universal tradition in all branches of the human family, with the sole exception of the black race." The Babylonian tradition is remarkably like the Hebrew account, and at the same time remarkably unlike. The coincidences suggest a community of origin, while the divergences show that there cannot have been any direct influence of Babylonia on the Hebrew account.

It is hardly likely that the Jews would have copied it from any Exilic records possessed by their inveterate foe. As is well known, the Babylonian account is grossly polytheistic, while the Hebrew is as purely monotheistic, and no theory of their relationship will ever be satisfactory unless the divergences as well as the coincidences are accounted for. It is much more natural to believe that the Hebrew preserves for us the pure spiritual version of the tradition, and that the Babylonian account is a corrupt version.

The antecedents of Abraham are ample to account for the Hebrew tradition, and if we may assume that he brought it with him to Canaan we can quite understand how the purer account was preserved. Civilization in the days prior to Abraham shows that this view is perfectly reasonable and even likely.

V. *The Flood in Genesis.*—It is urged that two, if not three, accounts are united, not by the blending of excerpts, as in previous sections, but by close interweaving. This is argued on the grounds that each account is complete in itself, and that only thus can the repetitions and alternations of the Divine names be accounted for. It may, however, be pointed out that each account is not complete, for if the sections attributed to each source respectively are read continuously, it will be found that there are gaps of great importance, and no real continuity of the narrative.

The story as it stands has a unity, and certainly was intended by the compiler to be regarded as a whole. If we allow the recognized thirty days to the month, and commence with Noah's six hundredth birthday as in chapter vii. 11, we shall find that there is no inconsistency in the chronology.

The use of the Divine names gives us the two aspects of the Flood in relation to the God of Judgment (Elohim) and the God of Grace (Jehovah). Both titles are used, and that with remarkable discrimination, while on the partition theory the differences of use are inexplicable. It is admitted by one leading critic that other phraseological criteria, apart from the use of the Divine names, are slight; while another critic holds that the theory of a division of the narrative based upon this distinction of usage of Divine names is now "manifestly exploded, and the disproof is absolute and irrefragable."

Above all, the theory of two documents entirely fails to account for the Chaldæan narrative of the Flood, which contains the characteristics both of the alleged author who uses Elohim and of the one who uses Jehovah. There are at least twenty-five items of the story of the Flood common to Genesis and the Assyrian tablet; and as these items cover nearly the entire story they necessarily include nearly all the literary characteristics upon which criticism bases its claim of two documents. As this tablet is said to be as old as 3000 B. C. (Hastings' *Bible Dictionary*), it is difficult to understand how we are to account for the separate narratives of the two authors, who are said to have lived more than a thousand years later.

The story in Genesis undoubtedly appears before us as a unity; and even if there were originally two stories they have been remarkably well blended into one. Certainly contradictions only arise when the attempt is made to dissect the narrative as it now stands (Green, *Unity of Genesis, in loc.*; Everts, *Homiletic Review*, vol. xl. p. 124; Sayce, *Monument Facts and Higher Critical Fancies*).

If in chapter vi. we find we have a portrait of the servant in relation to God, in chapter vii. we have a number of statements concerning God in relation to His servant.

1. *The Divine Invitation* (ver. 1).—"Come thou." This is the first time that the familiar word "Come" occurs. It is found some six hundred times in the rest of the Bible. It is noteworthy that God said "Come" into the ark, not "Go." Surely we have here the suggestion that in some sense God would be with him there. "His presence is salvation." The personal character of the invitation is also noteworthy, "Come *thou*." Yet again, the inclusion of his family in the invitation should be observed, "Come thou and all thy house."

2. *The Divine Observation* (ver. 1).—"Thee have I seen." The thought of God watching His servants is at once a joy and a responsibility, an inspiration and a warning. When the life is wholly surrendered to God and lived in genuine sincerity the thought of "Thou God seest me" is a delight. Not seldom in Holy Scripture have we expressions telling us that God is "well pleased" with His faithful servants. The thought that our life can give pleasure to God is one of the greatest incentives to holy living.

3. *The Divine Requirement* (ver. 1).—"Righteous before Me." This practically sums up everything that God demands from man. Article XI. of the Church of England defines justification as "accounted righteous before God." Somewhat similar in idea is the description of Zacharias and Elizabeth. "They were both righteous before God" (see Gen. xvii. 1; 1 Kings ix. 4; 2 Kings xx. 3; Job i. 1; Acts xxiii. 1; Phil. iii. 6). The Old Testament is necessarily concerned only with the divine requirement of righteousness. It remained for New Testament times to reveal the provision of a perfect righteousness in Christ Jesus (Rom. iii. 20-26).

4. *The Divine Testimony* (ver. 1).—"Righteous before Me in this generation." Once again we have the thought of Noah's contemporaries brought before us, but this time from the divine side. God here proclaims His servant's righteousness, and bears witness thereto. Like Abel and Enoch before him, "he obtained witness that he was righteous, God testifying of" his life (Heb. xi. 4-7).

"When a man's ways please the Lord" God always lets other people know it.

5. *The Divine Commandment* (ver. 5).—"The Lord commanded him." The Word of God is brought constantly before us in connection with Noah (chaps. vi. 13, 22; vii. 5, 9, 16; viii. 15, 21; ix. 1, 8, 12, 17), as indeed it is all through the Bible. God speaks, man listens; God commands, man obeys. The Word of God is at once the standard and the guide of life, and no life or service is possible unless it is ever subject thereto.

6. *The Divine Protection* (ver. 16).—"The Lord shut him in." This suggests that he was not dependent upon himself for safety, but upon the Lord. It was a divine, not a human fastening, that guaranteed his perfect shelter. Those whom God protects never need have any fear.

7. *The Divine Preservation* (chap. viii. 1).—"God remembered Noah." The servant was not forgotten by his Lord, and this point, which is the culminating thought of the section, shows the constant divine care of Noah and his family. There is only one thing that God forgets with reference to His children, that is, their sins. "Their sins and iniquities will I remember no more." As for God's people themselves, the words are blessedly and eternally true, "They shall not be forgotten of Me."

IX

AFTER THE FLOOD

GEN. viii.

AND God remembered Noah, and every living thing, and all the cattle that *was* with him in the ark: and God made a wind to pass over the earth, and the waters assuaged:

The fountains also of the deep and the windows of heaven were stopped, and the rain from heaven was restrained;

And the waters returned from off the earth continually: and after the end of the hundred and fifty days the waters were abated.

And the ark rested in the seventh month, on the seventeenth day of the month, upon the mountains of Ararat.

And the waters decreased continually until the tenth month: in the tenth *month*, on the first *day* of the month, were the tops of the mountains seen.

And it came to pass at the end of forty days, that Noah opened the window of the ark which he had made:

And he sent forth a raven, which went forth to and fro, until the waters were dried up from off the earth.

And he sent forth a dove from him, to see if the waters were abated from off the face of the ground:

But the dove found no rest for the sole of her foot, and she returned unto him into the ark, for the waters *were* on the face of the whole earth: then he put forth his hand, and took her, and pulled her in unto him into the ark.

And he stayed yet other seven days, and again he sent forth the dove out of the ark;

And the dove came in to him in the evening; and, lo, in her mouth *was* an olive leaf pluckt off: so Noah knew that the waters were abated from off the earth.

And he stayed yet other seven days; and sent forth the dove; which returned not again unto him any more.

And it came to pass in the six hundredth and first year, in the first *month*, the first *day* of the month, the waters were dried up from off the earth: and Noah removed the covering of the ark, and looked, and, behold, the face of the ground was dry.

And in the second month, on the seven and twentieth day of the month, was the earth dried.

And God spake unto Noah, saying,

Go forth of the ark, thou, and thy wife, and thy sons, and thy sons' wives with thee.

Bring forth with thee every living thing that *is* with thee, of all flesh, *both* of fowl, and of cattle, and of every creeping thing that creepeth upon the earth; that they may breed abundantly in the earth, and be fruitful, and multiply upon the earth.

And Noah went forth, and his sons, and his wife, and his sons' wives with him:

Every beast, every creeping thing, and every fowl, *and* whatsoever creepeth upon the earth, after their kinds, went forth out of the ark.

And Noah builded an altar unto the Lord; and took of every clean beast, and of every clean fowl, and offered burnt offerings on the altar.

And the Lord smelled a sweet savour; and the Lord said in His heart, I will not again curse the ground any more for man's sake; for the imagination of man's heart *is* evil from his youth; neither will I again smite any more every thing living, as I have done.

While the earth remaineth, seedtime and harvest, and cold and heat, and summer and winter, and day and night shall not cease.

AGAIN we are impressed with the remarkable detail of the history. Yet human history, as such and in itself, has no real place in the Old Testament. It is only human life, as seen in the light of the divine purpose, that is recorded in the Word of God. The divine and the human elements are here blended and contrasted, and along these lines the chapter will best be studied.

I. *The Lord's Action* (vers. 1-5).—The divine judgment is now drawing to its close. The servant is remembered by God and the covenant established is now to be carried out in full. The waters from above and below were restrained, and the ark now rests in safety upon the mountains of Ararat. The place of rest seems to have been the territory known by the name of one of the peaks (*cf.* 2 Kings xix. 37, R.V.).

II. *The Servant's Attitude* (vers. 6-14).—It was an attitude of Faith. Noah was on the alert and responsive to the divine movements. Having opened the window, he sent forth a raven, which wandered hither and thither and did not return. Then he sent forth a dove, but the dove found no resting-place and returned to him in the ark.

It was also an attitude of Hope. Having waited seven days more, again he sent forth a dove, and the dove came back with an olive leaf, so that Noah now knew that the waters were abating.

It was also an attitude of Patience. He waited seven days longer before sending out the dove a third time, and when the dove did not return, Noah must have known that the day of deliverance was at hand.

When God pledges His word and establishes His covenant, His servants have a strong foundation for their faith, hope, and patience.

> "How firm a foundation, ye saints of the Lord,
> Is laid for your faith in His excellent Word!
> What more can He say, than to you He hath said—
> To you, who for refuge to Jesus have fled."

III. *The Lord's Command* (vers. 15-17).—At last the time had come for Noah to leave the ark, and the Word which had so clearly told him to enter, now with equal clearness tells him to come forth with his family, and to bring forth with him everything that he had taken in. God never commands before the time required for obedience. Step by step He makes known His will. He is never too soon and never too late.

IV. *The Servant's Obedience* (vers. 18, 19).—As the servant had obeyed implicitly, accurately, and immediately before the Flood, so he does now. He went forth at once at the command of God. Obedience to be real must be prompt and full. This is one of the supreme tests of genuine living.

V. *The Servant's Consecration* (ver. 20).—Noah's first act on landing upon the earth was to build an altar and to offer sacrifices. Thereby he testified at once (a) to his gratitude to God for deliverance, (b) to his need of sacrifice in approaching his God, and (c) to the consecration of his life to the service of God as symbolized by the burnt offering.

VI. *The Lord's Revelation* (vers. 21, 22).—In response there is a twofold movement of God. First there is the acceptance of the sacrifice, "The Lord smelled a sweet savour." Quite literally the phrase is, "a savour of rest," the word apparently being a play upon the meaning of Noah (chap. v. 29). God thus signified His acceptance of what His servant had done in offering "a sacrifice to God for a sweet smelling savour" (Eph. v. 2).

Following the acceptance of the sacrifice was the divine assurance with special reference to the future of the earth. There was to be no more curse in the form of a flood, and there was to be an absolute guarantee of the permanence of the seasons, year by year, as long as the earth remained.

Thus the Lord and His servant revealed their attitudes towards each other all through this chapter, and we have in it one of the most suggestive pictures of God in relation to man, and of man in relation to God.

Let us now review these three chapters (vi.-viii.), and read them afresh in the light of New Testament teaching. In view of the words of the Apostle Peter (1 Pet. iii. 20), it is not wrong to regard the story of the flood as a great pictorial and symbolical lesson full of spiritual truths. It is sometimes said that history never repeats itself, but there is a sense in which it does in relation to spiritual and moral realities. Our Lord distinctly tells us that the history of Noah will repeat itself in the day of His coming (Matt. xxiv. 37-42). What were the days of Noah, and what will be the days of the Son of Man?

1. *Days of sin.*

(*a*) God's Way was abandoned. The earth had become corrupt through sin, and man's heart was only evil continually.

(*b*) God's Word was speaking. The Ark was the Divine protest against sin; while Noah, a preacher of righteousness, ever witnessed to the certainty of retribution and the limited time of God's Spirit among men (chap. vi. 3).

(*c*) God's Will was unheeded. For 120 years Noah preached without obtaining a single convert. This shows the awful extent of man's depravity, and the certainty of that wrath of God which is the manifestation of the Divine holiness against sin. "It is a fearful thing to fall into the hands of a living God."

2. *Days of sorrow.*

We think of the people at the time of the Flood, and our thought goes on to those who will be living similarly in the days of the Son of Man.

(*a*) God's Message was neglected. Every nail driven into the ark was like an appeal from God, and yet all the testimony was fruitless year after year.

(*b*) God's Refuge was rejected. There was no other way of salvation except the Ark; no human device was sufficient. They might get up to the highest peak of the highest hill, and yet there would be no salvation.

(*c*) God's Gift was lost. They had the offer of salvation and life. They neglected and then rejected it, and as a consequence they lost it.

3. *Days of salvation.*

(*a*) God's Grace was working. Noah was the solitary saint of those days, and this shows that goodness is possible, even amidst the most adverse circumstances. He lived as well as preached; his life testified as well as his words to the reality and opportunity of the grace of God.

(*b*) God's Love was planning. The instructions about the Ark, the invitation to enter, the protection within the Ark, the cessation of the Flood, and the deliverance of Noah and his house, all testify to the reality of God's love in providing this way of salvation.

(*c*) God's Power was keeping. How significant it is to read, "The Lord shut him in"! There was ample room and perfect provision in the Ark. No anxiety, no possibility of leakage or wreck; one door of entrance, and that protected by Divine power. The Ark was a home for saved people. So far as we know, there was no sail, no mast, no rudder; only God! And that was enough!

Thus, as it was in the days of Noah, so will it be in the days of the Son of Man. Days of evil and yet of good. Amid the evil days an opportunity for salvation and an invitation to partake of the Divine mercy. Days of peril and of loss; and yet the opportunity of pardon, peace, protection, preservation. "Now is the accepted time; now is the day of salvation."

X

THE NEW ERA

GEN. ix. 1-17

AND God blessed Noah and his sons, and said unto them, Be fruitful, and multiply, and replenish the earth.

And the fear of you, and the dread of you, shall be upon every beast of the earth, and upon every fowl of the air, upon all that moveth *upon* the earth, and upon all the fishes of the sea; into your hand are they delivered.

Every moving thing that liveth shall be meat for you; even as the green herb have I given you all things.

But flesh with the life thereof, *which is* the blood thereof, shall ye not eat.

And surely your blood of your lives will I require: at the hand of every beast will I require it, and at the hand of man; at the hand of every man's brother will I require the life of man.

Whoso sheddeth man's blood, by man shall his blood be shed: for in the image of God made He man.

And you, be ye fruitful, and multiply; bring forth abundantly in the earth, and multiply therein.

And God spake unto Noah, and to his sons with him, saying,

And I, behold, I establish my covenant with you, and with your seed after you;

And with every living creature that *is* with you, of the fowl, of the cattle, and of every beast of the earth with you; from all that go out of the ark, to every beast of the earth.

And I will establish My covenant with you; neither shall all flesh be cut off any more by the waters of a flood; neither shall there any more be a flood to destroy the earth.

And God said, This *is* the token of the covenant which I make between Me and you and every living creature that *is* with you, for perpetual generations:

I do set My bow in the cloud, and it shall be for a token of a covenant between Me and the earth.

And it shall come to pass, when I bring a cloud over the earth, that the bow shall be seen in the cloud:

And I will remember My covenant, which *is* between Me and you and every living creature of all flesh; and the waters shall no more become a flood to destroy all flesh.

And the bow shall be in the cloud; and I will look upon it that I may remember the everlasting covenant between God and every living creature of all flesh that *is* upon the earth.

And God said unto Noah, This *is* the token of the covenant, which I have established between Me and all flesh that *is* upon the earth.

NOAH now takes his place as the second head of the human race. There was to be a new beginning, a fresh start, full of hope and with every Divine guarantee of blessing. Sin had been punished, grace was working, and God was ready to guide and bless those through whom the earth was to be peopled and ruled.

I. *The Elements of a New Commencement* (vers. 1-7).—The new start is made at the only possible point, that of the Divine blessing (ver. 1). "God blessed Noah and his sons." Just as God blessed Adam and Eve (chap. i. 28), so it was necessary that the same Divine blessing should rest upon the new progenitors of the human race.

Divine exhortation naturally follows Divine blessing (ver. 1). "Be fruitful, and multiply, and replenish the earth." Again we are reminded of the primeval command (chap. i. 28). God thereby took the necessary steps for the propagation of life.

The Divine promise appropriately follows (ver. 2). Noah is assured that fear and dread should be upon everything on the earth for his sake. Into his hands they were all to be delivered, thereby assuring him of protection and power.

Divine provision was also assured to him (ver. 3). Food and sustenance were thus assured. It would seem from a comparison of this verse with chapter i. 29, that it was only after the Flood that animal food was permitted to man.

Divine prohibition is included in this new commencement (ver. 4). The sacredness of life is taught by this prohibition about the eating of blood, and still more the thought of what that blood was to symbolize in atonement is probably here first brought before us (Lev. iii. 17).

Divine warnings are another element in this passage (ver. 6). Noah and his sons are told still more about the sanctity of life.

Blood shed will be required, and this great principle is based upon the highest sanction, for "in the image of God made He man."

Divine expectations fitly close the section (ver. 7). God again exhorts and encourages Noah and his sons to fruitfulness, thus indicating that He expected them to fulfil the conditions of life and blessing, and to realize thereby the Divine purpose.

II. *The Establishment of a New Covenant* (vers. 8-17).—It is often said that God never gives a command without providing the grace needed to obey, and we have a striking illustration of this great principle in the passage before us. Following naturally and appropriately after the Divine counsels given in the preceding section we have the assurance of needed grace in connection with the Divine covenant.

The Source of the covenant naturally comes first (ver. 9). Its author was God. Human covenants were entered into mutually between two parties, but here the entire initiation was taken by God. "I, behold, I" (ver. 9); "I will" (ver. 11); "I make" (ver. 12), "I have established" (ver. 17). The significance of this is due to the fact that it was of God's free grace alone that the covenant was made. His blessings were to be bestowed even though nothing had been done by man to deserve them. Everything is of grace from first to last.

The Scope of the covenant is also noteworthy (vers. 9, 10). It comprehended Noah and his seed, and not only these, but "every living creature." Thus the blessings of God were to be extended as widely over the earth as they could possibly be. This is not the only place in Scripture where the destiny of the lower creation is intimately connected with that of man (Isa. xi. 6-8; Rom. viii. 19-22).

The Purpose of the covenant should be carefully noted (ver. 11). It was associated with the assurance that human life should not be cut off or the world destroyed any more by a flood. The appropriateness of this revelation is apparent, for at that time it must have been a real perplexity to know whether there would be any repetition in the future of what they had experienced in the Flood. Everything connected with their relations to God had been altered by that catastrophe, and now God does not leave man ignorant. but, on the contrary, pledges Himself not to bring another similar judgment upon the earth.

The Sign of the covenant is specially emphasized (vers. 12, 13). The rainbow is now given a specific spiritual meaning, and nature for the first time becomes a symbol of spiritual truth. We know from subsequent passages what a great principle is brought before us in this way. It is what is known as the "sacramental principle." In one of the Homilies of the Church of England, Sacraments are defined as "visible signs to which are annexed promises," and the rainbow was the first of such visible signs illustrative of spiritual truths. We think of the Passover Lamb, the Brazen Serpent, Gideon's Fleece, and especially of Baptism and the Lord's Supper as illustrations of this Divine method of revealing and assuring us of spiritual truth. As Lange beautifully says, "God's eye of grace and our eye of faith meet in the Sacraments." Our faith lays hold of the promise annexed to the sign, and the sign strengthens and confirms our faith that God will fulfil His word. At the same time it must never be forgotten that if there is no faith in the promise there can be no assurance in the sign. The word and the sign necessarily go together, and can never be separated. This revelation of the spiritual meaning of the rainbow was God's response to Noah's altar. Divine faithfulness thus answered to human faith, and it is of real interest that in the symbol of the prophet Ezekiel (chap. i. 28), and of the Apocalypse (Rev. iv. 3; x. 1), the rainbow is again brought before us.

The Message of the covenant should be carefully pondered (vers. 14, 15). It was an assurance of God's faithfulness. He was prepared to carry out all His promises, notwithstanding all the previous failures of mankind. The emphasis upon *My* covenant and *My* bow should be noted (*cf.* vi. 18), and it is specially to be observed that the sign of the covenant is associated with God's remembrance rather than man's. "I will remember" (ver. 15). "I will look upon it, that I may remember" (ver. 16).

The Duration of the covenant is also revealed (vers. 12, 16). "For perpetual generations," "The everlasting covenant." The unconditional and permanent character of the covenant is thus emphasized. God did not demand any pledge of obedience in response to the covenant, but assured Noah of the unconditional Divine faithfulness to His word throughout all generations.

The Guarantee of the covenant is not to be overlooked (ver. 17). "God said unto Noah, This is the token of the covenant." The covenant is thus based upon the Divine word. It is God's character and word that guarantee the fulfilling of His promises. "Two immutable things, in which it was impossible for God to lie" (Heb. vi. 18). Here is our strong and invincible assurance, the unchanging faithfulness of the word of the living God.

The word "covenant" is one of the great Bible words. It means "a coming together" (co-venant, *convenire*). As used of a human transaction, it implies a bargain, one party giving and the other receiving. It also sometimes partakes of the nature of a voluntary undertaking or pledge, without any expectation of a return. This latter view is its characteristic in the passage before us, for we read only of God's covenant with Noah, not Noah's covenant with God. God binds Himself, and lays down the line of His relationship to man. It was for Noah simply to receive this, to reckon upon it, and to rely upon its blessings. It was essentially a covenant of grace, and like the New Covenant of the Gospel, the essence of it is a gift.

1. *The Contents of the Covenant.*—It declared God's mercy in relation to the past. It told Noah that there would not be another flood of judgment.

It declared God's power in relation to the present. It reminded the patriarch and his sons that they could depend upon the regular order of nature not being disturbed, and not being subject to chance and mere caprice.

It declared God's faithfulness in relation to the future. It bid them look forward, and rest quietly in the assurance, that as each day came, all would be well with their life.

It declared God's grace in relation to man. There is a clear distinction between mercy and grace. Mercy partakes largely of the element of pity and compassion for those who are in need. Grace is much more than this, and is God's attitude of unmerited, undeserved favor towards those who are not merely negatively non-deserving, but also to those who are positively undeserving. The covenant of grace is at the foundation of everything which God bestows upon us.

It was intended to elicit faith. This was to be the human response to the Divine faithfulness. Man's trust was to answer to God's truth, and in this confidence man would find peace and strength.

It was intended to elicit hope. Hope differs from faith in this respect, that it looks onward to the future rather than being limited to the present. Faith accepts a present gift, hope expects a future gift. Faith looks upward to the Promiser, hope looks forward to the thing promised. Faith appropriates here and now, hope anticipates the coming blessing. Day by day Noah and his sons were intended to exercise hope as they rested upon the covenant of God.

It was intended to elicit love. Just as the altar expressed Noah's gratitude, so we may be perfectly sure that this renewal and establishment of the covenant would stir him to grateful and adoring love. "We love, because He first loved us."

2. *The Characteristics of the Covenant.*—Let us dwell on the rainbow as illustrating the Divine Covenant.

Consider its naturalness. A temporal feature was used to express and symbolize spiritual truths. God definitely associated nature with grace. This is but one out of many instances in which nature is a symbol of the supernatural.

Consider its conspicuousness. All could see the rainbow, and the covenant of God in like manner was intended to be seen by all without difficulty or hindrance.

Consider its universality. As the rainbow in the heavens so was the universal scope of the covenant. All the earth was included in it, not one of God's creatures was exempted.

Consider its uniqueness. The rainbow has been rightly described as the joint product of storm and sunshine. It comes from the effects of the sun on the drops of rain in a rain-cloud. So is it with the covenant of God. On the one hand it is due to the cloud of human sin, on the other to the sunshine of Divine grace.

Consider its beauty. There is scarcely anything more exquisitely beautiful than the rainbow, and assuredly there is nothing in this universe more beautiful than the grace of God. The term "grace" has for one of its meanings that of "beauty," and the Apostle Peter speaks of "the variegated grace of God" (1 Pet. iv. 10). John Wesley aptly writes of the "Victorious sweetness of the grace of God."

> "Grace, 'tis a charming sound,
> Harmonious to the ear."

Consider its union of earth and heaven. As the rainbow spans the sky and reaches the earth, so is it with the covenant of grace. Like Jacob's ladder, it is set up on the earth and the top reaches to heaven.

Consider its permanence. Mr. Eugene Stock (*Lesson Studies in Genesis*) calls attention to the fact that while we do not always see a rainbow owing to the clouds hiding the sun, yet if we could get above the clouds we should see the rainbow on them. Thus "there is never rain without a rainbow being visible if we could only get to the right spot to see it, but God is always above the clouds and He always sees it." This is exactly what is taught us. "The bow shall be in the cloud, and I will look upon it." It is not our sight of the rainbow, but God's, that constitutes the power and peace of this covenant.

> The clouds may go and come,
> And storms may sweep my sky—
> This blood-sealed friendship changes not:
> The cross is ever nigh.

> My love is oft-times low,
> My joy still ebbs and flows;
> But peace with Him remains the same—
> No change Jehovah knows.

> I change, He changes not,
> The Christ can never die;
> His love, not mine, the resting-place,
> His truth, not mine, the tie.

XI

A BELIEVER'S FALL

GEN. ix. 18-29.

AND the sons of Noah, that went forth of the ark, were Shem, and Ham, and Japheth: and Ham *is* the father of Canaan.

These *are* the three sons of Noah: and of them was the whole earth overspread.

And Noah began *to be an* husbandman, and he planted a vineyard:

And he drank of the wine, and was drunken; and he was uncovered within his tent.

And Ham, the father of Canaan, saw the nakedness of his father, and told his two brethren without.

And Shem and Japheth took a garment, and laid *it* upon both their shoulders, and went backward, and covered the nakedness of their father; and their faces *were* backward, and they saw not their father's nakedness.

And Noah awoke from his wine, and knew what his younger son had done unto him.

And he said, Cursed *be* Canaan; a servant of servants shall he be unto his brethren.

And he said, Blessed *be* the Lord God of Shem; and Canaan shall be his servant.

God shall enlarge Japheth, and he shall dwell in the tents of Shem; and Canaan shall be his servant.

And Noah lived after the flood three hundred and fifty years.

And all the days of Noah were nine hundred and fifty years: and he died.

THE events recorded in the preceding section might well suggest that henceforth everything would be well with Noah and his sons. A new start had been made amid great hopes, with perfect provision and a Divine assurance. Yet here comes the record of failure. As we read it our hearts are full of disappointment, and yet, if we may use human language, what must the Divine disappointment have been? As God afterwards said about Israel, "What could have been done more to My vineyard, that I have not done in it" (Isa. v. 4)? It is evident that the Divine judgment at the Flood had not extirpated the evil in human nature, and as we ponder this solemn lesson, we should take care to apply it to ourselves. It is much easier to feel sad about Noah than to be on the watch about our own life.

I. *The Sons* (vers. 18, 19).—The names of Noah's sons have been given before (v. 32; vi. 10; vii. 13); they are given again here because the narrative specially concerns them. In the reference to Canaan we have an anticipation of chapter x. 6, in order to prepare for what is recorded of him in verse 25 of the present section. The three sons of Noah are described as the heads of the three divisions of the human race (ver. 19), and it is by reason of their importance in this connection that the incident now recorded finds its full significance. Their action is soon seen to affect others.

II. *The Sins* (vers. 20, 21).—The occasion of the sins of Noah, it should be observed, was his daily occupation. They were committed in the course of his ordinary work. It was a perfectly legitimate calling as a husbandman to plant a vineyard, and no blame is attached to him in this respect. It is a point worthy of careful notice, that legitimate occupations may easily become the occasions of wrong doing.

The first of Noah's sins was that of drunkenness. Now whatever views Christian men may hold as to the lawfulness or wisdom of moderate drinking, there is no question whatever about the fact and heinousness of the sin of drunkenness as revealed in the Scriptures. It is writ large on all parts of the Word of God. Warnings and denunciations abound in the Old Testament, while in the New, drunkenness is included in St. Paul's catalogue of the works of the flesh with all the nameless and most shameful of evils (see Prov. xxiii. 20; Isa. v. 11, 22; xxviii. 1-7; Luke xxi. 23; Rom. xiii. 13; 1 Cor. v. 11, and vi. 10; Gal. v. 21; Eph. v. 18; 1 Thes. v. 8). The story of Noah is the first recorded instance of a sin that has since become well known and even prevalent almost all over the world.

Associated with drunkenness was the sin of immodesty. The Hebrew clearly indicates a deliberate act, and not a mere unconscious effect of drunkenness. The two sins of intemperance

and impurity have often been associated, and indeed the association has become proverbial. Of the unutterable sadness of this
sin of a servant of God it is quite unnecessary to speak.

III. *The Shame* (ver. 22).—Although the narrative does not
mention the shame that accrued to Noah, it is not difficult to realize
what it must have been. To think that one who had passed through
the thrilling and unique experiences of the Flood and the associated
events should have been guilty of such conduct was a fact full of
unspeakable shame. The corruption of the best is always the worst
thing possible.

Still more shameful was the conduct of his son Ham. He had
no sense of filial love or even of common decency. We seem to see
depravity here, of no ordinary degree. Not only was he guilty of
the plain sin of omission in failing to shield and hide his father's
shame; he was guilty also of a sin of commission in calling attention
to the circumstances, and endeavoring to get his brothers to share
in his sin. It has been pointed out that Noah's sin must surely have
been a solitary act, for Ham would not have done this to his father
if the circumstances had been familiar. Candlish suggests that in
the light of Canaan's probable association with his father, the act
was a token of a deliberate opposition to Noah on religious grounds.
Be this as it may, the sin against filial respect and honor is sufficiently heinous.

IV. *The Sorrow* (vers. 23, 24).—The two brothers refused to
share in Ham's sin. With filial love, true purity, and, as we can
believe, profound sorrow, they took immediate steps to cover their
father's shame. After all, he was their father, they owed everything to him, and however deeply he had fallen, it was not for them
to do anything but hide his and their unspeakable sorrow and
shame. They restored him in the spirit of love and meekness (Gal.
vi. 1), perhaps not unmindful of the possibilities of sin in themselves.

And what must Noah's sorrow have been when he awoke and
knew all? When he realized what he himself had done, and when
he discovered what his son had done to him, we can well imagine
the profound sorrow and sense of shame that filled his heart. He

who had "found grace in the eyes of the Lord" (vi. 8), he who had
been testified of by God as the only upright one in that age (vii.
1), he who had been the honored instrument of declaring and
doing God's will in circumstances such as would never happen
again—he it is who had now awakened to a consciousness of awful
sin in himself and his home.

V. *The Retribution* (ver. 23).—The curse pronounced on Canaan
was not the result of any personal feeling on the part of Noah,
for Ham the father is not mentioned as included in the curse. Noah
is here, as it were among the prophets, and foresees the future in
which the curse of Canaan shall be realized. It is real difficulty how
to explain the connection of Canaan with the sin that is attributed
to his father Ham. It is perhaps best to understand the matter according to the old Jewish tradition, that Canaan was somehow involved in the sin and was associated with his father in the mockery
of Noah. It has been well said that Ham sinned as a son and was
punished in his son. This is the third curse mentioned in Genesis
(chaps. iii. 14-17; iv. 11).

The servitude of Canaan here foretold was subsequently seen in
the course of history. "Servant of servants" is the Hebrew superla-
tive for "greatest possible servitude," and we know how true this
has worked out. Canaan was to be a slave both to Shem and
Japheth. The land of Canaan was subjugated by Israel, and the
Canaanites became the servants of the Semitic race. In a still
wider sense the descendants of Ham in Africa have for centuries
been the slaves of the Japhethic races.

VI. *The Reward* (vers. 26, 27).—The supremacy of Shem is
foretold with reference to their religious privileges. Jehovah is
to be their God, and, if the Hebrew may thus be rendered, it is
Jehovah Who is to dwell in the tents of Shem. The truth of this
is readily seen when we think of the preservation of Monotheism
amongst the Jews amidst all the false religions that surrounded them.
Above all, Christ belonged to the race of Shem, and Christianity
was first proclaimed and spread abroad by Semites.

The prophecy about Japheth indicates great prosperity and the
multiplication of descendants. "God shall enlarge Japheth." If

the rendering of the English versions is correct that Japheth is to "dwell in the tents of Shem," we know that as a matter of fact the Christian Gentile nations have indeed superseded the family of Shem in religious privileges, and have entered upon their inheritance of spiritual blessing and earthly power. It is at least striking that the political control of human affairs is now in the hands of the Japhetic line.

It is impossible to say how long after the Flood this sad event took place, but inasmuch as Noah lived three hundred and fifty years after the Flood we may rightly assume that he lived long after this fall, and did not repeat his terrible sin. His fall is never mentioned elsewhere in Scripture, and we may fairly believe in his complete restoration. Still, the memory must necessarily have. remained to cloud the glory of his former days.

1. *A Believer is never immune from sin.*—However far we may advance in the Christian life, however rich and deep our experiences, the evil principle still remains, and may at any time gain the upper hand. The infection of sin remains in the regenerate, and this is a fact that needs to be faced day by day.

2. *A Believer often finds small temptations the most dangerous.* —It was in his ordinary duty that Noah found the occasion of his fall. Many a man can meet a great crisis who fails before a simple duty. The little things of life frequently constitute the most searching test.

3. *A Believer is always liable to experience entirely new temptations.*—As the days go on evil often takes entirely novel forms. A man may have had a special weakness in youth and fought against it for years, only to find other weaknesses breaking out and new sins coming upon him in mature and old age.

4. *A Believer may be the occasion of sin in others.*—How sad to think of the influence of Noah on his sons. It is only one solitary instance of the great law that no one ever sins alone. The solidarity of human life is such that others are inevitably affected by the evil that we do.

5. *A Believer will suffer most bitterly for his backsliding.*—We may be perfectly certain that Noah was never without the shadow

of his sin, although his life might have been wholly bright. The Spirit of God makes the repentant believer more and more sensitive, and he does not cease to grieve over aberrations from the pathway of right.

6. *A Believer is always conscious of the utter impartiality of God.*—No vice or sin is ever hidden or extenuated. The sins and faults of the men of God are dealt with with perfect frankness and impartiality in the Word of God, and so it is in daily experience. God has no favorites.

7. *A Believer need never fall into sin.*—Although the evil principle remains with us to the end of this life, the provision of grace is such that sinning is absolutely unnecessary. The promise stands absolute and universal in its application. "Sin shall not have dominion over you" (Rom. vi. 14), and the explanation is accordingly given, "Ye are under grace." The grace of God is more than sufficient to meet every need. The Spirit of God dwelling in the heart and possessing it is able to counteract the strongest force of the evil nature; and while, according to Romans vii., the evil nature, in and by itself, will always assert itself, the true full Christian life is that which is depicted in Romans viii., which commences with "No condemnation," and ends with "No separation," since "we are more than conquerors through Him that loved us."

XII

A WIDE OUTLOOK

GEN. x.

Now these *are* the generations of the sons of Noah; Shem, Ham, and Japheth: and unto them were sons born after the flood.

The sons of Japheth; Gomer, and Magog, and Madai, and Javan, and Tubal, and Meshech, and Tiras.

And the sons of Gomer; Ashkenaz, and Riphath, and Togarmah.

And the sons of Javan; Elishah, and Tarshish, Kittim, and Dodanim.

By these were the isles of the Gentiles divided in their lands; every one after his tongue, after their families, in their nations.

And the sons of Ham; Cush, and Mizraim, and Phut, and Canaan.

And the sons of Cush; Seba, and Havilah, and Sabtah, and Raamah, and Sabtechah: and the sons of Raamah; Sheba, and Dedan.

And Cush begat Nimrod: he began to be a mighty one in the earth.

He was a mighty hunter before the Lord: wherefore it is said, Even as Nimrod the mighty hunter before the Lord.

And the beginning of his kingdom was Babel, and Erech, and Accad, and Calneh, in the land of Shinar.

Out of that land went forth Asshur, and builded Nineveh, and the city Rehoboth, and Calah,

And Resen between Nineveh and Calah: the same *is* a great city.

And Mizraim begat Ludim, and Anamim, and Lehabim, and Naphtuhim,

And Pathrusim, and Casluhim (out of whom came Philistim), and Caphtorim.

And Canaan begat Sidon his first-born, and Heth,

And the Jebusite and the Amorite, and the Girgasite,

And the Hivite, and the Arkite, and the Sinite,

And the Arvadite, and the Zemarite, and the Hamathite: and afterward were the families of the Canaanites spread abroad.

And the border of the 'Canaanites was from Sidon, as thou comest to Gerar, unto Gaza; as thou goest unto Sodom, and Gomorrah, and Admah, and Zeboim, even unto Lasha.

These *are* the sons of Ham, after their families, after their tongues, in their countries, *and* in their nations.

Unto Shem also, the father of all the children of Eber, the brother of Japheth the elder, even to him were *children* born.

The children of Shem; Elam, and Asshur, and Arphaxad, and Lud, and Aram.

And the children of Aram; Uz, and Hul, and Gether, and Mash.

And Arphaxad begat Salah; and Salah begat Eber.

And unto Eber were born two sons: the name of one *was* Peleg; for in his days was the earth divided; and his brother's name was Joktan.

And Joktan begat Almodad, and Sheleph, and Hazarmaveth, and Jerah,

And Hadoram, and Uzal, and Diklah,

And Obal and Abimael, and Sheba,

And Ophir, and Havilah, and Jobab: all these *were* the sons of Joktan.

And their dwelling was from Mesha, as thou goest unto Sephar, a mount of the east.

These *are* the sons of Shem, after their families, after their tongues, in their lands, after their nations.

These *are* the families of the sons of Noah, after their generations, in their nations: and by these were the nations divided in the earth after the flood.

A T first sight this chapter seems quite remote from the spiritual character of the preceding and following sections, but further consideration shows that it is in direct line with the religious purpose of Genesis. In chapter v. we have a list of the descendants of Adam ending with Noah, and in this chapter there naturally follows a list of Noah's descendants, until we reach Terah, the father of Abraham. In chapter x. 1 the sons of Noah are mentioned in the familiar order, Shem, Ham, and Japheth, but in the remainder of the chapter their descendants are taken in the opposite order, Japheth, Ham, Shem. This is an example of the characteristic, already mentioned, of dealing with collateral branches first, and only after that considering the main stream in the descendants of Shem. The religious purpose of the chapter must therefore be continually kept in view. This table of nations shows their kinship with the chosen race, out of which all spiritual blessing is to come. Then the nations are dismissed from the Scripture record, and attention concentrated on the Semitic line. Saphir (*The Divine Unity of Scripture*) truly says, "The tenth chapter of Genesis is a very remarkable chapter. Before God leaves, as it were, the nations to themselves and begins to deal with Israel, His chosen people from Abraham downward, He takes a loving farewell of all the nations of the earth, as much as to say, 'I am going to leave you for a while, but I love you. I have created you: I have ordered all your future'; and their different genealogies are traced."

It is impossible to enter in detail upon the classification of this chapter. It must suffice to call attention to its ethnological, genealogical, geographical, and biographical aspects. The four words (ver. 31), "families," "tongues," "lands," "nations," show the varied character of the classification. The precise principle of classification must thus include all these elements; the personal aspect is sometimes individual and sometimes tribal.

It is also to be carefully observed that there is no attempt at completeness in the list. Several of the more modern nations which came later into close contact with Israel, as Moab, Ammon, Edom, Amalek, find no mention here, while on the other hand not all the most ancient of the nations are included. The names of seventy nations are found here, fourteen associated with Japheth, thirty with Ham, and twenty-six with Shem. This number seventy is familiar from other parts of Scripture (chaps. xlvi. 27; Exod. xxiv. 1-9), and is evidently symbolical. Lange rightly speaks of the "high antiquity" of the chapter, and this is confirmed by Professor Sayce in his Archæological Commentary on Genesis. There is no reference in the chapter to the time posterior to Abraham. For the purpose of detailed study of the many interesting and important points which arise out of it, reference may be made to Sayce's Archæological Commentary on Genesis (*Expository Times*, vol. viii. 82 ff.); Cave (*Inspiration of the Old Testament*, Lecture iii.); Lange (*Commentary on Genesis*, p. 346 ff.); Urquhart (*The Bible and How to Read It*, vol. ii. p. 2 ff.). It is only possible to call attention to a few of the outstanding features with special reference to the spiritual meaning of the chapter.

I. *The Family of Japheth* (vers. 2-5).—Here it is unnecessary and perhaps impossible to identify the names with those of subsequent races and countries, but attention should certainly be concentrated on verse 5 with its reference to Gentiles. Viewed from the standpoint of the Jews it is clear that the Gentile nations arose from Japheth. This early reference to "the nations," to use the Hebrew phrase of later books, is very significant, and shows that amid all the Jewish exclusiveness the Old Testament never loses sight of the great fact of universality and God's purposes for all the world.

It was the crowning sin of the Jews in later ages that they forgot this and concentrated attention upon themselves as the chosen people of God, stopping short of the great truth of their revealed religion that they were chosen only for the purpose of being the instrument and channel of God's mercy and grace to "the nations" of the whole earth. Even today there is a great deal of ignorance among Christian people as to the note of universality that is struck so often in the Old Testament. A study of the Psalms and the Prophets in the Revised Version, with special reference to the phrase in the plural, "the nations," would do much to correct this.

II. *The Family of Ham* (vers. 6-20).—The first point that stands out with prominence in regard to the family of Ham is the reference to Nimrod (vers. 8, 9), and the word "mighty" in these verses is the same in the Hebrew as that used in chapter vi. 4. It would seem as though Nimrod represented a revival of the antediluvian spirit of independence and rebellion with its disregard of God and His authority. Nimrod, however, is specially associated with the founding of Babel, or Babylon, and this first mention of a word which is so familiar elsewhere should be specially noted. Babylon henceforward stands for everything that is godless, and for the great opponent of the people of God. It was a "Babylonish garment" (Josh. vii. 21) that led to the first sin in the promised land, and it was Babylon in one form or another that caused most of the trouble to the nation of Israel. In the Old Testament Babylon is a godless city and empire, in the New Testament it is a godless system, and it would form a study of the greatest possible significance and value to look at all the passages where Babylon is mentioned, until at length we come to its destruction as recorded in the Apocalypse (chap. xviii.). The other point in this section is the prominence given to Canaan and his descendants (vers. 15-19). This is doubtless because of the connection of Canaan with Israel in the light of subsequent history. Sayce (*ut supra*) says, "The age to which the chapter takes us back is indicated by the position given to Canaan. It is a position that was true of it only during the age of the eighteenth and nineteenth Egyptian dynasties. . . .

After that age no one would have dreamed of coupling Canaan and Egypt together."

III. *The Family of Shem* (vers. 21-31).—Shem is described as "the father of all the children of Eber," and this prominence given to Eber seems to bear out the suggestion that "Hebrew" comes from Eber. Eber is also mentioned (ver. 25) as having two sons, Peleg and Joktan. It was in the time of the former that the earth was divided, the reference probably being an anticipation of the confusion of Babel recorded in detail in the next chapter.

Thus we have this brief and suggestive account of the families of Noah, and the division of the earth by means of them. The authenticity and genuineness of the chapter may be seen from the simple fact that as late as the date of 1 Chronicles nothing more was known of the origin of the nations, and consequently the writer of Chronicles followed this list, for with only slight variations it is repeated there (1 Chron. i.). Canon Rawlinson remarks that these lists have "extorted the admiration of modern ethnologists, who continually find in them anticipations of their greatest discoveries." Up to the present moment ethnology cannot get behind the division of mankind into three primary groups. It remains to be added that archæological studies have gone to confirm the facts recorded here.

Keeping in view the religious and spiritual purpose of the chapter when read in the light of the entire book of Genesis, we notice several spiritual lessons.

1. *All Nations are of one blood.*—Or as the A.V. reads, "He made of one every nation of men." This is surely one of the most remarkable facts arising out of this chapter. Such representative critics as Dillmann, and the Bishop of Winchester, call attention to the spiritual significance of this chapter in the Hebrew Scriptures "It reminded the Israelite that God had made of one blood all the nations of the earth, and that the heathen who knew not Jehovah were nevertheless brethren of Israel. It reminded him that his own nation was only one among the nations of the earth by origin, and in no way separated from them, but only by the grace of God selected and chosen to be the bearer of His revelation to the world" (Ryle, *Early Narratives of Genesis*). Dillmann is equally clear

as to the uniqueness of this feature. "The fundamental idea of the survey is to point out the ultimate relationship of all these peoples. This idea is important . . . not much attention was paid as a rule to foreigners, unless national or trade interests were at stake. Often enough they were despised as mere barbarians, and in no case were they included with the more cultured nations in a higher community. It is otherwise in our text. Here, many with whom the Israelites had no sort of actual relationship are taken into consideration. . . . All men and peoples are of the same race, of the same rank, and with the same destiny, brothers and relatives of one another" (Dillmann, *Genesis*, vol. i. p. 314). When it is remembered that no other nation ever taught the brotherhood of man, but on the contrary despised and opposed it, we can surely see marks of divine inspiration in the way in which all nations are mentioned in this chapter. Ranke says of this chapter, "It is impossible to read it without seeing that there is something here different from all other history, and that the national pride and separation which we see everywhere else has been entirely subjugated by the religious idea, that all the different tribes of the earth are related to one another by their common descent from Shem, Ham, and Japheth." There is also a practical lesson for ourselves. There is no such thing as "foreign" missionary work. "All souls are Mine," and no one can say where home missions end and foreign missions begin. Here, then, is our great charter of world-wide evangelization. "Go ye, and teach all nations" (Matt. xxviii. 19). "Before Him shall be gathered all nations" (Matt. xxv. 32). "All nations" (Rev. vii. 9).

2. *All Nations have one need.*—The thought of sin is clearly implied throughout this chapter, as indeed throughout the book. Common trouble and disease rest upon all. "There is no difference, for all have sinned." Amid every variety of race, circumstance, place, and temperament, this one great fact of sin, deep-seated, ineradicable by human means, is experienced by all. It is this thought that gives point to the proclamation of the Gospel everywhere, that it meets one and the same great need.

3. *All Nations have one way of salvation.*—God's method of redemption, while working through Shem, is intended to include in

its beneficent scope the descendants of Ham and Japheth as well. The Jewish Messiah is the world's Saviour, and the blessing of Abraham is intended to come on the Gentiles through Jesus Christ (Gal. iii. 7-14). All workers for missions will find not a little of their warrant and inspiration as they ponder this chapter in the light of the subsequent teaching of the Word of God.

XIII

THE TOWER OF BABEL

GEN. xi. 1-9

AND the whole earth was of one language, and of one speech.

And it came to pass, as they journeyed from the east, that they found a plain in the land of Shinar; and they dwelt there.

And they said one to another, Go to, let us make brick, and burn them thoroughly. And they had brick for stone, and slime had they for mortar.

And they said, Go to, let us build us a city, and a tower whose top *may reach* unto heaven; and let us make us a name, lest we be scattered abroad upon the face of the whole earth.

And the Lord came down to see the city and the tower, which the children of men builded.

And the Lord said, Behold, the people *is* one, and they have all one language; and this they begin to do: and now nothing will be restrained from them, which they have imagined to do.

Go to, let us go down, and there confound their language, that they may not understand one another's speech.

So the Lord scattered them abroad from thence upon the face of all the earth: and they left off to build the city.

Therefore is the name of it called Babel; because the Lord did there confound the language of all the earth: and from thence did the Lord scatter them abroad upon the face of all the earth.

THE events of this section apparently happened earlier than some of those recorded in chapter x., for it is probable that this gives us the detailed account of that division of the earth which happened in the days of Peleg (chap. x. 25). Dispersion may have been divinely intended, and notified to the sons of Noah, and this episode of Babel may have been the human response of unwillingness to follow the divine command. It should be observed that there is no trace of Babylonian origin in this story, and no indications of its being based upon Babylonian myth, the mythical element being entirely absent.

I. *Human Life* (vers. 1-3).—Mankind is described as possessing at the time oneness of language, whatever that language was. There was also a natural nomadic element, for they were journeying from place to place. The conditions of agricultural life would doubtless necessitate a great deal of movement. In their journeyings they at last arrived at the land of Shinar, the plain in which Babylon was afterwards situated (chap. x. 10). The fertility of this plain would be of special value, and we are not surprised to read that "they dwelt there."

They soon conceived the plan of a prolonged stay and definite association, for they proposed to one another to make brick and build a city and a tower. The alluvial soil of the plain would give them facilities for clay and brickmaking, thereby providing materials for building. This was quite natural, because of the absence of stone in that region.

The primary motive in building the city, apart from the story of the tower, may well have been the innocent desire to remain associated, and to be protected by means of the city. At any rate, unless there had been a Divine revelation, it is difficult at this stage to charge them with any breach of a known law of God.

II. *Human Sin* (ver. 4).—Before long their objects (if innocent) degenerated into evil. To have a rendezvous might not in itself have been wrong, though there may have been associated with this desire a wish to remain together which possibly conflicted with the purposes of God for mankind at that stage. Whether this was so or not, the desire for a tower "whose top might reach to heaven" seems to have been prompted by something like pride and self-sufficiency. It is thought by some authorities that a religious question was involved in this tower, and that it was intended for an idolatrous temple. At any rate it is certainly true that Babylon afterwards became one of the worst and most terrible strongholds of idolatry and false religion.

One thing, however, is perfectly clear—they were filled with a godless ambition. "Let us make us a name, lest we be scattered abroad." In view of the fact that the Hebrew word for "name" is *"shem,"* it is not altogether impossible that the suggestion "to make a *shem"* had in it some covert sneer against the family of Shem, which had been assured of the Divine presence and blessing (chap. ix. 26); and the fear lest they should be scattered abroad is fairly chargeable with distrust in God, Whose purpose it was that they should be dispersed and people the whole earth. He who commanded them to scatter abroad would not leave them unsafe and unprotected. Altogether, this is a revelation of human sin in the form of rebellion against God, and it has not been wrongly described as the first organization of the scheme of godlessness and irreligion.

III. *Divine Consideration* (vers. 5, 6).—The description of God's attitude here recorded is striking in its simplicity. "The Lord came down to see." Man had just attempted to go *up* in his sin. God now comes *down* in judgment. Again we have what has been already seen several times in these early chapters, the revelation of the Divine scrutiny and examination, showing that God is intent upon His people's ways and cannot be indifferent to their attitude to Him. The result of this scrutiny is that God anticipates what the people will do, and He decides that nothing will restrain them from that which they have purposed to effect. The fact of their oneness of language would give them this remarkable power of united effort on a large scale. It was necessary, therefore, to face the problem and deal with it in the best possible way.

IV. *Divine Action* (vers. 7, 9).—The method employed was that of the confusion of their language, and their subsequent dispersion. We are told that they left off to build the city, and it is not known whether or not they finished the tower. Into the question of the identity of the tower ruins found on the site of Babylon it is unnecessary to enter here.

Dr. Dale thinks that dissension among the workmen was the first step leading to dispersion, and that the confusion of language came as the necessary consequence of this dispersion, the language being modified by separation from one another. It is worth noticing that history and archæology bear clear testimony to the fact of confusion of languages. Bunsen (quoted in Lange's *Commentary*) says:—"Comparative philology would have been compelled to set forth as a postulate the supposition of some such division of languages in Asia, especially on the ground of the relation of the Egyptian language to the Shemitic, even if the Bible had not assured us of the truth of this great historical event. It is truly wonderful, it is a matter of astonishment, that something so purely historical, something so conformable to reason, is here related to us out of the oldest primeval period, and which now, for the first time, through the new science of philology, has become capable of being historically and philosophically explained."

The memorial of their confusion remained in the city that they had built, and Babel from this time forward occupies a definite, not to say prominent part, in the record contained in the Scriptures. Babylon is never long out of sight, until at length it finds its complete and final overthrow in the Apocalypse.

1. *The danger and disaster of life without God.*—It is very striking, that in connection with Cain we have the first elements of human civilization, and here again we have the building of a city connected with those who were evidently indifferent to God. At first it was not so much iniquity as simple indifference. God was not in their life, but from indifference soon came rebellion, as is always the case. Whenever a religious system glorifies humanity and makes man everything, it is not long before it minimizes God and makes Him nothing. Culture, civilization, intellect, cleverness, progress. are all among the natural gifts of God to human life, and there is no reason whatever why they should not all be consecrated to the Divine service. When they are thus yielded to Him they become doubly powerful, and are the means of blessing on every hand. When, however, they are not handed over to God who gives them, but are. kept in man's own power and authority, they lead men farther and farther from God, and are the means of nothing but trouble on every hand.

2. *The danger and disaster of all false unity.*—These people attempted to keep themselves together by means of the outward and visible tie of a common dwelling-place and rallying-point. They had nothing in common except the city which they built. This however, proved fatal, and always will prove fatal to real unity. Unity must come from within. When outward unity is attempted

the result will be, as in this case, separation, dispersion, confusion. What a lesson we have here in connection with all attempts at church unity. How often churches have attempted to keep Christians together by means of outward elements only or mainly. Sometimes it has been unanimity of opinion, and this has proved impossible. Sometimes it has been uniformity of observance and ceremonial, but this has proved equally futile. Sometimes it has been a unity of organization, but this has never once succeeded. Unity must be a unity of life, of love, of interest, of intention, of spirit, of service, and this unity can be obtained and maintained amidst a great variety of organization, of opinion, of ceremonial. Our Lord speaks of the Jewish *fold*, and then of the unity of a *flock* including other than Jews (John x. 16, R. V.), the latter being far the more important, for it is possible to have one flock consisting of very different kinds of sheep and in many folds, yet all belonging to the one Master.

3. *The blessedness of true unity.*—There are three pictures in God's Word which ought always to be considered together. The confusion of tongues in Genesis xi.; the real unity amid diversities of tongues as the result of the gift of the Holy Spirit on the Day of Pentecost in Acts ii.; and the magnificent picture of "all nations, and kindreds, and tongues" in Revelation vii. as they stand before the throne. With the Babel of earth we set in contrast the Jerusalem that is above. To the city of man we oppose the city of God. True unity is always primarily the result of an organism, and only secondarily of an organization. It is based upon God and upon spiritual life in Him. "There is one body, and one Spirit, even as ye are called in one hope of your calling, one Lord, one faith, one baptism, one God and Father of all, Who is above all, and through all, and in you all" (Eph. iv. 4-6).

XIV

THE CALL OF ABRAHAM

GEN. xi. 10—xii. 9.

THESE *are* the generations of Shem: Shem *was* an hundred years old, and begat Arphaxad two years after the flood.

And Shem lived, after he begat Arphaxad, five hundred years, and begat sons and daughters.

And Arphaxad lived five and thirty years, and begat Salah.

And Arphaxad lived, after he begat Salah, four hundred and three years, and begat sons and daughters.

And Salah lived thirty years, and begat Eber.

And Salah lived, after he begat Eber, four hundred and three years, and begat sons and daughters.

And Eber lived four and thirty years, and begat Peleg.

And Eber lived, after he begat Peleg, four hundred and thirty years, and gcat sons and daughters.

And Peleg lived thirty years, and begat Reu.

And Peleg lived, after he begat Reu, two hundred and nine years, and begat sons and daughters.

And Reu lived two and thirty years, and begat Serug.

And Reu lived, after he begat Serug two hundred and seven years, and begat sons and daughters.

And Serug lived thirty years, and begat Nahor.

And Serug lived, after he begat Nahor, two hundred years, and begat sons and daughters.

And Nahor lived nine and twenty years, and begat Terah.

And Nahor lived, after he begat Terah, an hundred and nineteen years, and begat sons and daughters.

And Terah lived seventy years, and begat Abram, Nahor, and Haran.

Now these *are* the generations of Terah: Terah begat Abram, Nahor, and Haran; and Haran begat Lot,

And Haran died before his father Terah in the land of his nativity, in Ur of the Chaldees.

And Abram and Nahor took them wives: the name of Abram's wife *was* Sarai; and the name of Nahor's wife, Milcah, the daughter of Haran, the father of Milcah, and the father of Iscah.

But Sarai was barren; she *had* no child.

And Terah took Abram his son, and Lot the son of Haran, his son's son, and Sarai his daughter-in-law, his son Abram's wife; and went forth with them from Ur of the Chaldees, to go into the land of Canaan; and they came unto Haran, and dwelt there.

And the days of Terah were two hundred and five years: and Terah died in Haran.

Now the Lord had said unto Abram, Get thee out of thy country, and from thy kindred, and from thy father's house, unto a land that I will show thee.

And I will make of thee a great nation, and I will bless thee, and make thy name great; and thou shalt be a blessing:

And I will bless them that bless thee, and curse him that curseth thee: and in thee shall all families of the earth be blessed.

So Abraham departed, as the Lord had spoken unto him; and Lot went with him: and Abram *was* seventy and five years old when he departed out of Haran.

And Abram took Sarai his wife, and Lot his brother's son, and all their substance that they had gathered, and the souls that they had gotten in Haran; and they went forth to go into the land of Canaan; and into the land of Canaan they came.

And Abram passed through the land unto the place of Sichem, unto the plain of Moreh. And the Canaanite *was* then in the land.

And the Lord appeared unto Abram, and said, Unto thy seed will I give this land: and there builded he an altar unto the Lord, who appeared unto him.

And he removed from thence unto a mountain on the east of Beth-el, and pitched his tent, *having* Beth-el on the west, and Hai on the east: and there he builded an altar unto the Lord, and called upon the name of the Lord.

And Abraham journeyed, going on still towards the south.

WITH this section the Book of Genesis takes a new and very distinct departure. From the consideration of the entire human race (chaps. x. and xi.) our attention is directed to one family and one man as the chosen channel of the Divine purpose of redemption for the race. The earlier chapters are but a preface, though a necessary explanatory preface, to the remainder. They cover at least two thousand years, and yet we seem to be, as it were, hurried along, until we reach the fulness of the narrative about Abraham and his seed. The first eleven chapters are the foundation of which the other thirty-nine are the superstructure. They trace back the Divine redemption until its cause is found in the sin of the human race, and its scope is shown to embrace all mankind. This done, we are now free to consider the precise method whereby God accomplished His purpose, and redeemed mankind through the instrumentality of one man, his family, and his nation. It is the importance of Abraham in this connection that gives its meaning and importance to chapter xii. of this book. As the root to the stem so are chapters i-xi. to xii.-1., and as the stem to the tree so is Genesis to the rest of the Bible. It is the foundation, the explanation, the preface, the key to the rest of the Word of God.

There is only one man of those whose lives are recorded in the Old Testament who has the high privilege of being called the "friend of God." Isa. xli. 8, "Abraham, My friend"; 2 Chron. xx. 7, "Abraham, Thy friend"; (cf. Jas. ii. 23). To this day Abraham is known among the Arabs as *El Khalil* (Friend of God). The study of his life is one of the deepest interest on two grounds: (1) Personal: he is one of the noblest and most heroic figures in ancient history; (2) Spiritual: he was God's chosen instrument for the realization of the divine purposes of redemption.

The importance of Abraham can readily be seen by the space given to him in the record, nearly fourteen chapters out of fifty being devoted to him. It may be well to summarize the record of his life for the purpose of obtaining a general view of its history.

(*a*) Chapters xii.-xiv., the Call given and accepted.

(*b*) Chapters xv., xvi., the Covenant made and received.

(*c*) Chapters xvii.-xxi., the Confirmation of the Covenant.

(*d*) Chapter xxii., the Crowning Event.

(*e*) Chapters xxiii.-xxv. 10, the Closing Years.

We now commence by studying the circumstances of his early days and the Divine call as recorded at the head of this chapter.

I. *Abraham's Early Life.*—Abraham lived at Ur of the Chaldees, usually identified with Mugheir, near the Persian Gulf. The coastline, however, was at that time about one hundred and forty miles north of the present line. He comes of the line of Shem. His father was Terah (chap. xi. 24), and he had two brothers (chap. xi. 26). His wife was Sarai (chap. xi. 29) and she was childless (chap. xi. 30). Most probably Abraham was the youngest, not the eldest son, the names not being given in the order of their birth, but in the order of importance, since Abraham was God's chosen instrument. Similar circumstances are found in Gen. v. 32 with reference to Shem, Ham, and Japheth, and in Gen. x. 2, where Japheth comes first in the order of genealogy (cf. 1 Chron. i. 5, 8,

17). The analogy of God's choice of the younger of the sons of Adam, Isaac, Joseph, Jesse, suggests the probability that Abraham was Terah's youngest son.

Abraham evidently belonged to a family of shepherds accustomed to move about as pasture was needed.

Either Terah or his ancestors were idolaters (Joshua xxiv. 2, 15). Four hundred years had elapsed since the Flood, and there had thus been time for the degeneration of the sons of Shem. Possibly Abraham himself may have been an idolater (cf. Isa. li. 1, 2).

II. *The Divine Call.*—A third start is made with humanity. Adam had failed, Noah's descendants had failed, and now another attempt was to be made. The former attempts were made with the race, but this one was made by means of an individual as the founder of a nation which should in turn bless the race. Abraham, as the founder of the Jewish nation, was intended by God as (*a*) a witness to him to the rest of mankind (Isa. xliv. 8), (*b*) a depository of God's revelation (Rom. iii. 2), (*c*) a preparation for the Messiah and Saviour (Isa. liii.), (*d*) a channel of blessing to the world (Rom. xv. 8-12).

The first call came at Ur of the Chaldees (Acts vii. 2-4). "The God of Glory" called him. This unique title of God is very noteworthy. It was doubtless due to this call that Terah left Ur (Gen. xi. 31). Then came a second call in Haran after Terah's death (Gen. xii. 1). Some authorities consider Gen. xii. 1 to refer to the first call at Ur, and this is why the Authorized Version and the Revised Version render the Hebrew words "the Lord *had* said." As, however, there is no pluperfect tense in the original, it seems better to regard Gen. xii. 1 as referring to the second call, especially in the light of Acts vii. 2-4.

The Lord said, "Get thee out of thy country, and from thy kindred, and from thy father's house." These were very searching and pressing demands upon one who was the youngest son. Yet God's call to separation was a necessary condition of blessing. Separation was the keynote of Abraham's life from first to last, and in that separation to the will of God he found all his peace and blessing.

God never places burdens on His people's shoulders without giving them power to respond. "God's biddings are His enablings." He encouraged Abraham with a threefold promise: (*a*) A land (xii. 1), (*b*) a seed (xii. 2), (*c*) a world-wide blessing (xii. 3).

III. *The Human Response.*—Nothing is more striking than the immediate response made by Abraham. At the outset he manifests that faith which characterized him almost the whole of his life. The following aspects of his faith are worthy of consideration:—

The Confidence of Faith (ver. 4).—"So Abraham went, *as the Lord had spoken* unto him." He took God at His word without hesitation and without questioning.

The Obedience of Faith (vers. 4-6).—In leaving Ur and staying at Haran his obedience was only partial, whatever may have been the precise cause and explanation. Perhaps Terah lacked spiritual sympathy with Abraham, or else age and infirmity may have prevented him going further than Haran. In any case, Abraham did not obey fully until after his father's death. Then came entire and prompt obedience in his departure from Haran with all that he possessed. It is evident that the stay in Haran was a protracted one (ver. 5). The "souls" refer to the persons of the slaves and other dependents.

The Influence of Faith (ver. 5).—Abraham's response to the Divine call evidently led Lot to join his uncle and journey to Canaan. There was no compulsion on Lot; he might have stayed where he was. The influence of Abraham's faith constrained him to go. True faith in God often inspires others and leads them to blessing.

The Confession of Faith (vers. 6, 7).—Abraham came to Sichem (Sychar, John iv.), the later Shechem. The "oak" may be the "terebinth," or turpentine tree, whose leaf is very similar to that of the oak. "Moreh" may be the name of the owner of the terebinth, or, according to some, it means a soothsayer, implying that under this tree the art of divination was practised among the Canaanites. In verse 7 we have the first visible appearance of God to man. Hitherto only the Divine voice had been heard. Now there was a manifestation of the Divine presence, probably in the form of the

Angel of the Covenant (chap. xviii. 22; Josh. v. 13; Judges xiii. 3). To this revelation of God Abraham at once responded by building an altar. This was his acceptance and acknowledgment of the Divine revelation, the revelation being thus followed by his personal response. At the same time the altar was a testimony to the Canaanites who were then in the land.

The Endurance of Faith (vers. 8, 9).—Notwithstanding the promises of God, Abraham had to wait. He had no seed, though one had been promised; he had no abiding place, pitching his tent, not building a home; and the Canaanites in the land prevented him from possessing an inch of the country. All this was a renewed call to continued faith.

In this opening episode of Abraham's life we have clearly brought before us some of the most frequent experiences of the believer's early days.

1. *The Divine Call.*—To us also comes the call for absolute trust, the faith that takes God simply at His word, feeling assured that it cannot fail. Like Abraham, we are to trust in the dark (Heb. xi. 8).

2. *The Divine Claim.*—Separation is still the believer's duty. Sometimes it involves separation from dearest kindred, sometimes from congenial surroundings, and always from sin and self-will. Separation thus tests the reality of our life, and at the same time strengthens our spiritual fibres. "The nearer to heaven the steeper the mountains."

3. *The Divine Consecration.*—Abraham responded by building an altar and pitching his tent in place after place. By the altar he confessed himself a worshipper and by the tent a stranger and a pilgrim. Thus was his life wholly surrendered to his God. The altar and the tent together sum up the believer's life.

4. *The Divine Cheer.*—How beautifully God meets those who respond wholly to Him. They are assured of His presence (xii. 7), of His promises (xii. 2, 3), of His power, and of His peace. No life has ever had any demand made upon it without receiving the Divine cheer and encouragement which enables the soul to abide in the Lord and go forward with joy and courage.

XV

THE TESTING

GEN. xii. 10—xiii. 4.

AND there was a famine in the land: and Abram went down into Egypt to sojourn there; for the famine *was* grievous in the land.

And it came to pass, when he was come near to enter into Egypt, that he said unto Sarai his wife, Behold now, I know that thou *art* a fair woman to look upon:

Therefore it shall come to pass, when the Egyptians shall see thee, that they shall say, This *is* his wife: and they will kill me, but they will save thee alive.

Say, I pray thee, thou *art* my sister: that it may be well with me for thy sake; and my soul shall live because of thee.

And it came to pass, that, when Abram was come into Egypt, the Egyptians beheld the woman, that she *was* very fair.

The princes also of Pharaoh saw her, and commended her before Pharaoh: and the woman was taken into Pharaoh's house.

And he entreated Abram well for her sake: and he had sheep, and oxen, and he-asses, and men-servants, and maid-servants, and she-asses, and camels.

And the Lord plagued Pharaoh and his house with great plagues because of Sarai, Abram's wife.

And Pharaoh called Abram, and said, What *is* this *that* thou hast done unto me? Why didst thou not tell me that she *was* thy wife?

Why saidst thou, She *is* my sister? so I might have taken her to me to wife: now therefore behold thy wife, take *her*, and go thy way.

And Pharaoh commanded *his* men concerning him: and they sent him away, and his wife, and all that he had.

And Abram went up out of Egypt, he, and his wife, and all that he had, and Lot with him, into the south.

And Abram *was* very rich in cattle, in silver, and in gold.

And he went on his journeys from the south even to Beth-el, unto the place where his tent had been at the beginning, between Beth-el and Hai;

Unto the place of the altar, which he had made there at the first: and there Abram called on the name of the Lord.

THE young believer's life is soon tested, especially after seasons of communion (see 2 Chron. xxxii. 1, and xxxi. 20, 21, R.V.). It was so with the Apostle Peter (Matt. xvi. 17-23), and even with our Lord (Luke iii. 22, and iv. 1). We now see this great principle in the life of Abraham.

118

I. *The Special Circumstances* (ver. 10).—One of the frequent famines arose. As there was no artificial irrigation, Palestine necessarily depended on the annual rainfall and the heavy sea mist that came up from the Mediterranean at certain times of the year (the "dew" of the Old Testament).

This was a very real test to Abraham. Notwithstanding the recent revelation of God with all its promises (xii. 7), there was actually a famine in the land of promise. Doubtless Abraham remembered the rich alluvial plains of Mesopotamia and Syria. Thus he was soon tested. and his faithfulness put to the proof. We are sometimes apt to identify the peace and calm of outward circumstances with the peace arising from a consciousness of the Divine presence. It was to make this distinction clear that Abraham was tested.

II. *The Long Journey* (ver. 10).—This journey is the first point of contact between Israel as represented in Abraham and Egypt. We well know the baneful influence exercised in later ages. The famine was, of course, the sole cause of Abraham's journey, and in itself the most obvious and natural thing for him to do.

It was the "natural" thing for him to do; but then Abraham's position was not merely natural, for he had supernatural relationships. The right way is not always the easiest, and the easiest is not always the right way. Difficulties do not necessarily indicate that we are out of the pathway of God's will. It would certainly seem that Abraham was now thinking solely of the land and its famine, and forgetting God and His promises.

III. *The Proposal* (vers. 11-13).—Abraham suggested that Sarai should say that she was his sister instead of his wife. This was a "half-truth" (cf. xx. 12). Verbally it was correct; but really it was a lie.

It is to be observed, too, that the proposal was clearly actuated by selfishness; there was no regard for Sarai, but only for his own safety. How strange this is! He had journeyed all the way from Ur of the Chaldees, and yet could not trust God with his wife or with his own life. How small great people can be! How weak strong men can be! How bad good people can be!

IV. *The Result* (vers. 14-16).—What Abraham anticipated came to pass; Sarai was taken into the King's harem. Abraham's very precaution led to Pharaoh's action.

The patriarch's life is thus saved, and gifts are showered upon him, doubtless as the recognized dowry on the marriage of his sister with Pharaoh. Yet what must have been his thoughts as he was alone in his tent! He had gained his end, but at a very great cost to Sarai and himself. Thus Abraham fell at the point where he was supposed to be strongest—his faith. So it was with Moses, the meek man (Num. xx. 10).

V. *The Divine Displeasure* (ver. 17).—Serious illness came upon Pharaoh and his house, showing them clearly that some extraordinary meaning was in it. God could not allow His promises to Abraham to be frustrated or His will unfulfilled. It was therefore necessary to save Abraham from himself and rescue Sarai.

VI. *The Rebuke* (vers. 18-20).—We can picture Abraham's surprise at Pharaoh's expostulation. The Egyptians, with all their sins, seem to have laid great store by truth, and abhorred all kinds of lying. The King thereupon ordered Abraham to take her and go out of the land, Pharaoh's servants being charged to see them both safely out of Egypt.

VII. *The Restoration* (vers. 1-4).—We can imagine Abraham's feelings as the caravan slowly wended its way out of Egypt and as he came back to the land of Canaan. Note the phrase "at the beginning" (ver. 3), and "unto the place of the altar, which he had made there at the first" (ver. 4), and "called on the name of the Lord" (ver. 4). We read of no such altar or prayer in Egypt. Abraham seems to have been out of communion there. Now, however, he does the only possible thing—he returns to where he had been at the commencement; he came back to the true surrender and simple worship of his earliest days in Canaan. Whenever we backslide there is nothing else to do but to come back by the old gateway of genuine repentance and simple faith (Ps. xxiii. 3; 1 John i. 9).

1. *A Believer's false step.*—Abraham went aside out of the path of God's will; he was occupied with circumstances instead of with

God. He only saw the famine, not the divine faithfulness. "He that trusteth in his own heart is a fool" (Prov. xxviii. 26). "A crust with God is better than a feast without Him."

2. *A Believer's definite backsliding.*—The possibilities of a true child of God wandering into sin and unfaithfulness are very clear from Scripture. This is one of the saddest and most mysterious facts of spiritual experience. In Abraham's case it manifested itself first in fear due to forgetfulness of God, then in selfishness, and lastly in hypocrisy and deceit. There is nothing more solemn than the well-known fact that through sin a believer can be out of touch with God for a long time.

3. *A Believer's sad experience.*—One part of this was the knowledge that his wrongdoing had brought ill effects on others. Both Sarai and Pharaoh's house suffered through Abraham's sin. Another element in his bitter cup was the plain rebuke from the heathen Pharaoh. We have truly touched the depths of a spiritual unfaithfulness when a believer has to be openly rebuked by the ungodly.

4. *A Believer's only safeguard.*—This preservative is twofold— *trust* and *truth* every moment.

Abraham was taught three lessons about God in relation to *trust*: (1) That God was essential to his every step, and that nothing can be done apart from Him (John xv. 5); (2) that God was able— notwithstanding the famine God could have provided for Abraham; (3) that God was faithful: He had not forgotten His promises to His servant (xii. 1-3). Thus Abraham came back with a deepened idea of God and a louder call for simple, absolute, continual trust.

He was also taught the lesson of *truth*. The child of God is to be straightforward in all his attitude, and to go straight forward in all his actions. The end does *not* justify the means, whatever men may say. Even though our objects may be perfectly right, our means to attain those objects must be without blemish. This has special application to methods of Church work, ideas of social status, aspects of family life, and objects of personal ambition. Not only must the end we seek be true, the means we use must also be true.

XVI

THE SEPARATION

GEN. xiii. 5-18

AND Lot, also, which went with Abram, had flocks, and herds, and tents.

And the land was not able to bear them, that they might dwell together: for their substance was great, so that they could not dwell together.

And there was a strife between the herdmen of Abram's cattle, and the herdmen of Lot's cattle. And the Canaanite and the Perizzite dwelt then in the land.

And Abram said unto Lot, Let there be no strife, I pray thee, between me and thee, and between my herdmen and thy herdmen; for we *be* brethren.

Is not the whole land before thee? Separate thyself I pray thee, from me: if *thou wilt take* the left hand, then I will go to the right; or if *thou depart* to the right hand, then I will go to the left.

And Lot lifted up his eyes, and beheld all the plain of Jordan, that it *was* well watered everywhere, before the Lord destroyed Sodom and Gomorrah, *even* as the Garden of the Lord, like the land of Egypt, as thou comest unto Zoar.

Then Lot chose him all the plain of Jordan; and Lot journeyed east: and they separated themselves the one from the other.

Abram dwelt in the land of Canaan, and Lot dwelt in the cities of the plain, and pitched *his* tent toward Sodom.

But the men of Sodom *were* wicked, and sinners before the Lord exceedingly.

And the Lord said unto Abram, after that Lot separated from him, Lift up now thine eyes, and look from the place where thou art northward, and southward, and eastward, and westward:

For all the land which thou seest, to thee will I give it, and to thy seed for ever.

And I will make thy seed as the dust of the earth: so that if a man can number the dust of the earth, *then* shall thy seed also be numbered.

Arise, walk through the land, in the length of it, and in the breadth of it: for I will give it unto thee.

Then Abram removed *his* tent, and came and dwelt in the plain of Mamre, which *is* in Hebron, and built there an altar unto the Lord.

GOD teaches His children new lessons at every step of life's pathway. We are now to gain a deeper insight into the reality of Abraham's life, as well as a fuller revelation of God's will concerning him.

I. *A Serious Problem* (vers. 5, 6).—Abraham and Lot were rich. The accessions which came to them in Egypt had increased their flocks and herds. This is the first instance of riches in the Bible (ver. 2), and we also have here the interesting problem of wealth connected with the believer's life. What is the teaching of Scripture about wealth as possessed by a child of God? A careful study of the entire Bible seems to show that there is no sin in being wealthy provided the riches have been honorably obtained, are regarded as belonging to God, and are being constantly used as in the sight of God. At the same time, wealth very seriously increases the responsibility of a believer, and his riches will soon become a sin if they are not used properly and with a sense of stewardship, not of ownership. Another experience of human life is seen in this story—the danger of quarrels between relatives on account of wealth. How often this deplorable fact has been experienced since Abraham's day!

The possession of such flocks and herds prevented the uncle and nephew from continuing to dwell together. The need of increasing pasturage, together with the need of water, must have been very acute, and the problem was intensified by the presence of the Canaanites with their pastoral requirements.

II. *A Deplorable Strife* (ver. 7).—The quarrel originated with the servants, and was limited to them. Doubtless each herdman endeavored to gain the best locality for his own flocks.

Very significantly we read that "The Canaanite and Perizzite dwelled then in the land." This statement suggests not only the circumstance that accentuated the difficulty of obtaining pasturage, but also the fact that the heathen around must have seen and overheard this quarrel between the servants of God's children. Herein lay one of the saddest elements of the matter.

III. *A Generous Proposal* (vers. 8, 9).—Abraham takes the initiative, and begs that there shall be no strife. The quarrel might easily rise above the servants to the masters, and Abraham speaks in time to prevent this, urging as the great reason, "We are brethren." Notice his large-hearted suggestion. Although he is older than Lot and chief of the tribe or clan, and although the land had been promised by God to him, he allows his nephew the first choice. "The servant of God must not strive" (2 Tim. ii. 24). How beautifully Abraham had recovered from his fall in Egypt! While there he had learned the great lesson that no one needs to descend to deceit in order to obtain his desires. The true child of God can afford to be magnanimous, simply because he is a child of God.

IV. *A Selfish Choice* (vers. 10-13).—Lot thereupon took the generous Abraham at his word, and, seeing that the plain of Jordan was "well watered everywhere," he chose that region, and departed thither. This was the sole reason that prompted his choice. He saw the great advantage to him and his possessions in that most fertile of regions.

The land was indeed fertile, but as he "moved his tent as far as Sodom" (ver. 12, R.V.) it soon became evident what danger he was in. The material blessing was accompanied by moral blight. There are many modern counterparts to Lot's action; even professedly Christian people often choose their home in a locality simply for its scenery, or its society, or its other material advantages without once inquiring what Church privileges are there. The souls of their children may starve amid worldliness and polite indifference. The same disastrous choice is often made in connection with public schools, to which boys are sent simply for the position and reputation of the school, regardless of the moral and spiritual atmosphere of the institution. This was the great mistake of Lot's life, from which he ever afterwards suffered.

V. *A Divine Revelation* (vers. 14-17).—"After that Lot was separated from him." Abraham was now alone, and perhaps in his solitude be began to wonder whether he had done right, or whether his offer to Lot was due to weakness and the lack of true assertion of rights. There is often a temptation to reaction after a great moral decision has been made. Just at this time, then, and when he was alone, God came to him with Divine assurances and blessed compensation.

The revelation of the Divine purposes was fuller than any that preceded it (cf. xii. 1 and 7). Notice its three aspects:—

(a) The prospect afforded (ver. 14). Lot had "lifted up his eyes" (ver. 10), and with remarkable force and significant emphasis God says to Abraham, "Lift up now *thine* eyes." How different the action is in each case! Abraham's prospect was not only wider, but infinitely more glorious, because of the Word of God behind it.

(b) The promise given (vers. 15, 16). For the first time God promises the land to Abraham himself. "To thee will I give it"; hitherto the land had only been promised to his seed (xii. 7). Let us ponder these wonderful promises. They are to be interpreted literally and spiritually. They are already having their primary fulfilment in the Church of Christ as Abraham's spiritual seed (Gal. iii. 7-9, 16), but there will surely be a literal fulfilment in the future to the Jewish nation (Rom. xi. 26-29).

(c) The possession enjoined (ver. 17). Abraham is to "walk up and down," and, as it were, appropriate and claim for himself in detail that which God gives (cf. Josh. i. 3). The promises of God are to be appropriated by faith, and it is thus the purpose of God becomes realized in individual experience.

"Then Abraham moved his tent." Immediately he responded to God and pitched his tent "at Mamre, which is in Hebron." Hebron means "fellowship," and we may spiritualize the thought by saying that prompt whole-hearted obedience always leads to fellowship with God.

"Built there an altar." Again we see the real man in this simple, whole-hearted testimony to the Divine presence and promises. His tent and his altar indicate the pilgrim and devout life of the true child of God.

1. *Differences in Believers.*—What a contrast between Lot and Abraham! Except for 2 Peter ii. 7, 8, we should have hardly credited Lot with any vital religion. Although "righteous," he is yet living by sight, seeking only his own advantages and pleasure; worldliness is his dominant characteristic, his one thought is the well-watered plains. He is a type and illustration of the Christian who is not fully consecrated—one who is trying to make the best of both worlds, endeavoring to stand well with God, while pushing to the full his own earthly interests. Yet one part of his life must

necessarily suffer; so it was with Lot; so it is always. Contrast Abraham with his large-heartedness of spirit, his simple acceptance of God's promises, his whole-hearted obedience to God's will, and his courageous testimony in the altar of worship. He is a type and illustration of the consecrated believer, the one who puts God first, and to whom God's presence, God's will, God's way are everything. These differences in believers are as striking and as puzzling today as ever, yet they ought not to exist in the Church of Christ.

2. *Differences between Believers.*—Even the children of God from time to time have their differences of opinion, which often lead to trouble and strife. If only they are met with magnanimity like Abraham's, they will soon be resolved. Note the New Testament emphasis on mutual submission (Eph. v. 21; 1 Peter v. 5). The Christian paradox of everybody submitted to everybody else would soon heal all dissensions between believers. Magnanimity in Abraham was the result of his faith in God. He could afford to be large-hearted because God was so real to him. Those who put God first will never be bereft of their just rights. God is pledged on their behalf (Prov. iii. 5, 6).

3. *Differences for Believers.*—The results in the lives of Lot and Abraham were vastly different. Lot obtained what he wanted, earthly prosperity, but spiritually it may be questioned whether he was ever happy after making that choice. There was no witness for God, no real blessing on his home, and in the end came spiritual and social disaster. Abraham's experience was very different; God became an increasing reality to him, there was a glory and power in his life, and we are sure that he never regretted his action in putting God first. God's children always experience His Divine favor and blessing in proportion to their faithfulness, and if we are inclined to question and seek for the reason of differences in the spiritual experiences of the children of God we may find them in the difference of response to God on the part of His followers.

XVII

A NEW EMERGENCY

GEN. xiv. 1-16

AND it came to pass, in the days of Amraphel king of Shinar, Arioch king of Ellasar, Chedorlaomer king of Elam, and Tidal king of nations;

That these made war with Bera king of Sodom, and with Birsha king of Gomorrah, Shinab king of Admah, and Shemeber king of Zeboiim, and the king of Bela, which is Zoar.

All these were joined together in the vale of Siddim, which is the salt sea.

Twelve years they served Chedorlaomer, and in the thirteenth year they rebelled.

And in the fourteenth year came Chedorlaomer, and the kings that *were* with him, and smote the Rephaims in Ashteroth-Karnaim, and the Zuzims in Ham, and the Emims in Shaveh Kiriathaim.

And the Horites in their mount Seir, unto Elparan, which *is* by the wilderness.

And they returned, and came to Enmishpat, which *is* Kadesh, and smote all the country of the Amalekites, and also the Amorites, that dwelt in Hazezon-tamar.

And there went out the king of Sodom, and the king of Gomorrah, and the king of Admah, and the king of Zeboiim, and the king of Bela (the same *is* Zoar); and they joined battle with them in the vale of Siddim;

With Chedorlaomer the king of Elam, and with Tidal king of nations, and Amraphel king of Shinar, and Arioch king of Ellasar; four kings with five.

And the vale of Siddim *was full of* slime-pits: and the kings of Sodom and Gomorrah fled, and fell there: and they that remained fled to the mountain.

And they took all the goods of Sodom and Gomorrah, and all their victuals, and went their way.

And they took Lot, Abram's brother's son, who dwelt in Sodom, and his goods, and departed.

And there came one that had escaped, and told Abram the Hebrew: for he dwelt in the plain of Mamre the Amorite, brother of Eshcol, and brother of Aner: and these *were* confederate with Abram.

And when Abram heard that his brother was taken captive, he armed his trained *servants*, born in his own house, three hundred and eighteen, and pursued *them* unto Dan.

And he divided himself against them, he and his servants, by night, and smote them, and pursued them unto Hobah, which *is* on the left hand of Damascus.

And he brought back all the goods, and also brought again his brother Lot, and his goods, and the women also, and the people.

THE life of restful fellowship with God (xiii. 18) is now to be disturbed by a new emergency issuing in new experiences. Communion with God is constantly found to be the preparation for new crises in the believer's daily life.

I. *The Great Battle* (vers. 1-11).—Clearly we have here a contemporary record of the events described. Elam is seen to be supreme over Assyria and Babylon, and it was of the utmost importance to Elam to keep the Jordan valley free and open on account of the trade route to Egypt, with all that intercourse in commerce meant to those Eastern lands. Five kings of Eastern Palestine (ver. 2) had been subject to Chedorlaomer, the leader of the four kings of the East. Then came a rebellion on the part of the Palestine tributaries, followed by the expedition of Chedorlaomer and the kings that were with him (vers. 5-7). The vale of Siddim was the scene of the battle, with the rest that the kings of Sodom and Gomorrah were entirely vanquished.

It is well known that up to quite recent years certain schools of modern criticism rejected this chapter as wholly unhistorical. The discovery of tablets, however, has altered this view, and goes far towards demonstrating the essential historicity of the entire chapter. Chedorlaomer appears on the tablets as Kudur Lagamar and Amraphel as Hammurabi. The discovery of the code of Hammurabi during the last few years has given a further confirmation to the historical character of this chapter. (For a popular discussion on this subject, see Sayce's *Monument Facts and Higher Critical Fancies,* chapter iv.)

II. *The Significant Capture* (ver. 12).—Among the captures from the kings of Sodom and Gomorrah was Lot, who was taken prisoner, and carried off to the East. It is evident that Lot had overlooked the fact that others besides himself were thoroughly aware of the fertility of that neighborhood. It was not likely that he could expect to enjoy sole and unmolested possession of so advantageous a position. As he journeyed in the train of his captors we wonder what were his feelings, and whether he thought of his uncle Abraham in perfect safety, although only a few miles off.

How was it that Lot was taken captive, for we read only that he pitched his tent *towards* Sodom (xiii. 12)? It is evident that this did not satisfy him, for now we read that he dwelt *in* Sodom (xiv. 12). The consequences of this false step were as disastrous as they were thoroughly deserved. No godly man can ever deliberately dwell in Sodom with impunity.

An escaped prisoner came and told Abraham of what had happened, and for Abraham to hear that "his brother was taken captive" was to decide at once on his rescue. How very touching are the words "when Abraham heard that his brother was taken" (ver. 14). There is no root of bitterness here. He does not say "It serves him right" or "Let him alone."

III. *The Bold Undertaking* (vers. 13, 14).—Abraham now appears before us in a new aspect, showing himself to be a man of thought and skill, and of bravery. There may also be a touch of patriotism in it in relation to Canaan, his adopted country. New emergencies call out new powers. Apart from these circumstances no one would have credited Abraham with these remarkable qualities. He arms his trained servants and sets off in pursuit, arriving quickly at the northern end of Palestine at Dan.

The pursuit extended to 120 miles, and by a bold stroke of strategy, dividing his servants into separate companies, he smote the enemy from different directions, and pursued them far beyond the limits of Palestine, and nearly as far north as Damascus. The prompt action, the skilful leadership, and the brave, determined attack are interesting revelations of this new side of Abraham's nature.

Abraham was entirely successful, for he rescued Lot and all his household, besides the recovery of the goods belonging to the kings of Sodom and Gomorrah. As they journeyed back, uncle and nephew, we again wonder what were Lot's thoughts. There is no record of any expression or even feeling of gratitude, and the fact that he deliberately went back to Sodom is another illustration of the essential shallowness and worldliness of his mind in contrast to the magnanimity and genuine spirituality of Abraham.

1. *Some elements of a godly life.*—Looking closely at the narrative we cannot fail to see in it some essential features and most beautiful aspects of the life of a child of God.

(*a*) His Sympathy. Abraham showed no resentment, but with utter unselfishness he at once desires and determines to set out to the rescue of Lot.

(*b*) His Decision. We generally associate godliness with the passive rather than the active virtues, but in view of Hebrews xi. we must not forget the two sides of the Christian life. In Gen. xiii. Abraham is seen manifesting the passive virtues of unselfishness, humility, and willingness to yield his rights. In chapter xiv., however, there is all the decision and initiative of the brave and fearless man. Courage is as real a Christian virtue as humility.

(*c*) His Capability. Abraham's strategy and skill show that he was "a man of parts." There is no necessary connection between godliness and incapacity. The Christian man should neither be a coward nor an incapable. The Spirit of God Who equipped Bezaleel (Exod. xxxi. 3) is able to give inventiveness, and intellectual and executive ability.

2. *The explanation of these elements.*—It is all summed up by "faith in God." "By faith Abraham" was enabled to feel and show this sympathy, for the simple reason that God was all in all to him, and he could in the true sense afford to be tender-hearted and unselfish. "By faith Abraham" possessed and manifested decision, because he was in constant touch with the Source of all power, and was strong in his God to attempt and do great things. "By faith Abraham" was enabled to cultivate and reveal his capacity as a man of affairs because God is the God of all grace, and provides grace sufficient for all His servants in every emergency, and even when the believer's life commences with only a partial capability in certain directions, it is wonderful how grace can cultivate this faculty and enable the man to do wonders for God. Faith thus purifies and instructs the mind, softens and stirs the heart, and strengthens and controls the will. "This is the victory . . . our faith."

XVIII

THE TEST OF VICTORY

GEN. xiv. 17-24.

AND the king of Sodom went out to meet him after his return from the slaughter of Chedorlaomer, and of the kings that *were* with him, at the valley of Shaveh, which *is* the king's dale.

And Melchizedek king of Salem brought forth bread and wine; and he *was* the priest of the most high God.

And he blessed him, and said, Blessed *be* Abram of the most high God, possessor of heaven and earth:

And blessed *be* the most high God, which hath delivered thine enemies into thy hand. And he gave him tithes of all.

And the king of Sodom said unto Abram, Give me the persons, and take the goods to thyself.

And Abram said to the king of Sodom, I have lift up mine hand unto the Lord, the most high God, the possessor of heaven and earth.

That I will not *take* from a thread even to a shoelatchet, and that I will not take any thing *is* thine, lest thou shouldest say, I have made Abram rich;

Save only that which the young men have eaten, and the portion of the men which went with me, Aner, Eshcol, and Mamre; let them take their portion.

THE crowning hour of success is a good test of character. If "sweet are the uses of adversity," equally valuable in other directions are the uses of prosperity. How a man behaves at the moment of victory often affords a supreme revelation of character and spiritual power. We shall see this in the case of Abraham as we study his interview with the two kings.

I. *The Royal Recognition* (vers. 17, 18).—Gratitude alone would suffice to prompt the king of Sodom to go out to meet Abraham after his return from the slaughter of the kings who had caused such havoc to Sodom and Gomorrah. The meeting was the natural and fitting recognition of the great services rendered.

The other king (of Salem) who met the victorious patriarch was a very different personage, and in his capacity as priest of the Most High God brought forth bread and wine to greet the conqueror of the enemies of his country. It was another new experience to Abraham to be met by two kings and to be acknowledged by them before all their retinue as the saviour of their country.

II. *The Priestly Benediction* (vers. 18-20).—Who is this personage suddenly entering patriarchal history? He seems to have been one of the faithful few; one of those who still retained the purity of their allegiance to the one true God. He was a link with the past age of Shem, and amidst the surrounding departure from God still witnessed to the reality of the Divine presence and its claim upon men. The title of God is very noteworthy, "God Most High" (Hebrew, *El Elyon*). This title is very rare in the Old Testament, though it is found no less than four times in the verses now before us. The idea underlying it is that of God as the Supreme Being Who is above all local deities. We have its New Testament equivalent in "the Highest" (Luke i. 32, 35), and "the Most High God" (Acts xvi. 17). Melchizedek was "a priest of God Most High," and the root idea of priesthood is access into God's presence and the representation of man to God (Heb. v. 1). His typical character will come before us at a later stage.

We are told very distinctly that Melchizedek blessed Abraham and prayed the blessing of God Most High upon him, at the same time blessing God for the deliverance of Abraham. This solitary figure of the king thus standing between God and Abraham is very striking, and shows that true religion was still possible and actual outside the Abrahamic relation to God. The twofold blessing of Abraham and of God is also to be noted. When God blesses us it is a blessing in *deed*, a benefaction. When man blesses God it can of necessity only be a blessing in *word*, a benediction. Here we have both.

III. *The Loyal Acknowledgment* (ver. 20).—Abraham's attitude of immediate willingness to receive blessing is a striking testimony to his consciousness of the spiritual position and power of Melchizedek. This Divine blessing was received before his spiritual testing in the interview with the king of Sodom, and doubtless played its part in preparing him.

Abraham further acknowledged the position of the king of Salem by giving him tithes of all that he possessed. This reference to tithing is exceedingly interesting as suggesting the pre-Mosaic observance of this acknowledgment of God's claim on our gifts. If the principle of tithing was thus previous to the Mosaic economy there seems no reason to deny its essential fitness today in the economy of grace; the tenth being regarded as God's absolute right before any question arises about free-will offerings and other spontaneous gifts of the redeemed and grateful life.

IV. *The Natural Proposal* (ver. 21).—It was natural and inevitable that the king of Sodom should forthwith acknowledge his indebtedness to Abraham. The patriarch was now a great man in the eyes of the king, and it was the monarch's obvious duty to show his gratitude and appreciation of Abraham's great services. He proposed to Abraham the retention of the goods rescued from the Eastern kings, and that the men and women of Sodom should be handed over to their rightful sovereign. This was a natural and customary method of dividing the spoil after a victory, and from the point of view of existing usage it was as natural for the king to make the proposal as it would have been simply natural for Abraham to accept it. But Abraham had other than "natural" principles to guide him.

V. *The Noble Refused* (vers. 22-24).—He would not take anything, even the smallest gift. He had not entered upon the expedition for his own advantage, and consequently there was now no question about the spoil.

It would seem from the words, "I have lift up mine hand unto the Lord," that Abraham had anticipated the possibility of this or some similar proposal and had provided beforehand for it. Having thus faced the matter quietly before God, he was able to decide at once as to his course of action. It is always of great spiritual value, whenever the opportunity is afforded us, to face probable contingencies beforehand, and decide in the sight of God what we shall do if and when the event takes place.

"Lest thou shouldest say, I have made Abraham rich." His position in the sight of God was such that he could not endure the thought of being in any way dependent upon the king of Sodom. It is often found that when men rise in the world there are others who are only too ready to boast of the way in which they have helped these men in their upward progress. Very often this boasting is as natural as it is allowable, but it has its limits in any case, and sometimes it is very easily exaggerated. In Abraham's case help from the king of Sodom would have been help from a quarter to which he did not desire to be indebted. The worldliness of his nephew Lot had already shown the spiritual dangers of intimacy with Sodom.

The only qualification that Abraham makes is with reference to the Canaanitish young men who had assisted him in the victory, and who naturally would not be guided by the principles that actuated him. On their behalf he is willing to receive some of the spoil. Spirituality is thus able to discern and distinguish between circumstances when we are called upon to act for self and on behalf of others.

1. *The contrast of Abraham's attitude to the two kings.*—How very remarkable is this difference! To the king of Salem the acknowledgment of dependence; to the king of Sodom the assertion of independence. To the king of Salem the admission of inferiority; to the king of Sodom the attitude of equality. To the king of Salem the spirit of humility; to the king of Sodom the attitude of dignity. How striking and really wonderful is this perfect balance of qualities!

2. *The explanation of this striking attitude.*—Again we have to penetrate below the surface to discover the secret of Abraham's wonderful bearing. The explanation, of course, is "faith," and as we study the subject somewhat more closely we find a fourfold action and activity of Abraham's trust in God.

(*a*) Faith is able to recognize spiritual position. Melchizedek was God's representative, and Abraham's faith was quick to see this and to act accordingly.

(*b*) Faith is able to realize serious peril. Not always has a believer been able to see that success often means temptation, and victory the possibility of danger. Abraham saw this, and hence his unflinching attitude.

(*c*) Faith is able to resist strong pressure. It takes a real man to withstand honor paid by a king. "By faith" Abraham endured as seeing the King of kings.

(*d*) Faith is able to rest on special provision. The offer of the spoil was as nothing to Abraham compared with God's promise of the land and the attendant blessings. Thus Abraham could wait, and his faith expressed itself in patience, as he put God first. "In all thy ways acknowledge Him, and He shall direct thy paths."

XIX

THE GREAT ENCOURAGEMENT

GEN. xv. 1-6.

AFTER these things the word of the Lord came unto Abram in a vision, saying, Fear not, Abram: I *am* thy shield *and* thy exceeding great reward.

And Abram said, Lord God, what wilt Thou give me, seeing I go childless, and the steward of my house *is* this Eliezer of Damascus.

And Abram said, Behold, to me thou hast given no seed: and, lo, one born in my house is mine heir.

And, behold, the word of the Lord *came* unto him, saying, This shall not be thine heir; but he that shall come forth out of thine own bowels shall be thine heir.

And He brought him forth abroad, and said, Look now toward heaven, and tell the stars, if thou be able to number them: and He said unto him, So shall thy seed be.

And he believed in the Lord; and He counted it to him for righteousness.

TIMES of spiritual reaction are not uncommon among the people of God. Elijah experienced a great reaction (1 Kings xix.) after the eventful and critical day on Carmel (1 Kings xviii.) So it evidently was with Abraham. The new, remarkable, and in some respects exciting events connected with the rescue of Lot brought about the inevitable swing of the pendulum, as we can easily see in studying this chapter, which is closely connected with the preceding one.

I. *The Divine Revelation* (ver. 1).—There were nine successive manifestations of God to Abraham, of which this is the fifth. The phrase "the word of the Lord came" is very noteworthy as occurring first in this passage. It is found frequently afterwards throughout the Old Testament. (Cf. Exod. ix. 20; 1 Sam. iii. 1.) The revelation seems to have been in the form of a vision, not a dream (ver. 5).

When did it come? "After these things." The reference is, of course, to the events of chapter xiv., and shows the direct and es-

136

sential connection between the two chapters. God's revelations to His people are always intimately connected with their needs, as we see in this case.

Why did it come? "Fear not, Abraham." Then Abraham must have had some fear. What was this? Was it not a natural dejection after victory? May it not have been caused by inevitable physical, mental, and moral reaction after the strain involved in the recent events? Fear before battle is the characteristic of cowards; fear after battle is the mark of a hero. This is the first occurrence of the Divine "Fear not" which is afterwards found so often as God's message to His weary and tired servants. Either "Fear not," or its equivalent "Be not afraid," occurs some eighty-four times in Holy Scripture. The silence of six centuries after Malachi was broken by the Divine "Fear not" (Luke i. 13), and the announcement of the Incarnation was made in the same way (Luke i. 30).

What was it? "I am thy shield and thy exceeding great reward." How appropriate to the need of the moment was this twofold revelation of God to His servant! (a) God as a shield against all foes. (Cf. Psalm iii. 3; xviii. 2; xviii. 30! lxxxiv. 9; xci. 4.) (b) God as a reward after victory. Abraham had refused the spoil of Sodom and Gomorrah; but God would not allow Abraham to be a loser. He Himself would be His servant's "exceeding great reward."

II. *The Human Response* (vers. 2-3).—Notice his despondent inquiry. "What wilt Thou give me?" It is evident from this inquiry how over-strained Abraham was. The long waiting and the spiritual loneliness had been making their mark, and now he almost complains as he asks what reward there can be for him.

Mark his disappointed hope. "Seeing I go childless." Ten years had elapsed since his entrance into Canaan, and, in spite of the promise of a seed, there was no sign of fulfilment. Sarah and he were so much older, and everything seemed against even the possibility of the realization of God's promises.

Observe his discouraging prospect. "One born in my house is mine heir." Abraham seems to have almost lost hope, and was

settling down to the conviction that, after all, his steward would
be his heir.

III. *The Divine Assurance* (vers. 4, 5).—Now we shall see how
God dealt lovingly and faithfully with His tried and troubled
servant.

His faithlessness was corrected. "This shall not be thine heir."
God had not forgotten to be gracious. He was still mindful of His
promises (Gen. xii. 7, and xiii. 16).

His faith was instructed. "He that shall come . . . shall be thine
heir." Thus God particularized in a way that had not been done
previously in connection with the promise, and taught His servant,
by giving him new ground for trust.

His faith was encouraged. "Tell the stars . . . so shall thy seed
be." Abraham was bidden to look toward heaven, and in so doing
he would doubtless realize something of the wide sweep of God's
purposes for him and his seed. Notice the three metaphors connected with Abraham's seed: "The dust of the earth" (Gen. xiii.
16); "the stars of heaven" (Gen. xv. 5); "the sand of the seashore"
(Gen. xxii. 17).

IV. *The Human Acceptance* (ver. 6).—Now comes a wonderful
change and a definite progress upwards in Abraham's spiritual experience.

There was a prompt response to the Divine revelation. "Abraham believed." He had faith before, but now it was prominent
and emphatic, a clearer, stronger, fuller trust in God. The original
Hebrew for "believed" comes from a root whence we derive our
"Amen," and we might paraphrase it by saying that "Abraham said
Amen to the Lord." "Amen" in Scripture never means a petition
("May it be so'), but is always a strong assertion of faith ("It
shall be so," or "It is so"). Faith is thus the only, as it is the
adequate, response to God's revelation. The word of the Lord
comes, and we believe. Faith takes God at His word.

Then came an equally prompt rejoinder from God in answer to
His servant's trust. "And He counted it to him." That is, God
accounted Abraham's faith as the channel for the reception of the
gift of righteousness. Notice the Old Testament allusions to the

doctrine of imputation, or reckoning (Lev. vii. 18; xvii. 4; Num. xviii. 27; 2 Sam. xix. 19; Psalm xxxii. 2; cvi. 31. (See also Rom. iv. *passim.*)

The spiritual result is described in one significant word, "righteousness." This means the state or condition of being "right" with God, and we have here the first reference to this great word "righteousness" which is subsequently so characteristic of the Old Testament as well as the New Testament revelation. Abraham was originally destitute of righteousness, and is now reckoned as righteous through faith in God. God Himself is the Object of his faith, the Word of God is the ground of his faith, and righteousness is the result of his faith. It is to be noticed that the phrase "counted it to him *for* righteousness" is not to be confused with "counted it to him *instead* of righteousness." It means counted or reckoned with a view to his receiving righteousness. In Rom. iv. the preposition (for, unto) with "righteousness" cannot be equivalent to "as if" or "instead of." (See Haldane *in loc.*)

This passage is noteworthy for its first occurrences of remarkable and subsequently well-known words and phrases: (1) "The word of the Lord came"; (2) "Fear not"; (3) "Believed"; (4) "Counted"; (5) "Righteousness." It is hardly too much to say that all subsequent occurrences of these words and phrases find the key to their meaning here.

1. *The Possibility of spiritual despondency.*—This is a well-known fact in the life of the believer. It is often due to a three-fold strain which is partly physical, partly emotional, and partly spiritual. Great experiences make their mark upon us, and "by reason of the frailty of our nature we cannot always stand upright." At any rate we *do* not.

2. *The Peril of spiritual disheartenment.*—We may explain, but we can hardly excuse, spiritual depression, and it is often used of Satan to lead us away from God into the paths of spiritual despair. And even though we never reach despair, our depression may easily bring discredit upon the name of God. Herein lies one of the most serious elements of the peril.

3. *The Protection against spiritual discouragement.*—This is found first in God's continuous revelation of Himself to our hearts, and then our continued response in whole-hearted trust and confidence maintained through prayer and fellowship with the Word of God. God's truth and our trust. His grace and our faith. These are correlative facts and will ever protect the soul.

4. *The Preciousness of spiritual discipline.*—God's delays to Abraham were not denials. They were intended to bring him nearer to God and to lead him to depend more upon the Giver than on His gifts. Not what God gives so much as what He is, is the foundation and source of spiritual life, power and progress.

XX

THE CONFIRMATION OF FAITH

GEN. xv. 7-21

AND He said unto him, I *am* the Lord that brought thee out of Ur of the Chaldees, to give thee this land to inherit it.

And he said, Lord God, whereby shall I know that I shall inherit it?

And He said unto him, Take Me an heifer of three years old, and a she-goat of three years old, and a ram of three years old, and a turtle-dove, and a young pigeon.

And he took unto Him all these, and divided them in the midst, and laid each piece one against another: but the birds divided he not.

And when the fowls came down upon the carcases, Abram drove them away.

And when the sun was going down, a deep sleep fell upon Abram; and lo, an horror of great darkness fell upon him.

And He said unto Abram, Know of a surety, that thy seed shall be a stranger in a land *that is* not theirs, and shall serve them; and they shall afflict them four hundred years:

And also that nation, whom they shall serve, will I judge; and afterward shall they come out with great substance.

And thou shalt go to thy fathers in peace; thou shalt be buried in a good old age.

But in the fourth generation they shall come hither again: for the iniquity of the Amorites *is* not yet full.

And it came to pass, that, when the sun went down, and it was dark, behold a smoking furnace, and a burning lamp that passed between those pieces.

In that same day the Lord made a covenant with Abram, saying, Unto thy seed have I given this land, from the river of Egypt unto the great river, the river Euphrates:

The Kenites, and the Kenizzites, and the Kadomites,

And the Hittites, and the Perizzites, and the Rephaims,

And the Amorites, and the Canaanites, and the Girgashites, and the Jebusites.

IN response to Abraham's faith (ver. 6) God entered into solemn covenant with him, assuring him of the certainty, while revealing still more of the meaning, of the Divine promises concerning him and his seed. In this section "covenant" is the key-word.

I. *The Foundation of the Covenant* (ver. 7).—At the basis of the covenant was God's character and revelation to Abraham, and on this foundation everything else rested.

The covenant was introduced by the solemn announcement of the Divine Name, "I am Jehovah." This was the red-rock of all; God's unchanging and unchangeable presence and character.

Then came the significant reminder of what God had already done for him. "That brought thee out of Ur of the Chaldees." Abraham had already been redeemed, and this fact was the foundation of, and was intended to be a factor in, the rest of God's dealings with him.

Following this came the renewed declaration of the Divine purpose. "To give thee this land to inherit it." God again reminds and assures Abraham of His object in bringing him out of his own land. The purpose is once more stated clearly and plainly.

II. *The Desire for the Covenant* (ver. 8).—Abraham met this new assurance of God with an earnest desire for a proof.

He makes his appeal for knowledge. This was what he needed; knowledge, certitude.

He also sought from God some assurance. "Whereby shall I know." He desired some outward and visible guarantee and pledge.

And yet it must be observed that he did not require a sign in order to believe, but after and on account of believing. It was not faithlessness, but a desire for confirmation. He fully believed God's Word, and yet wondered how and when it would be fulfilled. Contrast Mary's attitude (Luke i. 34) with that of Zacharias (Luke i. 18), though her words were practically the same. Abraham's attitude might well be summed up and illustrated by the words, "Lord, I believe; help Thou mine unbelief" (Mark ix. 24).

III. *The Preparation for the Covenant* (vers. 9-10).—The Divine instructions are now given. "Take for Me an heifer," etc. The heifer, goat, and ram were to be three years old, signifying maturity in the offering. These, with the dove and pigeon, were afterwards found associated with the Mosaic law (Exod. xxix. 15; Num. xv. 27, xix. 2; Deut. xxi. 3).

Then Abraham proceeded to fulfil the requirements connected with the solemnities of a covenant. "Took . . . divided." See Leviticus i. 6. Having divided the animals, he places the corresponding pieces opposite to each other, and the one bird opposite to the other, leaving a passage between. This was the usual form of agreement and contract, the two parties walking in procession along the pathway just made, and thereby signifying their agreement (Jer. xxxiv. 18 f.). The idea underlying this was that of a covenant by means of sacrifice (Ps. l. 5). The blood-covenant was a well-known primitive method of ratifying solemn agreements.

We are now able to notice how Abraham prepared to receive God's assurance and further revelation.

IV. *The Readiness for the Covenant* (vers. 11, 12).—Faithfulness was the first and leading proof of Abraham's readiness. He had obeyed exactly according to the command of God, observing to the letter what God required. This is ever the true attitude for fuller teaching and deeper blessing.

Watchfulness was another feature of his attitude at this time. While waiting God's time he kept guard over the carcases, and kept away the birds of prey. We see how spiritual attitude underlies this act.

Nor are we wrong in thinking that receptiveness characterized him. The supernatural slumber (cf. Gen. ii. 21) prepared Abraham for the reception of God's revelation by detaching him from all things earthly which might divert his attention, and prevent the full teaching having its effect upon his life. The dread that fell upon him was doubtless due to the consciousness of a Divine presence overshadowing him.

V. *The Message of the Covenant* (vers. 13-16).—A fourfold revelation now comes from God, and Abraham is told of remarkable experiences which should accrue to his seed.

His seed is to endure great privation (ver. 13). Exile, bondage, and affliction are the three elements of this privation. He was to learn the meaning of heirship through suffering. (Cf. Rom. viii. 17).

N. B.—The term of 400 years seems to be a round number for 430 (Exod. xii. 40; Acts vii. 6; Gal. iii. 17). The 430 years may date from the birth of Isaac or from the death of Jacob, according to the computation chosen.

His seed is to witness the display of great power (ver. 14). The nation that would cause trouble to his seed would be punished, and his seed should come forth with abundant provision by God's help.

He himself is to experience great peace (ver. 15). This is the first hint that Abraham himself was not to realize personally the fulness of God's purpose. God leads us step by step without revealing everything at once; and as revelation after revelation came to Abraham the horizon of God's purpose extended wider and wider. Abraham is to die in peace and be buried in a good old age. He is to be gathered "to his fathers"—which means, as they were not buried in Canaan, that he would be with them in Sheol.

And he is called to exercise great patience (ver. 16). Another hint of the wide sweep of the Divine purposes. Other factors were at work, and many conditions had to be fulfilled before God's purpose could be completely realized.

VI. *The Making of the Covenant* (ver. 17-21).—After the revelation of God's will comes the Divine assurance in the form of a covenant.

The symbolical action is noteworthy (ver. 17). A cylindrical fire-pot and a fiery torch combined to symbolize and express the Divine presence (Exod. xix.) and in condescension to Abraham and his experience this symbol of the Divine presence passed along the pathway made between the birds and the animals, thus ratifying the covenant and giving God's servant a Divine guarantee.

Then comes a special assurance (vers. 18-21). God now reveals to His servant the precise limits of the land promised to him. It seems pretty clear that the two rivers referred to must be the Nile and the Euphrates, thus giving those complete boundaries of the Holy Land which have never yet been fully realized. (Cf. 1 Kings iv. 21; 2 Chron. ix. 26.) God's promises still await their perfect fulfilment, for His covenant with Abraham is absolutely unconditional, and will be realized in His own time.

The study of the Divine covenants of the Bible is full of the profoundest interest: (1) With Noah, (2) with Abraham, (3) with

Moses and Israel, (4) the New Covenant. Each has its own characteristic features and elements; and only one, the Mosaic, is conditional, a covenant of works. The other three are covenants "all of grace." Consider now the meaning and message of this Covenant.

1. *The Divine Action.*—It is noteworthy that God only passed through the pieces, and not Abraham as well. This clearly shows that a Divine covenant is not a mutual agreement on equal terms between two parties, but a Divine promise assured and ratified by means of a visible pledge of its fulfilment. This at once takes the Divine covenant out of the category of all similar human agreements. It is divinely one-sided. God promises, God gives, God assures (Heb. vi. 17).

2. *The Human Attitude.*—What, then, is man's part in this covenant? Simply that of a recipient. God gives; Abraham takes. "What shall I *render* unto the Lord? . . . I will *take*" (Ps. cxvi. 12, 13). The attitude of the believer in response to this covenant of grace is fourfold: (1) A feeling of deep gratitude, (2) a response of whole-hearted trust, (3) an expression of hearty thanksgiving, (4) a life of loyal obedience.

XXI

A FALSE STEP

GEN. xvi.

Now Sarai, Abram's wife, bare him no children: and she had an handmaid, an Egyptian, whose name *was* Hagar.

And Sarai said unto Abram, Behold now, the Lord hath restrained me from bearing: I pray thee, go in unto my maid; it may be that I may obtain children by her. And Abram hearkened to the voice of Sarai.

Sarai, Abram's wife, took Hagar her maid, the Egyptian, after Abram had dwelt ten years in the land of Canaan, and gave her to her husband Abram to be his wife.

And he went in unto Hagar, and she conceived: and when she saw that she had conceived, her mistress was despised in her eyes.

And Sarai said unto Abram, My wrong *be* upon thee: I have given my maid into thy bosom; and when she saw that she had conceived, I was despised in her eyes: the Lord judge between me and thee.

But Abram said unto Sarai, Behold, thy maid *is* in thy hand: do to her as it pleaseth thee. And when Sarai dealt hardly with her, she fled from her face.

And the angel of the Lord found her by a fountain of water in the wilderness, by the fountain in the way to Shur.

And he said, Hagar, Sarai's maid, whence comest thou? and whither wilt thou go? And she said, I flee from the face of my mistress Sarai.

And the angel of the Lord said unto her, Return to thy mistress, and submit thyself under her hands.

And the angel of the Lord said unto her, I will multiply thy seed exceedingly, that it shall not be numbered for multitude.

And the angel of the Lord said unto her, Behold, thou *art* with child, and shalt bear a son, and shalt call his name Ishmael; because the Lord hath heard thy affliction.

And he will be a wild man; his hand *will* be against every man, and every man's hand against him: and he shall dwell in the presence of all his brethren.

And she called the name of the Lord that spake unto her, Thou God seest me: for she said, Have I also here looked after him that seeth me?

Wherefore the well was called Beer-lahai-roi; behold, *it is* between Kadesh and Bered.

And Hagar bare Abram a son: and Abram called his son's name, which Hagar bare, Ishmael.

And Abram *was* fourscore and six years old when Hagar bare Ishmael to Abram.

IT might have been thought that after the experience recorded in chapter xv. Abraham would have been enabled to continue along the pathway of God's will without hesitation, mistake, or trouble. But we know by our own experience the proneness of the believer to blunder and fall into error and sin all through his earthly pilgrimage, no matter how far advanced his course or mature his experience. In the story of Hagar we come upon the record of another shadow which fell on Abraham's life. He is brought face to face with a specious temptation, and for lack of spiritual perception he falls into the snare, which leads to serious and very far-reaching consequences.

I. *The Sad Mistake* (vers. 1-3).—The temptation came originally from Sarah. Waiting had evidently told upon her, and this action was the result. Yet we must not overlook the fact that Abraham yielded even though the first suggestion came from his wife.

It had not yet been clearly revealed that Sarah was to be the mother of the promised seed, and probably this led to her impatience. Hagar, as bond-slave, was her mistress's personal property, "a living chattel," and any child of the bond-slave would necessarily belong to the mistress, not the mother.

There was evident faith in God's promise in this proposal of Sarah's. She fully believed that Abraham was to have the seed promised by God. We can therefore understand that her suggestion means a very genuine piece of self-denial. The practice was a common one, and Sarah was but the creature of her age in urging it on Abraham.

Nevertheless, though Sarah's motive was good, genuine, and involved self-sacrifice, the proposal was wrong in itself, and, at the same time, wrong in its method of obtaining the end sought. It was wrong against God, Whose word had been given and Whose time should have been waited. It was wrong against Abraham, leading him out of the pathway of patient waiting for God's will. It was wrong against Hagar, and did not recognize her individuality and rights in the matter. It was wrong against Sarah herself, robbing her of a high privilege as well as leading to disobedience.

II. *The Sorrowful Results* (vers. 4-6).—The outcome of Abraham's yielding was soon seen in the effects which came upon all.

The first effect was pride (ver. 4). Hagar's insolence was perfectly natural, and her reproach of her mistress, even though insolent, quite inevitable. Human nature is always human nature, and this reproach stung Sarah's pride to the quick, with the results that are well known.

The next result was jealousy (ver. 5). Now Sarah blames Abraham, a somewhat curious and very unfair attitude. "My wrong be upon thee." This may be interpreted, "My injury belongs to thee as well," or, "May the injury to me return to thee!" It is a little surprising that Sarah's quick womanly perception did not forewarn her of these results of pride and jealousy.

Then followed misery (ver. 6). This came upon Abraham with real force. He was, of course, powerless in the matter. as Hagar was her mistress's absolute property. He could not interfere, and was compelled to accept the inevitable, and say that Sarah must do "as it pleased" her.

And not least was the injustice (ver. 6). This came upon Hagar. with whom Sarah "dealt hardly." Hagar found herself once more a slave, and this time with personal maltreatment such as she had never experienced before.

It is easy for us to see as we read the story how inevitable these results were. Would that we ourselves realized beforehand all such inevitableness!

III. *The Special Interposition* (vers. 7-12).—What a picture of real life is found in this chapter! Man is seen blundering. sinning, and suffering, and then God intervenes with His overruling providence, wisdom, and grace.

We see the blessed truth of Divine interest in human troubles (ver. 7). "The angel found her." God had not overlooked what had taken place, and now He interposes in order to bring about the best possible results after the error and sin of His children. How often God has had to do this for His children since that day!

We observe, too, the Divine call for perfect submission (vers. 8, 9). The questions "whence" and "whither" recall Hagar to her position, and the slave woman tells the simple truth about her flight. The Divine command is that she should return and submit herself. It will be noticed that the quasi-marriage is not for an instant acknowledged. Sarah is still Hagar's mistress. This call for submission was the first step towards blessing in Hagar's life. The same is true today. If we have made mistakes which have led us into sin, the primary condition of restoration is complete submission to the will of God, whatever that may involve.

We have also the Divine assurance of definite blessing (ver. 10). God accompanies His call for submission by the promise of blessing to her child. He never makes a demand without giving us a promise. Thus He encouraged and incited her to the very submission from which she doubtless shrank.

And above all there is the Divine revelation of overruling providence (vers. 11, 12). God told her that she should have a son and also of his name and its meaning (Ishmael; "God shall hear"). Thus every time she mentioned his name she might be reminded of God's promises. Her son's character and relation to others were also revealed (ver. 12), an additional encouragement to the poor creature in her misery and trouble.

This interposition had its immediate and blessed effect on Hagar.

It led to a realization of the Divine presence (ver. 13). "She called the name. . . . Thou God seest me," or "The God of my vision." The Divine Presence thus came into her life with its blessing and cheer.

It prompted a memorial of the Divine promise (ver. 14). "The well was called Beer-lahai-roi." See margin, "The well of Him that liveth and seeth me"; that is, the well where life is preserved after seeing God.

It elicited obedience to the Divine will. She returned to her mistress, accepted the position, and all things were fulfilled according to the Divine revelation.

1. *The continuance of the old nature.*—How truly this fact of the spiritual life is proved by this chapter! Is it not also manifest in daily experience? The most deeply-taught believer is not exempt from the temptations, weaknesses, and tendencies of the old sinful nature.

2. *The occurrence of special dangers.*—Here again we are face to face with a well-known fact of the spiritual life. Our life may be lived for days, and weeks, and months without anything exceptional occurring, and then suddenly a special temptation may arise which leads us into sin.

3. *The unexpected sources of temptation.*—Abraham's temptation came from the nearest and dearest in his life, the very source whence trouble might have been least expected. So it often is today. Satan uses even the holiest of relationships and the closest of ties to bring about sin, and we ought not to be "ignorant of his devices."

4. *The combination of high motives and wrong actions.*—Sarah's motives were undoubtedly good, and we may fully believe that Abraham was actuated in the same way, and yet their actions were manifestly wrong. How frequently this remarkable combination of good motive and bad conduct occurs in history and daily life! The end does *not* justify the means, whatever people may say.

5. *The far-reaching effects of a believer's sin.*—Evil-doing on the part of a child of God is perhaps the very worst thing that can happen, and often has very widespread effects. It has been well pointed out by a modern writer that the existence of Mohammedanism today is really to be traced to Abraham's false step; Mohammedanism which is in some respects the deadliest opponent of Christianity. Isaac and Ishmael still struggle in fierce opposition.

6. *The necessity of prolonged waiting on God.*—God's will must be realized in God's way, and God's way often involves waiting God's time. The union of faith and patience (Heb. vi. 12) is one of the prime necessities of true spiritual life.

7. *The supreme secret of all true living.*—Abraham could hardly have been living in close touch with God, or his spiritual perception

would have been keen enough to detect the danger lurking in Sarah's temptation. The only protection against error in thought and action is found in abiding with God, living in fellowship with Him, listening to His voice in His word, and keeping the pathway to His presence clear by prayer and alertness of attitude before Him. "They that know their God shall be strong and do" (Dan. xi. 32. Heb.).

XXII

THE COVENANT RENEWED

Gen. xvii.

And when Abram was ninety years old and nine, the Lord appeared to Abram, and said unto him, I *am* the Almighty God; walk before Me, and be thou perfect.

And I will make My covenant between Me and thee, and will multiply thee exceedingly.

And Abram fell on his face: and God talked with him, saying,

As for Me, behold, My covenant *is* with thee, and thou shalt be a father of many nations.

Neither shall thy name any more be called Abram, but thy name shall be Abraham; for a father of many nations have I made thee.

And I will make thee exceeding fruitful, and I will make nations of thee, and kings shall come out of thee.

And I will establish My covenant between Me and thee, and thy seed after thee, in their generations, for an everlasting covenant, to be a God unto thee, and to thy seed after thee.

And I will give unto thee, and to thy seed after thee, the land wherein thou art a stranger, all the land of Canaan, for an everlasting possession; and I will be their God.

And God said unto Abraham, Thou shalt keep My covenant therefore, thou, and thy seed after thee in their generations.

This *is* My covenant, which ye shall keep, between Me and you, and thy seed after thee; Every man-child among you shall be circumcised.

And ye shall circumcise the flesh of your foreskin; and it shall be a token of the covenant betwixt Me and you.

And he that is eight days old shall be circumcised among you, every man-child in your generations, he that is born in the house, or bought with money of any stranger, which *is* not of thy seed.

He that is born in thy house, and he that is bought with thy money, must needs be circumcised: and My covenant shall be in your flesh for an everlasting covenant.

And the uncircumcised man-child, whose flesh of his foreskin is not circumcised, that soul shall be cut off from his people; he hath broken My covenant.

And God said unto Abraham, As for Sarai thy wife, thou shalt not call her name Sarai, but Sarah *shall* her name *be*.

And I will bless her, and give thee a son also of her: yea, I will bless her, and she shall be *a mother* of nations; kings of people shall be of her.

THE COVENANT RENEWED   153

Then Abraham fell upon his face, and laughed, and said in his heart, Shall *a child* be born unto him that is an hundred years old? and shall Sarah, that is ninety years old, bear?

And Abraham said unto God, O that Ishmael might live before Thee!

And God said, Sarah thy wife shall bear thee a son indeed; and thou shalt call his name Isaac: and I will establish My covenant with him for an everlasting covenant, *and* with his seed after him.

And as for Ishmael, I have heard thee: Behold, I have blessed him, and will make him fruitful, and will multiply him exceedingly; twelve princes shall he beget, and I will make him a great nation.

But My covenant will I establish with Isaac, which Sarah shall bear unto thee at this set time in the next year.

And He left off talking with him, and God went up from Abraham.

And Abraham took Ishmael his son, and all that were born in his house, and all that were bought with his money, every male among the men of Abraham's house, and circumcised the flesh of their foreskin in the selfsame day, as God had said unto him.

And Abraham *was* ninety years old and nine when he was circumcised in the flesh of his foreskin.

And Ishmael his son *was* thirteen years old when he was circumcised in the flesh of his foreskin.

In the selfsame day was Abraham circumcised, and Ishmael his son.

And all the men of his house, born in the house, and bought with money of the stranger, were circumcised with him.

GOD has always some fresh surprise of knowledge, grace and blessing with which to delight His children. We see this again and again in the life of Abraham, and not least of all in the story recorded in the present chapter. This episode was a great step forward in Abraham's spiritual relationship to God, as well as in his personal experience.

I. *The Fresh Revelation* (vers. 1-8).—Abraham was at this period ninety-nine years old. Thirteen years had elapsed since the trouble about Hagar (chap xvi. 16). Nothing is recorded of these years, and we may assume that there was no special or new revelation of God's will during the time. It was an opportunity of quiet waiting for, and waiting on God. Now once again the Lord appears to His servant.

This fresh appearance of God brought with it a new message (ver. 1). "I am the Almighty God." This was a new title of God (Hebrew: *El Shaddai*). The root idea seems to be that of power and ability, and is best rendered by the phrase "The Mighty God," the addition of "All" being no necessary part of the word. This special emphasis upon God's power was very appropriate to the new message about to be given.

New knowledge always carries new responsibilities and we are not surprised to note the definite claim (ver. 1). "Walk before Me, and be thou perfect" (upright). God called upon His servant to live and move in the Divine presence, and to be sincere, genuine, and true-hearted. Is this a hint that Abraham was settling down, satisfied with Ishmael, and no longer anxious about the special seed promised by God? Something of this seems to have been the case, or we should have hardly had this very definite call.

The personal result was soon seen (ver. 3). "Abraham fell on his face." This attitude of reverence and of readiness shows that Abraham realized at once the solemnity of the occasion.

And now for the first time we seem to become fully conscious of Abraham's high privilege (ver. 3). "God talked with him." Few of those whose lives are recorded in the Old Testament were on the same spiritual footing as Abraham. God once again shows His trust in His servant, and that He will not hide from him what He is about to do. How beautiful is the picture of this holy familiarity between the Mighty God and His servant!

Nor are we surprised to find that God gives to His servant a specially strong assurance (ver. 4). "As for Me, behold, My covenant is with thee." These words are evidently intended, by their emphatic reference to God Himself ("as for Me"), as a reminder to Abraham that, whatever he had forgotten, God had not been unmindful of His solemn promises. It is noteworthy that God reminds Abraham of an already existing covenant ("My covenant is with thee"), and then proceeds to tell him some of the forthcoming results of this existing fact. Not even the silence of thirteen years, still less the birth of Ishmael, can alter God's purposes or change His mind concerning Abraham.

The detailed promises of this new revelation deserve the most careful study (vers. 4-8). They deal with three great facts: (a) Abraham himself, (b) the land, (c) his seed. At this point a comparison should be made of the growth in the details of the revelation of God's purpose: chapter xii., "a great nation"; chapter xiii., "as the dust of the earth"; chapter xv., "as the stars of heaven"; chapter xvii., "many nations."

II. *The Necessary Requirements* (vers. 9-14).—Abraham is now told his part in the matter, and it is very striking and suggestive to notice that all that he has to do is to obey God's word in the one respect mentioned in these verses. This is another illustration of the fact that God's covenant of grace is divinely one-sided. God is the Giver; man the receiver, not the equal. The conditions to be fulfilled (vers. 10-14) are now stated. The ordinance of circumcision, already known widely in the East, is given a special meaning and deep sacredness. The truths connected with it seem to include at least four ideas: (*a*) designation, as belonging to God; (*b*) separation unto Him; (*c*) purity in Him; (*d*) possession by Him. It is also noteworthy that we are here brought face to face for the first time in Holy Scripture with young life in relation to God. God entered into covenant with little children, and as the covenant with Abraham was one of grace we see the true place of little children in the kingdom of God. Circumcision was not merely a mark of the Mosaic dispensation and Jewish covenant of works; it was, as here, pre-Mosaic, associated with the covenant of grace, and therefore independent of, and wider than, the Jewish national life (John vii. 22). God is here seen in the attitude of Father to little children, and He has never altered that attitude.

III. *The Further Revelation* (vers. 15, 16).—Not only Abraham's, but also his wife's name is now changed. This is another indication of God's purpose and a special assurance of blessing. And now for the first time Sarah is announced as the mother of the promised seed. Up to this moment everything had been couched in general terms as to "seed," but without special reference to Sarah. God's promises become more definite and detailed as time goes on and need arises.

IV. *The Immediate Response* (vers. 17, 18).—Abraham receives the new revelation of God with reverence, and yet with a certain trustful astonishment. The laugh is evidently not the laugh of unbelief, but of a faith which, while taking God at his word, considers the news almost too good to be true. God's revelations to His people often seem to be too good to be true, and yet they *are* true!

But there is one shadow over the scene. He is thinking of his growing son. How natural was this appeal on behalf of Ishmael! The boy had won his way to his father's heart, and it would have been surprising from the natural and human standpoint if Abraham had not desired Ishmael to be his heir. And yet, notwithstanding the naturalness of the appeal, there lies at the root of it a desire to have "some substitute for God's promises." It is as though anything else would really do as well. God knows better than His servant, and we have His answer at once.

V. *The Full Revelation* (vers. 19-22).—Not even the intense appeal can stand before God's purposes. God will maintain His own way, and so He assures Abraham that Sarah is indeed to be the mother of the seed, that the son's name shall be Isaac ("Laughter"), and that the covenant which is to be everlasting is to be realized through Isaac, and not through Ishmael.

Nevertheless Ishmael shall not be forgotten. He is Abraham's seed, and as the son of God's servant he will be blessed and made a great nation. Thus God overrules His children's mistakes, and in loving condescension and tender mercy brings blessing out of trouble.

VI. *The Loyal Reception* (vers. 23-27).—Now the time of communion has come to an end, and God leaves His servant to ponder what has been said and to respond to the revelation.

How prompt was his obedience (ver. 23). "In the selfsame day, as God had said." How striking in their simplicity are these words, indicating the immediateness of Abraham's trustful obedience! This is ever the pathway of blessing. "Whatsoever He saith unto you, do it," and do it at once!

How complete was his acceptance (ver. 27). Not only as to himself and Ishmael, but also as to all his house, Abraham fulfilled the Divine requirement and bestowed the sign of the covenant. They were all included in the Divine blessings, for God knew that Abraham would influence his whole household aright.

In this fresh revelation Abraham learned much about God, and the same lessons are needed by us today. The more we know of God, the stronger and richer will be our lives.

1. *A new view of God's Character.*—God revealed Himself to Abraham as a God of might and power (ver. 1), and, as such, able to fulfil all his hopes. God does not wish His children to be content with anything else than His fullest blessings, and for the accomplishment of this "He is able to do exceeding abundantly above all that we ask or think." The various passages in the New Testament where we read that "God is able" call for earnest meditation.

2. *A wider view of God's Purposes.*—Abraham little realized the far-reaching extent and universal scope of God's purpose concerning him. He was now taught this as he had never been taught before, in great wealth of detail and definiteness of meaning. It is always well to have our view of God's mind for the world extended and deepened and so "think His thoughts after Him."

3. *A clearer view of God's Will.*—God's will for us, as it was for Abraham, is loyal obedience. As the little child said of the angels in heaven who do God's will there, "they obey without asking any questions." This, and this alone, is the secret of power in daily living.

4. *A fuller view of God's Grace.*—The whole chapter is full of grace. It was grace that prompted, planned, and provided these blessings for Abraham. It was grace that condescended to Abraham's weaknesses, limitations, and faults. It was grace that persisted with Abraham in spite of every check and drawback, and it was grace that perfected everything concerning him. God is still "the God of all grace," and it is the believer's joy to experience the "unsearchable riches of His grace in His kindness toward us in Christ Jesus."

XXIII

FELLOWSHIP WITH GOD

GEN. xviii. 1-21

AND the Lord appeared unto him in the plains of Mamre: and he sat in the tent door in the heat of the day:

And he lift up his eyes and looked, and, lo, three men stood by him: and when he saw *them*, he ran to meet them from the tent door, and bowed himself toward the ground.

And said, My Lord if now I have found favor in thy sight, pass not away, I pray thee, from thy servant:

Let a little water, I pray you, be fetched, and wash your feet, and rest yourselves under the tree:

And I will fetch a morsel of bread, and comfort ye your hearts; after that ye shall pass on: for therefore are ye come to your servant. And they said, So do, as thou hast said.

And Abraham hastened into the tent unto Sarah, and said, Make ready quickly three measures of fine meal, knead *it*, and make cakes upon the hearth.

And Abraham ran unto the herd, and fetcht a calf tender and good, and gave *it* unto a young man: and he hasted to dress it.

And he took butter, and milk, and the calf which he had dressed, and set *it* before them; and he stood by them under the tree, and they did eat.

And they said unto him, Where *is* Sarah thy wife? And he said, Behold, in the tent.

And he said, I will certainly return unto thee according to the time of life; and, lo, Sarah thy wife shall have a son. And Sarah heard *it* in the tent door, which *was* behind him.

And Abraham and Sarah *were* old *and* well stricken in age: and it ceased to be with Sarah after the manner of women.

Therefore Sarah laughed within herself, saying, After I am waxed old shall I have pleasure, my lord being old also?

And the Lord said unto Abraham, Wherefore did Sarah laugh, saying, Shall I of a surety bear a child, which am old?

Is anything too hard for the Lord? At the time appointed I will return unto thee, according to the time of life, and Sarah shall have a son.

Then Sarah denied, saying, I laughed not; for she was afraid. And he said, Nay: but thou didst laugh.

And the men rose up from thence, and looked toward Sodom: and Abraham went with them to bring them on the way.

And the Lord said, Shall I hide from Abraham that thing which I do;

Seeing that Abraham shall surely become a great and mighty nation, and all the nations of the earth shall be blessed in him?

For I know him, that he will command his children and his household after him, and they shall keep the way of the Lord, to do justice and judgment; that the Lord may bring upon Abraham that which he hath spoken of him.

And the Lord said, Because the cry of Sodom and Gomorrah is great, and because their sin is very grievous;

I will go down now, and see whether they have done altogether according to the cry of it, which is come unto me: and if not, I will know.

OUR life in relation to God can be summed up in four words—sonship, worship, stewardship, fellowship. The believer is at once a son, a subject, a servant, and a friend of God. The last-named relationship marks the later period of Abraham's life, and seems to be (as always) associated with growth and maturity of spiritual experience. In this chapter there are several aspects of the believer's fellowship with God, and it is probable that from this period commence those experiences which led to Abraham being called the "friend of God" (2 Chron. xx. 7; Isa. xli. 8; Jas. ii. 23). He is the only one to whom this designation is given in the Old Testament.

I. *The Divine Appearance* (vers. 1-8).—The character of the appearance is noteworthy. It was not in the form of a vision (chap. xv.), nor was it merely a word or message (chap. xvii.). It was a Divine appearance as a Guest, thus marking Abraham's position of friendship and fellowship with God.

It is evident that the "three men" represent a personal manifestation of God in visible form, accompanied by two created angels (ver. 22 and xix. 1). The fact that the Church of England uses this chapter as a Lesson for Trinity Sunday indicates that this chapter has been regarded as in some sense a foreshadowing of the doctrine of the Trinity. We must, of course, be careful not to read too much of such a New Testament idea into it, though we are perfectly safe, and entirely warranted, in seeing in this unique manifestation and indication of certain essential distinctions in the Godhead which subsequently were fully revealed as the Trinity of the New Testament.

The response made by Abraham (vers. 2-8) is a characteristic picture of Eastern politeness and hospitality. The elements of courtesy (ver. 2), activity (vers. 6-7), hospitality (vers. 7-8), and respect (ver. 8) are very interesting and noteworthy, and strictly true to Eastern life today. The prominence given to hospitality in the New Testament is also to be pondered (Rom. xii. 13; 1 Tim. iii. 2; 3 John 5-7). Abraham indeed "entertained angels unawares" (Heb. xiii. 2).

II. *The Divine Assurance* (vers. 9-15).—The question "Where is Sarah thy wife?" showed that the strangers knew her name, and the words which immediately followed quickly told him Who the speaker was. The promise of a son was then repeated, with the assurance of the near approach of its fulfilment.

Sarah received this message with the utter astonishment of unbelief. She could not credit the possibility of it. This is only one out of several indications in the course of the story that Sarah's spiritual kinship with Abraham was not very close, and that she had never really risen with him to his clear faith in God.

Sarah was now taught a solemn and severe lesson. She was first of all reminded of God's power. "Is anything too hard for the Lord?" And when she denied her laughter, she was reminded of God's knowledge (ver. 15). Sarah now became aware of the real character of her visitors, and we see the result in her fear even while she denied the laughter.

III. *The Divine Announcement* (vers. 16-21).—The visitors then left the hospitable tent of Abraham, and with characteristic courtesy Abraham accompanied them on their journey. The time had come for a further revelation to Abraham.

How beautiful is the suggestion made by the Divine soliloquy! "Shall I hide from Abraham that thing which I do?" God's friends are permitted to know His secrets because they are His friends. Abraham is regarded by God as having a right to know what was about to be done (Ps. xxv. 4; Amos iii. 7).

God reveals His purpose to Abraham for very weighty reasons. He is to be the means of blessing to all nations (ver. 18), and it is therefore necessary for him to know the reason of this destruction of two of the cities of the earth—Sodom and Gomorrah. Further, Abraham's influence over posterity (ver. 19, R.V.) required that he should know of this judgment in order that it might be used as a solemn lesson in the days to come (Ps. lxxviii. 1-8). Again, it was his influence with those under his charge, and their obedience, that would in some way bring about the fulfilment of God's word to Abraham himself (ver. 19, last clause).

God now tells His servant of the terrible sin of Sodom and Gomorrah, and of His Divine determination to examine into it and to deal with it accordingly. Thus the servant of God learns the Divine will and enters more fully into the Divine purposes.

In this section we have an illustration of fellowship with God and some of its essential features. Fellowship is the crowning purpose of God's revelation (1 John i. 3). There is nothing higher than this, for man's life finds its complete realization in union and communion with God. Notice the following elements:—

1. *Sacred Intimacy*.—The picture of God as the guest of Abraham is a symbol of that spiritual relationship which is brought very clearly and beautifully before us in the New Testament. What an unspeakable privilege it is to have God as our Guest, and for us to be His guests (John xiv. 23; Rev. iii. 20).

2. *Genuine Humility*.—Abraham's attitude on this occasion is noteworthy. He quickly realized Who had come, and although he had all the privileges of fellowship, he never forgot his own true place and position. So is it always with the true believer. He never forgets that, notwithstanding all the privileges of fellowship, God is God, and he himself is nothing. Reverence is never separated from the fullest, freest realization of the Gospel of Grace. While we have "access," it is "access into the *Holiest*" (Heb. x. 19). There is no incompatibility, but the most beautiful fitness in the freedom, freeness, and fulness of Divine grace, combined with the attitude of reverential awe in those who are partakers of grace. "Holy and reverend is His Name" (Ps. cxi. 9).

3. *Special Revelation*.—Fellowship with God is always associated with the knowledge of His will. Servants do not know their master's purposes. but friends and intimates do. Our Lord taught this plain-

ly to His disciples (John xv. 15). There is no position like that of fellowship with God for knowing fully our Master's will. (Cf. John xiii. 25, R.V.).

4. *Unique Association.*—The man who is in fellowship with God does not merely know the Divine will, but becomes associated with God in the carrying out of that will. God deliberately and definitely associated Abraham with the realization of His purposes (vers. 17-19), and this has ever been the case. The friends of God become His fellow-workers, and are used to carrying out the wide-reaching purposes of His will to mankind. In view of all these glorious privileges and solemn responsibilities of fellowship with God, "what manner of persons ought we to be in all holy conversation and godliness?"

XXIV

THE MINISTRY OF INTERCESSION

Gen. xviii. 22-33—xix. 27-29

And the men turned their faces from thence, and went toward Sodom: but Abraham stood yet before the Lord.

And Abraham drew near, and said, Wilt thou also destroy the righteous with the wicked?

Peradventure there be fifty righteous within the city: wilt thou also destroy and not spare the place for the fifty righteous that *are* therein?

That be far from Thee to do after this manner, to slay the righteous with the wicked: and that the righteous should be as the wicked, that be far from Thee: Shall not the judge of all the earth do right?

And the Lord said, If I find in Sodom fifty righteous within the city, then I will spare all the place for their sakes.

And Abraham answered and said, Behold, now, I have taken upon me to speak unto the Lord which *am but* dust and ashes:

Peradventure there shall lack five of the fifty righteous: wilt thou destroy all the city for *lack of* five?   And He said, If I find there forty and five, I will not destroy *it.*

And he spake unto Him yet again, and said, Peradventure there shall be forty found there.   And He said, I will not do *it* for forty's sake.

And he said *unto Him,* O let not the Lord be angry, and I will speak: Peradventure there shall thirty be found there.   And He said, I will not do *it* if I find thirty there.

And he said, Behold now, I have taken upon me to speak unto the Lord: Peradventure there shall be twenty found there.   And He said, I will not destroy *it* for twenty's sake

And he said, O let not the Lord be angry, and I will speak yet but this once: Peradventure ten shall be found there.   And He said, I will not destroy *it* for ten's sake.

And the Lord went His way, as soon as He had left communing with Abraham: and Abraham returned unto his place.

And Abraham gat up early in the morning to the place where he stood before the Lord:

And he looked toward Sodom and Gomorrah, and toward all the land of the plain, and beheld, and, lo, the smoke of the country went up as the smoke of a furnace.

And it came to pass, when God destroyed the cities of the plain, that God remembered Abraham, and sent Lot out of the midst of the overthrow, when He overthrew the cities in the which Lot dwelt.

ONE of the essential and most blessed features of the believer's fellowship with God is the privilege and responsibility, the joy and duty of intercession. The Divine announcement concerning Sodom led Abraham to intercede for the doomed city. God's revelation thus finds its response in His servant's intercession. Some of the elements of intercession are clearly shown in the above passages.

I. *The Privileged Position* (vers. 22-23).—Intercession with God presupposes a spiritual relationship and position from which all else follows.

He was in God's presence. "Abraham stood yet before the Lord." the two angels had gone on to Sodom to fulfil the Divine will, leaving the Angel of the Covenant with Abraham.

He also realized God's nearness. "Abraham drew near." How like this language is to the teaching of the Epistle to the Hebrews (Heb. x. 22). Abraham was on a true footing of fellowship as he poured out his heart to God.

He also knew God's will. He had already been told what God was about to do, and this led him to prayer.

We have here a striking illustration of the future spirituality and power of Abraham's life. Several elements of real prayer are clearly seen.

II. *The Earnest Spirit* (vers. 23, 24).—His compassion is manifest. Abraham's prayer is evidently for the whole city and not merely for his nephew Lot. It is striking that he does not mention Lot from beginning to end, but only prays for the city.

His definiteness is noteworthy. He asked for what he wanted, and this is always the true attitude in prayer. God will tell us whether what we want is also what He thinks we need, but meanwhile our prayers should be definite.

His boldness is striking. There is no hesitation in his utterance, no fear in his attitude. Everything is frank, fearless, courageous, for the simple reason that he knows Whom he believes. Our Lord frequently inculcated boldness in prayer (Luke xi. 5-10; xviii. 1-8).

III. *The Urgent Plea* (vers. 23-25).—But Abraham was perplexed by the fact that the destruction of Sodom would involve the destruction of righteous men with wicked ones. With this difficulty in his mind he did the very best thing; he told God about it. Problems thus brought to God will either be resolved, or else sufficient grace will be given to wait for the perfect solution. Abraham had somehow got hold of the great principle that good people are as salt preventing surrounding corruption. How often one Christian in a family keeps back Divine judgment on sin! How often wandering boys are withheld from ruin through their mother's prayers!

Yet he cannot help entertaining a strong conviction. He felt that it was impossible that the righteous could be destroyed with the wicked. In the absence of any revelation of a future judgment redressing present inequalities, we are not surprised at Abraham's strong assertion of his sense of the injustice of indiscriminate destruction. He was evidently concerned for God also, and was particularly anxious that the heathen around should not get a wrong impression of the God of Abraham.

And all the while he rests in a sure confidence in God. "Shall not the Judge of all the earth do right?" He makes his appeal to God's righteousness rather than to His mercy, and in so doing he touches the very foundation of things. With a perfect trust in the absolute justice of God he pours out his heart and tells God his difficulties. This is the true spirit of the believer who is face to face with the great mysteries of life. He takes them all to God in prayer. and in the presence of Divine righteousness he finds that rest of heart which enables him to wait patiently for God (Psalms xxxvii. 6, 7; lxxiii. 16, 17).

IV. *The Divine Encouragement* (ver. 26).—Let us observe, moreover, how point by point the prayer was met by a Divine response: "And the Lord said." Thus God spoke to His servant in answer to prayer. So it ever is with the believer. God's Word is the complement of and response to our petitions.

"If I find . . . I will spare." God met his servant's request by a definite promise that if He found fifty righteous He would spare the place.

"For their sakes." Thus God responded to His servant's conviction that there was indeed a power and influence in good people. The whole city is to be spared, notwithstanding its sin, simply and solely on account of fifty people therein. Nothing can be clearer than this testimony to the salutary power and influence of godliness (Matt. v. 13).

V. *The Deep Humility* (ver. 27).—Abraham had a profound consciousness of God. "I have taken upon me to speak unto the Lord." Again we notice how his friendship with God is never allowed to make him forget his true position of dependence.

He also had an equally real and deep knowledge of himself. "Which am but dust and ashes." This is always the consciousness of the true child of God as he abides in the Divine presence. God's holiness and our sinfulness, God's greatness and our nothingness, are the overwhelming experiences.

VI. *The Earnest Persistence* (vers. 29-32).—Six times Abraham intercedes for the wicked cities. His heart is drawn out in pity and compassion, and he pleads again and again. Persistence in prayer is one of the prominent features of New Testament teaching. "Continuing instant" (Rom. xii. 12). Steadfastness in intercession is one of the sure marks of reality and earnestness.

Six times God responded to His servant's prayer. After each petition came the definite answer. So it is always; as long as we ask, God will answer. Notice the threefold promise with its element of increasing persistency in Matt. vii. 7.

VII. *The Natural Limitation* (ver. 33).—Why, then, did Abraham stop praying when he reached the number ten? Probably because of his ignorance of the extent and effect of Sodom's sin, and, from another point of view, probably because of his ignorance of the extent of the Divine mercy and longsuffering.

As it has often been said, Abraham ceased asking before God ceased giving. The reason why Abraham did not go lower than ten was possibly due to the fact that now he did not think there were anything like that number in the city.

We naturally compare and contrast Abraham's words, "I will speak yet but this once," with the intercession of our Lord Jesus Christ, Whose pleading on our behalf knows no limitation whatever. "He is able to save to the *uttermost* . . . seeing that He *ever liveth* to make intercession" (Heb. vii. 25).

VIII. *The Gracious Answer* (xix. 27-29).—"Abraham rose up early in the morning and looked towards Sodom." Somehow or other he must have expected that God would at least deliver the one righteous man that was in Sodom, and not destroy him with the rest.

It is not very significant that Lot's preservation is here directly connected with Abraham's intercession? Thus Abraham saved his nephew for the second time. The first time by the sword (chap. xiv.), the second time by supplication (chap. xviii.).

1. *The solemn responsibilities of Intercession.*—How striking are the words of Samuel teaching us that we are actually sinning against God if we do not pray for others! (1 Sam. xii. 23). Do we clearly realize this? Does it not make us ashamed and even afraid when we remember how little we pray for others as compared with our prayers for ourselves? And yet there is scarcely any part of prayer more prominent in the New Testament than prayer for others (Jas. v. 16; 2 Thess. iii. 1; Eph. vi. 17, 18; 1 Tim. ii. 1). The reason why intercessory prayer is thus so plainly taught is that it is the best opportunity we possess of showing spiritual interest in others. Our Christian life will never be really healthy and strong until we make intercession a very prominent and even predominant feature of our private devotions. The Lord's Prayer gives us the model in this as in other respects.

2. *The marvellous possibilities of Intercession.*—"The Lord turned the captivity of Job, when he prayed for his friends" (Job. xlii. 10). This shows the reflex blessing of intercessory prayer, but far beyond this is the social value of intercession. God has included in His great purpose of redemptive love the power and blessing of prayer for others, and if only God's people would realize what their prayers could do for the world, they would take up this work of priestly intercession in a way that they have never realized before. Only the great day will reveal what has been done by intercessory prayer. The Apostle Paul depended greatly on it in his ministry, and was frequently asking his friends to remember him and his work in prayer.

3. *The essential conditions of Intercession.*—We can only intercede in proportion as we abide in close fellowship with God. "If
ye abide in Me, and My words abide in you, ye shall ask what ye
will, and it shall be done unto you" (John xv. 7). Asking in our
Lord's Name (John xiv. 13; xvi. 23) is another way of stating the
need of union and communion with God. "In My Name" means,
not simply using His Name as a plea, but praying in union with
Him and with all that we know of His will. When these conditions are fulfilled the Lord's words become blessedly true. "Ye
shall ask what ye will, and it shall be done unto you." "Ask, and
ye shall receive, that your joy may be full." (Cf. 1 John iii. 22; v.
14, 15).

XXV

THE STORY OF LOT

GEN. xix.

AND there came two angels to Sodom at even; and Lot sat in the gate of Sodom: and Lot seeing *them*, rose up to meet them; and he bowed himself with his face toward the ground:

And he said, Behold now, my lords, turn in, I pray you, into your servant's house, and tarry all night, and wash your feet, and ye shall rise up early, and go on your ways. And they said, Nay; but we will abide in the street all night.

And he pressed upon them greatly; and they turned in unto him, and entered into his house: and he made them a feast, and did bake unleavened bread, and they did eat.

But, before they lay down, the men of the city, *even* the men of Sodom, compassed the house round, both old and young, all the people from every quarter.

And they called unto Lot, and said unto him, Where *are* the men which came in to thee this night? Bring them out unto us, that we may know them.

And Lot went out at the door unto them, and shut the door after him.

And said, I pray you, brethren, do not so wickedly.

Behold now, I have two daughters which have not known man; let me, I pray you, bring them out unto you, and do ye to them as *is* good in your eyes: only unto these men do nothing: for therefore came they under the shadow of my roof.

And they said, Stand back. And they said *again*, This one *fellow* came in to sojourn, and he will needs be a judge: now we will deal worse with thee than with them. And they pressed sore upon the man, *even* Lot, and came near to break the door.

But the men put forth their hand, and pulled Lot into the house to them, and shut to the door.

And they smote the men that *were* at the door of the house with blindness, both small and great: so that they wearied themselves to find the door.

And the men said unto Lot, Hast thou here any besides? son-in-law, and thy sons, and thy daughters, and whatsoever thou hast in the city, bring *them* out of this place:

For we will destroy this place, because the cry of them is waxen great before the face of the Lord; and the Lord hath sent us to destroy it.

And Lot went out, and spake unto his sons-in-law, which married his daughters, and said, Up, get you out of this place; for the Lord will destroy this city. But he seemed as one that mocked unto his sons-in-law.

And when the morning arose, then the angels hastened Lot, saying, Arise, take thy wife, and thy two daughters, which are here; lest thou be consumed in the iniquity of the city.

And while he lingered, the men laid hold upon his hand, and upon the hand of his wife, and upon the hand of his two daughters; the Lord being merciful unto him: and they brought him forth, and set him without the city.

And it came to pass, when they had brought them forth abroad, that he said, Escape for thy life; look not behind thee, neither stay thou in all the plain: escape to the mountain, lest thou be consumed.

And Lot said unto them, Oh! not so, my lord.

Behold now, thy servant hath found grace in thy sight, and thou hast magnified thy mercy, which thou hast shewed unto me in saving my life; and I cannot escape to the mountain, lest some evil take me, and I die.

Behold now, this city *is* near to flee unto, and it *is* a little one: Oh! let me escape thither (*is* it not a little one?) and my soul shall live.

And he said unto him, See, I have accepted thee concerning this thing also, that I will not overthrow this city, for the which thou hast spoken.

Haste thee escape thither; for I cannot do any thing till thou be come thither. Therefore the name of the city was called Zoar.

The sun was risen upon the earth when Lot entered into Zoar.

Then the Lord rained upon Sodom and upon Gomorrah brimstone and fire from the Lord out of heaven.

And He overthrew those cities, and all the plain, and all the inhabitants of the cities, and that which grew upon the ground.

But his wife looked back from behind him, and she became a pillar of salt.

And Abraham gat up early in the morning to the place where he stood before the Lord.

And he looked toward Sodom and Gomorrah, and toward all the land of the plain, and beheld, and, lo, the smoke of the country went up as the smoke of a furnace.

And it came to pass, when God destroyed the cities of the plain, that God remembered Abraham, and sent Lot out of the midst of the overthrow, when He overthrew the cities in which Lot dwelt.

And Lot went up out of Zoar, and dwelt in the mountain, and his two daughters with him; for he feared to dwell in Zoar: and he dwelt in a cave, he and his two daughters.

And the first-born said unto the younger, Our father *is* old, and *there is* not a man in the earth to come in unto us after the manner of all the earth:

Come, let us make our father drink wine, and we will lie with him, that we may preserve seed of our father.

And they made their father drink wine that night: and the first-born went in, and lay with her father; and he perceived not when she lay down, nor when she arose.

And it came to pass on the morrow, that the first-born said unto the younger, Behold, I lay yesternight with my father: let us make him drink wine this night also; and go thou in, *and* lie with him, that we may preserve seed of our father.

And they made their father drink wine that night also: and the younger arose, and lay with him; and he perceived not when she lay down, nor when she arose.

Thus were both the daughters of Lot with child by their father.

And the first-born bare a son, and called his name Moab: the same is the father of the Moabites unto this day.

And the younger, she also bare a son, and called his name Ben-ammi: the same is the father of the children of Ammon unto this day.

THERE are lives recorded in the Bible which have well been called beacons. There are men like Balaam, Saul, and Solomon, who started well, with every possible advantage, and then closed their careers in failure and disaster. Such a life was that of Lot the nephew of Abraham. He came out of Mesopotamia with his uncle, and continued with him in Canaan until their possessions necessitated a separation (chapters xii., xiii.). He thereupon pitched his tent towards Sodom, but soon entered and abode in the city. As a consequence he was involved in its captivity by the kings of the East (chapter xiv.). Even his rescue by Abraham did not suffice to warn him from the place, for he returned and lived there as before.

There is scarcely a life recorded in Scripture which is fuller of serious and solemn instruction for every believer.

I. *The Angelic Visit* (vers. 1-3).—While the Divine personage remained in company with Abraham, the two attendant angels journeyed on to Sodom, where Lot was sitting in the gate, the place of concourse, the place of importance. It is not improbable that he sat there in an official capacity as judge. With the true spirit of Eastern courtesy he rose to meet them, and greeted them with profound obeisance, also offering to them hospitality. At first they declined his invitation, alleging a somewhat remarkable reason, "We will abide in the street all night." They were there for the purpose of exploration with a view to judgment, and perhaps this was why they suggested remaining all night in the open street. But Lot urged them, and at last they yielded, and accepted his hospitality.

II. *The Awful Depravity* (vers. 4-11).—Into the fearful story recorded in these verses it is impossible to enter for more than the barest comment. Everyone knows that the sin hinted at here is perpetuated forever by a word in our language to which this chapter has given rise. Perhaps two other cities have equalled Sodom in this respect, the cities of Pompeii and Herculaneum, both of which have suffered in a similar way from devastation, and one of them to this very day reveals the unspeakable depravity of its inhabitants. One other point dare not be overlooked in this hideous recital of sin, and that is, the selfish readiness of Lot to sacrifice his daughters in order to save his own life and peace.

III. *The Solemn Warning* (vers. 12-14).—The angels now enquire of Lot as to his kinsfolk, and command him to bring them out of the wicked city. They also announce in the plainest terms the purpose of their errand. "The Lord hath sent us to destroy it." Lot does not hesitate to believe their testimony, and at once goes forth to urge upon his sons-in-law the absolute necessity of getting quickly out of the city. "But he seemed as one that mocked." His testimony had no power. He had lived too long as one of themselves, without any very real difference, to allow of his message being of any avail. When the testimony of the life does not agree with the testimony of the lips the latter always goes unheeded. It is the life that is the true light.

IV. *The Urgent Deliverance* (vers. 15-22).—At daybreak the angels had to urge Lot to take his wife and two daughters out of the city, "lest they be consumed." Even then Lot lingered, until at last the men laid hold upon him, his wife, and his daughters, and compelled them to go outside the city, "the Lord being merciful." On reaching the confines of the city another urgent appeal was made. "Escape for thy life; look not behind thee, neither stay thou in all the plain; escape to the mountain." Even now, with almost incredible weakness, Lot pleads that the mountain is too far away, and begs to be permitted to go to the neighboring city of Zoar. The Divine messengers concede this point, urging him once more to escape, since God was unable to do anything till His servant was in safety. What a marvelous picture of the Divine condescension and patience with one of the frailest of His creatures.

V. *The Divine Judgment* (vers. 23-26).—Lot, together with his wife and his daughters, had only reached Zoar when the Lord poured out His judgment on the wicked cities and overthrew them and all their people. Lot's wife seems to have been equally attracted to Sodom, for we are told that she looked back, and was soon engulfed in the lava by which the cities were destroyed. With husband and wife both weak, hesitating, and yielding, there can be no surprise at what we know of their family life.

VI. *The Powerful Intercession* (vers. 27-29).—Abraham rose early that morning on his way to a place from which he could see the plain of the Jordan valley. As he looked towards the cities he saw a smoke like that of a furnace, and yet with exquisite suggestiveness we have inserted at this point the indication that Abraham's prayer was answered so far as concerned his nephew. "God remembered Abraham, and sent Lot out." Abraham had ceased praying at the mention of ten righteous, but God was better than his prayers, and heard him for four only.

VII. *The Unutterable Shame* (vers. 30-38).—Again it is impossible to comment on this unspeakably sorrowful scene. Drunkenness and impurity are once more seen in association. It perhaps says one thing for Lot that it was only by means of the sin of drunkenness that his daughters could accomplish their ends. Yet this is but an infinitesimal point by comparison, for we cannot forget that Moab and Ammon (though they were kinsmen to Abraham) were in after years among the most implacable foes of Abraham's descendants. As for Lot he had sounded the lowest depths of shame, and passes away into the darkness and oblivion that were his due.

1. *Lessons from Sodom.*—(a) We observe the awful extent of human depravity. This is one of the most terrible chapters in the Bible, and is a reminder of the hideous possibilities of sin, and the extent to which evil can take hold of human nature. When the restraints of the Divine law are removed or set at naught there are scarcely any limits to human degeneracy and depravity (Rom. i. 21-31; 2 Pet. ii. 8; Jude 7, 8).

(b) We mark the certainty of Divine judgment. The iniquity of Sodom was indeed full. "The cry of them is waxen great before the face of the Lord," and when human sin reaches its awful fruit the judgment is as certain as it is unerring. There is no fact in God's universe more certain and assured than this, that He is not, and cannot, and will not be indifferent to human sin.

(c) We note the marvel of Divine mercy. From the narrative it might seem that Lot was not worth saving. His weakness amounted to wickedness, and yet again and again God bore with him, waited for him, pleaded with him, urged him, and at length did not bring down the Divine judgment until he was safe out of Sodom. Is there anything in this world so wonderful as the mercy that waits for us, follows us, hedges our path, and short of compulsion does everything to keep us from ruin?

2. *Lessons from Lot.*—(a) His dangers may easily be ours also. His first danger was from things lawful. It was not wrong to desire a good place for his flocks and herds. The sin was in putting earthly ease and prosperity first. "More men are killed by meat than poison." More souls are lost by abuse of things lawful than by the use of things unlawful. It is not wrong to have possessions, it is only wrong to let possessions have us. A ship in the water is perfectly right, but the water in the ship would be perfectly wrong. The Christian in the world is right and necessary, but the world in the Christian is wrong and disastrous. Another danger of Lot's was that of compromise. At first he pitched his tent *towards* Sodom, but soon entered the city and stayed there. He doubtless thought he could testify to the wicked people, but his words were nothing without deeds. They were quick enough to see that he was as sharp about money-making as the rest of them. A Christian must be outside Sodom in order to testify against it. To go into the world to influence it is futile and fatal. The world does not need influencing but saving, and for this the Christian must live a life of separation, "in the world, but not of the world." This suggests yet a third danger that Lot incurred, that of worldliness. He did testify and showed genuine hospitality, but his character was weakened, and his life was essentially selfish from the moment that he chose the best part of the land to the moment when he was pre-

pared to sacrifice his daughters for his own safety. Some men are utterly unable to bear worldly success. It affects their character and their home life. Not least of all, this worldliness endangered his happiness. He "got on" in the world, he sat in the gate as a leading citizen, but he was miserable. He "vexed his soul" day by day in seeing and hearing their wickedness (2 Pet. ii. 8). It is always so with those who do not put God first. Those who put Him second are the most miserable of men.

(b) His weakness may be ours also. He lacked the spirit of true independence. He was all right as long as he was with the stronger nature of Abraham, but he never seems to have been right afterwards. When the prop was removed he fell. It is often the case with Christian people today. Their religion is one of association. As long as they are surrounded with Christian friends, and connected with a Christian Church, their life seems to be perfectly right; but let these supports be removed, and they themselves placed alone in difficult surroundings, and their weakness is at once seen. Lot also lacked decision. At every point of the story from his separation from Abraham indecision is stamped on his career. Mark in this chapter the urgency of the angels, and the references to his lingering, and to their hastening him. Even Zoar had to be left and the mountain reached after all. Every true life needs decision and firmness of character. Otherwise when emergencies come circumstances are too strong and we fall. "The flighty purpose never is o'ertook, unless the deed go with it."

(c) Lot's needs may be ours also. The one supreme and all-embracing requirement was whole-hearted trust in and consecration to God. But for the phrase "righteous Lot" (2 Pet. ii. 7) we should have scarcely believed him to be in any sense a believer. From the Old Testament narrative he seems to be apparently godly, but really worldly, and the explanation is that there was nothing whole-hearted about his relation to God. His religion, though real as far as it went, was so entirely superficial that it did not cover more than a small part of his life. And so he was a backslider, an awful failure, his soul saved, but his life lost. "Saved, so as by fire." What a call it is to keep close to God and to His people, to witness for God to the world around, never to indulge in any half-way house between godliness and worldliness, but to let our light shine, and live by faith in the Son of God Who loved us and gave Himself for us.

XXVI

AN OLD SIN REPEATED

GEN. xx.

AND Abraham journeyed from thence toward the south country, and dwelled between Kadesh and Shur, and sojourned in Gerar.

And Abraham said of Sarah his wife, She *is* my sister: and Abimelech king of Gerar sent and took Sarah.

But God came to Abimelech in a dream by night, and said to him, Behold, thou *art but* a dead man, for the woman which thou hast taken; for she *is* a man's wife.

But Abimelech had not come near her: and he said, Lord, wilt thou slay also a righteous nation?

Said he not unto me, She *is* my sister? and she, even she herself said, He *is* my brother. In the integrity of my heart, and innocency of my hands, have I done this.

And God said unto him in a dream, Yea, I know that thou didst this in the integrity of thy heart; for I also withheld thee from sinning against me: therefore suffered I thee not to touch her.

Now therefore restore the man *his* wife; for he *is* a prophet, and he shall pray for thee, and thou shalt live: and if thou restore *her* not, know thou that thou shalt surely die, thou, and all that *are* thine.

Therefore Abimelech rose early in the morning, and called all his servants, and told all these things in their ears: and the men were sore afraid.

Then Abimelech called Abraham, and said unto him, What hast thou done unto us? and what have I offended thee, that thou hast brought on me and on my kingdom a great sin? thou hast done deeds unto me that ought not to be done.

And Abimelech said unto Abraham, What sawest thou, that thou hast done this thing?

And Abraham said, Because I thought, Surely the fear of God *is* not in this place; and they will slay me for my wife's sake.

And yet indeed *she is* my sister: she *is* the daughter of my father, but not the daughter of my mother; and she became my wife.

And it came to pass, when God caused me to wander from my father's house, that I said unto her, This *is* thy kindness which thou shalt shew unto me; at every place whither we shall come, say of me, He *is* my brother.

And Abimelech took sheep, and oxen, and men-servants, and women-servants, and gave *them* unto Abraham, and restored him Sarah his wife.

And Abimelech said, Behold, my land *is* before thee: dwell where it pleaseth thee.

And unto Sarah he said, Behold, I have given thy brother a thousand *pieces* of silver: behold, he *is* to thee a covering of the eyes, unto all that *are* with thee, and with all *other.* Thus she was reproved.

So Abraham prayed unto God; and God healed Abimelech, and his wife, and his maid-servants; and they bare *children.*

For the Lord had fast closed up all the wombs of the house of Abimelech because of Sarah, Abraham's wife.

THE continuance and power of the evil nature in believers are among the most patent and potent facts of universal spiritual experience. That the "infection doth remain in the regenerate" is as certain as it is sad and serious. We have here a solemn example and warning of this in Abraham.

I. *The Deplorable Sin* (vers. 1, 2).—Abraham journeyed onward from Mamre (xviii. 1) towards the south, that southern district of Palestine known as the Negeb. This may have been due to the need of new pasturage for his increasing flocks, or it may have been caused by his call to a continued pilgrimage with no settled habitation in the Land of Promise. Some think that it was prompted by a desire to remove from the surroundings made so painful to him from the events recorded in chapter xix. His place of sojourning was Gerar, in the land of the Philistines.

As before (cf. chap. xii. 13) Abraham said that Sarah was his sister. Thus Abraham attempted to protect himself at the expense of his wife. This repetition of an old sin would be astonishing were it not for the close consistency it bears to human nature, even among the people of God. Believers are often found to slip and fall where they have fallen previously.

Abimelech, the King of Gerar, at once acted upon the information received about Sarah, and took her with the intention of making her his wife. He doubtless realized the value of an alliance with a powerful man like Abraham. It is sometimes said that this story is only a variation of that which is recorded in chapter xiii., and is not a separate incident, but the numerous variations in the narrative, as well as its place in the history of Abraham, disprove this theory. Besides, it is too true to human nature that a sin of this kind should be repeated to make it incredible that Abraham should again transgress.

II. *The Divine Intervention* (vers. 3-8).—Very appropriately we have the title "God" employed (ver. 3) when the relation of God with the heathen is in question. "Jehovah" is the Covenant Name. The Lord's intervention was for the purpose of preserving Sarah, and at the same time of fulfilling the Divine purposes concerning the seed. Thus God's children are saved from themselves.

It was necessary that Abimelech should be restrained from doing that which in all ignorance and innocence he was about to do. There was also the thought of instruction and testimony concerning Abraham and his relation to God. Notwithstanding Abraham's sin, God would not allow him to be dishonored in the face of the ungodly.

The character of Abimelech shines out beautifully, and is in marked contrast with Abraham's at this point. Men of the world stand out superior at times to the people of God, and this is one of the great perplexities and problems of the spiritual realm. Abimelech's words bear witness to a true knowledge of God, and a genuine fear of God outside the covenant with Abraham (ver. 8). Abimelech had no intention of sinning, only of doing that which was perfectly natural to that age and state of life.

III. *The Deserved Rebuke* (vers. 9-16).—Again Abimelech's character and attitude shine as he reproaches Abraham with what he had done. It is very sad when a man of God has to be rebuked by a man of the world.

There are three points in Abraham's statement by which he attempted to justify his conduct. (*a*) He thought there was no fear of God (ver. 11) in Abimelech and his people. We can see how distinctly he was mistaken on this point. (*b*) Sarah was really his sister; that is, a half-sister. Abraham here clearly crossed over the boundary between concealment and lying, and by suppressing the truth he suggested only too plainly what was false. (*c*) It was an old compact made thirty years ago (ver. 13). This, spoken in extenuation, really intensifies his sin, for it means that all through the thirty years of fellowship with God in Canaan this old compact had been in existence and never broken. How true, this is to experience! A believer often finds some old habit or sin cropping up, and if it is not at once dealt with it will assuredly bring trouble and sorrow.

Abimelech gave gifts to Abraham, doubtless as an acknowledgement and as a kind of propitiation of the wrong that would have been done. To Sarah also Abimelech addressed himself, telling her that the gifts which he had given to her husband were of a propitiatory kind, so that the recent events might be covered and forgotten. This must have been a very definite rebuke to Sarah, who, whatever the old compact may have meant, should have at once told Abimelech the true state of affairs. *N.B.*—Perhaps the words "he is to thee" (ver. 16) should be rendered "it is to thee," referring to the gift rather than to Abraham.

All through we see the manifest moral superiority of a heathen man over children of God. When believers are out of the line of God's will they will sometimes go lower than other people. Abimelech is at his best. Abraham is at his worst. We must, of course, take care not to judge the entire life of either by this one incident, but the facts of the incident itself convey their own special lesson. How sad and deplorable it is when a believer does not keep in touch with God! "The corruption of the best is the worst." "'Tis true, 'tis pity; and pity 'tis 'tis true."

IV. *The Definite Results* (vers. 17, 18).—In answer to prayer, God's blessing came down upon Abimelech and his household. Thus God overruled these sad mistakes and brought blessing.

Sarah's position as Abraham's wife was preserved, and she would still be the instrument of fulfilling God's purposes by means of the promised seed.

Divine protection was vouchsafed to Abraham, and his sin overruled by the mercy and love of God. If God had not interposed on His servant's behalf what an unspeakable catastrophe would have been the result!

1. *The possibilities of sin in believers.*—It is almost incredible, after the experiences recorded in chapters xv. and xviii., that Abraham should have sinned in this way against God. Notice the elements included in this sin: (*a*) The fear of man; (*b*) innate selfishness; (*c*) deliberate untruth; (*d*) distrust of God through fear of

circumstances. And what degradation it was to be rebuked by a man of the world! It is truly a picture full of sadness and shame.

2. *The perils of sin in believers.*—There was peril to Abraham *himself.* Old habits broke out afresh which had been restrained and kept in the background for years. This is often a believer's experience. Former weaknesses and inveterate tendencies which we think no longer powerful suddenly arise and bring about our downfall. There is also a peril to our *fellow-believers* through our example. What a bad influence on Sarah! Younger Christians are shocked, and even led into sin, when they see an old believer fall. There is also a peril to the *world*, for the sin of a child of God dishonors God, and so far prevents the world from being impressed with the Divine character.

3. *The persistence of sin in believers.*—Abraham's experience proves New Testament truth that the old nature abides in the believer to the very end. Nowhere in Scripture is there any warrant for the idea that the root of sin is taken out in this life. The teaching of Article IX. of the Church of England is in exact correspondence with the Word of God. Neither in the regenerate nor in the sanctified (a distinction often made, but without warrant) is "the infection of nature" taken away. The realization of this solemn and patent fact would save many a believer from spiritual trouble.

4. *The protection against sin in believers.*—God took Abraham's part before Abimelech, but assuredly must have dealt very differently with him in private. The believer's standing before God is one thing; his state is quite another. While God's people are all "accepted in the Beloved," they are not all equally *acceptable to* the Beloved, and the question of protection against indwelling sin is vital for Christian living. This protection God has provided in abundant sufficiency for every need. The promise is clear: "Sin shall not have dominion over you." God's provision of power is in union with the death of Christ, and this, by the power of the Spirit, affords the guarantee of perpetual protection and victory. This provision must, however, be used. We are to "live in the Spirit and walk in the Spirit" (Gal. v. 25). "The law of the Spirit

of life in Christ Jesus" is the law, not of eradication, but of counter-action. If we will live and walk in the Spirit we shall not yield to and fulfil the lusts of the flesh (Gal. v. 16). Fuller surrender to the Holy Spirit will keep the inner being sensitive to the approaches of sin. We shall become conscious of the Satanic devices to lead us astray; and as we continue to yield ourselves to the incoming, full possession, and entire control of the Spirit of God the old nature will be kept under, the new life will have complete power, and we shall be "more than conquerors through Him that loves us."

XXVII

JOY AND SORROW

GEN. xxi. 1-21

AND the Lord visited Sarah as He had said, and the Lord did unto Sarah as He had spoken.

For Sarah conceived, and bare Abraham a son in his old age, at the set time of which God had spoken to him.

And Abraham called the name of his son that was born unto him, whom Sarah bare to him, Isaac.

And Abraham circumcised his son Isaac, being eight days old, as God had commanded him.

And Abraham was an hundred years old, when his son Isaac was born unto him.

And Sarah said, God hath made me to laugh, *so that* all that hear will laugh with me.

And she said, Who would have said unto Abraham, that Sarah should have given children suck? for I have born *him* a son in his old age.

And the child grew, and was weaned: and Abraham made a great feast the *same* day that Isaac was weaned.

And Sarah saw the son of Hagar the Egyptian, which she had born unto Abraham, mocking.

Wherefore she said unto Abraham, Cast out this bondwoman and her son: for the son of this bondwoman shall not be heir with my son, *even* with Isaac.

And the thing was very grievous in Abraham's sight because of his son.

And God said unto Abraham, Let it not be grievous in thy sight because of the lad, and because of thy bondwoman; in all that Sarah hath said unto thee, hearken unto her voice; for in Isaac shall thy seed be called.

And also of the son of the bondwoman will I make a nation, because he *is* thy seed.

And Abraham rose up early in the morning, and took bread, and a bottle of water, and gave *it* unto Hagar (putting *it* on her shoulder), and the child, and sent her away: and she departed, and wandered in the wilderness of Beer-sheba.

And the water was spent in the bottle, and she cast the child under one of the shrubs.

And she went, and sat her down over against *him* a good way off, as it were a bow-shot: for she said, Let me not see the death of the child. And she sat over against *him,* and lift up her voice, and wept.

And God heard the voice of the lad: and the angel of God called to Hagar out of heaven, and said unto her, What aileth thee, Hagar? fear not; for God hath heard the voice of the lad where he *is*.

Arise, lift up the lad, and hold him in thine hand; for I will make him a great nation.

And God opened her eyes, and she saw a well of water; and she went, and filled the bottle with water, and gave the lad drink.

And God was with the lad; and he grew, and dwelt in the wilderness, and became an archer.

And he dwelt in the wilderness of Paran: and his mother took him a wife out of the land of Egypt.

THE believer never comes, never can come, to a point in his experience when God has nothing new to teach him or to give to him. Further and deeper lessons come constantly, lessons about God and about life in relation to Him. This is now very clearly and strikingly brought before us in connection with Abraham.

I. *The Promised Seed* (vers. 1-8).—At last the word of God was fulfilled, and Sarah received the long-promised son. Her joy can readily be understood, and it is suggestive to see the emphasis upon the Lord's action being in strict accordance with His word. "The Lord did . . . as He had spoken" (ver. 1). "At the set time of which God had spoken" (ver. 2). The comment of the Apostle is very significant in this connection. According to the Authorized Version (Rom. iv. 19) Abraham "considered not his own body now dead," implying that his faith disregarded the physical circumstances which, humanly speaking, might make it impossible for God to do as He had promised. According to the Revised Version, which omits the negative, and reads, "He considered his own body now dead," we have a still more striking suggestion as to his faith, for it implies that he deliberately thought on the subject of his own age and circumstances, and, notwithstanding this careful consideration, he exercised faith in God and His Word. And now at length this faith was justified, and God was true to His promise.

The naming of the child "Isaac" and his circumcision were two prompt and definite proofs of Abraham's thorough trust in God. As already seen (chap. xvii.), the root idea of circumcision is designation, God marking off the life as belonging to Him.

Sarah now laughs the laugh of joy and satisfaction. The fulfilment of the promise was almost too good to be true; and yet it *was* true, as she shows by her joyous surprise. She doubtless remembers her former laugh of incredulity (chap. xviii. 13) as well as Abraham's laugh of faith and hope (chap. xvii. 17).

In due course the child was weaned; according to Eastern custom, at a much later date than in Western lands. Isaac must have been at least three, if not five, years old when this event took place. Abraham made a great feast to celebrate this occasion. The difference between East and West in this matter, and the spiritual ideas associated with it, can be seen from a careful comparison of Psalm cxxxi. 2; Isaiah xxviii. 9; Matt. xxi. 16.

II. *The Profound Sadness* (vers. 9-11).—The results of Abraham's sin as to Hagar now show themselves acutely. Up to the time of Isaac's birth Ishmael occupied the foremost place in Abraham's life, but now he has to give place to Isaac. The disappointment to a growing and wild lad of seventeen must have been keen, and we are not surprised to read of his mockery of the little child. St. Paul (Gal. iv. 29) speaks of the action of Ishmael as "persecuting," and no wonder, from Ishmael's point of view, since Isaac's arrival meant that he was robbed of his former position.

Sarah was quick to see this action of Ishmael, and resented it. It was now her turn to do what Hagar had done under similar circumstances. Thus the tangled web becomes still more tangled as jealousy, anger, and malice bear their sad fruit.

Sarah at once demands that Hagar and Ishmael shall be cast out. The terms in which she speaks of "this bondwoman and her son" show the pitiable spirit of jealousy and anger. She insists that Ishmael shall not be heir with her son, as though Abraham had any idea of the two boys being co-heirs. Sarah had either forgotten, or else distrusted God's definite promise about Isaac's sole heirship (chap. xvii. 21).

It is no surprise that this was a poignant grief to Abraham. After all, Ishmael was his own child, and for seventeen years had been the joy and light of his life.

III. *The Perfect Strength* (vers. 12-14).—We are now to see how God interposed amidst this strife and sorrow, overruling His children's mistakes and sin, and doing the very best that was possible for them.

We can hear the voice of God comforting him (ver. 12). God urged Abraham not to grieve. In all ages God's cheering message to His people has been "Let not your heart be troubled."

We can observe the wisdom of God guiding him (ver. 12). God tells Abraham to listen to what Sarah had said. Her counsel is to be followed, even though her conduct could not be approved. Ishmael's presence in the home would doubtless have been an ever-increasing difficulty, and a very genuine hindrance to the complete realization of God's will and purposes for Isaac. Thus in sending Ishmael away Abraham was really removing the cause of possible failure in regard to Isaac. Moreover, Ishmael had arrived, or would soon arrive, at a point in his life where he would need room to grow, and a change would therefore be good for him as well.

We can mark the promise of God encouraging him (ver. 13). God would not forget Ishmael, and he also was to become a great nation because of his relationship to Abraham. It is interesting to notice this reason assigned by God for His care of Ishmael. It is "because" he is the child of one of God's children. Thus Abraham was encouraged to do what must have been one of the hardest things in his experience, to put away from him his own child, and to realize that that child was no longer to be in any close and definite sense part of his life.

We can see the servant of God responding (ver. 14). Abraham at once obeys the Divine word. We see him rising up early in the morning, and with thoughtfulness and tenderness he bids Hagar and Ishmael farewell. It requires very little imagination to enter into his feelings as he saw them depart, realizing that a break had come into his life which could never be altered or set aside. It is striking to notice the entire absence of any remonstrance on the part of Hagar. She seems to have taken everything quietly. Ishmael, too, although seventeen years old, showed no signs of rebellion. Perhaps there was something behind which would explain all, as, indeed, seems to be hinted at in the Apostolic treatment of this incident (Gal. iv.).

1. *The unchanging faithfulness of God.*—The birth of Isaac was a beautiful and striking reminder that God is ever true to His word. "As He had spoken" is the keynote of the narrative. This is the experience of God's people in all ages. Joshua said that not one thing had failed of all that God had spoken; all had come to pass (Josh. xxi. 45; xxiii. 14). This is the bedrock of the believer's life. "God is faithful." A careful study of all the passages of the New Testament (and they are not few) which bring before us the faithfulness of God will show the prominence of this great truth in the Bible. "He abideth faithful"; and the more closely we enter into fellowship with Him through His Word, the more definitely we shall realize the preciousness of this great fact. "The counsel of the Lord standeth for ever, the thoughts of His heart to all generations" (Ps. xxxiii. 11).

2. *The perfect wisdom of God.*—We can easily realize the aching heart and troubled spirit of Abraham as he prepared to bid farewell to Ishmael, and yet, the initial mistake having been made (chap. xvi.), this severance was really the very best thing that could have happened for all concerned. Discipleship always involves *discipline,* and discipline is always necessary to spiritual blessing. God was taking up the tangled threads of His servant's life, weaving them into His own Divine pattern, and overruling everything for good. Happy for us if, like the Apostle Paul, we can rest our heart day by day on "the depth of the riches both of the wisdom and knowledge of God" (Rom. xi. 33).

3. *The absolute sufficiency of God.*—God's call to Abraham was met by Divine grace sufficient for his need. The Lord never puts upon His people more than they are able to bear. He encourages them by His promises, He assures them of His presence and power, and in response to all these encouragements His people yield trustful obedience, and find that His grace is sufficient for them. "As thy days, so shall thy strength be."

XXVIII

THE DAILY ROUND

GEN. xxi. 22-34

AND it came to pass at that time, that Abimelech and Phichol the chief captain of his host spake unto Abraham, saying, God *is* with thee in all that thou doest:

Now therefore swear unto me here by God that thou wilt not deal falsely with me, nor with my son, nor with my son's son: *but* according to the kindness that I have done unto thee, thou shalt do unto me, and to the land wherein thou hast sojourned.

And Abraham said, I will swear.

And Abraham reproved Abimelech because of a well of water, which Abimelech's servants had violently taken away.

And Abimelech said, I wot not who hath done this thing: neither didst thou tell me, neither yet heard I *of it*, but today.

And Abraham took sheep and oxen, and gave them unto Abimelech; and both of them made a covenant.

And Abraham set seven ewe lambs of the flock by themselves.

And Abimelech said unto Abraham, What *mean* these seven ewe lambs which thou hast set by themselves?

And he said, For *these* seven ewe lambs shalt thou take of my hand, that they may be a witness unto me, that I have digged this well.

Wherefore he called that place Beer-sheba; because there they sware both of them.

Thus they made a covenant at Beer-sheba; then Abimelech rose up, and Phichol the chief captain of his host, and they returned into the land of the Philistines.

And *Abraham* planted a grove in Beer-sheba, and called there on the name of the Lord, the everlasting God.

And Abraham sojourned in the Philistines' land many days.

THE ordinary uneventful days of a believer's life are usually a better test of his true character than an emergency or crisis. It is sometimes possible to face a great occasion with wisdom and courage, and yet to fail in some simple, average experiences of daily living. We have already had illustrations of what Abraham could do in great crises and striking situations. We shall now see him in an ordinary episode, and be able to consider some of the elements of his inner life and character.

I. *A Striking Testimony* (ver. 22).—Abimelech, King of Gerar, together with Phichol, the chief captain of his host, came to Abraham on a special errand, using the striking words, "God is with thee in all that thou doest." "Abimelech" is probably a title of a dynasty, like "Pharaoh" (cf. xx. 2; xxvi. 1, 16). "Phichol" also seems to be an official title answering to "Vizier" (cf. xxvi. 26).

This testimony to God's presence with Abraham seems to have been based on the occurrences of chapter xx. and on Abimelech's subsequent experiences of Abraham's life and prosperity. It showed that the patriarch's daily life was a genuine witness for God. The fact that a heathen king should be able to draw this conclusion clearly indicates the genuineness and reality of Abraham's life.

II. *A Significant Request* (ver. 23).—Abimelech, realizing the presence of God with Abraham, is specially desirous of peace for himself, his kindred, and his land. He therefore appeals to Abraham to take a solemn oath to insure this result. Abimelech also reminds him of their past intercourse, and the kindness shown on a former occasion (xx. 15).

Abimelech is evidently afraid of Abraham's power, and this, with his growing prosperity and influence, might easily lead to difficulty, and even differences, in the immediate future. Perhaps, too, Abimelech might not have felt quite satisfied about Abraham's future attitude in the light of his former experiences. Yet it is very probable that religious influence was not wanting as a reason for making this request. Abimelech was finding out what many others have found out since his day, that the friendship of good men is often an advantage, even in things temporal.

III. *A Sincere Response* (ver. 24).—At once Abraham responds to the invitation of Abimelech, and shows his readiness to do as the heathen king desires. He expresses his readiness and determination to take the oath required, and to give the solemn undertaking that there shall be peace between him and Abimelech. Abraham stands out at this point to distinct advantage. He is truly a man of God, and shows this by his heartiness and willingness in meeting the desires and fears of Abimelech. His readiness would at once go far to show that he was not bent on any conquest or purely selfish ends.

IV. *A Serious Remonstrance* (ver. 25).—Abraham now points out one difficulty in the way and clearly implies that any compact of peace is really impossible until the difficulty is settled. Abimelech's servants had violently taken away a well of water which belonged to Abraham, and it was with reference to this that Abraham complained. Water was everything to nomadic tribes, and its absence necessarily involved the greatest possible inconvenience, injury, and loss.

The fact that Abimelech's servants had dealt unjustly with the well has suggested to some writers that the well may have been made by Abraham for the convenience of Ishmael when he was sent out from his father's home, and that Abimelech's servants were not aware of the connection of Ishmael with Abraham. This is a very probable explanation, though at the same time it is equally likely that in the movement of their flocks and herds the servants of Abimelech might easily have trespassed in Abraham's neighborhood. Such disputes have always been very common.

V. *A Satisfactory Explanation* (ver. 26).—Abimelech, however, disclaims all knowledge of what had been done. He was entirely ignorant of the action of his servants. Thus, so far as Abimelech is concerned, a simple misunderstanding is at the root of Abraham's remonstrance. How often this is the case between friends and neighbors! Happy are they who are enabled to clear away misunderstandings as quickly and as easily as these two.

Abimelech not only disclaims knowledge and responsibility, but complains of Abraham for not telling him of this. The man is evidently sincere, upright, and genuine, a fine specimen of natural goodness, apart from the special spiritual revelation involved in the Abrahamic covenant.

VI. *A Solemn Covenant* (ver. 27-32).—Abraham thereupon sets before Abimelech the usual covenant presents (verse 27. Cf. 1 Kings xv. 19; Hosea xii. 1). Then he sets seven lambs of the flock by themselves, and, on being asked why this difference was made, he replies that they are a special gift, an additional security for the future with reference to the well (verse 30).

Abraham then calls the name of the place "Beer-sheba," which may mean "the well of the oath" or "the well of the seven." There is an etymological connection between the Hebrew words for "swear" and "seven," probably because of the seven sacrifices (ver. 28). It is, however, very interesting to know that seven wells have actually been found at the place which has been identified with Beersheba, twelve hours south-west of Hebron. Thus the covenant is made, and the two men become united in a solemn compact of brotherhood and peace. Abimelech and Phichol return to their country. Abraham remains at Beer-sheba.

VII. *A Special Revelation* (vers. 33, 34).—Abraham now adds on his own account another testimony to his recent experiences. He plants a grove, probably a tamarisk tree, one of the evergreens of the East, and a fit memorial of the perfect peace which he desired between himself, his God, and his fellow-men. But now there came a new revelation of the meaning of his relation to God. In the course of his prayer and communion he learnt a new Name of God, and the new Name was no mere additional title, but contained a new truth about God; "the Everlasting God" (*El Olam*). He was thus reminded of God's unchangeableness and his dependableness. This was a distinct advance on his previous knowledge of God as "Most High" (xiv. 22), and "Almighty" (xvii. 1). Thus, in the course of Abraham's daily life and his faithful attitude to those around him, came fresh mercies and blessings and new experiences of his God.

1. *The spiritual value of ordinary everyday life.*—It is impossible for Christians to be ever living in a constant succession of crises and great occasions. These exceptional experiences must of necessity be very rare. Ordinary life is the normal experience of the overwhelming majority of God's people; and "the trivial round, the common task, will furnish all we need to ask" of opportunities for faithfulness, as well as of experience of God. The prophet Isaiah

seems to suggest the three general experiences of life (xl. 31)—(a) There is the exceptional moment of exalted communion with God; "mount up with wings as eagles." (b) There is the special emergency; "they shall run." (c) There is the ordinary, normal, average, daily life; "they shall walk." The last-named is at once the hardest and really the most blessed. Ordinary is, after all, the "ordered," and therefore the truly "ordained" life. If we wait for great occasions in order to show our character we shall utterly fail to do God's will. It is for us to make every occasion great by faithful loyalty to His grace.

2. *The true attitude of believers to "them that are without."*— This episode is a helpful illustration of the relation of God's people to those who are not yet within the fold. The Apostle urges us more than once to live in view of the non-Christians around us. "Walk in wisdom toward them that are without" (Col. iv. 5). "Walk becomingly toward them that are without" (1 Thess. iv. 12). "A good report of them which are without" (1 Tim. iii. 7). The very phrase "them that are *without*" tells of the unutterable sadness and loss of being outside the fold and separated from all the great privileges of grace in Christ Jesus. This fact alone should make us the more careful to live aright in order that those who are now without may be attracted to come within. And, further, as a witness for God and His grace it is of the utmost necessity that we should "walk circumspectly," or, as St. Paul more literally wrote, "walk accurately" (Eph. v. 15), "providing things beautiful [or attractive] in the sight of all men" (Rom. xii. 17, Greek).

3. *The unspeakable blessedness of new experiences of God*— A profound satisfaction is realized by the believer as he discovers more and more of the glories of God and His grace. The believer is "ever learning," and from the moment of his conversion, in proportion to his faithful obedience day by day, God becomes better known in all the fulness and manifold variety of His revelation. These new experiences as they come are, however, not merely a matter of personal satisfaction, blessed though that is; they tend to prepare the soul for still greater accomplishments. God's revelations are not mere luxuries for personal enjoyment, but are given

for the purpose of preparing the soul for fuller service and still clearer testimony for God. We shall see how this new revelation of God to Abraham was a distinct preparation for a crisis that was to come in his life. It is the same today. God reveals Himself more and more fully in order that we may be more and more thoroughly equipped for greater efforts in the kingdom of God.

XXIX

THE SUPREME CRISIS

GEN. xxii. 1-19

AND it came to pass after these things that God did tempt Abraham, and said unto him, Abraham: and he said, Behold, *here* I *am*.

And he said, Take now thy son, thine only *son* Isaac, whom thou lovest, and get thee into the land of Moriah; and offer him there for a burnt offering upon one of the mountains which I will tell thee of.

And Abraham rose up early in the morning, and saddled his ass, and took two of his young men with him, and Isaac his son, and clave the wood for the burnt offering, and rose up, and went unto the place of which God had told him.

Then on the third day Abraham lifted up his eyes, and saw the place afar off.

And Abraham said unto his young men, Abide ye here with the ass; and I and the lad will go yonder and worship, and come again to you.

And Abraham took the wood of the burnt offering, and laid *it* upon Isaac his son: and he took the fire in his hand, and a knife; and they went both of them together.

And Isaac spake unto Abraham his father, and said, My father: and he said, Here *am* I, my son. And he said, Behold the fire and the wood: but where *is* the lamb for a burnt offering?

And Abraham said, My son, God will provide himself a lamb for a burnt offering; so they went both of them together.

And they came to the place which God had told him of; and Abraham built an altar there, and laid the wood in order, and bound Isaac his son, and laid him on the altar upon the wood.

And Abraham stretched forth his hand, and took the knife to slay his son.

And the angel of the Lord called unto him out of heaven, and said, Abraham, Abraham: and he said, Here *am* I.

And he said, Lay not thine hand upon the lad, neither do thou anything unto him: for now I know that thou fearest God, seeing that thou hast not withheld thy son, thine only *son*, from me.

And Abraham lifted up his eyes, and looked, and behold behind *him* a ram caught in a thicket by his horns: and Abraham went and took the ram, and offered him up for a burnt offering in the stead of his son.

And Abraham called the name of that place Jehovah-jireh: as it is said *to* this day, In the mount of the Lord it shall be seen.

And the angel of the Lord called unto Abraham out of heaven the second time.

And said, By myself have I sworn, saith the Lord, for because thou hast done this thing, and hast not withheld thy son, thine only *son*:

That in blessing I will bless thee, and in multiplying I will multiply thy seed as the stars of the heaven, and as the sand which *is* upon the sea shore; and thy seed shall possess the gate of his enemies;

And in thy seed shall all the nations of the earth be blessed; because thou hast obeyed my voice.

So Abraham returned unto his young men, and they rose up and went together to Beer-sheba: and Abraham dwelt at Beer-sheba.

LIFE is a succession of tests, for character is only possible through discipline. In many lives there is some supreme test to which all others are secondary and preparatory. It was so with Abraham, and we are now to consider the record of the crowning event of his life. For him it was the avenue leading to his closest fellowship with God and his greatest spiritual blessing. For us today it still reveals the secret of spiritual power and victory.

I. *The Test* (vers. 1, 2).—The time is noteworthy. "After these things." It was immediately after the new experiences of God recorded in the former chapter (xxi. 33, 34). It is frequently the case that severe tests follow special times of blessing. Our Lord's temptation followed immediately upon the spiritual experiment of His baptism, and the two events are closely associated by the Evangelists (Matt. iv. 1; Luke iv. 1). Discipline thus proves whether our spiritual experiences have really become part of our life and character, instead of being mere temporary enjoyments and luxuries.

What are we to understand by the words, "God did tempt Abraham"? The word "test" better expresses the Divine intention and action. God tests us to bring out the good. Satan tempts us to bring out the evil (James i. 12-15).

The description (ver. 2) is worthy of careful notice: "Thy son, thine only son, whom thou lovest, even Isaac." (R.V.). Thus by point after point Abraham is reminded of the dearest possession of his life, and is asked to give to God his best. Trials that are put upon us with no reason given at the time are the severest tests of all. They call for absolute unquestioning faith, and when responded to in this spirit invariably lead the soul higher and nearer to God. Moriah is mentioned again only once (2 Chron. iii. 1), where the reference is to one of the mountains on which Jerusalem is situated. Some writers think that, as the journey from Beer-sheba to Jerusalem would only take about seventeen hours, it is impossible to believe that Mount Moriah is intended in this chapter. At the same time the tradition that this was the spot is at least as old as Josephus, and, to say nothing of its spiritual appropriateness in view of Calvary, there does not seem any valid reason for rejecting it.

II. *The Trial* (vers. 3-10).—The alacrity of Abraham's reply to God's call is very striking, and is evidently intended to be regarded as a prominent feature of the narrative. Some writers are fond of depicting his silent agony, and emphasizing that he did not tell Sarah a word of what God had ordered. There is, however, nothing of this in the narrative. No reluctance, no hesitation, no doubt mark Abraham at this point. He "made haste, and delayed not" to keep God's commandment (Ps. cxix. 60). He "conferred not with flesh and blood" (Gal. i. 16). This alacrity should be borne in mind as one of the leading and most significant points of the story.

On the third day Abraham came to the end of his journey. His words to the young men need special attention (verse 5). "Abide ye here . . . I and the lad will go yonder and worship, and come again to you." It is therefore evident that Abraham fully expected Isaac would come back with him. The conversation between the father and the son is noteworthy and beautiful. The son's natural question about the lamb is followed by the father's whole-hearted and confident reply that God will provide it. Notice the repetition of the phrase in verses 6 and 8, "they went both of them together."

The part of Isaac in this matter is always a subject of great interest. Was there any concurrence on his part? It must be remembered that he had already arrived at man's estate. Probably as they neared the place Abraham revealed to his son that God had commanded, and also told him what he himself expected as the result of that command. There is no idea in Abraham's mind that

he is doing wrong in sacrificing his son. He was familiar with the
practice of human sacrifices from the Canaanites around him, and
there was consequently no shock to his conscience in this command.
As to the Divine aspect of it, it must be ever remembered that God
accommodates His instructions to the moral and spiritual standards
of the people at any given time. He knew the end from the beginning, and that He never meant Isaac to be sacrificed. What
God desired was not Isaac's life but Abraham's loyalty, thus separating between the false and the true in relation to human sacrifice.

III. *The Triumph* (vers. 11-14).—At the right moment and not
before (Ps. cvii. 27, 28), God interposed and stayed Abraham's
hand. By this action God bore unmistakable testimony to the
error of the heathen as to human sacrifices, and it is a striking fact
that from this time forward the Jews never adopted the practice of
human sacrifices until they had sunk to the level of the heathen
around them. In this respect the superiority of the Old Testament
to the worship and practices of the heathen around is evident to
all. God could not have given a better object lesson as to the sin
of sacrificing our offspring with the thought that it would be pleasing to Him. God sets His seal upon His servant's faith, and says,
"Now I know that thou fearest God." Abraham was prepared to
give God his very best. Faith can do no more.

Abraham not only finds that God interposes to prevent him from
killing his son, but that his word to his son, "God will provide,"
is also literally fulfilled. The ram was offered up as a burnt offering in the stead of Isaac.

"Abraham called the name of the place Jehovah-jireh," thus bearing his testimony to the reality of God's presence and provision.
"The Lord will see to it." This was the secret and assurance of
Abraham's faith, and the same is true today. As God has saved
our souls and made us His own children and servants, so assuredly
with reference to the whole of our life "The Lord will see to it"
(cf. Rom. v. 10). The place became sanctified to Abraham by a
very holy and blessed memory. It is well when we can look back
over life's pathway and point to a particular place or time when
God revealed Himself to us in blessing.

IV. *The Testimony* (vers. 15-19).—Again the Voice from heaven
was heard. It called to Abraham and acknowledged what had been
done: "Because thou hast done this." God clearly teaches the
patriarch that He regarded the sacrifice as actually offered. The
will was taken for the deed.

God now introduces a renewal of the promises by a specially
solemn oath: "By Myself have I sworn." This expression is only
found very rarely in Scripture, and indicates the most solemn oath
possible (Isaiah xlv. 23; Jer. xxii. 5; xlix. 13; Heb. vi. 13, 14).
These promises should be compared with those given on the former
occasions (chaps. xii. 2, 3; xiii. 16; xv. 5; xvii. 4-8).

We can easily picture the glad satisfaction with which Abraham
returned to the young men with Isaac his son. He had said they
would come back, and they had. He had proved that God was
true, and, having loyally accepted and fulfilled God's will, he was
filled with joy and peace.

1. *The simplicity of faith.*—Faith in the case of Abraham, as
indeed in every other instance, is taking God at His word. True
faith is nothing more, as it is nothing less, than this. God speaks:
man believes. This is the true idea involved in the phrase "im-
plicit trust," a trust that relies upon God without having his reasons "unfolded" to us. This simple faith, taking God at His word,
is always at the foundation of the believer's peace and restfulness,
strength and progress.

2. *The strength of faith.*—The entire absence from the narrative
of any suggestions about Abraham's emotions or self-sacrifice is
surely very significant. He had received certain promises from
God about his son, and he was perfectly certain that those promises
would be fulfilled. In the strength of this assurance he went forward, his attitude being that of Job: "Though He slay me, yet
will I trust in Him" (Job. xiii. 15). Abraham's faith showed its
strength in the way in which he fully expected his son Isaac to return with him to the young men (ver. 5). "We will come again
to you." Nothing can affect the force of this splendid expectation
of Abraham. What, then, did the words imply? Simply this: that
whilst he believed at that moment that God intended him to slay

his son, he nevertheless felt perfectly certain that God would there and then raise Isaac from the dead and send him back alive. Only thus could Abraham then see that the promises concerning his seed were to be fulfilled. What a magnificent exercise of faith this was! There had never been such an event as a resurrection, and so Abraham had no previous example to suggest this result or to encourage his faith thereby. But with a splendid sweep of God-given imagination, based upon God's personal relation to him, he said to himself, "God will raise my son from the dead."

3. *The source of faith.*—The foundation of this remarkable confidence was Abraham's conviction of the power of God: "Accounting that God was able" (Heb. xi. 17-19). The whole passage from the Epistle to the Hebrews shows that this is the true explanation of this incident, and so far from this view being, as is sometimes alleged, a mere *coup de thèâtre,* it was in reality a marvelous exercise of faith when it is remembered that no instance had then been known of God's power being exercised in the resurrection from the dead. God was such a reality to Abraham, and His promises were so certain, that the patriarch at once drew the inevitable and natural conclusion that God's power could and would effect this.

4. *The secret of faith.*—How was it that Abraham was able to exercise this unquestioning and even astonishing trust in God? The explanation is found in the phrase, which occurs twice in this chapter, "Here am I." Abraham lived in close fellowship with God, ready for His new revelations and responsive to His continual calls. Abiding close to God, he learnt more and more of the character of the One with Whom he was in covenant. "The secret of the Lord is with them that fear Him," and when we thus abide in Him He abides in us, and our faith grows strong, our love grows deep, our hope grows high. Then it is we "stagger not through unbelief" (Rom. iv. 20), and we are able to say: "The Lord God will help me; therefore shall I not be confounded; therefore have I set my face like a flint, and I know that I shall not be ashamed" (Isaiah 1. 7).

XXX

DEATH IN THE HOME

Gen. xxiii.

And Sarah was an hundred and seven and twenty years old: *these were* the years of the life of Sarah.

And Sarah died in Kirjath-arba; the same *is* Hebron in the land of Canaan: and Abraham came to mourn for Sarah, and to weep for her.

And Abraham stood up from before his dead, and spake unto the sons of Heth, saying,

I *am* a stranger and a sojourner with you: give me a possession of a buryingplace with you, that I may bury my dead out of my sight.

And the children of Heth answered Abraham, saying unto him.

Hear us, my lord: thou *art* a mighty prince among us: in the choice of our sepulchres bury thy dead; none of us shall withhold from thee his sepulchre, but that thou mayest bury thy dead.

And Abraham stood up, and bowed himself to the people of the land, *even* to the children of Heth.

And he communed with them, saying, If it be your mind that I should bury my dead out of my sight; hear me and intreat for me to Ephron, the son of Zohar.

That he may give me the cave of Machpelah, which he hath, which *is* in the end of his field; for as much money as it is worth he shall give it me for a possession of a buryingplace amongst you.

And Ephron dwelt amongst the children of Heth: and Ephron the Hittite answered Abraham in the audience of the children of Heth, *even* of all that went in at the gate of his city, saying,

Nay, my lord, hear me: the field give I thee, and the cave that *is* therein, I give it thee; and in the presence of the sons of my people give I it thee: bury thy dead.

And Abraham bowed down himself before the people of the land.

And he spake unto Ephron in the audience of the people of the land, saying, But if thou *wilt give it*, I pray thee, hear me: I will give thee money for the field; take *it* of me, and I will bury my dead there.

And Ephron answered Abraham, saying unto him.

My lord, hearken unto me: the land *is worth* four hundred shekels of silver; what *is* that betwixt me and thee? bury therefore thy dead.

And Abraham hearkened unto Ephron; and Abraham weighed to Ephron the silver, which he had named in the audience of the sons of Heth, four hundred shekels of silver, current *money* with the merchant.

And the field of Ephron, which *was* in Machpelah, which *was* before Mamre, the field, and the cave which *was* therein, and all the trees that *were* in the field, that *were* in all the borders round about, were made sure

Unto Abraham for a possession in the presence of the children of Heth, before all that went in at the gate of his city.

And after this, Abraham buried Sarah his wife in the cave of the field of Machpelah before Mamre: the same *is* Hebron in the land of Canaan.

And the field, and the cave that *is* therein, were made sure unto Abraham for a possession of a buryingplace by the sons of Heth.

AFTER the great crisis (Gen. xxii.) Abraham had twenty-five years of apparent uneventful life. Three scenes illustrative of home and personal experiences are successively brought before us: (*a*) the news of relatives from afar (chap. xxii. 20-24); (*b*) the death of the wife and mother (chap. xxiii.); (*c*) the marriage of the son (chap. xxiv.). We are now to consider the second of these, the death of Sarah.

I. *Death* (vers. 1, 2).—At the age of one hundred and twenty-seven, forty years after the birth of Isaac (Gen. xviii. 12), Sarah died. She is the only woman whose age is recorded in the Bible. The following points with reference to her death are worthy of consideration and meditation.

It was the death of a believer. Certain hints in the story suggest that Sarah's spiritual life and experience were not quite on the high level of her husband's, but at the same time it is equally evident that her spiritual life was real, and her faith in the promises of God strong. The New Testament also adds its witness to the fact of Sarah's spiritual oneness with Abraham (Heb. xi. 11-13; 1 Pet. iii. 5, 6).

It was the death of a life-long companion. For sixty years Sarah had lived in Canaan with Abraham, and with the exception of the incident about Hagar, which was itself prompted by Sarah, nothing marred the fellowship of these two as husband and wife. They afford to us a picture of true married life, a husband and wife united in the Lord and in each other in Him.

It was the death of a mother. To Isaac the death of Sarah was a very great loss. Although he was now nearly forty years of age, he had always lived at home and was the recipient of his mother's love and devotion and the subject of her constant hope and prayer. We are distinctly told of his sorrow on her death (chap. xxiv. 67).

It was a death in the home. The removal of one member of a household, especially if that member is a beloved wife and mother, causes a blank which nothing else can fill. The quiet influence of such a life in the home is of untold value, and the loss at death is proportionately great.

II. *Sorrow* (ver. 2).—Sarah's life came to its end at Hebron, and it would almost seem from the words "Abraham came to mourn" that he was away at the time of her death. It is possible, if not probable, that Abraham had two establishments with separate flocks and herds, one at Beer-sheba (chap. xxii. 19), and the other at Hebron, where Sarah then was.

This is the first occasion in Scripture of the record of a man's tears, and they were neither idle, nor unmanly, nor morbid, but the genuine and rightful expression of Abraham's deep sorrow on the death of his wife.

III. *Duty* (ver. 3).—There is danger lest sorrow overwhelm us and we should give way beyond measure. The great safeguard against this danger is work. So Abraham rose up and applied to the children of Heth with reference to a burial-place.

Abraham's desire for a resting place for the body of his wife is a simple but striking testimony to the innate feelings about the care of the body. The possessive pronouns "his dead" (ver. 3), "my dead" (ver. 4), "thy dead" (ver. 6), are very noteworthy in this connection. The body of his beloved wife was precious to him and was regarded by him and by others as his own property, of which he was about to take special and loving care.

IV. *Faith* (vers. 4-18).—The dialogue between Abraham and the sons of Heth is full of touching and deep interest, and is especially noteworthy as a revelation of Abraham's inner life.

Abraham confesses that he is a "stranger and sojourner," and yet by his request for a burial-place he clearly indicates that he intends to stay in the land of Canaan, and not to return to Mesopotamia. When Eastern sentiment as to burial with ancestors is remembered, this request for a piece of ground in Canaan is a striking testimony to Abraham's faith. He was fully assured that Canaan was the place for him and his descendants, and on this account Sarah is to be buried there.

We notice the perfect courtesy of Abraham in reply to the offers of the people of the land. Whether, as some writers think, all this was mere parleying with a view to a bargain, or whether, as others urge, it was a genuine and sincere offer on the part of the children of Heth, Abraham's attitude stands out in a very beautiful way. Religion is not intended to decrease, but to increase natural politeness, gentlemanliness, and courtesy. Indeed, courtesy is one of the truest marks of a genuine believer.

Abraham persisted in declining the offer (if it was really intended as an offer) of a burying-place. He was determined that Sarah should not be buried in any land but his own. It must not be hired; it must not be given. Till God's time came Abraham would not be a debtor to those who were to be dispossessed. "By faith" he refused.

Payment was consequently made, and everything was done in due form in the presence of witnesses. Thus, the first foothold in the land of Canaan that Abraham ever had was bought. Notwithstanding all God's promises of that land to him and to his seed, Abraham would not deal unjustly, even in appearance, with those then in possession of Canaan.

V. *Love* (vers. 19, 20).—The funeral brings us to the first grave of which we have any record in Holy Writ. The last offices of respect were paid, and the lonely old man went back to his home.

The possession of the property was guaranteed to Abraham and "made sure" for a perpetual possession. Visitors to Hebron today are still shown what is called Abraham's Tomb, and, although no Christian is allowed to enter and explore for himself, there does not seem much doubt as to the genuineness of the tradition which associates the present place with the cave of Machpelah. What an inspiring thought to realize that very likely the bodies of the patriarchs are still there, and that some day they will be exposed to view!

From this simple and touching story of death in the home we may learn how we should behave in times of bereavement. The true attitude at such times is threefold:—

1. *Sorrowing Love.*—The expression of love in sorrow is as natural as it is inevitable and beautiful. A consciousness of loss cannot fail to produce sorrow, and no one is to be blamed for feeling and expressing a sense of bereavement. It would be utterly unnatural if death were to come without eliciting sorrow.

2. *Faithful Service.*—At the same time, in order that the soul may not be swallowed up with over-much sorrow, there comes to us all at such occasions the call to and opportunity for definite service. The memory of a loved one is best treasured by doing what that loved one would wish were she here. Service always prevents sorrow from becoming dissipated in idle regrets and mere remembrance.

3. *Blessed Hope.*—Abraham laid Sarah's body to rest "in sure and certain hope" of a joyful resurrection (Heb. xi. 14). It was this above all things that upheld and strengthened him as he bade farewell to the wife who had shared his joys and sorrows for so many years. The expectation and anticipation of reunion in Christ on the Day of Resurrection is still the real hope, the blessed comfort, and the strong inspiration of the people of God. It enables us to look upon death without fear, and to look forward without dread. "In the midst of death we are in life" through Him who is the Resurrection and the Life.

XXXI

THE EVENING OF LIFE

GEN. xxiv. 1-9—xxv. 1-10.

AND Abraham was old, *and* well stricken in age: and the Lord had blessed Abraham in all things.

And Abraham said unto his eldest servant of his house, that ruled over all that he had, Put, I pray thee, thy hand under my thigh:

And I will make thee swear by the Lord, the God of heaven, and the God of the earth, that thou shalt not take a wife unto my son of the daughters of the Canaanites, among whom I dwell:

But thou shalt go unto my country, and to my kindred, and take a wife unto my son Isaac.

And the servant said unto him, Peradventure the woman will not be willing to follow me unto this land: must I needs bring thy son again unto the land from whence thou camest?

And Abraham said unto him, Beware thou that thou bring not my son thither again.

The Lord God of heaven, which took me from my father's house, and from the land of my kindred, and which spake unto me, and that sware unto me, saying, Unto thy seed will I give this land; he shall send his angel before thee, and thou shalt take a wife unto my son from thence.

And if the woman will not be willing to follow thee, then thou shalt be clear from this my oath: only bring not my son thither again.

And the servant put his hand under the thigh of Abraham his master, and sware to him concerning that matter.

Then again Abraham took a wife, and her name *was* Keturah.

And she bare him Zimran, and Jokshan, and Medan, and Midian, and Ishbak, and Shuah.

And Jokshan begat Sheba, and Dedan. And the sons of Dedan were Asshurim, and Letushim, and Leummim.

And the sons of Midian; Ephah, and Epher, and Hanoch and Abidah, and Eldaah. All these *were* the children of Keturah.

And Abraham gave all that he had unto Isaac.

But unto the sons of the concubines, which Abraham had Abraham gave gifts, and sent them away from Isaac his son, while he yet lived, eastward, unto the east country.

And these *are* the days of the years of Abraham's life which he lived, an hundred threescore and fifteen years.

Then Abraham gave up the ghost, and died in a good old age, an old man, and full *of years*; and was gathered to his people.

And his sons Isaac and Ishmael buried him in the cave of Machpelah, in the field of Ephron the son of Zohar the Hittite, which *is* before Mamre;

The field which Abraham purchased of the sons of Heth: there was Abraham buried, and Sarah his wife.

THERE is scarcely anything more beautiful and inspiring than the calm, bright, peaceful close of a long and honored life. Like a summer sunset, it floods the whole scene with brightness and glory. "The hoary head is a crown of glory" as it sinks to rest after a life's long day spent "in the way of righteousness." So it was with Abraham, as we can see from the passages which record his closing years.

I. *Crowning Experiences* (xxiv. 1-9).—Abraham's was an old age happily spent in continued enjoyment of the Divine blessing (ver. 1). "The Lord had blessed Abraham in all things." These words sum up the whole of Abraham's life and experiences, and now in old age he is still rejoicing in the consciousness of God's presence and favor. "The blessing of the Lord it maketh rich, and He addeth no sorrow with it" (Prov. x. 22; cf. Ps. xxxvii. 22).

His was an old age marked by persistent faithfulness to the Divine will (vers. 2-4). Abraham still clings with undiminished faith and persistence to the revelation of God concerning him and his seed. He is therefore urgent that his son should not take a wife from the daughters of the Canaanites. The commission which he now gives to his trusted servant (perhaps Eliezer, chap. xv. 2) shows clearly that he desires and determines to follow closely the Divine will. The oath mentioned here and in chapter xlvii 29 only occurs in these two passages in the Old Testament. It betokens a specially solemn engagement, though the reason of the precise form and method is practically unknown, and is therefore variously interpreted. A somewhat similar form of oath has been found in Australia (Driver, *Genesis*, p. 231).

His was an old age characterized by deep insight into the Divine purpose (vers. 6, 7). The servant naturally asks what is to be done if the woman of his kindred is unwilling to take the long journey into Canaan. Abraham promptly and briefly replies that in any case his son is not to be taken out of Canaan. Whatever happens, Abraham is perfectly clear that God's will must be done and His purpose maintained.

His was an old age possessed of absolute assurance of the Divine favor (vers. 7-9). He tells the servant that God, who had been with him all through his long life, would prosper the errand, and bring about that which was desired. At the same time the servant is once more enjoined not to take his son out of the land, and in the event of the unwillingness of the woman to come the servant will be clear of his oath. Thereupon the solemn promise was made, and the servant at once set out on that errand which, as we shall see, was crowned with Divine favor and success. The details of the story of his meeting with Rebekah, and the subsequent marriage, will come before us in the next chapter. We would now merely call renewed attention to this beautiful picture of an honored old age, loyal to God at all costs, "satisfied with favor, full with the blessing of the Lord."

II. *Closing Events* (xxv. 1-10).—It is evident that Abraham's closing years were marked by a fresh accession of bodily and mental vigor, as can be seen from the statements included in this section.

After the events recorded in the last chapter, culminating in the marriage of Isaac, Abraham in his solitude took to himself another wife, Keturah. At the same time the narrative makes it quite evident that she did not occupy the same rank of equality as Sarah did (ver. 6; 1 Chron. i. 32). It is interesting and significant to notice that one of the sons of Abraham's second marriage was Midian, whose descendants became the intensely bitter foes of the descendants of Isaac.

Abraham was careful to make Isaac's position perfectly clear, and, by providing for his other sons and sending them away "eastward, unto the east country," he took the necessary steps to maintain Isaac's position free from possible difficulties. Abraham thus sets possessors of wealth a good example in the careful and complete provision which he made during his lifetime for his family.

At length, at the age of one hundred and seventy-five years he passed away, seventy-five years after the birth of Isaac and thirty-five years after the marriage of the latter with Rebekah (chap. xxi. 5; xxv. 20). The description of his death (ver. 8) is very beautiful, and it is interesting to note that he was "gathered to his people," referring to their reunion in the unseen world. It is obvious that this phrase cannot possibly refer to his burial, since only Sarah's body was in that tomb (Cf. chap. xxxv. 29; xlix. 33).

The two sons, Isaac and Ishmael, met over their father's dead body to pay the last tokens of respect. Death is the great healer of family differences and personal feuds.

III. *Characteristic Elements.*—Looking over the whole of Abraham's life, we cannot but be struck with certain outstanding points in his character. Dr. Candlish, in his suggestive lectures on Genesis, divides the patriarch's life into two main sections; the first of these (chaps. xii.-xv.) he characterizes as the time of *faith,* when Abraham was *accepting* the present gifts of God; the second (chaps. xvi.-xxiv.) he characterizes as the period of *patience,* when Abraham was *expecting* the future inheritance promised to him. The following elements may, however, be seen throughout the whole of his life.

His Faith.—He took God at His word at each step of his career, and his simple trust in the Divine promise is the predominant feature of his life.

His Faithfulness.—He is rightly described as "faithful Abraham" (Gal. iii. 9), for he not only believed, but expressed his belief in life. God's promise had its outcome in Abraham's practice; his faith was proved by faithfulness.

His Fear.—By this is meant his attitude of reverence. Notwithstanding the familiar terms on which he lived with God, he never forgot the relative position of the Divine Majesty and his own nothingness.

His Fellowship.—As we have already seen, the latter portion of his life was marked by a great access of spiritual experience and blessing, which led him into full friendship and fellowship with God. This was with Abraham, as it is now with the believer, the culminating point of all spiritual life.

As we review the entire life of Abraham, and consider it specially from God's standpoint, we cannot help being struck with the threefold exemplification which is so evident all through the story.

1. *The Divine Purpose.*—One thing above all others marked the attitude of God in relation to Abraham: *His will was to be done.* From first to last this was God's purpose. He had in view not merely the manifestation of what a life could be, but also, and perhaps chiefly, the choice of Abraham as the instrument of furthering His great purposes of redemption through the promised Messiah. Whether we think of Abraham personally or as the ancestor of the Messiah, we cannot help learning this one lesson, that believers are placed upon this earth for the one purpose above all others of fulfilling the Divine will. "Thy will be done on earth, as it is in heaven."

2. *The Divine Power.*—God never commands without enabling, and in order that His purpose might be fulfilled He provided needful strength for Abraham. *God's grace was to be accepted.* It is as true today as ever that "As thy days so shall thy strength be," and the grace of God will always be found sufficient for carrying out His will and purpose.

3. *The Divine Plan.*—The practical question remains as to how, and by what means, the Divine purpose can be accomplished and the Divine power utilized by man. The answer is found in the life of Abraham. *God's word was to be believed.* When faith responds to the Divine promise the Divine power is at once given, and through that power the Divine purpose is perfectly accomplished. On the one hand God assures the believer, "My grace is sufficient for thee"; and on the other the believer responds, "I can do all things through Him Who is empowering me."

XXXII

THE MODEL SERVANT

GEN. xxiv. 10-67

AND the servant took ten camels of the camels of his master, and departed; for all the goods of his master *were* in his hand: and he arose, and went to Mesopotamia, unto the city of Nahor.

And he made his camels to kneel down without the city by a well of water at the time of the evening, *even* the time that women go out to draw *water*.

And he said, O Lord God of my master Abraham, I pray Thee, send me good speed this day, and shew kindness unto my master Abraham.

Behold, I stand *here* by the well of water; and the daughters of the men of the city come out to draw water:

And let it come to pass, that the damsel to whom I shall say, Let down thy pitcher, I pray thee, that I may drink; and she shall say, Drink, and I will give thy camels drink also: *let the same be* she *that* Thou hast appointed for Thy servant Isaac; and thereby shall I know that Thou hast shewed kindness unto my master.

And it came to pass, before he had done speaking, that, behold, Rebekah came out, who was born to Bethuel, son of Milcah, the wife of Nahor, Abraham's brother, with her pitcher upon her shoulder.

And the damsel *was* very fair to look upon, a virgin, neither had any man known her: and she went down to the well, and filled her pitcher, and came up.

And the servant ran to meet her, and said, Let me, I pray thee, drink a little water of thy pitcher.

And she said, Drink, my lord: and she hasted, and let down her pitcher upon her hand, and gave him drink.

And when she had done giving him drink, she said, I will draw *water* for thy camels also, until they have done drinking.

And she hasted, and emptied her pitcher into the trough, and ran again unto the well to draw *water*, and drew for all his camels.

And the man wondering at her held his peace, to wit whether the Lord had made his journey prosperous or not.

And it came to pass, as the camels had done drinking, that the man took a golden earring of half a shekel weight, and two bracelets for her hands of ten *shekels* weight of gold;

And said, Whose daughter *art* thou? tell me, I pray thee: is there room *in* thy father's house for us to lodge in?

And she said unto him, I *am* the daughter of Bethuel the son of Milcah, which she bare unto Nahor.

She said moreover unto him, We have both straw and provender enough, and room to lodge in.

And the man bowed down his head, and worshipped the Lord.

And he said, Blessed *be* the Lord God of my master Abraham, Who hath not left destitute my master of His mercy and His truth: I *being* in the way, the Lord led me to the house of my master's brethren.

And the damsel ran, and told *them of* her mother's house these things.

And Rebekah had a brother, and his name *was* Laban: and Laban ran out unto the man, unto the well.

And it came to pass, when he saw the earring and bracelets upon his sister's hands, and when he heard the words of Rebekah his sister, saying, Thus spake the man unto me; that he came unto the man; and, behold, he stood by the camels at the well.

And he said, Come in, thou blessed of the Lord; wherefore standest thou without? for I have prepared the house, and room for the camels.

And the man came into the house: and he ungirded his camels, and gave straw and provender for the camels, and water to wash his feet, and the men's feet that *were* with him.

And there was set *meat* before him to eat: but he said, I will not eat, until I have told mine errand. And he said, Speak on.

And he said, I *am* Abraham's servant.

And the Lord hath blessed my master greatly; and he is become great: and He hath given him flocks, and herds, and silver, and gold, and menservants, and maidservants, and camels, and asses.

And Sarah my master's wife bare a son to my master when she was old: and unto him hath he given all that he hath.

And my master made me swear saying, Thou shalt not take a wife to my son of the daughters of the Canaanites, in whose land I dwell:

But thou shalt go unto my father's house, and to my kindred. and take a wife unto my son.

And I said unto my master, Peradventure the woman will not follow me.

And he said unto me, The Lord, before whom I walk, will send His angel with thee, and prosper thy way; and thou shalt take a wife for my son of my kindred, and of my father's house:

Then shalt thou be clear from *this* my oath, when thou comest to my kindred; and if they give not thee *one*, thou shalt be clear from my oath.

And I came this day unto the well, and said, O Lord God of my master Abraham, if now Thou do prosper my way which I go:

Behold, I stand by the well of water: and it shall come to pass, that when the virgin cometh forth to draw *water*, and I say to her, Give me, I pray thee, a little water of thy pitcher to drink;

And she say to me, Both drink thou, and I will also draw for thy camels: *let* the same *be* the woman whom the Lord hath appointed out for my master's son.

And before I had done speaking in mine heart, behold, Rebekah came forth with her pitcher on her shoulder; and she went down unto the well, and drew *water*: and I said unto her, Let me drink, I pray thee.

And she made haste, and let down her pitcher from her *shoulder*, and said, Drink, and I will give thy camels drink also: so I drank, and she made the camels drink also.

And I asked her, and said, Whose daughter *art* thou? And she said, The daughter of Bethel, Nahor's son, whom Milcah bare unto him: and I put the earring upon her face, and the bracelets upon her hands.

And I bowed down my head, and worshipped the Lord, and blessed the Lord God of my master Abraham, which had led me in the right way to take my master's brother's daughter unto his son.

And now if ye will deal kindly and truly with my master, tell me: and if not, tell me; that I may turn to the right hand, or to the left.

Then Laban and Bethuel answered and said, The thing proceedeth from the Lord: we cannot speak unto thee bad or good.

Behold, Rebekah *is* before thee, take *her*, and go, and let her be thy master's son's wife, as the Lord hath spoken.

And it came to pass, that, when Abraham's servant heard their words, he worshipped the Lord, *bowing himself* to the earth.

And the servant brought forth jewels of silver, and jewels of gold, and raiment, and gave *them* to Rebekah: he gave also to her brother and to her mother precious things.

And they did eat and drink, he and the men that *were* with him, and tarried all night; and they rose up in the morning, and he said, Send me away unto my master.

And her brother and her mother said, Let the damsel abide with us *a few* days, at the least ten; after that she shall go.

And he said unto them, Hinder me not, seeing the Lord hath prospered my way; send me away that I may go to my master.

And they said, We will call the damsel, and enquire at her mouth.

And they called Rebekah, and said unto her, Wilt thou go with this man? And she said, I will go.

And they sent away Rebekah their sister, and her nurse, and Abraham's servant, and his men.

And they blessed Rebekah, and said unto her, Thou *art* our sister, be thou *the mother* of thousands of millions, and let thy seed possess the gate of those which hate them.

And Rebekah arose, and her damsels, and they rode upon the camels, and followed the man: and the servant took Rebekah, and went his way.

And Isaac came from the way of the well Lahai-roi; for he dwelt in the south country.

And Isaac went out to meditate in the field at the eventide: and he lifted up his eyes, and saw, and, behold, the camels *were* coming.

And Rebekah lifted up her eyes, and when she saw Isaac, she lighted off the camel.

For she *had* said unto the servant, What man *is* this that walketh in the field to meet us? And the servant *had* said, It *is* my master: therefore she took a vail, and covered herself.

And the servant told Isaac all things that he had done.
And Isaac brought her into his mother Sarah's tent, and took Rebekah, and she became his wife; and he loved her: and Isaac was comforted after his mother's *death*.

WE have already considered Abraham's part in this search of a bride for his son Isaac, but the chapter is so full of interesting and vivid detail that it needs careful attention from the standpoint of Abraham's servant, whose attitude and action illustrate in the highest degree the qualities of true service. We may, therefore, fitly regard him as a model for all who are called upon to work for God. Several characteristics of his service call for attention.

I. *Intelligent Obedience* (vers. 1-9).—He was at hand ready for work, and upon being told what was required of him met his master's commands by an evident desire for information (ver. 5). His service was an intelligent service, and he wished to know what was to be done under certain contingencies that might present themselves. God always welcomes inquiries from His servants concerning His will (John xvi. 19). On being assured by his master of the Divine guidance he at once pledged himself to Abraham, and took a solemn oath of faithfulness to duty.

II. *Zealous Interest* (vers. 10-14).—With promptitude the servant set out on his important errand, and we can see from the entire narrative that he was fully identified with the object of his quest. His was no mere slavery, for it was an evident delight to him to do his master's bidding, and to seek for a bride for his son.

The true spirit of the man is seen in his earnest prayer for guidance (ver. 12); his task was a difficult one. He was on a very unlikely and unusual errand, and so he prays that the God of his master would give him good success. Not only does he pray for guidance, but for grace (vers. 13, 14). He seeks to know the road, and then asks for power to walk along it. He requests opportunities, and then grace to use them. There is scarcely anything more touching and beautiful than this prayer, especially in its emphasis upon his master, and his desire that God would show kindness to Abraham. Happy are those masters who have such a servant as this, and happy are those servants able to pray in this way for their masters.

III. *The Holy Tact* (vers. 15-33).—It is impossible for us to dwell in exhaustive detail on all the interesting and beautiful touches of this full narrative. We cannot, however, fail to notice his perfect courtesy (ver. 17). Manner counts for a very great deal in all Christian work. We may spoil a good cause by our lack of considerateness and courtesy. We observe, too, his patience (ver. 21). He will not force matters, for there must be no hurry. The man is filled with a holy watchfulness for every indication of the will of God. "The man looked steadfastly on her, holding his peace, to know whether the Lord had made his journey prosperous or not."

The wisdom of the man is equally evident (ver. 22). He brings out what would be perfectly known to the young girl as bridal gifts, and offers them first before approaching the subject of his errand, or mentioning the person of his master or his master's son. We cannot fail to observe his reverence and thankfulness as he realizes that his prayer has been answered, and that God has indeed guided him in the way. Not least of all is the man s intense earnestness (ver. 33). He would not eat or rest until he had told his errand; his master's cause must come first.

IV. *Loving Faithfulness* (vers. 34-49).—Again we are impressed with the combination of wisdom and faithfulness in all that the servant says and does. He states his position at once with dignity and humility (ver. 34). He is loud in the praises of his master, and tells them in brief his history (vers. 35, 36). He then declares definitely the object of his errand (vers. 37-48), and makes the proposal, offering a definite choice to the relatives of the young woman whom he had met at the well (ver. 49).

V. *Blessed Success* (vers. 50-67).—There are difficulties in the way, as they point out, but they are willing that Rebekah should go, only they ask him to allow her to remain a few days before the departure. The man, however, is decided; his master's business requires haste, and he urges upon them the necessity of instant decision. Rebekah at once, and with definiteness, says, "I will go," and thus the journey home was commenced.

Soon the purpose of the servant is accomplished. He introduces Rebekah to Isaac, and the servant retires to tell his aged master what he has done. The servant disappears from view at this point with fitness and appropriateness, but we are sure that he received his "well done" from Abraham, and entered into the joy of his master in the accomplishment of the task appointed to him.

In the addition to the lessons of Christian service already observed in our study of the chapter it is possible, and we believe legitimate, to regard this story as an illustration of still higher truths. The length of the chapter in a book whose spiritual purpose is evident at every stage seems to compel the thought that the full detail in these sixty-seven verses must have some deeper meaning than appears on the surface. Spiritual commentators have consequently not been slow to find herein the seeds of profound spiritual truths. Doubtless our forefathers went too far in the direction of spiritualizing the Old Testament narratives, but it is equally possible for us to go to the other extreme, and to see nothing of the kind in them. If it be ever borne in mind that such a spiritual use of the narrative is secondary and not primary, that it is application not interpretation, and if moreover we avoid fanciful details and confine ourselves to leading lines of spiritual suggestion, the method is not only legitimate but essentially helpful. Let us therefore look at some of these suggestions that are often brought out of this chapter.

1. *The purpose of the father.*—The father has but one purpose in this chapter, to seek a bride for his son. "A certain king made a marriage feast for his son" (Matt. xxii. 2).

2. *The position of the son.*—The son is the father's one thought, and in him all his purposes are to be fulfilled (ver. 36). So also is it in regard to the Son of God (Eph. i. 20-22).

3. *The prospects of the bride.*—The bride was thought of before she herself knew it (ver. 4), and arrangements were made for her to be offered the position of wife to Isaac. "He chose us in Him before the foundation of the world, that we should be holy and without blemish before Him in love" (Eph. i. 4).

4. *The proclamation of the servant.*—The one object of the servant was the announcement of Abraham's purpose, which carried with it the revelation concerning the son, and the offer to Rebekah. How wonderfully he proclaimed the vast resources of the father (ver. 35), and the glory of the son (ver. 36). In like manner the Holy Spirit through the mouths of Christian preachers is continually proclaiming the glory of Christ. Is it not something more than a coincidence that we have such striking words in St. John xvi. 14, 15?

5. *The power of the message.*—The success of the servant in attracting Rebekah to go with him is very noteworthy. In like manner, Christ, if He be lifted up, will draw men to Himself. There is nothing so attractive as the preaching of a free and full Gospel (John xii. 32).

6. *The progress of the soul.*—The decision of Rebekah and her determination to go is another striking point of the narrative. She believed the servant's word based upon the evidences of Abraham's good faith. She ventured everything and went. So is it with the soul that rests upon the Word of God based upon the certainty of those things wherein we have been instructed. Faith ventures and finds itself justified. Faith steps on the seeming void and finds the rock beneath.

7. *The prospect of the home.*—Rebekah in coming to Canaan finds a husband, her true life, and her permanent home. The soul coming to Christ enters into true fellowship, rejoices even now in eternal life, and knows that in God's good time there will be the Canaan above, the rest for the people of God.

XXXIII

THE FATHER OF THE FAITHFUL

BEFORE passing on to the story of Isaac, and the record of the development of the Divine purpose with Abraham and his descendants, it will be useful to dwell once more on the life and character of Abraham as a whole.

None of the lives recorded in the Old Testament made a deeper impression or became more prominent in after ages than that of Abraham. His position as the founder of the Jewish nation, and his character as the pattern and type of believers in all ages, have given him a very important place in Holy Scripture. The following summary of passages may serve as a guide to fuller and detailed study.

I. IN THE OLD TESTAMENT—

The Scripture Record.—It is evident to the most casual reader that wherever Abraham is mentioned he is always assumed to have been a veritable historic personage. There is no possibility of his being regarded as an "eponymous hero." That he existed, that he had the experiences recorded in the Book of Genesis, and that he was the personal, definite, historic founder of the Jewish nation are always regarded as simple matters of fact.

The Gracious Covenant (Exod. ii. 24).—"God remembered His covenant with Abraham." This Abrahamic covenant is often referred to in times subsequent to the patriarch, and is regarded as the foundation of everything in connection with God's dealings with Israel.

The Divine Title (Exod. iii. 6).—"I am . . . the God of Abraham." This title of God in relation to the patriarch is full of

spiritual reality and blessedness, and is dwelt on in later books
with evident satisfaction. It is especially precious as a spiritual fact
in the light of Heb. xi. 16: "God is not ashamed to be called their
God."

The Special Appeal (Isa. li. 2).—"Look unto Abraham your
father . . . for I . . . blessed him." God here uses Abraham and
His own dealings with the patriarch as a reminder to Israel and an
assurance to His people in captivity that He will bless them also, as
He had blessed their ancestor. The unchanging faithfulness of God
is one of the foundation truths of Holy Scripture.

The Definite Plea (1 Kings xviii. 36).—"Lord God of Abraham."
Elijah bases his prayer on God's relation to Abraham. He uses it
as a reason for God's answer to His prayer, and His manifestation
in the face of idolatry. In like manner Moses put forth the same
plea: "Remember Abraham . . . to whom Thou swarest . . . and
saidest" (Exod. xxxii. 13; Deut. ix. 27). Believers have a blessed
and holy right to plead God's faithfulness to their forefathers as a
reason for continued help.

The Unique Relationship (2 Chron. xx. 7).— "Abraham, Thy
friend." (Cf. Isa. xli. 8). He is the only personage in the Old
Testament who has this high and privileged title. To this day in
Arabia *El Khalil* ("God's friend") is used of Abraham.

A careful study of these and other passages, especially in the
Psalms, will reveal a wealth of spiritual teaching associated with
Abraham and the Divine Covenant made with him.

II. IN THE NEW TESTAMENT—

The Record of his Life.—Here again we are face to face with the
simple fact that all the New Testament writers regard Abraham as a
genuine personage, and no mere mythical hero. Whether we study
passages like Acts vii, or Romans iv. or Hebrews xi., or dwell upon
particular verses in the Gospels and elsewhere, there is only one
interpretation possible; the New Testament accepts, endorses, and
uses the Old Testament testimony to Abraham, and it is not too
much to say that no one with his New Testament in his hand can
hesitate for an instant as to the true meaning and genuine implica-
tions of the references to the patriarch.

His Relation to the Messiah.—The genealogy given by St. Matthew (i. 1) traces our Lord's connection with Abraham and clearly teaches that the Messiah "took on Him the seed of Abraham" (Heb. ii. 16). This fact in the first Gospel, which is essentially the Gospel for the Jews, shows the historic root of the Messianic expectation. Looking at Abraham's relation to the Messiah from another standpoint, we notice what may be called his spiritual anticipation of the Messiah: "Abraham rejoiced to see My day" (John viii. 56) What this sight of the Messianic day really meant and included it is now impossible to say. We must be on our guard against assuming too much spiritual knowledge or against almost entirely denying it. Probably on the occasion of the great events recorded in Gen. xv., and especially in Gen. xxii., Abraham had a spiritual vision given of Him in Whom all the promises were to be completely fulfilled.

His Relation to the Jews.—We can see from several passages the national and individual pride felt in Abraham (Matt. iii. 9; John viii. 39). A poor woman is spoken of by our Lord as "a daughter of Abraham" (Luke xiii. 16), and the highest and most precious view of the future life to the Jews seems to have been "Abraham's bosom" (Luke xvi. 22). We can see from all this how profound was the Jewish reverence for their great ancestor. The pride was in some respects perfectly natural and legitimate, though in the result it became a stumbling-block and a danger to them, since they rested in their lineal descent and forgot the need of spiritual affinity and kinship.

The above passages are concerned with general references to Abraham. In the four passages that follow he is used by the writers for the purpose of conveying special spiritual teaching, and it is to be noted carefully that each passage by itself has one main thought about Abraham. There is no repetition, but four different aspects of his spiritual life are dwelt upon.

His Righteousness by Faith (Rom. iv.).—This is the main thought of the entire chapter, in which the Apostle sets out to prove that Abraham became righteous not by works but by faith. Righteousness in Romans, as also in Genesis xv., is much more than justifica-

tion, and from first to last we are to understand that Abraham became righteous by faith in God (vers. 3, 13, 21, 22).

His Spiritual Seed (Gal. iii.; iv. 22-31).—Another aspect of
Abraham's life is here considered. The key-thought of the whole
passage is the relation of Abraham to the great spiritual seed of
believers of whom he is the father (iii. 9, 16, 26, 29; iv. 31). The
Apostle is emphasizing the great outstanding reality of spiritual
kinship with Abraham through faith, and all that faith brings of
sonship to God and liberty.

His Life of Faith (Heb. xi. 8-19).—It is interesting to notice
that three times in the New Testament the words of the prophet,
"The just shall live by faith" (Hab. ii. 4), are quoted, but each
time with a special emphasis. Taking the words as they stand in
the Greek, "The just by faith shall live," we notice that in Romans
i. 17 the emphasis is on *"the just"*; in Galatians iii. 11 it is on
"by faith"; in Hebrews x. 38 it is on *"shall live"*; and the result is
that the great chapter, Hebrews xi., is concerned with illustrations
of the life of faith—that is, with faith as the spiritual principle and
power of the entire life of the believer from the beginning to the
end. Consequently Abraham is there described as manifesting
various characteristics of the attitude of faith—*e.g.* his obedience of
faith (ver. 8); his patience of faith (ver. 9); his expectation of faith
(ver. 10); his consecration of faith (ver. 17). The entire passage
shows the various ways in which faith manifests itself as the fundamental power of daily living.

His Faith and Works (Jas. ii. 21-24).—This passage, as is well
known, has given rise to great controversy, but there surely was no
need of much difference of opinion. St. Paul uses the story recorded
in Genesis xv. as a proof that Abraham was justified by faith. St.
James uses the event recorded in Genesis xxii., which occurred
twenty-five years after, as a proof that Abraham was justified by
works. Seeing, then, that for twenty-five years Abraham's relationship with God was of faith, it is evident that Genesis xxii. is the

crown and culmination of that faith, and is proved by Abraham's act of offering Isaac. "Faith wrought with his works, and by works was faith made perfect" (Jas. ii. 22). Works are the evidential proof of faith. As Calvin has aptly said, while it is faith alone that justifies, the faith that justifies is never alone.

Let us now sum up the entire record of Abraham's life as found in Holy Scripture, and dwell upon it from God's standpoint and from his own. We may see in it a revelation of true life.

1. *Life's choicest privilege.*—What is this? It is to be associated with God, as was Abraham; to be lifted up into union with God and into fellowship with His Divine purposes of blessing for the world. We can easily imagine what Abraham would have been without this privilege. Now, however, he is forever associated with God, and God is called "the God of Abraham" (Luke xx. 37). Such is the case with every believer. God lifts him out of the mire of sin and raises him to a position of high privilege, transforming his life and enabling him to realize the Divine will.

2. *Life's strong foundation.*—What is this? It is God's covenant with man. This was at the basis of everything with Abraham. This, too, was what David rested on and rejoiced in; "the everlasting covenant, ordered in all things and sure" (2 Sam. xxiii. 5). This is still the foundation of the believer's life and tower of hope, the new covenant in Christ (Heb. viii. 10-12). A life lived in the consciousness of an everlasting covenant made between God the Father and God the Son on behalf of the believer and sealed to him by the Holy Spirit makes life strong, peaceful, and satisfied.

3. *Life's greatest glory.*—What is this? It is faithfulness to God. The one thing needful is not success, but sincerity; not glory, but goodness; not honor, but holiness. A humble, consistent, earnest life, lived to the praise of God, is the greatest life that can be lived; and this, on the whole, was the characteristic of Abraham's life. He witnessed to the reality of God and His grace.

4. *Life's simple secret.*—What is this? It is faith—faith believing God's word and trusting God Himself. Faith rests on God,

receives from God, responds to God, relies on God, realizes God, rejoices in God, and reproduces His life and character. In proportion to our faith will everything else be. "By faith" is the simple but all-embracing secret of daily living. So it was with Abraham, so it has ever been, so it ever will be until "Faith is changed to sight and hope with glory crowned."

XXXIV

THE BIRTH OF JACOB

GEN. xxv. 11-28

11. And it came to pass after the death of Abraham, that God blessed his son Isaac; and Isaac dwelt by the well Lahai-roi.

12. Now these *are* the generations of Ishmael, Abraham's son, whom Hagar the Egyptian, Sarah's handmaid, bare unto Abraham:

13. And these *are* the names of the sons of Ishmael, by their names, according to their generations: the firstborn of Ishmael, Nebajoth; and Kedar, and Adbeel, and Mibsam,

14. And Mishma, and Dumah. and Massa,

15. Hadar, and Tema, Jetur, Naphish, and Kedemah:

16. These *are* the sons of Ishmael, and these *are* their names, by their towns, and by their castles; twelve princes according to their nations.

17. And these *are* the years of the life of Ishmael, an hundred and thirty and seven years: and he gave up the ghost and died; and was gathered unto his people.

18. And they dwelt from Havilah unto Shur, that *is* before Egypt, as thou goest toward Assyria: *and* he died in the presence of all his brethren.

19. And these *are* the generations of Isaac, Abraham's son: Abraham begat Isaac:

20. And Isaac was forty years old when he took Rebekah to wife, the daughter of Bethuel the Syrian of Padan-aram, the sister to Laban the Syrian.

21. And Isaac intreated the Lord for his wife, because she *was* barren: and the Lord was intreated of him, and Rebekah his wife conceived.

22. And the children struggled together within her; and she said, If *it be* so, why *am* I thus? And she went to enquire of the Lord.

23. And the Lord said unto her, Two nations *are* in thy womb, and two manner of people shall be separated from thy bowels; and *the one* people shall be stronger than *the other* people; and the elder shall serve the younger.

24. And when her days to be delivered were fulfilled, behold, *there were* twins in her womb.

25. And the first came out red, all over like an hairy garment; and they called his name Esau.

26. And after that came his brother out, and his hand took hold on Esau's heel; and his name was called Jacob: and Isaac *was* threescore years old when she bare them.

27. And the boys grew: and Esau was a cunning hunter, a man of the field; and Jacob *was* a plain man, dwelling in tents.

28. And Isaac loved Esau, because he did eat of *his* venison: but Rebekah loved Jacob.

"GOD buries His workmen and carries on His work." This is the simple but significant truth taught in the verse that immediately follows the record of the burial of Abraham. "And it came to pass after the death of Abraham that God blessed his son Isaac." God calls His servants to Himself, but His purposes abide. Abraham dies, but God lives, and the Divine blessing continues to rest upon the son of His servant. Abraham's seed was already experiencing the commencement of the fulfilment of the Divine promise, "In thee and in thy seed shall all the families of the earth be blessed." We have now to follow the course of the Divine purpose and see how it was carried out; how the unchanging God continued with His servants, blessing them and fulfilling His own word of truth and grace.

The second half of Genesis contains the generations of Ishmael (xxv. 12-18), of Isaac (xxv. 19—xxxv. 29), of Esau (xxxvi. 1-43), and of Jacob (xxxvii. 2—l. 26). The record deals very briefly with the stories of Ishmael and Esau, the brevity indicating the definite purpose of Genesis, which is to show the fulfilment of the promise to Abraham and the development of God's purpose of redemption (iii. 15).

The lives of Abraham and Jacob stand out prominently in the record. Of Isaac much less is said. His life was practically devoid of striking incident, his character was quiet and passive, and, except as a link in the chain of the fulfilment of the Abrahamic promise, he is of no special importance in the patriarchal history. It is different with Jacob. God is known as the God of Abraham, but still more definitely as the God of Jacob. The latter title is particularly appropriate in view of the fact that Jacob was the direct and immediate ancestor of the twelve tribes of Israel.

The life of Jacob is of interest and value, not merely as revelation of human character, but also and chiefly as a manifestation of Divine grace. Viewed from the standpoint of his nature, Jacob is unattractive and even repulsive; but as we study his history step by step we become conscious that God's grace is at work, moulding and fashioning him by the discipline of sorrow, suffering, and loss. There is no character in Holy Scripture which more clearly manifests the glory of Divine grace in dealing with the most forbidding of materials. And because the record in Genesis holds the mirror up to nature and also reveals the glory of grace, the story of Jacob has a perennial interest for us all. We see ourselves in the story of Jacob; our weaknesses, and yet our aspirations; our failures, and yet our fresh starts; our cowardice, and yet our endeavour to trust God.

At the point at which we take up the story of Genesis, we are introduced to the family life of the patriarch Isaac. He has been married many years, his father is still alive, and nothing of moment in connection with the development of the Divine purposes seems to have occurred since the day of his marriage. Consider carefully each element in this picture of family life.

I. *The Husband* (vers. 20, 21).—Isaac was experiencing a great disappointment. It was now nearly twenty years (ver. 26) since that memorable day when he first saw the wife of God's choice. And yet his home was still without a child. Year after year had passed, and there was no fulfilment of the Divine promise. This was a real trial and a definite test of his faith. The Divine message had been clear that in Isaac, not in Ishmael, Abraham's seed was to be called; and yet now it seemed almost impossible that the promise could be fulfilled. God's delays, however, are not necessarily denials, and the fulfilment of the promise was not the only element in the Divine purpose. The training of faith and the discipline of character were also in view, and we feel sure God delayed the fulfilment of His word in order that all human hope which rested solely on natural powers should give way, and the Divine action might be made still more prominent.

In his difficulty and trial Isaac did the very best possible thing; he took it to the Lord in prayer.

The answer soon came. God had only been testing His servant's faith, and we are clearly intended to understand that the gift of the children was a definite grant from God, a Divine interposition in order to make it still more evident that the promise to Abraham was by grace and not by nature. God often delays in the bestowal of His grace in order that we may the more thoroughly rely upon

Him and the more definitely realize that our expectation is from Him, and not merely from secondary causes or natural laws.

II. *The Wife* (vers. 22, 23).—Even now everything was not clear, and it was Rebekah's turn to experience distress and perplexity. She could not understand God's dealings with her, and wondered as to the cause of it. Like her husband, however, she did the very best thing; she turned to God and inquired of Him. How often it has occurred since that day that God's children have received answers from Him very different from what they have expected, and have experienced perplexity as to the meaning of the Divine discipline! Sometimes in the pathway of duty, when the soul is sincerely conscious of uprightness and whole-hearted consecration to God, there is trouble, trial, difficulty, and anxiety. A man believes he has been right in following a certain pathway, only to find himself surrounded by almost overwhelming anxieties and difficulties. The forces of evil seem more active than ever, and he begins to wonder whether he was right, after all, in doing what he has done. Like Rebekah, he must again resort to God and seek out the Divine will.

The answer is very striking. Rebekah was taught that her trouble involved great and far-reaching results. She was first of all told that she was to have two sons, not one; then that the two sons would represent two nations which are to be opposed to each other from the very first; and, last of all, that the elder was to serve the younger. Thus Rebekah was the unconscious instrument of carrying out the Divine purpose. Her trouble had nothing whatever to do with herself individually, but was part of a great Divine plan which God was about to work out for His own glory.

In all this we see the marvel and glory of the Divine sovereignty. Why the younger son should have been chosen instead of the elder we do not know. It is, however, very striking to find the same principle exercised on several other occasions. It is pretty certain that Abraham was not the eldest son of Terah. We know that Isaac was the younger son of Abraham, and that Joseph was not the eldest son of Jacob. All this goes to emphasize the simple but significant fact that the order of nature is not necessarily the order of grace. All through, God desired to display the sovereignty of His grace as contrasted with that which was merely natural in human life. The great problem of Divine sovereignty is of course insoluble by human intellect. It has to be accepted as a simple fact. It should, however, be observed that it is not merely a fact in regard to things spiritual; it is found also in nature in connection with human temperaments and races. All history is full of illustrations of the Divine choice, as we may see from such examples as Cyrus and Pharaoh. Divine election is a fact, whether we can understand it or not. God's purposes are as certain as they are often inscrutable, and it is perfectly evident from the case of Esau and Jacob that the Divine choice of men is entirely independent of their merits or of any pre-vision of their merits or attainments (Rom. ix. 11). It is in connection with this subject that we see the real force of St. Paul's striking words when he speaks of God as acting "according to the *good pleasure* of His will" (Eph. i. 5); and although we are bound to confess the *"mystery* of His will" (Eph. i. 9), we are also certain that He works all things "after the *counsel* of His will" (Eph. i. 11). There is nothing arbitrary about God and His ways, and our truest wisdom when we cannot understand His reasons is to rest quietly and trustfully, saying, "Even so, Father, for so it seemeth good in Thy sight." "In His Will is our peace."

III. *The Sons* (vers. 24-28).—From the moment of their birth the sons differed in appearance, and their unlikeness was a symbol of that hostility which characterized their after-life and the history of their descendants. The outward signs were expressive of real differences. As they grew they were also very different in pursuits, Esau being a clever hunter, a man of outdoor life; while Jacob was just the opposite—a quiet (Revised Version, margin), home-keeping man. Their names were given with reference to the facts which were evident at their birth. Esau was so called because of his hairy aspect, and Jacob from his laying hold of his brother's heel at their very entrance upon life.

They also differed in regard to the paternal affection bestowed upon them. Esau was his father's favorite, Jacob his mother's. Isaac, the quiet, passive man, saw in Esau, the bold hunter, the energetic nature of the woman whom he had loved as a wife all those years. Rebekah, the strong, self-assertive woman, saw in the quiet, gentle Jacob the quiet, passive husband whom she had loved so long. It is often found that the father loves the boy or girl who resembles the mother, while the mother is frequently found to favor the boy or girl whose nature is most akin to the father; but when, as in this case, partiality is carried to great extremes, nothing but trouble can be the result. God's revelation about the younger ruling the elder was obviously no secret. Both parents and sons must have known of it, and it is this knowledge that makes the partiality more heinous, and at the same time more deplorable in its results.

1. *In times of difficulty or perplexity let us wait and pray.*—Both Isaac and Rebekah experienced the real difficulty of not knowing how God's will and purpose were to be fulfilled. They did the very best possible thing; they handed their difficulty over to God in trust and prayer. In the midst of perplexity it is not wise or well to be too much occupied in telling others of our troubles. Our wisdom and comfort will be found in telling the Lord Himself. "Half the breath thus vainly spent" should be sent to Heaven in supplication. Waiting for God and waiting on God will always be our greatest consolation.

2. *In the face of deep problems of life let us trust and pray.*—Rebekah could not understand the circumstances which were causing difficulty and anxiety; and even after the revelation of God concerning the younger son there must have been not a little perplexity to know the meaning of it all. Our greatest wisdom in all such circumstances is found in simple trust and earnest prayer. God's ways are not our ways, nor His thoughts our thoughts (Isa. lv. 8). We may perhaps have no real thought beyond our own little horizon, but it may be that God is working out His purpose through us on a large scale. What matters it what we endure, so long as God's will is being done through us? Let us abide in humble trust and hopeful prayer and "believe to see the goodness of the Lord in the land of the living."

3. *In the presence of home troubles and trials let us watch and pray.*—Isaac and Rebekah clearly brought upon themselves a great

deal of their trouble by their partiality for the sons, and when home life is thus disturbed by jealousies and quarreling we may be sure that God's blessing is withheld. "Watch and pray lest ye enter into temptation" is as important in connection with home life as it is with anything else, and those are most likely to meet all such difficulties successfully who *watch* that the enemy shall not take occasion to lead them astray, and who *pray* for needed grace daily to do the will of God.

XXXV

THE BIRTHRIGHT

GEN. xxv. 29-34.

29. And Jacob sod pottage: and Esau came from the field, and he *was* faint:
30. And Esau said to Jacob, Feed me, I pray thee, with that same red *pottage;* for I *am* faint: therefore was his name called Edom.
31. And Jacob said, Sell me this day thy birthright.
32. And Esau said, Behold, I *am* at the point to die; and what profit shall this birthright do to me?
33. And Jacob said, Swear to me this day; and he sware unto him: and he sold his birthright unto Jacob.
34. Then Jacob gave Esau bread and pottage of lentils; and he did eat and drink, and rose up, and went his way: thus Esau despised *his* birthright.

THE revelation of the Divine will concerning the two brothers (ver. 23) was evidently no secret. It is clear that both Esau and Jacob knew of it. This fact is in some respects the key to the true interpretation of this incident.

I. *The Bargain of the Brothers.*—The contrast in appearance which marked the two boys was continued in their characters as men. Their daily pursuits were expressive of their natures and temperaments. Esau comes in one day from hunting, tired and hungry. The savour of the pottage is enticing, and the hungry and weary man cries out to his brother to feed him with that red stuff of which he does not even know the name. Now is Jacob's opportunity, for which he has probably been waiting. He had doubtless already taken his brother's measure and knew how to deal with him, and so he proposes a bargain: "Sell me this day thy birthright." The birthright seems to have included temporal and spiritual blessings; it carried with it a double portion of the paternal inheritance (Deut. xxi. 17; 1 Chron. v. 1, 2); it gave the holder precedence as head of the family or tribe; above all, it constituted the possessor priest and spiritual head of his people. All this Jacob evidently knew, and in the light of what God had said to his mother he already appreciated the value of the birthright.

It is not at all improbable that long before this moment Esau had learned to set little store by the family privileges which belonged to him as the firstborn son. To him the position and opportunity meant little or nothing; and now he impulsively cries out that as the birthright is of no profit to him, since he is at the point of death, he is willing to sell it for a meal of red lentils. It seems clear from the narrative that there was no likelihood whatever of his dying for want of food. The words are expressive of his utter disregard of and indifference to the position and privileges associated with the birthright.

Jacob, knowing his brother's weakness and bearing in mind the issues involved in the transaction, calls upon Esau to take a solemn oath. This Esau is quite ready to do, and so the transaction is closed. He sold his birthright and in return received the meal that he so eagerly desired. "Thus Esau despised his birthright." In these few words we have the illuminating touch which explains the whole position. This was no sudden impulse on the part of Esau, just as it was no sudden brilliant idea on the part of Jacob. On the one hand, there was the attitude of despising the birthright and on the other the attitude of full appreciation. These things do not spring up suddenly and at once; they are plants of longer growth. It is this fact that compels us to go beneath the surface and try to discover the explanation of both sides of the transaction.

II. *The Characters of the Brothers.*—On the surface of the story Esau is a good specimen of the man of the world—frank, warm-hearted, and every inch a man. There is a superficial attractiveness about him, and we easily dub him a fine fellow. In reality, however, he was at once sensuous and sensual. The one word "profane" (Heb. xii. 16) in its literal meaning sums up his character. It come from *pro-fanum*, "outside the temple," and refers to that plot of ground just in front of the fane which was common to everyone, as being outside the sacred enclosure. Gradually the word came to mean that which was purely earthly and common, as opposed to that which was sacred, consecrated, and dedicated to God. Esau's life was entirely earth-bound. God was not in all his thoughts. He was intent only on present gratification, and set no value on the Divine gifts. To him future blessings were intangible and unreal, and as he thought he was going to die he did not see any reason why he should grasp at blessings which could never be personally enjoyed. Everything about the present was real to him, while everything about the future was unreal, vague, and misty; and so, whatever we may say about Jacob's part in the transaction, Esau cannot be exculpated. So far from being an injured man he really supplanted himself. To him this world was everything and God nothing.

"He is the kind of man of whom we are in the habit of charitably saying that he is nobody's enemy but his own. But, in truth, he is God's enemy, because he wastes the splendid manhood which God has given him. Passionate, impatient, impulsive, incapable of looking before him, refusing to estimate the worth of anything which does not immediately appeal to his senses, preferring the animal to the spiritual, he is rightly called a "profane person." "Alas!" while the body is so broad and brawny, must the soul lie blinded, dwarfed, stupefied, almost annihilated?" (Carlyle)."[1]

Jacob's character, on the other hand, was unattractive and even repulsive on the surface. He was cool and calculating, could hold his appetites and desires in check, and wait—if necessary for years—for the accomplishment of his purpose. He evidently knew his brother well, and had been watching his opportunity. When the psychological moment came he took advantage of it at once. All this tends to repel us from the man as unworthy and contemptible, and no one for a moment can doubt that his crafty and subtle method was in every way objectionable and deplorable. And yet underneath the surface there was not a little in him of an entirely opposite character. He had a keen and true appreciation of that which Esau despised. He realized the spiritual nature of the birthright; and though we utterly object to the method by which he attempted to obtain it we must never forget that his object was good, and that he desired to obtain that which he knew God intended for

---

1. Strachan, *Hebrew Ideals*, p. 23.

him. Thus Jacob was appreciative of the spiritual meaning of the birthright, and was at any rate to some extent truly sensitive to the Divine word. He wanted spiritual blessings, even though he went the wrong way to obtain them. He also shines out in contrast with his brother in his constancy. Esau was one of the most inconstant of men, everything by turns and nothing long, a shallow nature full of impulse and ungoverned feelings; today despising his birthright, tomorrow wanting it back; today absolutely indifferent, tomorrow sorrowing over his loss. Jacob on the other hand was tenacious and persistent, and possessed a reserve of strength which, even though it was often directed into wrong channels, was in itself one of the most valuable features of human life.

Thus while superficially we are attracted to Esau and repelled by Jacob, as we penetrate towards the depth of their characters we see the true natures of the brothers and their differences of attitude to and outlook on life and things spiritual.

1. *Lessons from Esau.*—(a) The real proof of life is personal character. It was the act in Esau's case that revealed the true state of affairs and showed what he was. We see in him "that inexorable law of human souls, that we are preparing ourselves for sudden deeds by the reiterated choice of good or evil that gradually determines character" (George Eliot). No one becomes base all at once, and we may be perfectly sure that Esau's character had already deteriorated before he made this choice. Character is continually growing, and when the crisis comes we act, not solely according to what we wish at the moment, but according to what we really are, for our wishes are the expressions of our actual character. Esau possessed no spiritual insight, no appreciation whatever of the blessings of the great Abrahamic covenant. He cared only for this life and for present enjoyment. The result was that when the test came the true man was revealed. According as he had lived previously, so his character showed itself.

> "The tissues of the life to be
>   We weave with colors all our own;
> And in the field of Destiny
>   We reap as we have sown."

(b) The supreme test of character is found in little things. It
seemed but a small matter, a feeling of hunger and a desire for
food, and yet it was the means of testing and revealing Esau's real
character. It is a sad and solemn picture, a strong man who cannot wait a moment for food and cries out to be fed. How often in
history have insignificant events been turning points of human lives!
We are tested more by trifles than by great crises. Many men can
shine in emergencies who are not able to stand the test of faithfulness in little things.

(c) The imperative necessity in life is to subdue the flesh to the
spirit. Esau failed to see, because he had lost the power to see,
that the mind and soul need food as well as the body. And if life
is "harmony with environment," then nothing purely physical can
nourish the soul. It is only too easy to crush and kill our higher
aspirations by undue attention to the demands of our lower nature.
This is true not only of the purely earth-bound like Esau, but also of
great and noble natures like Darwin's, who by absorption in intellectual pursuits become atrophied in taste and feeling. No part
of our complex nature must remain unnourished, but we must see
to it that physical and even intellectual enjoyments do not dwarf
and eventually kill the spiritual side of our being. When the animal
and spiritual collide, it will involve sacrifice if the spiritual is to be
considered. The little girl's explanation of St. Paul "keeping under
his body" was not far wrong: "by keeping his soul *on top*."

(d) The one thing needful is to put God first in our life. So
far as we can see, God had no place in the life of Esau. With all
his bodily vigor and general attractiveness there was one part of his
nature entirely uncultivated. He was God-less. He lived for the
present, not for the future; for things physical, not spiritual; for
time, not eternity. In this he is like many men today. They have
everything that this world can give—wealth, money, natural powers,
position—everything but God. And yet, with all their advantages,
they must necessarily fail. "In the beginning God." And when
God is first, then all else finds its place—purpose, power, and
perpetual peace and progress.

2. *Lessons from Jacob.*—(*a*) The necessity of right principle. Jacob's purpose in desiring the birthright was undoubtedly genuine and exemplary, but the way in which he went to work to obtain the birthright was in every way deplorable and wrong. He was one of the earliest, but unfortunately has not been by any means the last, of those who have considered that the end justifies the means. This is one of the deadliest foes of true living. The end does *not* justify the means; and right ends must always be accomplished by right means, or else left unaccomplished.

(*b*) The value of waiting for God. If only Jacob had been willing to wait God's time and way, what a difference it would have made to him! The birthright would have been his in any case, but he was unwilling to allow God to give it to him. How like we are to Jacob in this respect! We take God at His word, and yet we will not wait God's time; and the result is we bring untold sorrow and trouble upon ourselves and others. It is essential that we keep in view the two requirements of the true life, *faith and patience* (Heb. vi.). It is not enough to believe what God has said; we must "wait patiently for Him."

(*c*) The certainty of righteous retribution. We must never forget that God permitted Jacob no possession of the birthright until he had first of all acknowledged Esau as his lord (Gen. xxxii. 4, 5 ff.), and had renounced all claim to it as the result of this evil bargain. He did not enter upon the birthright until it came quite naturally into his possession after Esau had abandoned it (Gen. xxxvi. 6). How different his life would have been if only he had believed that God was able to carry out His purposes unaided—at least, unaided by cleverness and deceit!

(*d*) The conclusion of the whole matter is that the only guarantee of true living is God in the heart and life as absolutely and permanently supreme. When God dwells in the heart as Saviour, in the conscience as Master, in the life as Lord, then—and only then—do we become assured of the possession of God's spiritual birthright and of its enjoyment in God's own way.

XXXVI

ISAAC

GEN. xxvi. 1-33

1. And there was a famine in the land, beside the first famine that was in the days of Abraham. And Isaac went unto Abimelech king of the Philistines unto Gerar.

2. And the Lord appeared unto him, and said, Go not down into Egypt; dwell in the land which I shall tell thee of:

3. Sojourn in this land, and I will be with thee, and will bless thee; for unto thee, and unto thy seed, I will give all these countries, and I will perform the oath which I sware unto Abraham thy father;

4. And I will make thy seed to multiply as the stars of heaven, and will give unto thy seed all these countries; and in thy seed shall all the nations of the earth be blessed;

5. Because that Abraham obeyed my voice, and kept my charge, my commandments, my statutes, and my laws.

6. And Isaac dwelt in Gerar;

7. And the men of the place asked *him* of his wife; and he said, She *is* my sister: for he feared to say, *She is* my wife; lest, *said he,* the men of the place should kill me for Rebekah; because she *was* fair to look upon.

8. And it came to pass, when he had been there a long time, that Abimelech king of the Philistines looked out at a window, and saw, and, behold, Isaac *was* sporting with Rebekah his wife.

9. And Abimelech called Isaac, and said, Behold, of a surety she *is* thy wife: and how saidst thou, She *is* my sister? And Isaac said unto him, Because I said, Lest I die for her.

10. And Abimelech said, What *is* this thou hast done unto us? one of the people might lightly have lien with thy wife, and thou shouldest have brought guiltiness upon us.

11. And Abimelech charged all *his* people, saying, He that toucheth this man or his wife shall surely be put to death.

12. Then Isaac sowed in that land, and received in the same year an hundredfold: and the Lord blessed him.

13. And the man waxed great, and went forward, and grew until be became very great:

14. For he had possession of flocks, and possession of herds, and great store of servants: and the Philistines envied him.

15. For all the wells which his father's servants had digged in the days of Abraham his father, the Philistines had stopped them, and filled them with earth.

16. And Abimelech said unto Isaac, Go from us; for thou art much mightier than we.

17. And Isaac departed thence, and pitched his tent in the valley of Gerar, and dwelt there.

18. And Isaac digged again the wells of water, which they had digged in the days of Abraham his father; for the Philistines had stopped them after the death of Abraham: and he called their names after the names by which his father had called them.

19. And Isaac's servants digged in the valley, and found there a well of springing water.

20. And the herdman of Gerar did strive with Isaac's herdmen, saying, The water is our's: and he called the name of the well Esek; because they strove with him.

21. And they digged another well, and strove for that also: and he called the name of it Sitnah.

22. And he removed from thence, and digged another well; and for that they strove not: and he called the name of it Rehoboth; and he said, For now the Lord hath made room for us, and we shall be fruitful in the land.

23. And he went up from thence to Beer-sheba.

24. And the Lord appeared unto him the same night and said I am the God of Abraham, thy father: fear not, for I am with thee, and will bless thee, and multiply thy seed for my servant Abraham's sake.

25. And he builded an altar there, and called upon the name of the Lord, and pitched his tent there: and there Isaac's servants digged a well.

26. And Abimelech went to him from Gerar, and Ahuzzath one of his friends, and Phichol the chief captain of his army.

27. And Isaac said unto them, Wherefore come ye to me, seeing ye hate me, and have sent me away from you?

28. And they said, We saw certainly that the Lord was with thee: and we said, Let there be now an oath betwixt us, even betwixt us and thee, and let us make a covenant with thee;

29. That thou wilt do us no' hurt, as we have not touched thee, and as we have done unto thee nothing but good, and have sent thee away in peace: thou art now the blessed of the Lord.

30. And he made them a feast, and they did eat and drink.

31. And they rose up betimes in the morning, and sware one to another: and Isaac sent them away, and they departed from him in peace.

32. And it came to pass the same day, that Isaac's servants came, and told him concerning the well which they had digged, and said unto them, We have found water.

33. And he called it Shebah: therefore the name of the city is Beer-sheba unto this day.

ALTHOUGH Isaac lived the longest of all the patriarchs less is recorded of him than of the others. This is the only chapter exclusively devoted to his life. His was a quiet, peaceful, normal life. He was the ordinary son of a great father, and the ordinary

father of a great son. We are accustomed to speak of such lives as
commonplace and ordinary, and yet the ordinary life is the
"ordered" life, and in the truest sense the "ordained" life. Like
the rest of us, Isaac's experiences were marked by light and shade, by
sin and discipline, by grace and mercy. The chapter before us is
full of illustrations of how difficulties should and should not be met.

I. *Difficulty met by Divine Guidance* (vers. 1-5).—Once again
there arose a famine in the land of Canaan and the difficulty about
food quickly became urgent with Isaac and his large household.
Trials are permitted to come into the life of the best and holiest of
men, and it is by this means that God sometimes teaches His most
precious lessons. As the result of this famine Isaac left his home
and journeyed southwards into the land of the Philistines to Gerar.
The question naturally arises whether he was right in taking this
journey, whether he had consulted God about it, whether it was
undertaken by the will of God, or prompted by his own unaided
wisdom. In any case the Lord appeared to him and prevented
him from going further southward into Egypt as his father had
done under similar circumstances. "Go not down into Egypt."
Egypt was not the promised land, and there were dangers there
to body and to soul from which it was necessary that Isaac should
be safeguarded. With the prohibition came the definite Divine
instruction to remain in the land of Canaan, and the promises to
his father Abraham were thereupon repeated and confirmed. Careful study should be made of the various occasions on which the
Divine promise was given to Abraham, and then a comparison
should be instituted with these words to Isaac. It will then be
seen that each time there is some new feature of the Divine revelation and a confirmation of the Divine promise. It is impossible
to avoid asking the question whether in view of the sequel Isaac
was right in going even as far as to Gerar. It would almost seem
as though he had been walking by sight rather than by faith and
had not consulted God before starting out from home.

II. *Difficulty met by Human Sin* (vers. 6-11).—Isaac continued
to dwell in Gerar and it was not very long before he was asked
by the inhabitants of the place about his wife. Following his father's

evil example he told a deliberate lie and said, "She is my sister."
In this he was actuated by cowardly fear and by deplorable selfishness; "Lest the men of the place should kill me for Rebekah." It
is sometimes wondered how it was that Isaac did exactly what his
father before him had done, and the similarity of the circumstances has led some to think that this is only a variant of the
former story. Would it not be truer to say that this episode is
entirely consonant with what we know of human nature and its
tendencies? What would be more natural than that Isaac should
attempt to do what his father had done before him? Surely a little
knowledge of human nature as distinct from abstract theory is sufficient to warrant a belief in the historical character of this narrative. Besides, assuming that it is a variant of the other story, we
naturally ask which of them is the true version; they cannot both
be true, for as they now are they do not refer to the same event.
The names and circumstances are different in spite of similarities.

This belief in Rebekah as Isaac's sister was evidently held by the
people of Gerar for some time, for it was only after Isaac had been
there "a long time" that the King of the Philistines detected the
sin and became convinced that Isaac and Rebekah were husband and
wife. Like his predecessor before him Abimelech was a man of uprightness, for he very plainly rebuked Isaac and reminded him of the
serious consequences that might have accrued to him and to
Rebekah if the facts of the case had not become known. Is there
anything sadder in this world than that a child of God should be
rebuked by a man of the world? The corruption of the best is
indeed the worst, and when a believer sins and his sin has to be
pointed out to him by men who make no profession whatever of
religion, this is indeed to sound the depths of sorrow and disappointment. Abimelech took immediate steps to prevent any harm
coming to Isaac and Rebekah from what had been done, and it is
not difficult to imagine Isaac's feelings as he realized the results of
his deliberate untruth.

III. *Difficulty met by Divine Blessing* (vers. 12-17).—Isaac still
lived on at Gerar, and quite naturally occupied himself with his
daily agricultural work. He sowed seed, and in the very same year

received an hundredfold owing to the blessing of the Lord. This
was an exceptional result even for that exceptional land, and the
Divine blessing is of course the explanation. Not only so, but his
flocks grew and his household increased more and more "until he
became very great." This marked Divine blessing following soon
after his deliberate sin is at first sight a difficulty, for we naturally
ask how God's favor could possibly rest upon him so quickly after
the discovery of his grievous error. The answer may be found in a
somewhat frequent experience of the people of God. They are often
permitted to receive publicly a measure, and a great measure, of
the Divine blessing even when they may not be in private fully
faithful to the Divine will. God may at times honor His people in
the sight of men while dealing with them in secret on account of
their sins. As Richard Cecil once said, "A minister of Christ is
often in highest honor of men for the performance of one half of
his work, while God is regarding him with displeasure for the
neglect of the other half." It seems to have been something like
this with Isaac. In the presence of his enemies the Philistines God
indeed, "prepared a table" before him, but it is pretty evident from
what follows that God had other ways of dealing with him on account of his sin. God may not suffer His servants to be dishonored
before the world, but He will take care to discipline them in faithfulness, and even with severity in the secret of His fellowship with
them.

This prosperity soon had its inevitable outcome. "The Philistines
envied him," and this envy was shown in what was perhaps the
severest and most trying way. "All the wells which his father's
servants had digged in the days of Abraham his father, the Philistines
had stopped them and filled them with earth." The digging of
wells was a virtual claim to the possession of the land, and it was
this in particular that the Philistines resented. They were not prepared to allow Isaac to regard himself as in any sense the owner
of this property, and they therefore made it difficult and even impossible for him to remain there. Water especially for such a
household as his was an absolute necessity, and the stopping up of
the wells compelled him to take action. Abimelech too was not

happy about this increasing property, and begged Isaac to depart, saying that he was mightier than the Philistines. Isaac thereupon departed, and yet even then did not go back to his own home, but remained in the valley of Gerar and dwelt there. Once again we cannot help feeling conscious that Isaac was not exercising sufficient faith in the power of his father's God, or he would never have remained so near Gerar in the land of the Philistines.

IV. *Difficulty Met by Human Patience* (vers. 18-22).—This reluctance to go far away soon had its effect. Isaac was necessarily compelled to dig again the wells of water that had been stopped up, but this was at once met by a strife with the herdmen of Gerar for the possession of the wells. Again Isaac's herdmen dug a well, and the men of Gerar strove for that also. All this was evidently intended to make things uncomfortable for Isaac until he should be willing to return to his own home. Compelled by circumstances to make another move, a third attempt was made at well-digging, and at length the people of Gerar did not continue to strive. This was regarded by Isaac as a mark of Divine favor. "He called the name of it Rehoboth; and he said, For now the Lord hath made room for us, and we shall be fruitful in the land." The spirit of yielding is very noteworthy, more particularly as peacemakers are very rare in the East. A strife of this kind is scarcely ever likely to be met by such a spirit of willingness to yield. On the contrary, there is every likelihood of such action leading to further strife and insistence upon personal rights. God was at work gently but very definitely leading Isaac back again to his own home.

V. *Difficulty met by Divine Favor* (vers. 23-33).—At length Isaac was impelled, not to say compelled, to leave the land of the Philistines, "and he went up from thence to Beersheba." Let us observe carefully what follows these words. They are very striking and significant. "The Lord appeared unto him *the same night.*" Does not this show clearly that God never meant him to go even to Gerar? By this Divine appearance "the same night" it is evident that Isaac was at last in line with God's will, and could receive a Divine revelation. "I am the God of Abraham thy father: fear not, for I am with thee, and will bless thee, and multiply thy seed for

My servant Abraham's sake." This is the first time that we have the now familiar title, "the God of Abraham." Isaac is told not to fear, that he can rely upon the divine presence and blessing, and upon the fulfilment of the promise to his father Abraham. When God's servants get right with Him they are certain to receive His full revelation of truth and grace. "The secret of the Lord is with them that fear Him, and He will show them His covenant."

Isaac at once responded to this Divine revelation. "He builded an altar there, and called upon the Name of the Lord, and pitched his tent there: and there Isaac's servants digged a well." Let us mark carefully these four stages in the patriarch's restored life. First comes the altar with its thought of consecration, then prayer with its consciousness of need, then the tent with its witness to home, and then comes the well with its testimony to daily life and needs. The altar and the home sum up everything that is true in life. First the altar and then the home, not first the home and then the altar. God must be first in everything.

Personal blessing from God and the consciousness of a life right with God were not the only result of Isaac's return to Beersheba. "Then Abimelech went to him from Gerar." The point of time is very noteworthy, "*Then* Abimelech went," that is, when Isaac had returned to the pathway of God's will, those who were formerly his enemies came to him and bore their testimony to the presence of God with him. Isaac naturally asked why they had come, seeing that they had sent him away from them. Their reply is very significant, "We saw plainly that the Lord was with thee . . . thou art now the blessed of the Lord." How true it is that "when a man's ways please the Lord He maketh even his enemies to be at peace with him." It is scarcely possible to doubt in view of all these verses record that Isaac ought never to have left his home, but should have trusted God to keep him in spite of the famine in the land. But at last he was right with God, and both Divine favor and human acceptance wait upon him. He responded with alacrity to the desire of Abimelech for a covenant of peace, and after a feast of fellowship his visitors departed from him in peace. When God is honored by man, man is always honored by God.

Isaac's life, as recorded in this chapter, is full of simple yet searching lessons for people who, like him, are called upon to live ordinary, every-day lives.

1. *The Secret of true living is here revealed.*—God must at all costs be first. Divine revelation is the foundation of all true life, and Divine guidance is its only safety. Not a step must be taken without His direction, not a work undertaken without His grace and blessing. "In the beginning God" must actuate and dominate every life that seeks to live to His glory. It is a profound mistake to think that we need only concern ourselves with God's will in the great events, the crises of life. The story of Isaac shows with unmistakable clearness that there is nothing too trivial for God's guidance, and nothing too small for the need of His grace and power.

2. *The need of strength of character is here emphasized.*—There is always a very serious peril in being the son of a great father. Life is apt to be made too easy, and the son often occupies his father's position without having had his father's experience. Isaac entered upon his inheritance without having passed through the various ways of discipline that Abraham experienced, and the result was that things were so easy for him that he did not realize the need of individuality of character and definite personal assertion of himself in the Divine life. In opening the wells that had been filled up he was copying Abraham's example without obtaining Abraham's success, and he was doubtless thereby taught that it was necessary for him to have a personal hold on God and duty for himself instead of merely imitating what his father had done. It is always dangerous when life is made too simple and easy for young people; "it is good for a man to bear the yoke in his youth," and it was the absence of this yoke that doubtless ministered in great measure to that weakness of character which seems to have marked Isaac almost throughout his whole life.

3. *The importance of separation from the world is here seen.*—As long as Isaac was in or near Gerar he did not experience much

happiness. He was envied, thwarted, and opposed by the jealous Philistines. He was wanting not only in happiness but also in power, for it was not until he returned to Beersheba that Abimelech came to him bearing testimony to his conviction that God was with Isaac and blessing him. Thus for happiness, comfort and power with others, separation from the world is an absolute necessity. There is no greater mistake possible than to imagine that we can be one with the world and yet influence them for Christ. Lot found out this mistake to his cost, and so it has ever been. Separation from the world, paradoxical though it may seem, is the only true way of influencing the world for Christ. We must be in the world but not of the world if we would glorify God, bring blessing to our own souls, and be the means of blessing to others.

IV. *The spirit of meekness is here illustrated.*—It is noteworthy that all through his life Isaac's temperament was of a passive rather than of an active nature. During his childhood he was subject to the insults of Ishmael, in his manhood he was taken to Moriah and bound there for sacrifice, and a wife was chosen for him by his father. He accepted the rebuke of Abimelech with meekness, he and his servants yielded to the Philistines about the well, and in his later life we can see the same spirit of passive yielding in his relations with Rebekah and his two sons. And yet in spite of all this meekness the Philistines testified to him as a man of power and might, and begged that he would not do them any harm. What a testimony this is to the spirit of true gentleness and meekness. The world thinks very little of meekness, but it is one of the prime graces of Christianity. "Let your sweet reasonableness be known unto all men" is the apostolic word echoing the Master's beatitude, "Blessed are the meek for they shall inherit the earth." Not only so, but this meekness is an echo of God's own life, for does not the Psalmist say "Thy gentleness hath made me great"? As the French aphorism truly says, *La douceur est une force.* Meekness means the self-sacrifice of our own desires and interests, and in this spirit of gentleness is the secret of truest character and finest victory over self and others. Egoism is always a cause of weakness, for a constant consideration of ourselves is so absorbing that it tends to rob us of the very finest powers of our character. On the other hand, as we cease to regard self and concentrate attention upon others we find our own character becoming stronger as it becomes more unselfish, and with that is quickly added influence over others, and a beautiful recommendation of the grace of our Lord Jesus Christ.

XXXVII

THE BLESSING

GEN. xxvii. 1-40

1. And it came to pass, that when Isaac was old, and his eyes were dim, so that he could not see, he called Esau his eldest son, and said unto him, My son: and he said unto him, Behold, *here am* I.

2. And he said, Behold now, I am old, I know not the day of my death:

3. Now therefore take, I pray thee, thy weapons, thy quiver and thy bow, and go out to the field, and take me *some* venison;

4. And make me savoury meat, such as I love, and bring *it* to me, that I may eat; that my soul may bless thee before I die.

5. And Rebekah heard when Isaac spake to Esau his son. And Esau went to the field to hunt *for* venison, *and* to bring *it.*

6. And Rebekah spake unto Jacob her son, saying, Behold, I heard thy father speak unto Esau thy brother, saying,

7. Bring me venison, and make me savoury meat, that I may eat, and bless thee before the Lord before my death.

8. Now therefore, my son, obey my voice according to that which I command thee.

9. Go now to the flock, and fetch me from thence two good kids of the goats; and I will make them savoury meat for thy father, such as he loveth:

10. And thou shalt bring *it* to thy father, that he may eat, and that he may bless thee before his death.

11. And Jacob said to Rebekah his mother, Behold, Esau my brother *is* a hairy man, and I *am* a smooth man:

12. My father peradventure will feel me, and I shall seem to him as a deceiver; and I shall bring a curse upon me, and not a blessing.

13. And his mother said unto him, Upon me *be* thy curse, my son; only obey my voice, and go fetch me *them.*

14. And he went, and fetched, and brought *them* to his mother: and his mother made savoury meat, such as his father loved.

15. And Rebekah took goodly raiment of her eldest son Esau, which *were* with her in the house, and put them upon Jacob her younger son:

16. And she put the skins of the kids of the goats upon his hands, and upon the smooth of his neck:

17. And she gave the savoury meat and the bread, which she had prepared, into the hand of her son Jacob.

18. And he came unto his father, and said, My father: and he said, Here *am* I; who *art* thou, my son?

19. And Jacob said unto his father, I *am* Esau thy firstborn; I have done according as thou badest me: arise, I pray thee, sit and eat of my venison, that thy soul may bless me.

20. And Isaac said unto his son, How *is it* that thou hast found *it* so quickly, my son? And he said, Because the Lord thy God brought *it* to me.

21. And Isaac said unto Jacob, Come near, I pray thee, that I may feel thee, my son, whether thou *be* my very son Esau or not.

22. And Jacob went near unto Isaac his father; and he felt him, and said, The voice *is* Jacob's voice, but the hands *are* the hands of Esau.

23. And, he discerned him not, because his hands were hairy, as his brother Esau's hands: so he blessed him.

24. And he said, *Are* thou my very son Esau? And he said, I *am*.

25. And he said, Bring *it* near to me, and I will eat of my son's venison, that my soul may bless thee. And he brought *it* near to him, and he did eat: and he brought him wine, and he drank.

26. And his father Isaac said unto him, Come near now, and kiss me, my son.

27. And he came near, and kissed him: and he smelled the smell of his raiment, and blessed him. and said, See, the smell of my son *is* as the smell of a field which the Lord hath blessed:

28. Therefore God give thee of the dew of heaven, and the fatness of the earth, and plenty of corn and wine:

29. Let people serve thee, and nations bow down to thee: be lord over thy brethren, and let thy mother's sons bow down to thee: cursed *be* every one that curseth thee, and blessed *be* he that blesseth thee.

30. And it came to pass, as soon as Isaac had made an end of blessing Jacob, and Jacob was yet scarce gone out from the presence of Isaac his father, that Esau his brother came in from his hunting.

31. And he also had made savoury meat, and brought it unto his father, and said unto his father, Let my father arise, and eat of his son's venison, that thy soul may bless me.

32. And Isaac his father said unto him, Who *art* thou? And he said, I *am* thy son, thy firstborn Esau.

33. And Isaac trembled very exceedingly, and said, Who? where *is* he that hath taken venison, and brought *it* me, and I have eaten of all before thou camest, and have blessed him? yea, *and* he shall be blessed.

34. And when Esau heard the words of his father, he cried with a great and exceeding bitter cry, and said unto his father, Bless me, *even* me also, O my father!

35. And he said, Thy brother came with subtilty, and hath taken away thy blessing.

36. And he said, Is not he rightly named Jacob? for he hath supplanted me these two times: he took away my birthright; and behold, now he hath taken away my blessing. And he said, hast thou not reserved a blessing for me?

37. And Isaac answered and said unto Esau, Behold, I have made him thy lord, and all his brethren have I given to him for servants; and with corn and wine have I sustained him: and what shall I do now unto thee, my son?

38 And Esau said unto his father, Hast thou but one blessing, my father? bless me, *even* me also, O my father; And Esau lifted up his voice, and wept.

39. And Isaac his father answered, and said unto him, Behold, thy dwelling shall be the fatness of the earth, and of the dew of heaven from above;
40. And by thy sword shalt thou live, and shalt serve thy brother; and it
shall come to pass when thou shalt have the dominion, that thou shalt break
his yoke from off thy neck.

NOWHERE, perhaps, is the real character of the Bible more
evident than in this chapter. The story is given in all its
naked simplicity, and, although no precise moral is pointed, the
incidents carry their own solemn lesson to every reader. All four
persons concerned with the history are portrayed without hesitation
or qualification, and the narrative makes its profound impression upon the reader by its simple but significant recital of facts. It is an
unpleasant picture that we have here presented to us, a family life
full of jealousy and deceit. If love is not found in the home, where
may we expect it? And if, in particular, jealousies are found associated with the profession of faith in God, how terrible is the
revelation!

I. *The Father's Plot* (vers. 1-4).—Isaac's part in the history here
recorded is sometimes overlooked, and yet it is evident that he was
in large measure responsible for the sad results. In the time of old
age he calls his elder son and speaks of his own approaching death,
inviting his son to prepare food that he may eat, and at the same
time give his elder son the parental and patriarchal blessing. There
does not seem to have been any real sign of approaching death,
and, as a matter of fact, Isaac lived for over forty years after this
event. The hurry and secrecy which characterized his action are
also suspicious, and not the least of the sad and deplorable elements
is the association of old age with feasting, personal gratification,
and self-will. It is perfectly clear that he knew of the purposes of
God concerning his younger son (xxv. 23), and yet here we find
him endeavoring to thwart that purpose by transferring the blessing from the one for whom it was divinely designed. This partiality
for Esau, combined with his own fleshly appetite, led the patriarch
into grievous sin, and we cannot but observe how his action set
fire to the whole train of evils that followed in the wake of his
proposal.

Esau was quite ready to fall in with his father's suggestion. He must have at once recalled the transaction with his brother whereby the birthright had been handed over to Jacob. He must also have known the divine purpose concerning him and his brother; and although his marriage with a Canaanitish woman had still further disqualified him for spiritual primogeniture, it mattered nothing so long as he could recover what he now desired to have. He realized at last the value of that which his brother had obtained from him, and he is prompt to respond to his father's suggestion, since he sees in it the very opportunity of regaining the lost birthright.

II. *The Mother's Counter-Plot* (vers. 5-17).—We have now to observe with equal care the part played by Rebekah. Isaac had evidently not counted on his wife's overhearing his proposal to Esau, nor had he thought of the possibility of her astuteness vanquishing his plot. It is necessary that we should be perfectly clear about Rebekah's part in this transaction. Her object was to preserve for Jacob the blessing that God intended for him. Her design, therefore, was perfectly legitimate, and there can be very little doubt that it was inspired by a truly religious motive. She thought that the purpose of God was in danger, and that there was no other way of preventing a great wrong being done. It was a crisis in her life and in that of Jacob, and she was prepared to go the entire length of enduring the Divine curse so long as her favorite son could retain the blessing that God intended for him. Yet when all this is said, and it should be continually borne in mind, the sin of Rebekah's act was utterly inexcusable. We may account for it, but we cannot justify it. She was one of those who take upon themselves to regard God as unable to carry out His own purposes, thinking that either He has forgotten, or else that His will can really be frustrated by human craft and sin. And so she dared to do this remarkably bold thing. She proved herself to be quite as clever as Isaac and Esau.

Jacob's compliance was not immediate and hearty, for he evidently perceived the very real risk that he was running (ver. 12). He also saw the sin of it in the sight of God, and feared lest after all he should bring upon himself the Divine curse instead of the Divine blessing. Yet, influenced and overpowered by the stronger nature of the mother, he at length accepted the responsibility for this act, and proceeded to carry out his mother's plans.

III. *The Younger Son's Deception* (vers. 18-29).—The preparations were quickly and skilfully made, and Jacob approached his father with the food that his mother had prepared for him. The bold avowal that he was the first-born was persisted in, and his aged father entirely deceived. Lie follows lie, for Jacob had to pay the price of lies by being compelled to lie on still. Nothing in its way is more awful than this deception. We pity Jacob as the victim of his mother's love, but we scorn and deplore his action as the violation of his conscience and the silencing of his better nature. The terrible thoroughness with which he carried out his mother's plans is one of the most hideous features of the whole story.

The father's benediction is now given; and although it is mainly couched in terms of temporal blessing, we see underlying it the thought of that wider influence suggested by the promise of universal blessing given to Abraham and his seed.

IV. *The Elder Son's Defeat* (vers. 30-40).—It was not long before the true state of affairs came out. Isaac must have been astonished at the discovery for more than one reason. He had thought doubtless that in blessing, as he considered, his elder son, he had overreached both Rebekah and Jacob, and now he finds after all that the Divine purpose has been accomplished in spite of his own wilful attempt to divert the promise from Jacob. It is, however, to Isaac's credit that he meekly accepts the inevitable, and is now quite prepared to realize that God's will must be done.

We are not surprised at Esau's behavior, for we know the true character of the man. His bitter lamentation was due to the mortification he felt at being beaten. His cry of disappointment was probably, if not certainly, due to the fact that he had lost the temporal advantage of the birthright and blessing, not that he had lost the spiritual favor of God associated with it. His indignation at Jacob, like all other anger, is characterized by untruth; for whilst Jacob undoubtedly supplanted him, the taking away of the birthright was as much his own free act as it was due to Jacob's superior cleverness. We cannot help being touched by his tearful request to his father to give him even now a blessing. He realizes, when it is too late, what has been done, and although a partial blessing is bestowed upon him it is quite beyond all possibility that things can be as he had desired them to be. Esau had despised his birthright, but, however it came about, he was evidently conscious of the value of the blessing; and when the New Testament tells us that "he found no place for repentance," it means, of course, that there was no possibility of undoing what had been accomplished. He found no way to change his father's mind, though he sought earnestly to bring this about (Heb. xii. 17). There is a sense in which the past is utterly irretrievable, and it is only very partially true that "we may be what we might have been."

We have been concerned mainly with the four human actors in this family drama, and we have seen how one after another was dealt with; but that which lies behind the entire narrative is the thought of the God who reigns and rules over all. What does God teach us from this whole story?

1. "Let us *not* do evil that good may come." Right objects must be brought about by right means. It is one of the most remarkable features of human life in all ages that lofty purposes have been associated with the most sordid of methods, and one proof of this is found in that intolerable phrase "pious fraud." Yet clearly one of these words always contradicts the other. If a thing is pious it cannot be a fraud; if a thing is a fraud it cannot be pious. We must not convert our opponent by using untruth as an argument, we dare not win victories for Christ by any unworthy efforts. As it has been well said, the heights of gold must not be approached by steps of straw. Righteousness can never be laid aside, even though our object is yet more righteousness. In personal life, in home life, in Church life, in endeavors to win men for Christ, in missionary

enterprise, in social improvement, and in everything connected with the welfare of humanity we must insist upon absolute righteousness, purity, and truth in our methods, or else we shall bring utter discredit on the cause of our Master and Lord.

2. "Be sure your sin will find you out." This message is writ large on every line of the story. All four found this out to their cost, as we see in the subsequent history of Isaac, Rebekah, Jacob, and Esau. They were never the same afterwards, and their sins in some respects dogged their footsteps all the rest of their days. If only Isaac had realized this at the outset, how much he might have saved himself and his family!

"Oh! what a tangled web we weave,
When first we practise to deceive."

3. "Walk in the light as He is in the light." It has been well said (Eugene Stock, *Lesson Studies in Genesis*) that this chapter is a chapter of desires and devices. Isaac had his desires and devices; so had Rebekah, Jacob, and Esau. Each one of them attempts to accomplish their desires by means of the most unworthy devices; and sorrow, disappointment, trouble were the inevitable result. How different it would have been with them if they had lived in the presence of God! How different it always is with us if, instead of following the devices and desires of our own hearts, we are able to say like the Psalmist, "All my desires are before Thee"! For if only "we delight ourselves in the Lord" He will give us "the desires of our hearts." And as we delight ourselves in Him our desires become His desires, and His desires ours, by the transformation of Divine Grace.

4. "The Lord reigneth." This is perhaps the chief and fundamental lesson of the whole story. It is utterly futile to suppose that we can thwart the Divine purpose. "There are many devices in a man's heart; nevertheless the counsel of the Lord, that shall stand" (Prov. xix. 21). God maketh "the devices of man to be of none effect" (Psalm xxxiii. 10), and we well know that "the counsel of the Lord, that shall stand" (Isa. xlvi. 10). Whenever man has attempted to play the part of Providence, the issue has always

been distaster. "A man's heart deviseth his way; but the Lord direct-eth his steps" (Prov. xvi. 9). The true secret of living is to realize that we are not agents, but only instruments in carrying out the Divine will; and if with all our hearts we truly seek Him, waiting upon Him in prayer, trust, and obedience, we shall find ourselves taken up into the line of His wise providence, used to carry out His purposes, and enabled to live to His glory.

XXXVIII

AN INTERLUDE

GEN. xxvii. 41—xxviii. 9.

41. And Esau hated Jacob because of the blessing wherewith his father blessed him: and Esau said in his heart, The days of mourning for my father are at hand; then will I slay my brother Jacob.

42. And these words of Esau her elder son were told to Rebekah: and she sent and called Jacob her younger son, and said unto him, Behold, thy brother Esau, as touching thee, doth comfort himself, *purposing* to kill thee.

43. Now therefore, my son, obey my voice; and arise, flee thou to Laban my brother to Haran;

44. And tarry with him a few days, until thy brother's fury turn away;

45. Until thy brother's anger turn away from thee, and he forget *that* which thou hast done to him: then I will send, and fetch thee from thence: why should I be deprived also of you both in one day?

46. And Rebekah said to Isaac, I am weary of my life because of the daughters of Heth: if Jacob take a wife of the daughters of Heth, such as these *which* are of the daughters of the land, what good shall my life do me?

1. And Isaac called Jacob, and blessed him, and charged him, and said unto him, Thou shall not take a wife of the daughters of Canaan.

2. Arise, go to Padan-aram, to the house of Bethuel thy mother's father: and take thee a wife from thence of the daughters of Laban thy mother's brother.

3. And God Almighty bless thee, and make thee fruitful, and multiply thee, that thou mayest be a multitude of people;

4. And give thee the blessing of Abraham, to thee, and to thy seed with thee; that thou mayest inherit the land wherein thou art a stranger, which God gave unto Abraham.

5. And Isaac sent away Jacob: and he went to Padan-aram unto Laban, son of Bethuel the Syrian, the brother of Rebekah, Jacob's and Esau's mother.

6. When Esau saw that Isaac had blessed Jacob, and sent him away to Padan-aram, to take him a wife from thence; and that as he blessed him he gave him a charge, saying, Thou shalt not take a wife of the daughters of Canaan;

7. And that Jacob obeyed his father and his mother, and was gone to Padan-aram;

8. And Esau seeing that the daughters of Canaan pleased not Isaac his father;

9. Then went Esau unto Ishmael, and took unto the wives which he had Mahalath the daughter of Ishmael Abraham's son, the sister of Nebajoth, to be his wife.

THIS section seems to suggest the after-swell of a storm; the waters are pent up, longing to rush forth. After the crisis recorded in the preceding section we notice the actors in the drama evidently impressed and affected by the terrible experience through which they have passed.

I. *Esau's Anger* (vers. 41, 42).—Mortified at his loss of the blessing, and hating his brother on that account, Esau forms a resolve marked by cold-blooded calculation. He expects the death of his father at no distant date, and makes up his mind to wait for that event and then to kill his brother. He will not cause grief to his father, but he does not allow any feelings for his mother to enter into his project. It is evident from all this that there was no genuine repentance in him. While Isaac meekly accepted the Divine decision Esau was determined not to do so. To him life was nothing so long as he could not get rid of his brother. The words "comfort himself" (verse 42) show the grim satisfaction that actuated him as he contemplated his brother's murder.

But the days of mourning did not come. His father lived, and the postponement of the revenge led to the failure of the project. Full of passion and impulse he could not keep his plan to himself, for while at the outset he only spake "in his heart," it was not long before the project was heard of by Rebekah.

II. *Rebekah's Plan* (vers. 43-46).—To hear of Esau's determination was to take action, and with characteristic promptitude and vigor she tells Jacob what has happened, at the same time urging him to flee to his uncle at Haran and stay there a short time until his brother's anger should pass away. Rebekah well knew the short-lived passion of her elder son.

This, however, was not all that was in her mind. She saw much further ahead than the few days necessary for the dissipation of Esau's anger. She did not inform Jacob of any deeper project, but in her conversation with Isaac this entirely different idea is brought forward. Rebekah's characteristic cleverness is again in evidence.

She is quite at home in all these plans and projects. She will not speak to Isaac of her fears of Esau's murder of Jacob, but she introduces a suggestion about Jacob's marriage which has the desired effect. She tells her husband that she is sore troubled because of Esau's unfortunate marriage with the daughters of Canaan, and she fears still further trouble if Jacob should follow his example. There was no need to suggest to Isaac where Jacob was to go, for he would doubtless remember from whence he had taken his own wife. Rebekah's view of the marriage was assuredly correct, and it is perhaps true to say that there never has been any Divine blessing from mixed marriages between God's people and people of the world.

Rebekah, however, little knew what she was doing in proposing this scheme to Isaac. It was impossible for her to foresee every contingency. She could outwit her husband and her son, but it would seem as though she had either forgotten or did not know that in Laban she had a brother who was quite her own equal in craft and cleverness. Not for an instant did she imagine that she would never see Jacob again, and that her old age would be bereft of the company of her favorite son. Thus does shrewdness overreach itself, bringing sorrow and trouble upon its own head.

It is impossible to take leave of Rebekah without observing once again her remarkable cleverness and masterfulness. She is certainly one of the ablest women whose lives are recorded in Holy Writ. Full of plans and projects, ever impatiently questioning, she is typical of those resourceful people who leave nothing to chance, but take every precaution within their reach to accomplish what they desire to do. From the moment she first comes upon the scene we have suggestive hints of her capacity and power. Her first question is concerned with the great problem of her own acute suffering (xxv. 22). Her resourcefulness and determination are evident all through the story of the last section, while in the passage before us we see on the one hand her fear lest she should be deprived of both sons (or it may be of husband and favorite son) in one day, and also her intense sorrow and disappointment at the bare possibility of Jacob marrying a wife of whom she herself could not approve.

While vigor and capacity are very important, far more important and necessary are patient trust in God and consistent integrity. Most human catastrophes have been brought about by men and women regarding themselves as agents instead of instruments, and by thinking that the world cannot possibly be managed except by their shrewdness and sharp practice. Ability must be consecrated to God if it is to be of real service.

III. *Isaac's Blessing* (vers. 1-5).—Rebekah's suggestion is sufficient to compel Isaac to take action. He accepts the indication of Divine providence, and realizes now that Jacob is the real heir of the promise to Abraham. He therefore calls his son, and charges him not to take a wife of the daughters of Canaan, but to go to Padan-aram and take a wife of the daughters of Laban, his mother's brother. Then follows the patriarchal benediction; the blessing of "God Almighty" is invoked upon him, that title of God which was first revealed to his forefather Abraham (xvii. 1). Added to the blessing is a prayer that God would make him fruitful, and multiply him according to the blessing of Abraham.

It is touching to realize that Isaac lived over fifty years after this event, and nothing is recorded of him. His life generally was much quieter and far less full of incident than those of his father and of his son, and yet it would almost seem as though the utter silence concerning these fifty years was intended to remind us of the comparative failure of Isaac after his deliberate attempt to divert the blessing from his son Jacob. At any rate, God often has to set aside even honored workers by reason of unfaithfulness, and it is possible that Isaac's sin led to these years of quiet without any incident worthy of being recorded by Divine inspiration. At the same time this may not be the true interpretation of the silence, which may be due simply to the absence of anything in his life worthy of special note. Quiet lives can glorify God just as much as public ones. It is perfectly true that "full many a flower is born to blush unseen," but *not* to "waste its sweetness on the desert air." God can use the lives unseen of men to bring about blessing and glorify Himself.

IV. *Jacob's Obedience* (ver. 5). In all this section Jacob appears quite passive. First he listens obediently to his mother's voice about fleeing to Haran, and then with equal readiness he accepts his father's command and sets out on his long journey. Verse 5, according to the well-known Hebrew literary characteristic, anticipates the detailed record by stating quite briefly his journey and destination. Jacob little knew at the time what this all meant. Apparently it was but a small incident, a stay of a short time while his brother's anger cooled; but God had wider purposes to fulfil, and that which seemed an ordinary journey and a short stay was to be made part of a great project involving many other lives than his own. When he said "Good-bye" to his mother and father, in the full expectation of a speedy return, he was entering upon some of the profoundest experiences of his life. He went away ostensibly to avoid his brother's anger and to seek for himself a wife. He found very much more than this, for, as we shall see, he came in contact with God, and learned lessons that lasted him all his days. Events that seem trivial to us are often fraught with momentous results.

V. *Esau's Marriage* (vers. 6-9).—The narrative once more turns by contrast to Esau, who now makes another attempt to regain the blessing. He is quick enough to see at length that his father and mother disapprove of his own marriage, and had sent Jacob to seek a wife from Laban, and now Esau attempts to steal a march on Jacob and reverse the blessing. He tries to please his parents, for obviously he has no thought of doing what he proposes from any higher motive. He adds to his two Canaanitish wives a daughter of Ishmael, his own cousin. It makes no difference to him that Ishmael is not of the same direct line as himself, nor does it matter to him in the least that God had passed over Ishmael for his father. Esau has no idea of spiritual realities. All that he is concerned about is to please his parents, and if possible to win back the blessing. This again shows the real character of the man and the utter absence of any spiritual reality actuating his life. Esau is one of those who, as it has been truly and acutely said, tries to do what God's people do in the vain hope that somehow or other it will be pleasing to God (Dods, *Genesis, in loc.*). He will not do precisely what God requires, but something like it. He will not entirely give up the world and put God first in his life, but he will try to meet some of God's wishes by a little alteration in his conduct. Instead of renouncing sin he will cover it with the glory of small virtues; but it is one thing to conform to the outward practices of God's people, it is quite another to be thoroughly and truly godly at heart. Men of the Esau type may attend the House of God and join in its service, but at heart they are essentially without God and regardless of His claims on their lives.

1. *God has a plan for every life.*—One of Bushnell's great sermons has the title "Every Man's Life a Plan of God." God had a plan for Jacob's life, and that plan could not be hindered by the action of Isaac or Esau, nor could it be really furthered by the cleverness and craft of Rebekah. It gives dignity, force, and peace to life to realize that God has a plan for it, and it is at once our duty and privilege to seek out that plan and to discover God's will concerning us.

2. *God has His own ways of realizing His plan for us.*—Rebekah's thought in sending out Jacob was very different from God's idea. There were surprises in store that Jacob never dreamt of. God's ways are higher than ours, and it is our truest wisdom to let God show us His way and enable us to fulfil His purpose concerning us.

3. *God is willing to reveal His plan for us.*—Two requirements are necessary if we are to know God's plan for our lives. There must be the sympathy of trust and the faithfulness of obedience. Sympathetic trust is always the parent of spiritual insight. God ever reveals Himself to the trustful, loving heart. Faithful obedience is another and connected secret of spiritual insight. "If any man wills to do . . . he shall know" (John vii. 17). "Then shall we know, if we follow on" (Hos. vi. 3). Trustful obedience, step by step, is the sure guarantee of spiritual knowledge. "The secret of the Lord is with them that fear Him, and He will show them His covenant."

XXXIX

BETHEL

GEN. xxviii. 10-22.

11. And he lighted upon a certain place, and tarried there all night, because the sun was set; and he took of the stones of that place, and put *them for* his pillows, and lay down in that place to sleep.

12. And he dreamed, and behold a ladder set up on the earth, and the top of it reached to heaven: and behold the angels of God ascending and descending on it.

13. And, behold, the Lord stood above it, and said, I *am* the Lord God of Abraham thy father, and the God of Isaac: the land whereon thou liest, to thee will I give it, and to thy seed;

14. And thy seed shall be as the dust of the earth, and thou shalt spread abroad to the west, and to the east, and to the north, and to the south: and in thee and in thy seed shall all the families of the earth be blessed.

15. And, behold, I *am* with thee, and will keep thee in all *places* whither thou goest, and will bring thee again into this land; for I will not leave thee, until I have done *that* which I have spoken to thee of.

16. And Jacob awaked out of his sleep, and he said, Surely the Lord is in this place; and I knew *it* not.

17. And he was afraid, and said, How dreadful *is* this place, this *is* none other but the house of God, and this *is* the gate of heaven.

18. And Jacob rose up early in the morning, and took the stone that he had put *for* his pillows, and set it up *for* a pillar, and poured oil upon the top of it.

19. And he called the name of that place Beth-el: but the name of that city *was called* Luz at the first.

20. And Jacob vowed a vow, saying, If God will be with me, and will keep me in this way that I go, and will give me bread to eat, and raiment to put on,

21. So that I come again to my father's house in peace; then shall the Lord be my God:

22. And this stone, which I have set *for* a pillar, shall be God's house: and of all that Thou shalt give me I will surely give the tenth unto Thee.

THE story of God's special and personal dealings with Jacob commences with **this** incident. Hitherto he has not appeared in a very favorable light, and it is only indirectly that we have been able to gather anything of his relation to God. Now, however, we are to have a series of revelations of his character as he is being tested and trained by the wisdom and grace of God. The story is one of chastisement and mercy. Jacob again and again reaps the fruit of his sins, and yet we shall see the triumphs of Divine grace in one of the most naturally unattractive and even forbidding of temperaments.

1. *The Journey* (vers. 10, 11).—His departure from home in search of a wife was very different from that of his father's servant on the memorable occasion when Abraham sent him to bring back Rebekah. Jacob is alone, no steward to accompany him, no cavalcade, no companions; he is really fleeing for his life. It is not wholly imaginative to try to realize something of his thoughts and feelings on this memorable occasion, fresh from the loving farewell with his mother. It is almost certain that he commenced to review the past as well as contemplate the future. Should he ever return to his father's house in peace? Should he ever possess the blessing that had been bestowed upon him? Was it after all so very precious and valuable? In what respect was he better than his brother Esau? Would it not have been better if he had never sought the birthright and obtained the blessing? Such thoughts as these probably coursed through his mind as he realized that he was virtually being banished from all that was near and dear to him.

He is like many another since his day who has gone out from the old home to seek his fortune elsewhere, although in his case the departure was not the natural and inevitable development of young life, but was due to his sin. There is always something of a crisis when the old home is left and a new life is entered upon. Most young people have to face this fact and to experience all the emotions that are associated with it.

II. *The Dream* (ver. 12).—From Beersheba, 12 miles to the south of Hebron, Jacob journeys, and at length reaches the place afterwards known as Bethel, which was situated in the mountains of Ephraim, about three hours' journey north of Jerusalem. The place was a bleak moorland in the heart of Palestine. "The track winds through an uneven valley, covered, as with gravestones, by large sheets of bare rock; some few here and there standing up like the cromlechs of Druidical monuments."[1] Here he lies down to rest, and, influenced no doubt by the surroundings, in his sleep the stones seem to be like stairs reaching from earth to heaven. To the lonely man there seemed "a ladder set up on the earth, and the top of it reached to heaven," and on the ladder angels of God were ascending and descending. As on so many other occasions, God spoke by means of this dream. The ladder was intended first of all to remind Jacob of the gulf between his soul and God. By craft he had obtained his brother's birthright, by lying and deceit he had snatched away the blessing, and now the fugitive is reminded of the separation between his soul and God and the absolute necessity of some means of communication. The ladder also reminded him of the way in which his soul could come back to God in spite of his sin, and the fact that it reached from earth to heaven signified the complete provision of Divine grace for human life. Right down to his deepest need the ladder came, right up to the presence of God the ladder reached, and the vision of the angels on the ladder was intended to symbolize the freedom of communication, telling of access to God, and of constant, free, easy communication between earth and heaven.

III. *The Revelation* (vers. 13-15).—The ladder was only the symbolical part of his dream; he also received that which was far more and deeper than anything symbolical. Above the ladder stood the God of his father, and from that Divine presence came his first direct message from above. There was first of all the revelation of God as "Jehovah, the God of Abraham and of Isaac." Then came the specific revelation concerning the land whereon Jacob was lying, and the promise of that land to him and to his seed. It will be remembered that the blessings bestowed upon Jacob by Isaac his father (xxvii. 27-29 and xxviii. 3, 4) were couched in very general terms, but now Jacob received the specific, clear assurance that the covenant with Abraham and Isaac was to be continued with him, and through him to his seed.

Then followed a four-fold assurance which must have been very precious to the soul of the fugitive—(*a*) The Divine Presence: "I

---

[1] Stanley's *Sinai and Palestine.*

am with thee"; (*b*) the Divine protection: "and will keep thee"; (*c*) the Divine preservation: "and will bring thee again into this land"; (*d*) the Divine promise: "I will not leave thee until I have done that which I have spoken to thee of." Observe in this passage the threefold repetition of "Behold"; "Behold the angels" (ver. 12), "Behold the Lord" (ver. 13), "Behold, I am with thee" (ver. 15). Thus Jacob was encouraged and assured by a Divine revelation.

IV. *The Response* (vers. 16, 17).—The vision aroused Jacob out of his sleep, and he was astonished at finding God where he fancied himself alone. Hitherto he does not seem to have had personal knowledge of God, everything having been mediated to him through his father and mother. Now he understands and realizes God as his personal God, and is surprised to find that heaven is so near, though he is far from home. Henceforward life takes a different color and "earth's crammed with heaven" for him. No wonder he is afraid, for he realizes that this is the place where God dwells, the house of God, the gate of heaven. When the soul comes in contact with God for the first time it is a good sign that the result is awe, reverence, fear. "Holy and reverend is His Name."

V. *The Memorial* (vers. 18, 19).—Jacob seems to have gone to sleep again and rested until the morning, and then on rising he took the stone which he had put for his pillow and consecrated it to God in commemoration of that wonderful night. This was a fine and worthy idea; to him the place would be evermore sacred as the spot at which he first met God. He did not wish to lose any part of the impression of so memorable an occasion. The place of our conversion is one to be remembered and recalled.

"He felt that, vivid as the impression on his mind then was, it would tend to fade, and he erected this stone that in after days he might have a witness that would testify to his present assurance. One great secret in the growth of character is the art of prolonging the quickening power of right ideas, of perpetuating just and inspiring impressions. And he who despises the aid of all external helps for the accomplishment of this object is not likely to succeed" (Dods' *Genesis*, p. 288).

It is evident that Jacob was deeply impressed with the vision, the
ladder, and the voice of God, and his responsiveness to the Divine
revelation is worthy of careful notice in view of his former craft
and deceit. It shows that, in spite of everything, he had that in his
soul which reached out towards the Divine will, however unworthy
and wrong were the methods that he used. We cannot imagine
the purely secular, sensuous, and even sensual Esau entering into
the spirit of this vision or allowing it to have any influence upon
his life.

VI. *The Vow* (vers. 20-22).—With the memorial stone comes the
story of the first vow recorded in Scripture. Jacob acknowledges
his need of God, which is another testimony to the genuineness of
the man, and he vows, saying, "If God will be with me, and will
keep me in this way that I go, and will give me bread to eat, and
raiment to put on, so that I come again to my father's house in
peace; then shall the Lord be my God: and this stone, which I
have set for a pillar, shall be God's house: and of all that Thou
shalt give me I will surely give the tenth unto Thee." The precise
attitude of Jacob in this vow has been variously interpreted. Some
have thought that his "If" really means "*Since* God will be with
me," and following the margin of the Revised Version it is suggested that the protasis should not be in verse 21 but in verse 22,
and that we should read: "Since God will be with me and will keep
me . . . and will give me . . . *and* the Lord will be my Guide *then*
this stone . . . shall be God's house." Others think that Jacob cannot be excused a low and mercenary feeling in this vow. We must
be careful not to read too much into it, but it is equally necessary
not to read too little into it. Let us remember that this is what we
should call Jacob's conversion, the commencement of a life of grace,
and we are therefore not to be surprised if he is unfamiliar with
God and cannot at once rise to a high level of spiritual attainment.
Even supposing it is true that he met God's "I am with thee" with
"*If* God will be with me," he is only doing what Peter did under
very different circumstances. When the Lord said, "It is I," Peter
replied, "*If* it be thou." It is a great thing that Jacob realizes his
need of God and that he makes this resolution, under whatever

condition, acknowledging God as his God and pledging himself to God's service. If only some of those who are inclined to critize Jacob would do what he promised and give the tenth of their income to God, what a different state of affairs would obtain in connection with God's work at home and abroad!

The story of Bethel left its mark on the people of Israel, for it is found referred to, at least twice in after ages (Hos. xii. 4; John i. 51). It is full of lessons for the life of the believer, and we shall do well to ponder it closely as a revelation of Divine grace.

1. *God's condescending grace.*—The vision of Bethel was used by our Lord as a symbol and type of Himself: "Ye shall see heaven open, and the angels of God ascending and descending *upon the Son of Man.*" As the ladder was to Jacob so is the Lord Jesus Christ to mankind, a revelation of God's wonderful condescension and mercy. Set up on earth in Bethlehem, the top of it reached to heaven at the Ascension, and now the Lord Jesus is our Divine ladder, first of revelation and then of communication. All that we know of God comes through Him, and all that we receive from God comes through Him. Ever since the Incarnation of our Lord earth has been no desert, but a place where God is manifest to the eye and heart of faith.

2. *God's all-sufficient grace.*—How appropriate this story is for those who are standing on the threshold of life, who have just left home and are feeling all the loneliness associated with this time! It is on such an occasion that God meets us and offers us Himself, shows us the ladder between earth and heaven, assures us that His grace is all-sufficient, and that though we are far from home we are very near to him: "My grace is sufficient for thee."

3. *God's overruling grace.*—There was really no need for Jacob to have fled from his brother, for God could have dealt with Esau and put everything right; but Jacob has to suffer the results of his impatience and imprudence, and God will overrule his mistakes and sins and teach him still deeper lessons. Though he had left his father's house, God was still with him, and in this vision he was taught that God was now taking him in hand and would not leave him till the work of grace was done. How wonderfully God over-

rules our mistakes, and faults, and sins, and gathers up the threads of our troubles and even weaves them into His pattern for our life!

4. *God's sovereign grace.*—It was necessary that Jacob should learn how utterly helpless he was to bring about the Divine purposes concerning him. It was only when he was asleep, needy and helpless, that God revealed Himself. Jacob had hitherto considered it necessary to use craft and cleverness in order, as he thought, to bring about the purposes of God. He was now to be told that God could dispense with him and yet accomplish His own Divine aims. It is a very salutary lesson to learn the sovereignty of grace, to realize that we have no claim on God, to be conscious that God does not require our cleverness or ability, and to lean our hearts increasingly upon the Divine word: "Not by might, nor by power, but by My Spirit."

5. *God's teaching grace.*—At Bethel God really commenced the education and making of Jacob. To educate is to "educe" or draw out that which is within, and while we might have thought that there was no material worthy of God's consideration, the Divine Teacher could see the possibilities of this man, and was willing, in marvellous patience, to attempt the work of training. God did this in three ways: (*a*) He revealed Jacob's character to himself; He brought him to the end of himself and revealed to him something of his evil heart. (*b*) He also showed to Jacob his utter helplessness from earthly sources. Bereft of father and home, in danger from his brother, and powerless himself, Jacob was perforce compelled to turn to God. (*c*) Above all, the Lord revealed Himself to Jacob. He introduced him to a larger life and wider experience, reminding him that the Divine presence was to be found everywhere. So "He led him about, He instructed him, He kept him as the apple of His eye."

6. *God's long-suffering grace.*—When Jacob awoke after the vision his true life commenced. We are not altogether surprised at the low level of his spiritual life, for he was evidently unfamiliar with God and needed very much more experience before he could enter fully into all the Divine purposes concerning him. Even if we acquit him of bargaining we can still see that his knowledge

of God was only superficial, and he was not yet able to enter into the fulness and glory of the Divine thought concerning him and his seed. But God had commenced His work in Jacob's soul and with marvelous patience God continued His dealings with him. Since at our conversion we know very little of God, we and others must not be surprised if our lack of familiarity with Divine realities leads us into error; but the great thing is to commence the true life, for as we yield ourselves to God and wait upon Him we shall find ourselves taught, upheld, and blessed by the wonderful patience of His grace. Only let us be clear that when God says, "I am with thee" we do not reply with "If," but say, out of a full heart, "I believe God, that it shall be even as it was told me," and, like Abraham of old, go forward "fully persuaded that what He has promised He is able also to perform."

XL

THE NEW LIFE

GEN. xxix. 1-30

1. Then Jacob went on his journey, and came into the land of the people of the east.

2. And he looked, and behold a well in the field, and, lo, there *were* three flocks of sheep lying by it; for out of that well they watered the flocks: and a great stone *was* upon the well's mouth.

3. And thither were all the flocks gathered: and they rolled the stone from the well's mouth, and watered the sheep, and put the stone again upon the well's mouth in his place.

4. And Jacob said unto them, My brethren, whence *be* ye? And they said, of Haran *are* we.

5. And he said unto them, Know ye Laban the son of Nahor? And they said, We know *him*.

6. And he said unto them, *Is* he well? And they said *He is* well: and, behold, Rachel his daughter cometh with the sheep.

7. And he said, Lo, *it is* yet high day, neither *is it* time that the cattle should be gathered together; water ye the sheep, and go *and* feed *them*.

8. And they said, We cannot, until all the flocks be gathered together, and *till* they roll the stone from the well's mouth; then we water the sheep.

9. And while he yet spake with them, Rachel came with her father's sheep: for she kept them.

10. And it came to pass when Jacob saw Rachel the daughter of Laban his mother's brother, and the sheep of Laban his mother's brother, that Jacob went near, and rolled the stone from the well's mouth, and watered the flock of Laban his mother's brother.

11. And Jacob kissed Rachel, and lifted up his voice, and wept.

12. And Jacob told Rachel that he was her father's brother, and that he *was* Rebekah's son: and she ran and told her father.

13. And it came to pass, when Laban heard the tidings of Jacob his sister's son, that he ran to meet him, and embraced him, and kissed him, and brought him to his house. And he told Laban all these things.

14. And Laban said to him, Surely thou *art* my bone and my flesh. And he abode with him the space of a month.

15. And Laban said unto Jacob, Because thou *art* my brother shouldst thou therefore serve me for nought? tell me, what *shall* thy wages *be?*

16. And Laban had two daughters; the name of the elder *was* Leah, and the name of the younger *was* Rachel.

17. Leah *was* tender eyed; but Rachel was beautiful and well favored.

18. And Jacob loved Rachel; And said I will serve thee seven years for Rachel thy younger daughter.

19. And Laban said, *It is* better that I give her to thee, than that I should give her to another man: abide with me.

20. And Jacob served seven years for Rachel; And they seemed unto him *but* a few days, for the love he had to her.

21. And Jacob said unto Laban. Give me my wife, for my days are fulfilled, that I may go in unto her.

22. And Laban gathered together all the men of the place, and made a feast.

23. And it came to pass in the evening, that he took Leah his daughter, and brought her to him: and he went in unto her.

24. And Laban gave unto his daughter Leah Zilpah his maid *for* an handmaid.

25. And it came to pass, that in the morning, behold it *was* Leah: and he said to Laban, What is this thou hast done unto me? did not I serve with thee for Rachel? wherefore then hast thou beguiled me?

26. And Laban said, It must not be so done in our country, to give the younger before the firstborn.

27. Fulfil her week, and we will give thee this also for the service which thou shalt serve with me yet seven other years.

28. And Jacob did so, and fulfilled her week; and he gave him Rachel his daughter to wife also.

30. And he went in also unto Rachel, and he loved also Rachel more than Leah, and served with him seven other years.

JACOB is now in the greatest of all schools, that of experience, and there are many lessons to learn. These three chapters (xxix-xxxi.) cover forty years of his life, and are the record of a large part of his training.

1. *The New Start* (ver. 1).—The Hebrew is very suggestive: "Then Jacob lifted up his feet." A new hope had dawned in his breast, and now he starts on his way from Bethel with alacrity. The revelation of God and the assurance of God's presence and blessing had brought light and cheer to his heart, and, like every young convert fresh from the experience of meeting God for the first time, "he went on his way rejoicing." Who does not remember those early days, when everything seemed different, when joy illuminated the pathway, and hope sprang up, covering the pathway with its rainbow of blessed assurance! The long journey (450 miles from Beersheba) was at length accomplished, and he arrived in the country of his kinsfolk, "the people of the East."

II. *The Memorable Meeting* (vers. 2-14).—As he neared his journey's end he came across a well with flocks of sheep lying by it, and on asking the shepherds whence they were, received the answer, "From Haran." Another question followed about Laban, and he was soon told that his uncle was in health, and that Rachel his daughter was coming with the sheep. Then comes a point exceedingly characteristic of Jacob. He suggests to the shepherds that, as it is not yet time to gather together the cattle and fold them for the night, they should at least go and give the flocks of sheep food and water. What was the meaning of this suggestion of Jacob? There does not seem much doubt that it was made for the purpose of getting an opportunity to be alone with Rachel. Already he seems to realize that his way has been guided aright, and with characteristic forethought and promptitude he desires to make the most of the opportunity. The shepherds decline to accede to his request, urging that it would cause unnecessary trouble to give water to some of the sheep while the others had not yet gathered around the well.

Then comes the meeting with Rachel, and we are doubtless right in regarding Jacob's feelings as those of "love at first sight." With courtesy he went near and rolled away the stone from the mouth of the well, and then revealed himself to his cousin, telling her who he was and whence he had come. Rachel thereupon goes and tells the news to her father. The picture is one of idyllic beauty. Faith had come into his life through his meeting with God at Bethel, and now had entered that second best of God's gifts, a woman's love.

Laban at once comes out to meet him, and gives him the heartiest possible welcome. In spite of all that we have to see and note about Laban, it is evident that he was a man of warm-hearted and generous impulses, and was genuinely delighted to welcome his kinsman into his house.

III. *The Faithful Service* (vers. 15-20).—Laban again stands out well in the story at this point. He does not wish to presume his relationship to Jacob by expecting him to do service for nothing, so he asks him to say what wages he desires. Jacob thereupon proposes to serve seven years for Rachel, Laban's youngest daughter;

and to this Laban agrees, saying that he would much prefer giving Rachel to him than to a stranger.

"And Jacob served seven years for Rachel; and they seemed unto him but a few days, for the love he had to her." There are few verses more familiar in the story of Jacob than this beautiful description of his love; and whatever else may be said about him, his sharp practices, cleverness, and craft, it is impossible not to give adhesion to Coleridge's well-known words that "No man could be a bad man who loved as Jacob loved Rachel." For seven long years he toiled hard and faithfully in the service of Laban, and yet because of his great love the time passed rapidly and seemed but a few days. Love such as this takes little account of time; buoyed up and urged on by its joyous hope, it lives and labors and grows stronger and stronger.

V. *The Bitter Disappointment* (vers. 21-30).—The seven years are now over, and Jacob asks Laban for the fulfilment of his promise. Laban thereupon prepares for the usual wedding-feast, which, in the East, lasts seven days, and then, under cover of the darkness, and according to Eastern custom, he brings his daughter closely veiled to the tent of Jacob. Jacob is soon made aware of the treachery of Laban, to which Leah was a party, though probably with no real power to resist her father's will. Nor indeed was she likely in any case to resist it, since it is evident that a deep love for Jacob had sprung up in her heart. Laban's answer to Jacob's reproach is another indication of the true character of the man. He told Jacob that it was not customary in their country that the younger daughter should be married before the first-born; and yet surely Jacob ought to have been told this at the beginning, not at the end of the seven years. To add to the difficulty and confusion Laban proposes that at the end of the week of the marriage-feast for Leah Jacob should take Rachel also as his wife. Jacob agrees to this; and so, at the close of the marriage festivities in connection with his marriage with Leah, Jacob accomplishes his heart's desire and marries Rachel. It is clear, from a careful consideration of the story, that he married Rachel at the beginning, not at the end of his second seven years of service. His love for Rachel had never varied, and he was quite prepared to serve with Laban "yet another seven years."

Jacob is already in the training school of discipline. God is dealing with him in deed and in truth, and as we study the story we find several messages that ought to come home to our own hearts.

1. *Doing the will of God.*—After Bethel came the long journey to Haran, and Bethel was intended to fit Jacob for the journey and all that lay before him. Quiet times with God are intended to be the means of doing our ordinary work in "the daily round, the common task." Conversion is intended to be expressed in consecration. Mountain-top experiences are to be followed by service in the valley, and the real test of our life lies not in our profession, but in our character and conduct. One of the most practical, pointed, and pressing questions that we should ask ourselves day by day is this: What are our Bethels doing for us? "If ye know these things, happy are ye if ye do them." All our professions of fellowship with God will count for nothing unless those experiences are reproduced in our ordinary everyday life. "How call ye Me Lord, and do not the things which I say?"

2. *Experiencing the providence of God.*—The story before us is a very ordinary one. A journey, a meeting with shepherds near a well, a young woman coming up, an act of courtesy; and yet these small events led to great and far-reaching results. How very much depends upon very little! There is nothing really small in human life. We start out in the morning, and what we may call a chance meeting, or the receipt of an ordinary letter, or some very slight circumstance may affect the whole of the subsequent life of quite a number of people. We call this the "providence" of God, and we do well; and the true Christian heart will always love to trace the hand of God in the ordinary everyday experiences of life. For, after all, "ordinary" means "ordered," and it is the joy of the believer to realize that everything is ordered and that "all things work together for good to them that love God." The harmonious and beneficent combination of circumstances guided and overruled by the wisdom and will of God constitutes for the Christian soul the joy and cheer of everyday living.

3. *Discovering the justice of God*—Laban's deception came to Jacob as a great surprise, and yet he ought not to have been astonished in view of his past. He was now commencing to reap as he had sown. He was now being treated as he had treated his father and brother, and the deceiver is at length deceived. He had come to the school whence all his own powers of deceit had originally come. Laban is seen to be the equal of his clever sister Rebekah, and Jacob is being paid back with the family coin. God has no favorites, and if His own children wander from the pathway they have to suffer. And yet the sufferings are not punitive, but disciplinary. We are chastened and trained and it is the highest wisdom of every believer to accept and to learn all that God has to teach him. Old tendencies need to be corrected, old weaknesses made strong, old faults removed; and if only we yield ourselves into the hands of the great Potter He will fashion the clay, in spite of all our natural disadvantages, into vessels unto honor.

> "Yet take Thy way—for, sure, Thy way is best;
> Stretch or contract me, Thy poor debtor;
> 'Tis but the tuning of my breast
> To make the music better."

XLI

IN THE SHADOWS

GEN. xxix. 31—xxx. 43

31. And when the Lord saw that Leah *was* hated, he opened her womb: but Rachel *was* barren.

32. And Leah conceived, and bare a son, and she called his name Reuben: for she said, Surely the Lord hath looked upon my affliction; now therefore my husband will love me.

33. And she conceived again, and bare a son: and said, Because the Lord hath heard that I *was* hated, he hath therefore given me this *son* also: and she called his name Simeon.

34. And she conceived again, and bare a son; and said, Now this time will my husband be joined unto me, because I have born him three sons: therefore was his name called Levi.

35. And she conceived again, and bare a son: and she said, Now will I praise the Lord: therefore she called his name Judah; and left bearing.

1. And when Rachel saw that she bare Jacob no children, Rachel envied her sister; and said unto Jacob, Give me children, or else I die.

2. And Jacob's anger was kindled against Rachel: and he said, *Am* I in God's stead, who hath withheld from thee the fruit of the womb?

3. And she said, Behold my maid Bilhah, go in unto her; and she shall bare upon my knees, that I may also have children by her.

4. And she gave him Bilhah her handmaid to wife: and Jacob went in unto her.

5. And Bilhah conceived, and bare Jacob a son.

6. And Rachel said, God hath judged me, and hath also heard my voice, and hath given me a son: therefore called she his name Dan.

7. And Bilhah Rachel's maid conceived again, and bare Jacob a second son.

8. And Rachel said, With great wrestlings have I wrestled with my sister, and I have prevailed: and she called his name Naphtali.

9. When Leah saw that she had left bearing, she took Zilpah her maid, and gave her Jacob to wife.

10. And Zilpah Leah's maid bare Jacob a son.

11. And Leah said, A troop cometh: and she called his name Gad.

12. And Zilpah Leah's maid bare Jacob a second son.

13. And Leah said, Happy am I, for the daughters will call me blessed: and she called his name Asher.

14. And Reuben went in the days of wheat harvest, and found mandrakes in the field, and brought them unto his mother Leah. Then Rachel said to Leah, Give me, I pray thee, of thy son's mandrakes.

15. And she said unto her, *Is it* a small matter that thou hast taken my husband? and wouldst thou take away my son's mandrakes also? And Rachel said, Therefore he shall lie with thee to night for thy son's mandrakes.

16. And Jacob came out of the field in the evening, and Leah went out to meet him, and said, Thou must come in unto me; for surely I have hired thee with my son's mandrakes. And he lay with her that night.

17. And God hearkened unto Leah, and she conceived, and bare Jacob the fifth son.

18. And Leah said, God hath given me my hire, because I have given my maiden to my husband: and she called his name Issachar.

19. And Leah conceived again, and bare Jacob the sixth son.

20. And Leah said, God hath endued me *with* a good dowry; now will my husband dwell with me, because I have born him six sons: and she called his name Zebulun.

21. And afterwards she bare a daughter, and called her name Dinah.

22. And God remembered Rachel, and God hearkened to her, and opened her womb.

23. And she conceived, and bare a son; and said, God hath taken away my reproach:

24. And she called his name Joseph; and said, The Lord shall add to me another son.

25. And it came to pass, when Rachel had born Joseph, that Jacob said unto Laban, Send me away, that I may go unto mine own place and to my country.

26. Give *me* my wives and my children, for whom I have served thee, and let me go: for thou knowest my service which I have done thee.

27. And Laban said unto him, I pray thee, if I have found favor in thine eyes, *tarry*: for I have learned by experience that the Lord hath blessed me for thy sake.

28. And he said, Appoint me thy wages, and I will give *it.*

29. And he said unto him, Thou knowest how I have served thee, and how thy cattle was with me.

30. For *it was* little which thou hadst before I *came,* and it is *now* increased unto a multitude; and the Lord hath blessed thee since my coming: and now when shall I provide for mine own house also?

31. And he said, What shall I give thee? And Jacob said, Thou shalt not give me anything: if thou wilt do this thing for me, I will again feed *and* keep thy flock:

32. I will pass through all thy flock today, removing from thence all the speckled and spotted cattle, and all the brown cattle among the sheep, and the spotted and speckled among the goats: and *of such* shall be my hire.

33. So shall my righteousness answer for me in time to come, when it shall come for my hire before thy face: every one that *is* not speckled and spotted among the goats, and brown among the sheep, that shall be counted stolen with me.

34. And Laban said, Behold I would it might be according to thy word.

35. And he removed that day the he goats that were ring-straked and spotted, and all the she goats that were speckled and spotted, *and* every one that

had *some* white in it, and all the brown among the sheep, and gave *them* into the hand of his sons.

36. And he set three days' journey betwixt himself and Jacob: and Jacob fed the rest of Laban's flocks.

37. And Jacob took him rods of green popular, and of the hazel and chesnut tree; and pilled white stakes in them, and made the white appear which *was* in the rods.

38. And he set the rods which he had pilled before the flocks in the gutters in the watering troughs when the flocks came to drink, that they should conceive when they came to drink

39. And the flocks conceived before the rods, and brought forth cattle ringstraked, speckled, and spotted.

40. And Jacob did separate the lambs, and set the faces of the flocks toward the ringstraked, and all the brown in the flock of Laban; and he put his own flocks by themselves, and put them not unto Laban's cattle.

41. And it came to pass, whensoever the stronger cattle did conceive, that Jacob laid the rods before the eyes of the cattle in the gutters, that they might conceive among the rods.

42. But when the cattle were feeble, he put *them* not in: so the feebler were Laban's and the stronger Jacob's.

43. And the man increased exceedingly, and had much cattle, and maidservants, and menservants, and camels, and asses.

JACOB'S life at Haran was one long prolonged discipline in various ways. He was almost continually in the crucible, whether through the faults and sins of others or through his own unworthy and sinful expedients. The entire story is full of sad and sordid incidents, but as we read it we shall do well to bear in mind that the long-suffering patience of God was all the while at work with his unworthy servant.

I. *At Home* (xxix. 31—xxx. 24).—The results of Laban's deception were soon evident in Jacob's home life. The possession of two wives brought its inevitable results. Polygamy was only tolerated, never accepted, by the Hebrews in after-days. The experience of their progenitor doubtless weighed with them in the attitude they assumed towards it (Lev. xviii. 8). Yet even in this unhappy experience we can see the overruling hand of God, for when He saw Jacob's partiality for Rachel He taught him some needed lessons in connection with the birth of his first children. The way in which Leah's thoughts turned to God on the occasion of the birth of her first four sons is very striking. She realized that the Divine hand was being put forth on her behalf, and she trusted that through the birth of the sons her husband's feelings would be changed towards her.

The story then proceeds along familiar lines, in the envy and jealousy of the two sisters. First Rachel and then Leah manifests this spirit, with what results we know only too well. It is not too much to say that all this household friction had its dire influence upon the temperaments of the children, and we can hardly be surprised at what we read of them in after-days. There could not be righteousness, holiness, and peace amid such untoward surroundings. When there is trouble between parents, the children must necessarily suffer. It is impossible also to avoid noticing what seems to be a declension in Leah's spiritual life from the time of the birth of her fifth son (xxx. 17-21). In connection with the first four the Lord's hand was very definitely perceived, but now there is no longer any reference to the Covenant Name Jehovah, and the expressions indicate what is almost only purely personal and even selfish as two sons and a daughter are born to her.

At length God heard the prayers of Rachel and granted her her heart's desire in the birth of a son. It was now her turn to recognize the hand of the Lord and to acknowledge His mercy and goodness in dealing with her. As we review the whole story we are impressed more and more with the sadness of it all. It started with Laban's deception combined with Leah's co-operation; and although perhaps it would have been impossible for Jacob to have sustained any protest against this action, we can see the result of it in the years of sorrow and chastening that came to him and all the actors in this unhappy domestic tragedy. Where the home life is not full of love and peace, there can be no true witness for God or genuine helpfulness to one another.

II. *At Work* (xxx. 25-43.)—The birth of Rachel's son seems to have been a turning-point in Jacob's life, and to have prompted a desire to return to his own country. He had now been with Laban the best part of twenty years (xxxi. 38, 41), and the longing for the old country and the old home pressed heavily upon him. Laban, however, was altogether unwilling to lose so valued a servant, for far too much blessing had come into his life through Jacob to allow him willingly to depart. He therefore suggested to Jacob that he should stay and fix his own terms; but Jacob was not ready to do this. He had had experience already of the way in which Laban had not kept his engagements about wages (xxxi. 7, 41), and he therefore preferred to take matters into his own hands. The real Jacob comes out in his distrust of others and his determination to manage things for himself. He therefore proposes to leave with Laban all the animals of one color, and to keep for himself those that were spotted and speckled among the sheep and the goats. If we read Laban's words aright (ver. 34) it would seem as though he agreed to this proposal with reluctance; but his caution and greed are at once seen (vers. 34, 35), for he proceeds to remove the very animals that would be likely to fall to Jacob's lot, hands them over to the care of his sons and then puts the distance of three days' journey between them and Jacob. This again shows the character of the man with whom Jacob had to deal. Truly the deceiver is having a full payment in his own coin.

It is now Jacob's turn to plot and plan, and his retaliation is sharp and complete (vers. 37-43). He is quite the equal of his uncle, and his plan succeeds beyond his imagination, for he increased exceedingly and had large flocks as well as a great retinue of servants. He was not likely to be far behind in any effort for his own advantage, and we can see in this method of revenge the depth of his resentment against Laban. It was a case of equal meeting equal, for there is nothing to choose between them in the character and extent of their cleverness and craft.

The entire story is full of searching lessons as we contemplate the extent to which human nature will go in furthering its own ends and accomplishing its own will. At the same time it is not without a background of teaching concerning the overruling mercy of God.

1. *A Severe Discipline.*—The fact that God permitted the deception about Leah to be practised on Jacob seems to suggest that it was necessary for him somehow or other to be emptied of self and self-seeking. Circumstances were therefore used to break him down and bring him to the end of himself. It is certainly very

remarkable that, notwithstanding his intense love for Rachel, it was through Leah that the most permanent—that is, the Messianic—blessings were to come to and through him. It is a striking fact of experience that when he was about to enter upon the enjoyment of his seven years of toil God allowed something else, instead of that which he desired, to come into his life; something entirely unexpected; something that seemed the very opposite of what he wished. When such disappointments come—if, as in this particular case, they are not the result of our own sin—it is well for us by the Spirit of God to be able to transmute our disappointment into "His appointment," for very often by such discipline our life becomes more fruitful. What we *want* may be good, but what we *need* may be better; and God deals with our needs, not with our wants.

2. *A significant testimony.*—How very striking it is to read Laban's words in appealing to Jacob not to depart! "I have learned by experience that the Lord hath blessed me for thy sake" (xxx. 27). Laban had wit enough to see the value of having Jacob associated with him, and so he seeks to profit by the association, and use Jacob for his own ends. There does not seem to have been any real religion in Laban, but he was able to appreciate the value of it in Jacob. There are many Labans today who are not personally pious, but who are quite able to appreciate the good effects of piety in others. They do not become Church members and workers, but they attend church because of the social and other advantages that accrue to a profession of Christianity. It is a fine testimony to the value of religion when a man of the world is able to realize that there is something in it after all, and that, however indirectly, it "pays" to be associated with God's people. So far as the man's personal life is concerned we may rightly speak of it as mean and contemptible, but we must not overlook the fact that it is a genuine testimony to the value of religion.

3. *A sad downfall.*—When we read of Jacob's plot against Laban our hearts sink within us as we remember that this was done by a man who had been to Bethel, had seen angels, and heard the voice of God. We may not be surprised at Laban's deception; but for

one who had met with God to descend to the level of the worldling, was indeed a deplorable revelation. Here are two men trying to outwit each other, and one of these two men is a professed believer in God. It is absolutely impossible to excuse and to exculpate Jacob. On no account was he warranted in following Laban's example. Just as it had been almost from the first, he was afraid to trust God with his affairs. He must take them into his own hands, and use all kinds of unworthy means to bring about ends that were in themselves perfectly right and justifiable. It was right and true that he should be paid his wages for those long years of service, but it was utterly wrong that he should be paid as the result of such unworthy means. The corruption of the best is the worst; and when a Christian falls, great and awful is the descent.

4. *A striking manifestation.*—The human side of things is so prominent in this story that we almost fail to see and realize the Divine hand behind it all. How marvelous was God's patience with His unworthy servant! How much God must have seen in Jacob to have waited all these years, disciplining him, leading him, over-ruling his mistakes and sins! Is there anything comparable with the patience and mercy of God? As we read the narrative we find ourselves irritated and disappointed with Jacob's failures and falls after Bethel; and yet God was waiting His own time and way to bring about His purposes, to lead Jacob in the right path, to bring him to the end of himself and his self-seeking, and to manifest in that strong character the power and glory of His grace. Shall we not pray that we may have grace to exercise similar long-suffering patience with others, in spite of all disappointments and shattered hopes? If God be so long-suffering with us, surely we ought to be long-suffering one with another.

XLII

TURNING HOMEWARDS

GEN. xxxi.

1 And he heard the words of Laban's sons, saying, Jacob hath taken away all that *was* our father's; and of *that* which *was our* father's hath he gotten all his glory.

2. And Jacob beheld the countenance of Laban, and, behold, it *was* not toward him as before.

3. And the Lord said unto Jacob, Return unto the land of thy fathers, and to thy kindred; and I will be with thee.

4. And Jacob sent and called Rachel and Leah to the field unto his flock.

5. And said unto them, I see your father's countenance, that it *is* not toward me as before; but the God of my father hath been with me.

6. And ye know that with all my power I have served your father.

7. And your father hath deceived me, and changed my wages ten times; but God suffered him not to hurt me.

8. If he said thus, The speckled shall be thy wages; then all the cattle bare speckled: and if he said thus, The ringstraked shall be thy hire. then bare all the cattle ringstraked.

9. Thus God hath taken away the cattle of your father, and given *them* to me.

10. And it came to pass at the time that the cattle conceived that I lifted up mine eyes, and saw in a dream, and, behold, the rams which leaped upon the cattle *were* ringstraked, speckled, and grisled.

11. And the angel of God spake unto me in a dream, *saying*, Jacob: And I said, Here *am* I.

12. And he said, Lift up now thine eyes, and see, all the rams which leap upon the cattle *are* ringstraked, speckled, and grisled: for I have seen all that Laban doeth unto thee.

13. I *am* the God of Beth-el, where thou anointedst the pillar, *and* where thou vowedst a vow unto me: now arise, get thee out from this land, and return unto the land of thy kindred.

14. And Rachel and Leah answered and said unto him, *Is there* yet any portion or inheritance for us in our father's house?

15. Are we not counted of him strangers? for he hath sold us, and hath quite devoured also our money.

16. For all the riches which God hath taken from our father, that *is* our's, and our children's: now then, whatsoever God hath said unto thee, do.

17. Then Jacob rose up, and set his sons and his wives upon camels;

18. And he carried away all his cattle, and all his goods which he had gotten, the cattle of his getting, which he had gotten in Padan-aram, for to go to Isaac his father in the land of Canaan.

19. And Laban went to shear his sheep: and Rachel had stolen the images that *were* her father's.

20. And Jacob stole away unawares to Laban the Syrian, in that he told him not that he fled.

21. So he fled with all that he had: and he rose up, and passed over the river, and set his face *toward* the mount Gilead.

22. And it was told Laban on the third day that Jacob was fled.

23. And he took his brethren with him, and pursued after him seven days' journey; and they overtook him in the mount Gilead.

24. And God came to Laban the Syrian in a dream by night, and said unto him, Take heed that thou speak not to Jacob either good or bad.

25. Then Laban overtook Jacob. Now Jacob had pitched his tent in the mount: and Laban with his brethren pitched in the mount of Gilead.

26. And Laban said to Jacob, What hast thou done, that thou hast stolen away unawares to me, and carried away my daughters, as captives *taken* with the sword?

27. Wherefore didst thou flee away secretly, and steal away from me; and didst not tell me, that I might have sent thee away with mirth, and with songs, with tabret, and with harp?

28. And hast not suffered me to kiss my sons and my daughters? thou hast now done foolishly in *so* doing.

29. It is in the power of my hand to do you hurt; but the God of your father spake unto me yesternight, saying, Take thou heed that thou speak not to Jacob either good or bad.

30. And now, *though* thou wouldest needs be gone, because thou sore longedst after thy father's house, *yet* wherefore hast thou stolen my gods?

31. And Jacob answered and said to Laban, Because I was afraid: for I said, Peradventure thou wouldest take by force thy daughters from me.

32. With whomsoever thou findest thy gods, let him not live: before our brethren discern thou what *is* thine with me, and take *it* to thee. For Jacob knew not that Rachel had stolen them.

33. And Laban went into Jacob's tent, and into Leah's tent, and into the two maidservants' tents; but he found *them* not. Then went he out of Leah's tent, and entered into Rachel's tent.

34. Now Rachel had taken the images, and put them in the camel's furniture, and sat upon them. And Laban searched all the tent, but found *them* not.

35. And she said to her father, Let it not displease my lord that I cannot rise up before thee; for the custom of women *is* upon me. And he searched, but found not the images.

36. And Jacob was wroth, and chode with Laban: and Jacob answered and said to Laban, What *is* my trespass? what *is* my sin, that thou hast so hotly pursued after me?

37. Whereas thou hast searched all my stuff, what hast thou found of all thy household stuff? set *it* here before my brethren and thy brethren, that they may judge betwixt us both.

38. This twenty years *have I been* with thee: thy ewes and thy she goats have not cast their young, and the rams of thy flock have I not eaten.

39. That which was torn *of beasts* I brought not unto thee; I bare the loss of it; of my hand didst thou require it, *whether* stolen by day, or stolen by night.

40. *Thus* I was; in the day the drought consumed me, and the frost by night; and my sleep departed from mine eyes.

41. Thus have I been twenty years in thy house; I served thee fourteen years for thy two daughters, and six years for thy cattle: and thou hast changed my wages ten times.

42. Except the God of my father, the God of Abraham, and the fear of Isaac, had been with me, surely thou hadst sent me away now empty. God hath seen mine affliction and the labor of my hands, and rebuked *thee* yesternight.

43. And Laban answered and said unto Jacob, *These* daughters *are* my daughters, and *these* children *are* my children, and *these* cattle *are* my cattle, and all that thou seest *is* mine: and what can I do this day unto these my daughters, or unto their children which they have born?

44. Now therefore come thou, let us make a covenant, I and thou; and let it be for a witness between me and thee.

45. And Jacob took a stone, and set it up *for* a pillar

46. And Jacob said unto his brethren, Gather stones; and they took stones, and made an heap: and they did eat there upon the heap.

47. And Laban called it Jegar-sahadutha: but Jacob called it Galeed.

48. And Laban said, This heap *is* a witness between me and thee this day. Therefore was the name of it called Galeed;

49. And Mizpah; for he said, The Lord watch between me and thee, when we are absent one from another.

50. If thou shalt afflict my daughters, or if thou shalt take *other* wives beside my daughters, no man *is* with us; see, God *is* witness betwixt me and thee.

51. And Laban said to Jacob, Behold this heap, and behold *this* pillar, which I have cast betwixt me and thee;

52. This heap *be* witness, and *this* pillar *be* witness, that I will not pass over this heap to thee, and that thou shalt not pass over this heap and this pillar unto me, for harm.

53. The God of Abraham, and the God of Nahor, the God of their father, judge betwixt us. And Jacob sware by the fear of his father Isaac.

54. Then Jacob offered sacrifice upon the mount, and called his brethren to eat bread: and they did eat bread, and tarried all night in the mount.

55. And early in the morning Laban rose up, and kissed his sons and his daughters, and blessed them: and Laban departed, and returned unto his place.

IT was impossible that the relations just described between Laban and Jacob could last long. Everything was hurrying towards the climax of a necessary separation. Jacob's heart was also set on returning home (xxx. 25). As we study the various actors and movements we seem to see at first nothing but jealousy, craftiness, plotting, and hypocrisy. Yet, in spite of all these, we can hardly fail to notice how marvelously God overruled the confusions and made them subserve His purpose of grace for Jacob.

I. *The Crisis* (vers. 1-3).—Jacob's remarkable prosperity could not remain long unnoticed, and it was perhaps inevitable that Laban's sons should attribute it to craft and theft. And yet, in fairness to Jacob, we must observe that the charge was certainly exaggerated. They made no allowance for their father's craftiness (xxx. 35) which was the occasion, if not the cause, of Jacob's counter-move. Laban was evidently actuated by similar feelings of envy (ver. 2). He hardly expected to find his match in his apparently yielding and submissive nephew.

In the midst of this trying situation God interposed, and made known His will to Jacob, so that what had hitherto been an intense desire became also a plain duty (ver. 3). He is commanded to return, and with the command comes the promise of the Divine presence.

II. *The Consultation* (vers. 4-16).—Jacob acts with his accustomed promptitude, and the first step is to take counsel with his wives. To have them in accord with him would be a very great advantage. The journey home would be long, and the destination unknown and strange to them. Much therefore depended on his obtaining their acquiescence. He thereupon placed before them all the facts (vers. 4-13), speaking plainly of their father's injustice to him. Deception, change of wages no less than ten times, and all this in spite of faithful, strenuous, long-continued service, had been Jacob's experience of Laban. But God had not left him, and now had come the Divine message to return to his own land. In this recital Jacob claims for himself Divine protection and approval (vers. 5, 9, 11), and reveals no consciousness of any wrong-doing of his own. To him it was a deep-seated conviction, which marked his life from the outset, that the end justified the means, and it seems clear that he considered he was doing right in taking steps to increase his possessions by reason of Laban's actions in not paying the proper wages. Jacob had a long way to go yet before he came to the end of himself.

The true character of Laban is clearly seen from the fact that his daughters entirely sided with Jacob against their own father. Even though it was husband against father, they were very evidently and heartily one with Jacob. They too had experienced their father's selfishness and greed, and were ready to approve of their husband's project and to go with him. While not laying undue stress on this acquiescence and approval, it is impossible not to regard it as a testimony to Jacob's general faithfulness, so far as the wives had the spiritual discernment to judge of it.

III. *The Flight* (vers. 17-21).—Again Jacob acted with characteristic promptitude and initiative, that very striking feature which marked all his life. Collecting all that he had, he set out on his long journey. What his feelings were as he turned his face homewards we can well understand. Whether he had heard of his mother's death we know not; but if the news had not reached him, we can imagine the joyful anticipation of meeting her who had sacrificed much for him. There was, however, one crook in the lot, though happily Jacob was unaware of it. Rachel, his favorite and greatly beloved wife, still retained some of her Syrian superstitions, and had stolen the teraphim, or small household gods, belonging to her father. These idols seem to have been used as charms, whose presence was thought to bring good to the possessor. It is curious that Rachel, and not Leah, should have almost always turned out to be Jacob's greatest hindrance in life.

IV. *The Pursuit* (vers. 22-24).—Jacob had only been gone three days when Laban was told of what had happened. At once he started off in pursuit, evidently intending to bring back the fugitives by superior force, and compel Jacob once more to return to a service that, in spite of everything, was decidedly profitable to Laban. But Laban has to reckon with Someone Who was stronger than Jacob. God interposes on Jacob's behalf and warns Laban to do the fugitives no harm. This Divine warning is a clear proof of what Laban had intended to do. It is also a testimony that, in spite of all we with our clear light can now see objectionable in Jacob, right and truth were on the whole with Jacob, and not with Laban. "Laban's treatment of Jacob has naturally a bearing on the estimate we form of Jacob's behavior towards Laban. Laban is not only the first to break faith with Jacob, but is throughout the chief offender: and had Laban treated Jacob honestly and generously, there is no reason to suppose that he would have sought to overreach him" (Driver, *Genesis*, p. 290.)

V. *The Expostulation* (vers. 25-35).—Laban's attitude of injured innocence is very suggestive in the light of the whole story. It is a mixture of hypocrisy and exaggeration. His expressions of love for his daughters and grandchildren are either utterly unreal, or else so impulsively emotional as to be practically worthless. He had had many years of opportunity to show love to them, but the very reverse had been their experience, as they had told Jacob. Love expressed so late as this cannot be worth much. It is what we are prepared to do for our loved ones while they are with us, not the kind of things we say of them after they are gone, that is the real test and genuine measure of our affection.

Laban tells Jacob what he had power to do and what doubtless he would have done but for the warning from God the previous night. And so he contents himself by charging Jacob with the theft of his household gods. It is difficult to appraise at anything like a real spiritual value the religion of Laban. It seems to have been mainly of an indirect and second-hand character, a mixture of truth and error, a blending of a consciousness of the Divine presence with a belief in images. This superstitious use of household gods seems to have been a breach of the law of the second rather than of the first Commandment.

Jacob was of course entirely ignorant of Rachel's theft, and is therefore able to assert his innocence and allow Laban to search through the tents for the lost teraphim. Rachel was a true daughter of her father and a match for him in cunning. But she little knew the trouble she was bringing on Jacob and herself by this deceit.

VI. *The Vindication* (vers. 36-42).—The failure to discover the gods gave Jacob his opportunity to vindicate himself, and right bravely he does it. He recounts with telling force what he had done for Laban, and how he had been requited. And it should be carefully observed that the statements are allowed to "pass unchallenged"

(Driver, p. 290), a proof of their essential truth, for Laban was not the man to allow all this to be said if it had not been true. One thing at least cannot be laid to the charge of Jacob; he was not unfaithful in his long-continued service to Laban. These verses bear reading and pondering. Jacob clearly sees the true meaning of the Divine vision to Laban. It was nothing else than a rebuke for conduct that was in every way uncalled for and despicable. God may have much against His own servants which He will not allow to pass, but He will in any case defend their cause against the wrong-doer and champion them in the face of flagrant injustice. (Cf. Jer. xv. 19-21.)

VII. *The Covenant* (vers. 43-55).—Laban at length realizes the true position of affairs, and proposes to end the feud by a covenant. A pillar is first of all raised, and then a heap of stones. The heap is called by Laban, in Syriac, "Jegarsahadutha" ("the heap of witness"), and by Jacob, in Hebrew, "Galeed," which has exactly the same meaning. The pillar is called "Mizpah" ("watch tower"), and is regarded as the symbol of the Lord watching between the two parties to the covenant and keeping guard over the agreement, lest either should break it. Then comes the solemn oath in the Name of God, followed by the usual sacrifice and sacrificial feast. These two were now "blood-brothers" (see Trumbull's *Blood-Covenant*), pledged to eternal unity and fealty. The next morning Laban and his followers returned, and Jacob and his household went on their journey.

It is impossible to avoid noticing the curious misconception of the term "Mizpah" which characterizes its use today. As used for a motto on rings, Christmas cards, and even as the title of an organization, it is interpreted to mean union, trust, and fellowship; while its original meaning was that of separation, distrust, and warning. Two men, neither of whom trusted the other, said in effect: "I cannot trust you out of my sight. The Lord must be the watchman between us if we and our goods are to be kept safe from each other." Thus curiously does primary interpretation differ from spiritual application, and conveys a necessary admonition against the misuse of Scripture even by spiritual people.

1. *The will of God in daily life.*—Mark carefully the steps by which Jacob was led to return home. They afford a striking lesson on the Divine methods of guidance. First of all a *desire* to go home sprang up in Jacob's heart. Then *circumstances* between him and Laban began to make it impossible for him to remain. The nest was being stirred up, and his position rendered intolerable by envy, jealousy, and injustice. And, lastly, came the Divine *message* of command. Thus inward desire, outward circumstances and the Divine word combined to make the pathway clear. This is ever the way of God's guidance; the conviction of the spirit within, the Word agreeing with it in principle, and then outward circumstances making action possible. When these three agree, we may be sure of right guidance. When the first two alone are clear, the way may be right, but the time is not yet come. When the third only is clear and the two former are not, we may be certain that the way is *not* right. Only let us be spiritually alert, and then "the meek will He guide in judgment, the meek will He teach His way."

2. *The acknowledgment of God in daily life.*—We cannot fail to see the way in which Jacob, Leah, Rachel, and Laban, all in their turn and way, speak of God as either interposing on their behalf or else taking action to prevent them from accomplishing their purpose. Above all we observe the way in which Laban and Jacob make and complete the covenant, by invoking God's presence and power. It may not be possible always to discern God's hand aright, or to attribute to Him precisely the things that really come from Him, but it is surely one of the prime secrets of true life to be able to acknowledge God's presence and power, and to realize that there is "a Divinity that shapes our ends." The words of the wise man are as true today as ever, and true moreover, in spite of any mistakes we may make about God's hand: "In all thy ways acknowledge Him." To do this is to live as He desires us to live.

3. *The Providence of God in daily life.*—Amid much that is sad and even sordid in this story; amid "envy, hatred, malice, and all uncharitableness"; amid craft, deceit, and lying on almost every side, we cannot fail to see the hand of God overruling, and making even the wrath of man to praise Him. We are often perplexed by

the problems of sin and freewill, and we are baffled as we try to think out how God's will can possibly be done amid all the perverseness of human nature. But we can learn much from a story like this, as we observe each actor a perfectly free agent and yet see everything taken up into the Divine purpose and made to serve far-reaching ends. We may well speak of God's providence—pro-vidence, His "seeing beforehand" and making provision accordingly. It is this that gives quietness amidst perplexities, and enables the soul to rest in faith until all is made clear. God's providence is indeed the saints' inheritance.

XLIII

GOD'S HOST FOR MAN'S HELP

GEN. xxxii. 1-23

1. And Jacob went on his way, and the angels of God met him.
2. And when Jacob saw them, he said, This *is* God's host: and he called the name of that place Mahanaim.
3. And Jacob sent messengers before him to Esau his brother unto the land of Seir, the country of Edom.
4. And he commanded them, saying, Thus shall ye speak unto my lord Esau; Thy servant Jacob saith thus, I have sojourned with Laban, and stayed there until now:
5. And I have oxen, and asses, flocks, and menservants, and womenservants: and I have sent to tell my lord, that I may find grace in thy sight.
6. And the messengers returned to Jacob, saying We came to thy brother Esau, and also he cometh to meet thee, and four hundred men with him.
7. Then Jacob was greatly afraid and distressed: and he divided the people that was with him, and the flocks, and herds, and the camels, into two bands;
8. And said, if Esau come to the one company, and smite it then the other company which is left shall escape.
9. And Jacob said, O God of my father Abraham, and God of my father Isaac, the Lord which saidst unto me, Return unto thy country, and to thy kindred, and I will deal well with thee.
10. I am not worthy of the least of all the mercies, and of all the truth, which thou hast shewed unto thy servant; for with my staff I passed over this Jordan; and now I am become two bands.
11. Deliver me, I pray thee, from the hand of my brother, from the hand of Esau; for I fear him, lest he will come and smite me, *and* the mother with the children.
12. And thou saidst, I will surely do thee good, and make thy seed as the sand of the sea, which cannot be numbered for multitude.
13. And he lodged there that same night; and took of that which came to his hand a present for Esau his brother;
14. Two hundred she goats, and twenty he goats, two hundred ewes, and twenty rams,
15. Thirty milch camels, with their colts, forty kine, and ten bulls, twenty she asses, and ten foals.
16. And he delivered *them* into the hand of his servants, every drove by themselves; and said unto his servants, Pass over before me, and put a space betwixt drove and drove.

17. And he commanded the foremost, saying, When Esau my brother meeteth thee, and asketh thee, saying, whose *art* thou? and whither goest thou? and whose *are* these before thee?

18. Then thou shalt say, *They be* thy servant Jacob's; it *is* a present sent unto my lord Esau: and, behold, also he is behind us.

19. And so commanded he the second, and the third, and all that followed the droves, saying, On this manner shall ye speak unto Esau, when ye find him.

20. And say ye moreover, Behold, thy servant Jacob is behind us. For he said, I will appease him with the present that goeth before me, and afterward I will see his face; peradventure he will accept of me.

21. So went the present over before him: and himself lodged that night in the company.

22. And he rose up that night, and took his two wives, and his two womenservants, and his eleven sons, and passed over the ford Jabbok.

23. And he took them, and sent them over the brook, and sent over that he had.

GOD'S discipline for man sometimes takes the form of a lengthened process, like the years of Jacob with Laban. At other times it is experienced in the form of a short and perhaps sharp crisis, as at Bethel. We are now to consider another of these crises in the life of Jacob, a turning-point, a pivot in his career. Freed from the trammels endured at Haran, he soon becomes aware once again of the hand of God upon him and the Divine purpose concerning him. The grace of God which had never left him, is now to work upon him as never before. Let us mark closely the various stages of the process. Now and henceforward we shall see very clearly the conflict of nature and grace, and the way in which grace overcomes nature. There is scarcely any character in Scripture which is more full of profound yet practical lessons for the spiritual life.

I. *Messengers of God* (vers. 1, 2).—Delivered from the thraldom of Laban's service Jacob goes on his way towards the old home, only to realize before long that another difficulty confronts him in his brother Esau. But between the two difficulties comes this timely revelation from God; "the angels of God met him." How and by what way this manifestation was vouchsafed, whether by waking vision or midnight dream, we know not. Suffice it to say that it was one more proof of the Divine assurance that Jacob should not be left until the purpose of God had been accomplished in him (xxviii. 15). The angels of God had come to him at Bethel (xxviii. 12) and in Haran (xxxi. 11), and now met him again.

The ministry of angels to the children of God is one of the most interesting and precious elements of the Divine revelations in Scripture. No details are given to satisfy curiosity, but the fact is certain and the blessedness is real (Ps. xxxiv. 7; Dan. vi. 22; Heb. i. 14). And it is worth while remembering that angels, as they are brought before us in Holy Writ, are invariably depicted as the *servants* of the saints—their inferiors, not superiors. It is probably a mistake to think of angels as occupying an intermediate place between men and God, as something more than the one and less than the other. It may have been this error that has led to the worshipping of angels and the thought of them as mediators between an impure humanity and a holy God. Scripture, on the contrary, reveals them as always *ministers*, servants, of those who are higher than themselves in spiritual place and privilege, of those who are "heirs of salvation." (Cf. Heb. i. 14; 1 Pet. i. 12.)

This manifestation from God Jacob was quick to see. He recognized the Divine hand, and said, "This is God's host." Whatever may have happened during those years in Haran, Jacob still retained sufficient spiritual discernment to apprehend God's action in this meeting. And he at once raises a memorial of the occasion by calling it "Mahanaim"—"Two Hosts" or "Two Camps"—God's heavenly host and his own earthly host of possessions granted to him by God (xxxi. 9) and now to be protected by God. "Whether visible to the eye of sense or, as would appear, only the eye of faith, they *are* visible to this troubled man; and, in a glow of confident joy, he calls the name of that place "Mahanaim," Two Camps. One camp was the little one of his own down here, with the helpless women and children and his own frightened and defenceless self; and the other was the great one up there, or rather in shadowy but most real spiritual presence around about him, as a bodyguard making an impregnable wall between him and every foe" (Maclaren).

On the first great occasion of his life he had raised his memorial and called it "God's House" (xxviii. 17). On this, the second great

occasion, he is conscious of "God's Host." He has still a deeper
experience to pass through before he can raise his third and crowning memorial to "God's Face."

II. *Messengers of Man* (vers. 3-6).—It is impossible to avoid
seeing the connection and contrast between God's messengers to
Jacob and Jacob's messengers to Esau. The pity of it is that Jacob
did not fully learn the simple yet profound lesson of the connection.
As he nears the borders of the old country, memory begins to move
and conscience to work. He knows that there can be no peace and
quiet until his relations with Esau are assured and put on a proper
footing. Not until *that* matter was settled could Jacob feel certain
of his future. Is not this a great principle of the spiritual life? We
must put right what we know to be wrong before we can enjoy
settled peace. Unconfessed sin, unforgiven wrong, must be dealt
with and put right. Righteousness must precede peace (Isa. xxxii.
17; Ps. lxxxv. 10 and lxxii. 3).

Jacob's despatch of an embassy to his brother was obviously
to feel his way, to learn Esau's mind towards him. But the obsequiousness of the message, with its repeated emphasis on "my
lord Esau" and "thy servant Jacob," does not sound well from
one who had met the angels of God. The words indicate a servile
fear that seems strange and surprising in one who had already been
assured of the birthright and blessing, and whose personal position
as the owner of great possessions surely warranted a higher tone.
There is a world of difference between genuine repentance and
grovelling humiliation. Jacob could have shown the one without
the accompaniment of the other. The message is throughout marked by a spirit of fear of Esau which is unworthy of one who had
received such assurances from God. But Jacob was probably not
the first, as he certainly was not the last, to fail to realize the direct
and causative influence of his intercourse with God on his intercourse with man. While he is in God's presence he seems to be
learning aright his spiritual lessons; but when he is face to face
with a crisis he forgets the assurances derived from God and proceeds to act for himself as though his own initiative and natural
powers were everything.

The messengers return and bring news of the coming of Esau to meet his brother, accompanied by 400 evidently armed men. Not a word of friendly greeting in response to the fawning message, not a single indication of reconciliation in spite of all the intervening years. Not even Jacob's reminder of his long sojourn with Laban "until now," with its implication of having left Esau free all this time, had sufficed to put matters right. The old hostility which had died down by lapse of time seems to have been roused up, and the impulsive, easily-stirred Esau sets out to meet Jacob with a retinue which appears to bode nothing but ill. It may have been done merely to frighten Jacob, or it may have been prompted by a genuine determination to take revenge, but it had the immediate effect of driving Jacob into an exhibition of his old natural self, and thereby afforded a fresh proof of the small extent to which God's assurances of grace had as yet laid hold of his inner life.

III. *Fear of Man* (vers. 7, 8).—Jacob's intense fear and distress were evidently due to his conviction that Esau's coming meant hostility, that the past had not been forgotten or overlooked. But he soon recovers his balance, though, instead of at once casting himself on God, he begins his characteristic work of planning. Esau's host had for the time driven out of his mind the host of God, and now again he proceeds to display that natural resourcefulness which characterized him all his days from the beginning to the very end. He divided his possessions into two parts, so that in case Esau fell on one of them the other might escape and at least something be left. The employment of this stratagem clearly shows that with all his possessions armed resistance was quite impossible, and, still more, it shows that once again Jacob was not using for his own peace and assurance the real meaning of the revelation that God had vouchsafed to him. At that moment the "angels of God" were not in his mind, or he might easily have remembered that they who were with him were more than all Esau's host (2 Kings vi. 16).

IV. *Fear of God* (vers. 9-12).—And yet, in spite of all his clever planning, he cannot help turning to God, even though, like many others since, he arranges matters before he begins to pray (Acts i. 23, 24). He called God to help him in the due execution of his own projects, instead of reversing the order and asking, "Lord, what wilt Thou have me to do?" Let us now look at his prayer. It is worthy of careful consideration on several grounds; both for what it contains and also for what it lacks.

It is a prayer of real and yet partial faith (ver. 9). He calls on God, and so far well; yet is it not strange, after Bethel and Haran and Mahanaim, that he does not rise to the height of calling God his own God, but contents himself with the thought of God as the God of his fathers? Then, again, his faith is clear and true in his reminder to God of His commands and promises about the return from Haran, but is it not curious that he does not see that after these promises God would surely take care of him? By all means let us put God in remembrance and plead His promises, but let us also expect that God can and will fulfil His own word (Acts xxvii. 25). His faith, then, was real, but partial; true, but inadequate; and yet, though it is easy for us as we read the narrative to see where he failed, let us not forget that we are often doing the very same ourselves, with far greater light than Jacob had, and therefore with infinitely less reason. We must take care lest we miss the lesson for ourselves in all this, "lest we forget."

The prayer was also marked by true humility (ver. 10). He acknowledged his own unworthiness of all that God had done to and for him, and with heartfelt gratitude he testifies to the way in which blessings had been showered on him. There is perhaps nothing wanting here unless, as some think, it be a consciousness of sin. Certainly we find no indication that he realized any connection between his present fear of Esau and the events associated with the surreptitious possession of the blessing. But in any case the spirit of this humility is a marked advance on anything we have hitherto seen in Jacob. God was indeed at work in his soul.

The prayer was also one of intensely earnest entreaty (ver. 11). He cries out for fear of Esau, and craves deliverance. He assigns as his reason for protection the fear lest he, his wives, and children should be destroyed by his passionate and ruthless brother. The reference to the "mother with the children" is very touching and beautiful, revealing the tenderness of Jacob's nature. And yet it is impossible to overlook the characteristic lack of faith whereby, after expressing this fear of losing his children, he quotes God's promise about those very children being "as the sand of the sea." How like Jacob was this failure to draw the true conclusion of faith from the premises of the Divine promise! And if we call attention to it we are not desirous of blaming him, so much as of using his failure to point the moral for ourselves. "Hath He said, and shall He not do it?"

As we review this prayer we seem to see in it a revelation of a genuine work of grace after years of apparent fruitlessness. Like a stream that emerges into day after running for a long distance underground, Jacob's spiritual life comes out now after those years at Haran; and, though there is still much to seek, we can see the clear marks of the work of God directing, deepening, and purifying his soul. God had never left him (xxviii. 15), as these spiritual experiences abundantly indicate.

V. *Dread of Man* (vers. 17-19).—Once again we seem to be brought face to face with the other and less worthy side of Jacob. After prayer he is planning again. What is the connection between his praying and his planning? Was the latter the due use of precautions? Was it the proper way of answering his own prayer? It would hardly seem so. It appears rather to be an expression of his intense fear. He proceeds to arrange his possessions into droves of cattle, with distances separating them. He is intent on appeasing Esau with a present, and with remarkable skill he brings train after train to lay siege to his brother. He piles present upon present to break down opposition. When he first sent messengers to Esau (ver. 3) there was no indication of any present, for he thought perhaps none would be needed; but now his great fear compels him to take these steps. He is still concerned to manage Esau, instead of letting God do it for him; and the message to the servants breathes the same spirit of obsequious cringing to his brother. Truly "the fear of man bringeth a snare," and it is only "he who trusteth in the Lord" that is set on high above all such dread.

VI. *Distrust of God* (vers. 20-23).—It seems clear that all this careful preparation was unwarrantably made. We can see it now in the sequel (xxxiii. 9), but it was equally unwarranted before Esau appeared. The man who prayed that prayer (vers. 9-12) surely ought not to have spoken as he afterwards did (ver. 20). Had he not already forgotten his prayer? He was so filled with his own fears and prospects that he quite failed to rest his heart on God and trust Him to plan and protect. If we express our needs in prayer, it is obviously unfitting to go on arranging and scheming as though we had never prayed. It is one thing to seek wisdom from God and trust Him for it; quite another to ask God's blessing on our own wisdom. And it was this that Jacob had to learn before he met Esau. Only when God had brought him to an utter end of himself could the true position be taken and the full blessing granted. Meanwhile we pause here to gather up some of the most obvious lessons for ourselves.

1. *God's provision comes just when it is needed.*—The angelic host appeared just after Jacob had left Laban and before he encountered Esau. God is never too soon and never too late. "Thou *preventest* him with the blessings of goodness." The old theological phraseology of "prevenient grace" embodies one of the profoundest and most precious truths of the spiritual life. God anticipates our need, and provides His grace just when we require it. He sees beforehand, what we cannot see, the needs of the soul, and comes in love to meet them. Whatever the circumstance or emergency, God will be there; for not only has He said, "I will not forsake thee" (that is, when once He has come), but also "I will not fail thee" (that is, when the need first arises). As we go on our way we may rest assured that God's host will meet us.

2. *God's provision comes just as it is needed.*—Not only *when*, but *as*; not only timely, but appropriate. What was Jacob's one great need at that moment? Surely it was protection. And so God sent His *host* to assure him of it. God always suits His grace to His people's needs. When Israel was in Egypt they needed deliverance, and obtained it. When they reached Sinai they required instruction, and received the Law. When hostility from surround-

ing nations was at hand, then, and then only, came the entirely
new title "the Lord of *hosts*" (1 Sam. i. 3). So it is always. "*As
. . . so*" is God's great principle for His people. Whatever the need,
that will be the nature and measure of the supply.

3. *God's provision should remove the fear of man.*—The Divine
revelation to Jacob was intended to do for him exactly what he
needed most, and yet he never really lost the fear of his brother.
He could not fully trust God. He "committed his way to the Lord,"
but did not "trust *also* in Him." He still carried his burden himself, even after God's angels came, and after his own prayer to God.
And yet God's grace is intended to be a reality in our lives. We
miss very much when we do not trust Him fully. If only the swim-
mer yields to the water, the water bears him up; but if he continues
to struggle, the result is disastrous. Let us learn to trust, just as
we learn to float.

4. *God's provision renders clever scheming unnecessary and even
sinful.*—There is a very true sense in which everyone who prays
must also use means. "Trust in God and keep your powder dry."
But there is an equally true sense in which anxiety about means
and methods is the very reverse of the right attitude for the believer. Jacob's heart was more set on planning than on praying.
He plans before and after his prayer. He asks God, it is true, but
almost at the same time he seems to feel that he must depend entirely on his own resources. He leans on his plan more than on his
prayer; indeed, as we read of the plans, we forget that he ever
prayed, and he apparently forgot it also. To the true believer, the
man of real faith in God, there will be no real difficulty as to the
relation of prayer and work. His work, as well as his prayer, will
be manifestly permeated by trust in God. There is a very real sense
in which *orare est laborare;* for the man who prays trustfully, rest-
fully, hopefully, will find heart and mind so taken up with God that
instinctively he will be led to adopt such methods as will reveal his
trust and answer his own prayer. The soul that is truly and fully
occupied with God will never be at a loss to know the true relation
between prayer and work, work and prayer; for in answer to prayer

comes the spirit of wisdom, the spirit of a sound mind, the spirit of courage and fearlessness, the spirit of calm restfulness and equally calm progress. It will know when to "stand still" and when to "go forward," because God is its all in all.

NOTE.—The word rendered "appease" in verse 20 is *kipper*, the word afterwards used for "covering" or "atonement." This is its first occurrence in the Bible (xx 16 is different, but allied in thought), and, according to the principle of first occurrences in Scripture (see on xv. 1-4), the usage here helps to interpret the true meaning of atonement.

XLIV

PENIEL — THE FACE OF GOD

GEN. xxxii. 24-32

24. And Jacob was left alone; and there wrestled a man with him until the breaking of the day.

25. And when he saw that he prevailed not against him, he touched the hollow of his thigh; and the hollow of Jacob's thigh was out of joint as he wrestled with him.

26. And he said, Let me go, for the day breaketh. And he said, I will not let thee go, except thou bless me.

27. And he said unto him, What *is* thy name? And he said, Jacob.

28. And he said, Thy name shall be called no more Jacob, but Israel: for as a prince hast thou power with God and with men, and hast prevailed.

29. And Jacob asked *him*, and said, Tell *me*, I pray thee, thy name. And he said, Wherefore *is* it *that* thou dost ask after my name? And he blessed him there.

30. And Jacob called the name of the place Peniel: for I have seen God face to face, and my life is preserved.

31. And as he passed over Penuel the sun rose upon him, and he halted upon his thigh.

32. Therefore the children of Israel eat not *of* the sinew which shrank, which *is* upon the hollow of the thigh, unto this day: because he touched the hollow of Jacob's thigh in the sinew that shrank.

THE one absorbing thought with Jacob was his meeting with Esau. It never seems to have occurred to him that there was a far greater need—a meeting with God. Still less did he imagine that there could be any connection between the two meetings, that his meeting with God would prove the best preparation for meeting his brother. These two thoughts sum up the story before us: Jacob must meet God before he meets Esau, and the one meeting will be the only and sufficient way of preparing for the other. We are thus able to understand what a spiritual crisis this was to Jacob, and we can also perceive, what Jacob did not, how lovingly God provided for this by the embassy of the angels (ver. 1). More than this, we can see in the story an illustration of God's dealings with His children today. Are we faced with some difficult problem? Are we opposed by some apparently insuperable obstacle? Are we at our wit's end in view of some terrible need? Let us learn from the story of Jacob to put God first, and thereby to discover the secret of all real spiritual power and blessing. The story brings before us a striking contrast of the human and the Divine, and reveals the way in which the human is met, dealt with, overcome, and blessed by the Divine. Step by step as the narrative is unfolded we observe this contrast between nature and grace, between man and God, between self-effort and Divine power.

I. *Human Solitude* (ver. 24).—Jacob had sent all his family, household, and possessions over the ford Jabbok. But for some reason or other he remained that night on the opposite bank; he was "left alone." Why was this? He was clearly conscious that a great crisis had come in his life. Anything might happen on the next morning when Esau and his four hundred men arrived. He had planned and prayed, prayed and planned, and now there was nothing more for him to do. Inaction was the most difficult of all things for so resourceful and energetic a nature. For Jacob to *wait*, instead of to work, was the greatest of all efforts. And yet there he was, in the darkness of the night, alone, with all the events of the past day clear before him, with all the awful possibilities of the coming day well in view. Why, then, was he alone? Is there any spiritual meaning in it? Was there a spiritual need expressed by this sending over all his household and himself remaining outside the promised land? Was there any idea of the blessing of solitude as "the mother-country of the strong?" It is difficult to say, but the probability is that this solitude was merely for the purpose of taking every possible precaution. He had arranged his present to "appease" his brother, he had sent over the ford all that was nearest and most precious to him, and now he remains alone on guard, ready for any emergency, or any attack under cover of the night. Alert as ever, he will leave nothing to chance; he will not even sleep.

II. *Divine Discipline* (ver. 24).—Suddenly he is conscious of an assailant. A man wrestles with him. At once, the courageous, re-

sourceful Jacob closes with this opponent. It would seem as though
Jacob regarded him as an emissary of Esau who had come to bar
his way to the promised land. As such he is to be resisted and opposed with all possible strength. The struggle went on until daybreak, and all the while it was not Esau or any of his men. Let us
mark carefully the description: "There wrestled a man *with him*."
It is sometimes read as though Jacob wrestled with the man, and
from it is derived the lesson of prevailing prayer. But this is to
mistake altogether the point of the story. "There wrestled a man
with him." The wrestling was an endeavor on God's part to break
down Jacob's opposition, to bring him to an end of himself, to take
from him all self-trust, all confidence in his own cleverness and resource, to make him know that Esau is to be overcome and Canaan
obtained not by craft or flattery, but by Divine grace and power.
There is no lesson at all on prevailing prayer. Far from it; quite
the opposite. The self-life in Jacob is to be overcome, the old nature
is to be conquered, the planning is to be rendered futile, and the
resourcefulness made impotent. Instead of gaining Canaan by
cleverness he must receive it as a gift from God. Instead of winning
he must accept it from Divine grace.

Was this a literal physical struggle? Most assuredly it was. The
outcome shows this very clearly (vers. 25, 31, 32). And yet the
physical aspect is subservient to the spiritual, the bodily weakness
was to be a symbol of the spiritual need of the man.

III. *Human Opposition* (ver. 25).—In the darkness of the night
Jacob did not realize who and what his assailant was. And so he
put forth all his resources of bodily vigor. Keyed up by the stirring
events of the preceding day, and remembering that all his precious
possessions were involved, to say nothing of his own life, he resisted
this powerful opponent, and the struggle remained in the balance
hour after hour. His pertinacity was marvelous! Here was no
coward, no poltroon, but a man of unbounded energy, ready to fight
for his own to the last.

How like he is to many of us today! We do not realize that all
these untoward circumstances, these perplexities, these sorrows, are
part of the Divine discipline, and intended to bring us to the end

of ourselves. And so we struggle, and strive, and fight, and resist, and all to no purpose. God had been trying to get Jacob to trust Him all these years. He met him at Bethel with vision and promises, and yet how poor was the response (xxviii.). He met him again during those years in Haran, using disappointment (xxix.), trouble (xxx.), and opposition (xxxi.) to lead to trust, but to little or no effect. And then came the angelic host (xxxii. 1 ff.) ; but its effect was only transient, the self-effort was soon in the ascendant again. And now comes the crowning attempt to break down this man's self-confidence and lead him to lean, to trust, to wait on his covenant God. But he will not, he cannot; he must oppose, he must resist, he must act for himself. He might pray, and pray earnestly, but he must also act; and act he did, though the net result was only to thwart and delay the Divine purpose concerning him. So it is often with us; we refuse to trust God, to put Him first, in spite of all the assurance of His love and the revelation of His grace through many a long year. But God did not leave Jacob, and He does not leave us.

IV. *Divine Power* (ver. 25).—At last Jacob was made to realize the true state of affairs. So marvelous was the human opposition that nothing short of a special manifestation of Divine power would suffice to break it down. God could have done this earlier in the struggle, but He would not, for He wanted Jacob's willing surrender. Yet at length, as He could not obtain this, there was nothing else to be done but to deal with him in severity, and by an assertion of Divine power to bring this masterful man to an end of himself. God wished Jacob to realize that only by Divine grace he could meet Esau and enter Canaan; that he could not overcome by guile and enter by cleverness; that only by mercy, grace, and favor could his difficulties be met and his way prospered. And so "He touched the hollow of his thigh," took away the very power required for wrestling, brought him by one swift blow to the very end of his resources, and left him utterly powerless. Thus Divine love dealt with him in mercy and taught him, albeit in severity, the one lesson he needed most to learn.

Here again we see ourselves and God's dealing with us. God must bring us to Himself, and He can only do this by bringing us to an end of ourselves. And because of our senseless resistance and dull inability to see His fatherly hand in discipline, he has to touch our natural powers and resources, and reduce us to impotence before He can teach us the needed lesson and bestow the needed grace. And yet His "touch" is always one of love, of wisdom, of mercy, if only we would see it.

V. *Human Helplessness* (ver. 26).—As the dawn came on, Jacob recognized the mysterious assailant. No longer able to wrestle, he began to cling. Instead of opposition came tenacity, and Jacob proved himself to possess the latter as fully as the former. Disabled at the very point of strength for wrestling, Jacob could do nothing but cling. From cunning to clinging, from resisting to resting— this was the literal and symbolical experience of the crafty but now conquered Jacob. His words, 'I will not let Thee go except Thou bless me," are clear evidence of the change in him. He is conscious at last of the futility of all his efforts to appease Esau and overcome his animosity, and now he clings to God and seeks for blessing. At last he is in the right position, but at what cost! If only he had learnt the lesson sooner, how much trouble and anxiety he would have been spared! No fears of Esau, no need of planning to appease him, no concern for his wives and children, nothing but rest of heart in the love of God. Ah! if only he had learnt the lesson of Bethel, and the lesson of Haran, and the lesson of Mahanaim! But now it is learnt, and God is better to him than all his fears. What he struggled for, he lost; what he trusted for, he gained. So it is always. It is always worth while to trust God and put Him first.

VI. *Divine Blessing* (vers. 27-29).—"Except Thou bless me" was Jacob's desire (ver. 26). "And He blessed him there" was the Divine answer (ver. 29). But what was included in that Divine blessing? Very much that concerned Jacob's life and experience.

A new character was to be his. He is asked his name, and is compelled to call himself Jacob, "Supplanter." But this is to be changed to "Israel," "God's Prince" or "God's Perseverer" (Driver) ;

the one who is no longer the crafty one, but he who is worthy to prevail, to lead, to rule, to overcome.

A new power was also to be his. He had experienced power with God by clinging. He is now to have power with man by reason of having power with God. (Cf. Hos. xii. 3, 4.) When God is put first, power with man naturally and necessarily follows. The gloss of the Septuagint and the Vulgate seems to give the true idea of the verse: "Thou hast had power with God; much more shalt thou prevail with men." The one is the guarantee of the other.

A new experience was also to be his. The Divine Angel could ask Jacob's name (ver. 27), but Jacob was not allowed to know the Angel's (ver. 29; cf. Judg. xiii. 17). There seems little doubt that this was a Divine manifestation, not the visit of a created angel. (Cf. Gen. xviii. 1, 2, 16, 22.) But if Jacob might not know His name, he could experience His blessing, for "He blessed him there."

VII. *Human Gratitude* (ver. 30).—As on previous occasions, Jacob again raised his "Ebenezer," and made a memorial of the experience which had been vouchsafed to him. He called the name of the place "Peniel," God's Face, in token of that wonderful bestowal of God's favor and of the preservation of his life (Exod. xxxiii. 20; Deut. iv. 33; Judg. vi. 22f. and xiii. 22). He realized, in some measure at least, what it meant. God had met him, taught him, blessed him; and now he could meet Esau without fear, and face any emergency, in the strength of that glorious vision.

VIII. *Divine Glory* (vers. 31, 32).—"The sun rose upon him." There was sunshine within as well. The sun seemed brighter than ever that morning, and the very face of nature seemed changed by reason of that vision of the face of God. The sun of God's glory was reflected on Jacob's face too, and though he had to bear the marks of that contest (ver. 31), and though there was to be a perpetual record of it in the days to come (ver. 32), yet it had all been worth while, for the grace of God had overcome the self-effort of man, the fear of God had displaced the fear of man, the power of God had given assurances as to the power of man. Jacob was now a monument of Divine grace, and was intended henceforth to live to the Divine glory. Thus God justified and vindicated Himself in the life of His unworthy servant, "to the praise of the glory of His grace." Thus God's loving sympathy, marvelous patience, and perfect wisdom shone forth in His dealings with Jacob; grace was glorified, and God Himself magnified.

(For a summary of the true meaning of this episode, see the suggestive note in Driver's *Genesis*, p. 296.)

Peniel was a noteworthy landmark in Jacob's spiritual history. It was the third occasion and culminating point of a special Divine revelation. The first was Bethel, where "the House of God" reminded and assured him of the Divine *Presence*. The second was Mahanaim, where the "Host of God" taught him the Divine *Power*. The third was Peniel, where he was led beyond the ideas of God's presence and power to that of Divine *Favor* and *Fellowship*. The "Face" of God is used constantly in Scripture as a symbol of favor, friendship, fellowship (Exod. xxxiii. 11, 20; Deut. xxxiv. 10), and in the believer's life fellowship is the highest of our spiritual privileges (1 John i. 3). God desired and purposed to bring Jacob into this position of blessedness and power; and all the Divine dealings, from Bethel onwards, were intended to lead up to this. So it is now; everything that God has for us is expressed in terms of union and communion of which the New Testament is so full. What, then, will this fellowship accomplish?

1. *The "Face of God" is the place of transformation of character.* —Fellowship with God changes Jacobs to Israels. "Behold . . . we are being changed." From this time onward there was a very distinct change in Jacob; and although the old nature was still there, Peniel had its effect and exercised transforming influence. There is nothing like fellowship with God to change and transfigure our nature.

2. *The "Face of God" is the place of power for daily life.*—Like Jacob, we have to meet our Esaus and we are afraid. We strive, plan, struggle, and all to no purpose. But we see God's Face, and all is changed. Power with man comes from power with God. We have, it may be, a crisis today; but first of all we pray, and the victory is gained. We wonder who will roll away the stone, but find that it is already gone. Fellowship with God gives insight and

foresight, peace and patience, calm and courage in every emergency, and enables us to become "more than conquerors" over every foe. Just as power with God came by surrender, so also will power with men come by willing self-sacrifice on their behalf. Self is the greatest foe to blessing from God or influence with men.

3. *The "Face of God" is the place of spiritual blessing.*—In the presence of God it is impossible to use carnal weapons. "If I regard iniquity in my heart, the Lord will not hear me." When Jacob came to an end of struggling and commenced clinging, the blessing quickly came. Jacob hitherto had no idea of a blessing obtained by passive receptiveness. But in the life of a true believer God's best gifts come that way. Gain comes by loss, gathering by scattering. So it must be always. Fellowship with God dispenses with subterfuges, natural craft, and clever resourcefulness. The wisdom of this world is foolishness with God. Blessing must be obtained in the right way or not at all. The supreme need of man is the grace of God, and this is not only independent of, but opposed to all that is merely earthly and human. Just as salvation is of God by grace, so is every spiritual blessing derived in the same way. Whether we think of the individual believer or the community of God's people, all grace comes through fellowship with God. Not by unworthy expedients, not by mere human effort, not by natural energy, but in union and communion with God all grace and blessing become ours. We *must* see the Face of God.

XLV

AFTER PENIEL

Gen. xxxiii.

1. And Jacob lifted up his eyes, and looked, and, behold, Esau came, and with him four hundred men. And he divided the children unto Leah, and unto Rachel, and unto the two handmaids.

2. And he put the handmaids and their children foremost, and Leah and her children after, and Rachel and Joseph hindermost.

3. And he passed over before them, and bowed himself to the ground seven times until he came near to his brother.

4. And Esau ran to meet him, and embraced him, and fell on his neck, and kissed him: and they wept.

5. And he lifted up his eyes, and saw the women and the children; and said Who *are* those with thee? And he said, The children which God hath graciously given thy servant.

6. Then the handmaidens came near, they and their children, and they bowed themselves.

7. And Leah also with her children came near, and bowed themselves: and after came Joseph near and Rachel, and they bowed themselves.

8. And he said, What *meanest* thou by all this drove which I met? And he said, *These* are to find grace in the sight of my lord.

9. And Esau said, I have enough, my brother; keep that thou hast unto thyself.

10. And Jacob said, Nay, I pray thee, if now I have found grace in thy sight, then receive my present at my hand; for therefore I have seen thy face as though I had seen the face of God, and thou wast pleased with me.

11. Take, I pray thee, my blessing that is brought to thee; because God hath dealt graciously with me, and because I have enough. And he urged him, and he took *it*.

12. And he said, Let us take our journey, and let us go, and I will go before thee.

13. And he said unto him, My lord knoweth that the children *are* tender, and the flocks and herds with young *are* with me: and if men should over-drive them one day, all the flock will die.

14. Let my lord, I pray thee, pass over before his servant; and I will lead on softly, according as the cattle that goeth before me and the children be able to endure, until I come unto my lord unto Seir.

15. And Esau said, Let me now leave with thee *some* of the folk that *are* with me. And he said, What needeth it? let me find grace in the sight of my lord.

16. So Esau returned that day on his way unto Seir.

17. And Jacob journeyed to Succoth, and built him an house, and made booths for his cattle: therefore the name of the place is called Succoth.

18. And Jacob came to Shalem, a city of Shechem, which *is* in the land of Canaan, when he came from Padan-aram; and pitched his tent before the city.

19. And he bought a parcel of a field, where he had spread his tent, at the hand of the children of Hamor, Shechem's father, for an hundred pieces of money.

20. And he erected there an altar, and called it El-elohe-Israel.

WHEN the Angel at Peniel said, "Thy name shall be called no more Jacob, but Israel," the obvious meaning was that from that time forward the man was to be known by the new name only. In similar cases of change of name, Abram to Abraham, Saul to Paul, Simon to Peter, the new name persisted and, at least with Abraham and Paul, the old one was never used again. But what do we find in the story of Jacob? This; that after Peniel the name "Jacob" occurs no less than forty-five times, while "Israel" appears only twenty-three times. And what is equally significant, the usage to which we are familiar is "Abraham, Isaac, and Jacob," not "Abraham, Isaac and Israel."

Why, then, did not the name "Jacob" disappear entirely and "Israel" take its place? Was it not because Jacob went back from the new position and privilege given him at Peniel? He did not continue true to that Divine revelation; he did not abide in the position and power of a "Prince of God." It is unutterably sad when a believer recedes from a high position of spiritual privilege. To be disobedient to the heavenly vision and revert to the old type of life is one of the most terrible of sorrows and one of the profoundest of mysteries. It is bad for a man to refuse God altogether; it is in some ways infinitely worse for a believer to lose position, peace, and power through unfaithfulness. Let us give heed to this story of Jacob's failure, and as we mark his steps backward let us ponder well the secret of his fall.

I. *First Step Backward* (vers. 1-11).—The next morning after Peniel Jacob had yet to face his great problem of the meeting with Esau. The difficulty was still there, Esau and his 400 men, and not

even the intercourse with God had removed it. But that intercourse provided him with the secret and means of victory over it if
only he had used the opportunity. God does not always see fit to
remove obstacles from our pathway, but He always gives power to
triumph over them. Instead, however, of Jacob meeting Esau "in
the strength of that meat" received by Peniel, we find him still
actuated by fear. Leaving household and cattle as arranged the
preceding day (xxxii. 7, 8), he makes a new disposition of his
wives and children, placing them in such order that the best-loved
are hindermost. Thus he prepares for the worst, still contemplating
the possibility, not to say the probability, of Esau's vengeance. The
fear of man still brings a snare.

Then, putting himself at the head of his family procession, he
goes forward to meet his brother, bowing with very great deference
—far in excess, so it would seem, even of the customary Oriental
courtesy. He is intent on showing his brother all possible consideration, and apparently means to acknowledge Esau's superior
prerogatives. This, after obtaining the birthright and blessing is
strange, and perhaps is intended as a tacit acknowledgment of his
old sin of craft and deceit. But be this as it may, the response of
Esau is very striking. He runs to meet Jacob, and they greet each
other amid tokens of genuine feeling. Esau's anger had gone in
the rush of emotion on seeing his brother after all those years of
separation. Rebekah was quite right in her knowledge of her elder
son's feelings. He was impulsive, hasty, passionate, but his anger
did not last; there was no brooding revenge, no malevolence. And
thus, in an instant, Jacob's fears were proved to be groundless,
and all his elaborate precautions for safety seen to be entirely unnecessary.

After making the acquaintance of Jacob's family, Esau naturally
asked the meaning of "all this drove" that he had met. He was
told that it was a present, "to find grace in the eyes of my lord."
But all this obsequiousness also proved quite unnecessary, for Esau
refused the present, saying that he already had enough. Jacob
thereupon pressed him to take it, urging as his reason that he was
grateful for his favorable reception. He felt that just as God had

received him graciously, so Esau's favor was now equally evident, and in token of his gratitude he pressed the gift upon him.

It is, however, hardly possible to avoid seeing in this urgency a desire on the part of Jacob to purchase Esau's goodwill. He knew his brother's fickleness, and was therefore determined to take every possible precaution. We cannot but feel that Jacob does not come quite worthily out of this meeting. After Peniel it does not read well. In the face of that guarantee of power and grace we are disappointed to read of further precautions, manifest fear, obvious fawning, and continued planning. Jacob has still to learn the lesson of absolute trust in his God. It is worthy of note that all the recognition of God was on his side (vers. 5, 10, 11), not on Esau's; but in spite of it all we feel that he did not remain on the high level of Peniel, or derive all the spiritual power he might have obtained from that memorable occasion of fellowship with God.

II. *Second Step Backward* (vers. 12-17).—Esau proposed that they should journey together, he and his men going forward as the escort. This suggestion was another mark of friendliness, and here we cannot help observing how splendidly Esau showed up on this occasion. Warmth, generosity, unselfishness, willingness to help, friendliness—all these features characterized him. Men of the world often put to shame the children of God in the manifestation of the practical virtues of life. Yet this ought not to be so.

Jacob met this generous proposal in a very characteristic way, and thereby gave another revelation of himself. He called attention to the little children and to the flocks and herds with their young, and pleaded quite naturally for a slow journey, as the children and cattle could bear it. But it was a polite though shrewd way of declining his brother's invitation. He was evidently still mindful of the diversity of their temperaments, and feared that if they were long together, some occasion of friction would arise and again sever their friendly relations. There was, quite probably, real worldly wisdom in this attitude of Jacob. He had a keener insight into the facts of the case than his more superficial brother. Yet we would rather have seen a hearty response to the proposal and a more definite trust in God as to the consequences. And cer-

tainly we could have easily dispensed with the renewed obsequiousness that marked Jacob's language to Esau. It was surely unworthy
of a brother to a brother, an equal to an equal—yea, rather a child
of God to a man of the world. If a believer has to refuse a request
to a non-Christian he should not be afraid to give the right reason
for his refusal. Testimony to truth, if given in the right spirit and
with a right motive, will never be allowed to do harm.

But, whatever may be said of all this, there is one point in the
narrative in which Jacob clearly does definite wrong. In declining Esau's invitation to journey together on account of his own
need of a slower progress Jacob distinctly promised to rejoin Esau
in Seir. Whereupon Esau naturally offered to leave some of his
men as a guide and escort. This again Jacob very politely declined
(ver. 15), and at length Esau departed. What, then, was Jacob's
next step? Actually this: instead of going after Esau to Seir, which
was situated south-east of Peniel, he took his journey in an exactly
opposite direction, and went to Succoth, north-west of Peniel. And
thus he took the second step backward, deceiving his brother once
again. It is surely impossible even to palliate this falsehood. As
he had not the courage to give his brother the real reason of his
declining the journey together, so also he told an untruth in order
to put as much distance as he could between them. We wonder
what Esau must have thought when he found Jacob did not arrive.
We wonder whether he discounted Jacob's references to God which
he had made on their meeting together. What is the use of our
pious verbal acknowledgment of God if we deny Him by our actions
and give cause to the men of the world to reflect on our profession
of religion and even to blaspheme it? How long will it be before
we learn that orthodoxy of profession with unreality of conduct is
the most deplorable combination in this world?

III. *Third Step Backward* (ver. 17).—Jacob did not content himself with a temporary stay at Succoth. He "built him a house and
made booths for his cattle." Hitherto he had lived the pilgrim
life, as his father and grandfather before him; but now he seeks for
something more permanent, and builds a house. A tent was no
longer sufficient for him. But it may be asked, Was this wrong?

Not *per se,* perhaps, and yet pretty certainly wrong for him. There are many things not essentially sinful which become sinful under particular circumstances. Jacob had forgotten his vow at Bethel (xxviii. 21), and by making Succoth so evidently his home he was showing himself to be on a very low spiritual level in his forgetfulness of the claim of God upon him. When God revealed Himself in Haran it was as "the God of Bethel" (xxxi. 13), and the reminder at that time of the vow made by Jacob was evidence of the prominent and even predominant place Bethel was intended to occupy in the subsequent life of the patriarch. He thus fails to rise to the full height of God's purpose. He had overlooked all this, and was settling down, at any rate for a time, in earthly ease and prosperity. There were no fine pastures at Bethel! How easily we forget our Bethels and all that we have promised God! How disappointing to God must be the failures and unfaithfulness of His servants! How sad to ignore in prosperity the vows we made when we were in danger! And yet, alas! how true this is to life today!

IV. *Fourth Step Backward* (vers. 18-20).—After a time Succoth was left, and Jacob journeyed on. If we read the R. V., he "came in peace to the city of Shechem," which reminds us of his vow (xxviii. 21, "in peace"), although he did not go back to Bethel. In this case Shechem is the name of the owner of the place (Cf. xxxiv. 2). If, however, we read the A. V., he "came to Shalem," a city in the country or neighborhood of what was afterwards Shechem or Sychar (John iv. 5; Acts vii. 16). In pitching his tent "before the city" we see another indication of his low spiritual condition. If he had been true to God he would have recognized his danger in the proximity to the inhabitants of the land. And, as we know, this nearness brought untold trouble upon him.

Then, again, he bought some property there, purchasing the land on which his tent was pitched. He was thus actually buying his own promised possessions, the land assured to him by God! Was this necessary? Surely not. Abraham's purchase was for a very different reason. Why could not Jacob trust God, as Abraham had done? It was because his faith could not rise to the occasion. Jacob's motto was "A bird in hand is worth two in the bush," and apart from God the motto is no doubt full of wisdom. But when God is first in the life it makes all the difference. To the man of the world faith is unreal, there is nothing tangible about it; to him "seeing is believing." But to the believer faith is a reality; to him "seeing is believing." "Faith is the *title-deed* [so substance in the Papyri] of things hoped for, the proof of things unseen" (Heb. xi. I). If Jacob had possessed Abraham's faith he would not have bought an inch of ground.

But this was not all. Jacob proceeded to erect an altar in this place. He thought to counteract his disobedience by consecration to God. He had no right to be there at all. Bethel, not Shechem, was the place for the altar. Worldliness in the week-days is not overcome by early Communions on Sundays. Unfaithfulness to God in daily duty is not set aside by having family prayers night and morning, and Bible readings for our neighbors. Meanness to employes is not obliterated by a large gift to the Hospital Sunday Fund or the cause of foreign Missions. Even the name of the altar, "God the God of Israel," seems to indicate a low tone, in its reference to himself, especially as he was not living the life of "Israel," the Prince of God. The sin lay in being "near the city," and indeed in being there at all. And the results as we shall see were disastrous, as they always are when people try to blend worldliness and godliness, Society and Christ, Mammon and God. The world always wins; religion always recedes.

1. *The awful possibilities of spiritual degeneration.*—Jacob's experiences after Peniel are a solemn reminder that Conversion (Bethel) and Consecration (Peniel) are no guarantees of abiding faithfulness. They need to be followed by Concentration and Continuance. There are frequent hints throughout Holy Scripture of the ghastly possibilities of spiritual relapse after the most exalted fellowship with God. We think of David's sin after such a revelation as is recorded in 2 Sam. vii. We think of Simon Peter's denial after Caesarea Philippi (Matt. xvi.) and after the Transfiguration (Matt. xvii.). And we remember the solemn warning of Heb. v. 12, 14, with its revelation of the awful possibility of spiritual senility, of *second childhood,* (vers. 11, 12). It is possible for one

who has had great spiritual insight, received great spiritual gifts, done great spiritual service, to lose all by unfaithfulness. Backsliding is a terrible and awful fact, and sometimes the higher the rise the lower the fall. Spiritual experience, however true and rich, does not exempt from danger; rather does it call for greater watchfulness. "So Daniel continued." The grace of continuance is the greatest need of all. Have we not, perhaps, heard of some servant of God who had been honored and blessed, and afterwards fell into sin and shame? Can we not, perchance, think of some who commenced their Christian life, and it may be their ministry, full of hope and promise, but who are now "unfulfilled prophecies," by reason of lack of faithfulness to the heavenly vision? They have virtually ceased to pray, practically ceased to meditate on the Bible, ceased to be unworldly; they have adopted unworthy methods in their ministry, pandered to worldliness and earthly ambitions, and the result is dullness, darkness, dryness, deadness in life and ministry, souls not being saved, believers not being quickened, everything stale and unprofitable in their service. They are "cast away," not in the sense of losing their salvation, but of having lost their usefulness. They are "disapproved," rejected, set aside. While the regenerate can never become *un*regenerate, he can, alas! become *de*generate, and herein lies one of the gravest perils of the Christian life. Moody once said to Canon Hay Aitken that the one thing he feared most was the loss of his testimony for Christ. "I saw that there was a way to hell even from the gates of heaven, as well as from the City of Destruction."

2. *The simple secret of spiritual stability.*—This lies in obedience to the heavenly vision, faithfulness to the heavenly voice. If only Jacob had kept God first, and refused to listen to the voice of self, how different would have been his record! With absolute trust in God would have come victory over temptation, courage in danger, and preservation from worldliness. We fail because we distrust God, and distrusting we disobey Him. God's grace is sufficient for every emergency, and the light granted at Peniel would have detected every danger and protected from every disaster. Every spiritual victory lifts us to a higher plane of power and blessing,

and thus we go on from "strength to strength," from "glory to glory." There is no need for failure, for backsliding, for defeat, but every warrant for progress, power and preservation. We have only to obey the vision vouchsafed to us, to appropriate the grace provided for us, in order to experience stability, strength and ever-growing satisfaction, to the glory and praise of God.

XLVI

RESULTS OF UNFAITHFULNESS

GEN. xxxiv.

1. And Dinah the daughter of Leah, which she bare unto Jacob, went out to see the daughters of the land.

2. And when Shechem the son of Hamor the Hivite, prince of the country, saw her, he took her, and lay with her, and defiled her.

3. And his soul clave unto Dinah the daughter of Jacob, and he loved the damsel, and spake kindly unto the damsel.

4. And Shechem spake unto his father Hamor, saying, Get me this damsel to wife.

5. And Jacob heard that he had defiled Dinah his daughter: now his sons were with his cattle in the field: and Jacob held his peace until they were come.

6. And Hamor the father of Shechem went out unto Jacob to commune with him.

7. And the sons of Jacob came out of the field when they heard *it*; and the men were grieved, and they were very wroth, because he had wrought folly in Israel in lying with Jacob's daughter; which thing ought not to be done.

8. And Hamor communed with them, saying, The soul of my son Shechem longeth for your daughter: I pray you give her him to wife.

9. And make ye marriages with us, *and* give your daughters unto us, and take our daughters unto you.

10. And ye shall dwell with us: and the land shall be before you; dwell and trade ye therein, and get you possessions therein.

11. And Shechem said unto her father and unto her brethren, Let me find grace in your eyes, and what ye shall say unto me I will give.

12. Ask me never so much dowry and gift, and I will give according as ye shall say unto me: but give me the damsel to wife.

13. And the sons of Jacob answered Shechem and Hamor his father deceitfully, and said, because he had defiled Dinah their sister:

14. And they said unto them, We cannot do this thing to give our sister to one that is uncircumcised; for that *were* a reproach unto us:

15. But in this will we consent unto you: If ye will be as we *be*, that every male of you be circumcised;

16. Then will we give our daughters unto you, and we will take your daughters to us, and we will dwell with you, and we will become one people.

17. But if ye will not hearken unto us, to be circumcised; then will we take our daughter, and we will be gone.

18. And their words pleased Hamor, and Shechem Hamor's son.

19. And the young man deferred not to do the thing, because he had delight in Jacob's daughter: and he *was* more honorable than all the house of his father.

20. And Hamor and Shechem his son came unto the gate of their city, and communed with the men of their city, saying,

21. These men *are* peaceable with us; therefore let them dwell in the land, and trade therein; for the land behold, *it is* large enough for them; let us take their daughters to us for wives, and let us give them our daughters.

22. Only herein will the men consent unto us for to dwell with us, to be one people, if every male among us be circumcised, as they *are* circumcised.

23. *Shall* not their cattle and their substance and every beast of their's *be* our's? only let us consent unto them, and they will dwell with us.

24. And unto Hamor and unto Shechem his son hearkened all that went out of the gate of his city; and every male was circumcised, all that went out of the gate of his city.

25. And it came to pass on the third day, when they were sore, that two of the sons of Jacob, Simeon and Levi, Dinah's brethren, took each man his sword, and came upon the city boldly, and slew all the males.

26. And they slew Hamor and Shechem his son with the edge of the sword, and took Dinah out of Shechem's house, and went out.

27. The sons of Jacob came upon the slain, and spoiled the city, because they had defiled their sister.

28. They took their sheep, and their oxen, and their asses, and that which *was* in the city, and that which *was* in the field.

29. And all their wealth, and all their little ones, and their wives took they captive, and spoiled even all that *was* in the house.

30. And Jacob said to Simeon and Levi, Ye have troubled me to make me to stink among the inhabitants of the land, among the Canaanites and the Perizzites: and I *being* few in number, they shall gather themselves together against me, and slay me; and I shall be destroyed, I and my house.

31. And they said, Should he deal with our sister as with an harlot?

A CAREFUL comparison of passages shows that Jacob's stay at Succoth and Shechem must have extended over several years. Bethel and his vow (xxviii. 22) were evidently forgotten or ignored. The pastures at Succoth and Shehem were attractive, his possessions had so largely increased that movement was difficult, circumstances were perhaps conceived of as having changed, making the realization of the vow almost impracticable. And so Jacob settled down to ordinary life, having either put off or else put aside the fulfilment of his promise. He was not prepared for the unheaval that a move to Bethel would involve. Full of resource whenever danger threatened, he seemed to be "settling on the lees," content with his

favored position in Shechem and with his profession of religion as
indicated by the altar (xxxiii. 20).

"A spiritual experience that is separated from your present by
twenty years of active life, by a foreign residence, by marriage, by
the growing-up of a family around you, by other and fresher
spiritual experiences, is apt to be very indistinctly remembered. The
obligations you then felt and owned have been overlaid and buried
in the lapse of years. And so it comes that a low tone is introduced
into your life, and your homes cease to be model homes" (Dods,
Genesis, p. 313).

And this is the man who has seen the Face of God! This is the
man to whom the special Divine revelation of grace had been given!
This is the man whom God's goodness and mercy had followed all
the days of his life! He it is who is on this low ground of unfaithfulness, of spiritual declension, and who has to suffer for it
bitterly. So it is always; spiritual leakage means spiritual loss,
a lower tone, a cessation of power, a discontinuance of testimony,
and, not least of all, an unrest of soul and untold trouble of heart
and life. Let us now observe some of the sad effects of Jacob's
unfaithfulness.

I. *The Grave Danger* (cf. xxxiii. 18-20).—It seems clear that
the choice of Shechem was largely conditioned by its favorable
position for his family and flocks. Jacob pitched his tent "before
the city," in close proximity to the people and the place, in the
neighborhood of which he could find society and protection, with
pasturage for his flocks. The choice of a home or of a school today
is not seldom regulated by the same considerations. A professing
Christian man is retiring from business, and determines to reside
in the country. Where shall he go? What are his requirements?
Healthy surroundings, of course. But also a neighborhood where
his young people will be able to enjoy the advantages of good
society, where they can mix easily and freely on good terms with
the "best people," where social intercourse and entertainmer
abound, and where the family will soon take its place as one of tl
recognized centers of social influence. All very attractive and d
lightful; but does it ever occur to the man who is thus choosing hi

home to inquire as to the spiritual opportunities of the place? What sort of church has it? Is the Gospel preached there? Is Christ lifted up? Or is it a fashionable church where either formalism or mere intellectualism rules? But, says the man, "You cannot have everything you want; you must do the best you can with your opportunities, and hope for the best." Be it so; and spiritual trouble will be the result. Unless a family is deliberately going into a spiritually destitute neighborhood to witness for Christ and to win people to Him (in which case they will not be allowed many social advantages by their neighbors!), the first and supreme factor of choice of a new home should be, "What will it do for our spiritual life?"

Or it may be that parents have to choose a school for their boys and girls. They are able to send them to the very best known of public schools, and they quite naturally desire for their children the best opportunities, educational and social. But there are well-grounded reports that these particular schools, though socially advantageous, are morally disadvantageous, and attended with risk. What will the father and mother do? Will they take the risk? Or will they definitely make themselves familiar with the religious life of the school before sending their boy? Or will they not rather send him to a less known school, where all is well religiously, and sacrifice the social advantages of the other school for the sake of moral and spiritual safety? On the answer to these questions much will turn. Jacob chose to live near Shechem, with all the risks involved thereby, and no one ever follows his example without suffering quite as definitely, in some way or other.

II. *The Great Disaster* (vers. 1, 2).—The inevitable result of living near Shechem was soon seen. Dinah, the only daughter of Jacob (xxx. 21), "went out to see the daughters of the land." It was a perfectly natural thing for a young, inexperienced girl to do. The thought of visiting "the daughters of the land," was at once novel and interesting. We wonder, however, what Jacob and Leah were doing to allow it. Why did they not warn Dinah of the danger, and prevent her going? Was this inaction due to their lowered moral tone? Did they argue that there was "no danger" and that "we must not be too particular or strait-laced"? In any case, she was allowed to go, with the result that is well known. The sin of Shechem was, of course, in every way inexcusable, for it was against the youth of the girl, as well as against all known laws of hospitality. And yet in view of the fact that he and his people were people of the land, and not followers of the one true God, it would not be regarded by him and his in the same light of heinousness as it was regarded from Jacob's side. It is very striking that the word rendered "defiled" (vers. 5, 13, 27) means "desecrated," and is used later to describe the defilement or desecration of the Temple (Ps. lxxix.). "The dishonor of womanhood and the desecration of the Holy of Holies are regarded with the same feelings and described by the same word" (Strachan, *Hebrew Ideals, in loc.*). Thus does the Book of God regard personal purity, and denote and denounce the sin that dishonors it. But while we fail not to point out the sin of Shechem, we may not forget the weakness and unfaithfulness of Jacob that made possible his daughter's shame.

III. *The Unexpected Project* (vers. 3-12).—Shechem proceeded to make the only possible reparation. He had evidently become genuinely attached to Dinah and wished to make her his wife. He thereupon requested his father to take the necessary steps to this end according to the custom which made it the parents' business to obtain wives for their sons (Gen. xxiv. 4; Judges xiv. 2).

Jacob soon heard the terrible news of his daughter's fall, and as his sons were not then at home he "held his peace." We wonder why? Was it because of sorrow and shame as he thought of his daughter and of the circumstances that gave opportunity for it? Was conscience stirring within him, reminding him of Bethel? Or was it a case of real indecision, not knowing what to do, and therefore leaving the matter to be settled by Dinah's brothers? It is true that brothers seem to have had a great deal to say concerning their sister's life (xxiv. 50 f.), but at the same time Jacob's silence and inaction, as head of the household, are somewhat difficult to understand. The "silence" does not seem to have been in connection with the proposed marriage, but with reference to the sin and shame.

At length the brothers heard of it, and at the same time came Hamor's request on behalf of his son. The proposal for marriage was suggested as an opportunity for the beginning of a general amalgamation of the two families and peoples (ver. 9, 10). Shechem was also prepared to give whatever "dowry" they asked, the "dowry" being not a gift to the bride, in the modern sense, but a price paid to the parents for their daughter (Exod. xxii. 16f.; 1 Sam. xviii. 25).

These proposals are significant on several grounds. They show clearly the value set by the Canaanites on union with Jacob's family. It was not the first, and it has not been the last occasion when people of the world have thought it advantageous to be united with the people of God. Godliness, even of the kind then shown by Jacob, has promise of attractiveness and value for men of the world. Then, too, we cannot help noticing the true nobility of character shown by Shechem. In spite of his sin, or at least after it, he stands out well by comparison with the rest of the actors here mentioned. And it is a striking testimony to the candour of the Book that it depicts both this Canaanitish prince and the sons of Jacob so faithfully. The frankness of the Bible is not the least proof of its truthfulness and authenticity.

IV. *The Unworthy Pretext* (vers. 13-17).—The request and proposals of Hamor and Shechem were regarded by Dinah's brothers as impossible unless one particular condition were fulfilled. They took up the ground that it would be intolerable to allow an uncircumcised man to become the husband of one who was within the covenant of God, but they were quite ready to agree to the marriage if the Canaanites would agree to all their males receiving the sign of the covenant. Not only so, they would be prepared to enter into other marriages and to become "one people" with the Canaanites.

And this sounded quite fair and straightforward. It was taking up a perfectly intelligible attitude, and one that, if based on right motives, would have been not only necessary and justifiable, but would have brought about the best possible ending to the trouble concerning their sister. But it was the absence of the right motive that condemned their proposal. They had no idea of these men entering the covenant on religious grounds. They were proposing to use the sign of the religious covenant as the means of a purely human agreement. Circumcision without faith in the covenant God could not be anything but carnal and earthly. And, worse still, they were about to employ the solemn seal of the Divine covenant for the purpose of wreaking their vengeance on these unsuspecting men. Their suggestion was therefore nothing more than a pretext to cover treachery. There was the appearance of piety with the reality of intended murder. Could anything be more truly terrible? What a light it sheds on the state of Jacob's home life! And why was Jacob silent during all these proposals? True, he could not know the contemplated treachery, but his entire silence is remarkable. Had he no part or power in the matter of his daughter's life? Or was he weak and irresolute, conscious of his own unfaithfulness?

V. *The Trustful Acceptance* (vers. 18-24).—The requirements of Dinah's brethren were at once welcomed by Hamor and Shechem. The latter was prepared for instant acquiescence, so genuine was his love for Dinah. The proposals were also set before the men of the city, and their acceptance urged by Hamor and Shechem. They pointed out the peaceable character of Jacob and his family, and the size of the land as sufficient for them all to live in and trade together. It was also shown that amalgamation would prove advantageous in the acquisition of fresh possessions, since all would be as one in the event of marriages between the two races. The proposals thus ably urged were accepted, and the men of Shechem submitted to the condition laid down by Jacob's sons. And apart from any consideration of personal advantage urged as one of the reasons for acquiescence, it is impossible not to see the peaceable and trustful attitude of the Canaanites in the face of Jacob and his sons. The "heathen" show up well by contrast with those who were professedly the people of God.

VI. *The Treacherous Action* (vers. 25-29).—Very soon the true object of Dinah's brethren was revealed. Their apparently religious requirement was seen to be the cloak of vengeance, and at a convenient moment the trusting Canaanites were massacred, including Hamor and Shechem. Then, after taking their sister home, they returned to complete their fell task by sacking the city and capturing all the women, children, and flocks they could find. Thus they avenged sin by greater sin. It is sometimes said that this was all the result of "religious fanaticism," and that in it we have the first example of that Jewish fanaticism for religion which caused the Jews so much trouble (Dods, p. 314). It does not, however, appear clear that there was anything of religion in it, but only sheer cruelty and vindictiveness exercised under the guise of a religious rite. The men who could plot and wreak such vengeance did not possess one grain of religion, even of a fanatical kind. The story is one of unrelieved savagery. If only they had been actuated by true motives their sister's shame would have been covered, so far as it could be, by subsequent marriage; but as it was, she was robbed of that refuge, and had to live her life and end her days under the cloud of disgrace, due first to herself and then to her brothers' vengeance. And all this in the family of the chosen patriarch! Could anything be sadder or more disappointing? Could Divine grace overrule these awful troubles? Yes, it could and did, though they still stand recorded in all their hideousness, "written for our learning."

VII. *The Surprising Rebuke* (ver. 30).—At last Jacob speaks, having "held his peace" far too long. He rebuked his sons for their action, but the character of the rebuke is very noticeable. Jacob-like, the patriarch looks at the matter solely from his own point of view. "Ye have troubled *me* to make *me* to stink among the inhabitants . . . and *I* being few . . . they shall gather . . . against *me* and *I* shall be destroyed, *I* and *my* house." Could anything be feebler or more unworthy? No blame for the sin committed, only for the danger involved. He was afraid for his life, his home, the land he paid for, the possessions he enjoyed. Trouble comes through unfaithfulness, and then circumstances are blamed. Children bring trouble on parents, and perhaps the fault is originally and largely the parents' own.

Weakness and timidity are here as plainly marked as ever, showing clearly the low tone of the man through long-continued unfaithfulness to God. His apprehensiveness of danger shows that there was no spiritual satisfaction or assurance of safety. He had quite forgotten the Divine promise of protection (xxviii. 14 f.). People who live on the borderland between Church and world are like those who lived in the old days on the borders between England and Scotland—they are never safe.

VIII. *The Significant Rejoinder* (ver. 31).—The sons have the last word, and justify their action in words that partake of the nature of a *suppressio veri*, and therefore of a *suggestio falsi*. They omit all reference to the action of Shechem by which he would have done reparation and prevented Dinah from living all her days under the shadow of her sin. Their father allows them to have the last word, not that he admits the truth of their position, but perhaps because argument with such men would be useless, and possibly because he is conscious that his own choice of Shechem for a home was contributory in great measure to what had happened. When, however, the end of his life comes, the old man shows that he had not forgotten their action (xlix. 6, 7), for he stamps it in its true colors as disreputable and wrong in the sight of God.

The one lesson that stands out from all the rest is that which is associated with the life and character of Jacob at this time. It is the fact and danger of worldliness.

1. *Worldliness is a real spiritual peril.*—It is doubtless difficult to define "worldliness," and on this account it is easy to ridicule the idea and put it down to narrowness, straitlacedness, and censoriousness. But in all ages, under a variety of phases, the fact and force of "worldliness" have been felt and acknowledged by all spiritually-minded people. Does not Church history show a difference in the spiritual life of the Church in the second and third as compared with the fourth and fifth centuries? What was the explanation? Three words sum it up: Constantine, patronage, worldliness. We see it again and again in churches and congregations where sensational or other unworthy methods have been used to attract people, with the result that the ministry is robbed of power, Prayer meetings and Bible classes yield to concerts, "the hungry sheep look up and are not fed," and souls are not saved. We see it also in the individual lives of those who once "ran well," but who have yielded

to pressure and have lowered the standard of holiness for fear of being thought too "narrow" or "too particular." Yes, worldliness *is* hard to define, but it is very easy to feel, to detect, and to describe. It is an atmosphere, enervating, lowering, poisoning, deadening; and whenever individuals and churches are under its sway, the result, however long delayed, is as inevitable as it is disastrous to the soul and dishonoring to God.

2. *Worldliness prevents spiritual blessing.*—Not only did Jacob's worldliness lead to danger and disaster to himself and his household, it necessarily hindered him at the same time from bearing witness to God. "The Canaanite was then in the land," and, like Lot before him, there was no real testimony, because there was no real difference between him and them. What cared they for his altar, so long as he lived with them and did as they did? What good could the altar do in the face of his life day by day as one of themselves? So it is always. Worldliness lowers tone and prevents testimony. The banner is not displayed, because the life is not true. The standard is not maintained, and blessing is not obtained. There never has been a case where the adoption of worldly methods has justified itself by spiritual blessing. In the Middle Ages the Pope boasted to Thomas Aquinas, as he showed that great scholar the treasures of the Vatican, "The Church cannot now say, 'Silver and gold have I none.'" "True," said Thomas, "and neither can it say, 'In the Name of Jesus Christ of Nazareth, rise up and walk.'"

3. *Worldliness can only be prevented by separation.*—The Master in His High Priestly prayer (John xvii.) gives us the true (sevenfold) attitude of the believer and the Church to the world, and thereby reveals the safeguard against this insidious peril. We are given to Christ "out of the world" (ver. 6); we are "in the world" (ver. 11); we are "hated by the world" (ver. 14); we are "not of the world" (ver. 14); we are "not to be taken out of the world," but "kept from" its evil (ver. 15), and we are "sent into the world" (ver. 18) to witness to it as our Master did, "that the world may know" (ver. 23) who and what He is. All this can only be realized through true spiritual separation, and, however difficult it may be

to define exactly the limits of separation, the fact and necessity of it are undoubted. The principles, ideals, and methods of Christianity cannot possibly be mixed with those of the world without contamination; and if only we abide in Christ and continue in His love we shall live in an atmosphere of purity and power which will be our constant safeguard and our sufficient warning. One thing is perfectly clear: no one can read and study the teaching of the New Testament as to "the world" without becoming conscious at once of the danger and of the safeguard, of the enemy and of the protection, of the warfare and of the secret of perpetual victory.

XLVII

BETHEL AT LAST

GEN. xxxv. 1-15

1. And God said unto Jacob, Arise, go to Beth-el, and dwell there: and make there an altar unto God, that appeared unto thee when thou fleddest from the face of Esau thy brother.

2. Then Jacob said unto his household, and to all that *were* with him, Put away the strange gods that *are* among you, and be clean, and change your garments:

3. And let us arise, and go up to Beth-el: and I will make there an altar unto God, Who answered me in the day of my distress, and was with me in the way which I went.

4. And they gave unto Jacob all the strange gods which *were* in their hand, *all their* earrings which *were* in their ears; and Jacob hid them under the oak which *was* by Shechem.

5. And they journeyed: and the terror of God was upon the cities that *were* round about them, and they did not pursue after the sons of Jacob.

6. So Jacob came to Luz, which *is* in the land of Canaan, that *is*, Beth-el, he and all the people that *were* with him.

7. And he built there an altar, and called the place El-beth-el: because there God appeared unto him, when he fled from the face of his brother.

8. But Deborah Rebekah's nurse died, and she was buried beneath Beth-el under an oak: and the name of it was called Allon-bachuth.

9. And God appeared unto Jacob again, when he came out of Padan-aram, and blessed him.

10. And God said unto him, Thy name *is* Jacob: thy name shall not be called any more Jacob, but Israel shall be thy name: and he called his name Israel.

11. And God said unto him, I *am* God Almighty: be fruitful and multiply; a nation and a company of nations shall be of thee, and kings shall come out of thy loins:

12. And the land which I gave Abraham and Isaac, to thee I will give it, and to thy seed after thee will I give the land.

13. And God went up from him in the place where He talked with him.

14. And Jacob set up a pillar in the place where He talked with him, *even* a pillar of stone: and he poured a drink offering thereon, and he poured oil thereon.

15. And Jacob called the name of the place where God spake with him, Beth-el.

A CRISIS had arrived in the life of Jacob. His stay at Shechem was a time of spiritual unfaithfulness and therefore of spiritual unfitness, but the time had come when through a variety of circumstances he was to be brought back to God. "The thirty-fourth chapter of Genesis is God-less; "the thirty-fifth is full of God. The former describes the Shechem life of the Hebrews; the latter their Bethel life. The contrast between a believer's and an unbeliever's life is scarcely more marked than the contrast between a half-hearted and a whole-hearted believer's life" (Strachan, *Hebrew Ideals, in loc.*). When a believer is out of spiritual condition and is not living in spiritual touch with God, God does not leave him alone. In one way or another he is stirred up, troubled, and dealt with in discipline until he returns to his true life of fellowship. This, as we shall now see, was Jacob's experience.

I. *The Urgent Call* (ver. 1).—"And God said unto Jacob, Arise, go up to Bethel, and dwell there: and make there an altar unto God, that appeared unto thee when thou fleddest from the face of Esau thy brother." Bethel was only thirty miles away from Shechem, and yet it was quite ten years since Jacob's return into Canaan. And it was over thirty years since he had made his vow to return to Bethel and acknowledge God's hand if he were brought back in peace. The conditions had been exactly and completely fulfilled years ago, but the vow was yet unpaid. Now at length came the Divine call, for God could not let His servant rest in disobedience. He must bring him back to the point and place of faithful obedience. The only possible means of restoration after backsliding is the old familiar gateway of repentance and faith.

There was also a personal as well as a Divine reason for returning to Bethel. It was impossible for Jacob to detect the true state of affairs as long as he remained in Shechem. The atmosphere was impregnated with worldliness, and while he continued there he could not detect aright his unspiritual and sinful condition. We might have supposed that it was quite unnecessary for God to command him to go to Bethel "and make there an altar," for was there not already an altar in Shechem (xxxiii. 20)? But, as we have before seen, that altar had long lost all spiritual power for Jacob and his family, since their daily living was for the most part a direct contradiction of its testimony. If that altar had been of any real service we should not have had the awful story of the savagery of Jacob's sons (xxxiv.). It is scarcely too much to say that children brought up in an atmosphere of worldliness are the very hardest to impress with the realities of spiritual religion, even though they may attend a place of worship week by week. The life of worldliness during six days is far too powerful for anything that happens on the seventh day to counteract it.

There was also yet another and social reason for Jacob's removal. He and his family were henceforward in constant dread of trouble and danger from their Canaanitish neighbors. Up to that time everything seemed to be going quietly, and, in their judgment, satisfactorily; but now it was seen to be absolutely essential to make a move, for it would be no longer safe to abide near Shechem in view of the almost assured certainty of blood revenge on the part of the Shechemites.

These three reasons—the Divine, the spiritual, and the social—combined to lead Jacob out of Shechem. It was doubtless hard, and certainly it must have been costly and troublesome, but it had to be done.

II. *The Special Preparation* (vers. 2-4).—At length Jacob was thoroughly roused, and promptly set about obeying the Divine and urgent command. The first thing to be done was to make due spiritual preparation, and he called upon his household to put away the strange gods that were among them, to purify themselves, and to change their garments. What a revelation this is! It shows at once the true state of affairs. There had been spiritual declension, and Jacob clearly knew of, and had evidently connived at, the presence of idols and idolatrous practices in his household. His love to Rachel had led him to tolerate what he knew perfectly well was contrary to the mind and will of God. It is sad to realize that all this was true of the man who had been brought face to face with God at Peniel. It shows again the awful possibility of spiritual declension, even after the most exalted fellowship with God.

It is very striking to read of Jacob's influence at this time. His appeal to his household at once elicited a whole-hearted response. They saw that he was in earnest, and they gave to him "all the strange gods which were in their hand, and all the earrings which were in their ears." The household gods and amulets were all freely surrendered, and Jacob did the very best possible thing with them; he "hid them under the oak which was at Shechem." Shechem had been the place of spiritual trouble, and these causes of spiritual trouble were appropriately left behind there. It would not have been safe to have allowed them to remain a moment longer in the household. Surrender is the supreme secret and condition of spiritual blessing. As long as there is any mental or moral reservation, there cannot be any real satisfaction in the soul, strength in the character, or service for God. It is noteworthy that there are certain things in connection with the spiritual life that must be entirely given up and destroyed, for it is impossible to sanctify or consecrate them. They must be buried and left behind, for they cannot possibly be devoted to the service of God. It is this that gives point to our Lord's well-known words, "If thy right hand offend thee, cut it off." There are things that have to be cut off and cannot be consecrated. Books have to be burned (Acts xix. 19). Evil habits have to be broken. Sin must be put away. There are things that are beyond all reclamation.

> "The dearest idol I have known,
> Whate'er that idol be;
> Help me to tear it from thy throne,
> And worship only Thee."

It is impossible to avoid noticing the astonishing alacrity and remarkable power of Jacob at this juncture, especially in contrast with his weakness and powerlessness as recorded in the former chapter. He asserted his authority, and his position was accepted without any question even by his strong-willed and savage sons. Even they could not help being impressed with the fact that their father was now on the right ground before God, and was showing the truth of the wonderful revelation at Peniel that when a man has power with God he soon has power with man.

III. *The Remarkable Journey* (ver. 5).—"And they journeyed: and the terror of God was upon the cities that were round about them, and they did not pursue after the sons of Jacob." This is a wonderful verse, and is another testimony to the astonishing power of a life that is right with God. "When a man's ways please the Lord He maketh even his enemies to be at peace with him." So deeply impressed were the Canaanites round about them that there was no attempt whatever to hinder or injure the departing family. The supernatural fear that came upon them prevented them from taking revenge on the sons of Jacob. We see again the absolute necessity of separation from evil if there is to be true testimony for God. As long as they were at Shechem, there was no real witness; but now that they were separating themselves from it the people were impressed with the supernatural character of the travelers, and "the terror of God" was manifestly experienced by the Canaanites. What confidence this must have put into the heart of Jacob as he received the assurance that he was now at length in the pathway of God's will! "If our hearts condemn us not, then have we confidence toward God."

IV. *The Noteworthy Arrival* (ver. 6). "So Jacob came to Luz, which is in the land of Canaan, that is, Bethel, he and all the people that were with him." Jacob's sincerity is very evident in the way in which he accomplished his journey. There was no halting, and no lagging behind, for everything that belonged to him arrived with him; "he *and all the people* that were with him." He had become thoroughly roused to his true position and duty, and at last after thirty years' absence he was once more back at the place of the Divine vision (xxviii.). What memories the place must have called up as he reviewed the past with all his varied experiences! And how thankful he must have felt to be at length in the pathway of God's will, and assured of peace, rest, protection, and blessing!

V. *The Prompt Obedience* (vers. 7, 8).—"And he built there an altar, and called the place El-bethel: because there God appeared unto him when he fled from the face of his brother." This was the way in which Jacob fulfilled his vow (xxviii. 22). The name of the altar is worthy of special note in comparison with that of the altar at Shechem (xxxiii. 20). In Shechem the altar bore witness to God's relation to Jacob himself, "God the God of Israel"; but at Bethel self is entirely lost and God alone is mentioned, "the God of Bethel," or "God of the House of God." This was a higher and nobler thought. Instead of thinking of God in relation to himself, Jacob thought of God alone. His spiritual condition being higher, his conception of God was higher also. The constant recurrence of this name of God, "El," in Jacob's history is very interesting. It will be remembered that Abraham built an altar near Shechem (xii. 7), though his altar was not built unto El, but unto Jehovah. In the case of Jacob there had been a special revelation of God under this name of El, both at Bethel and at Peniel, which was incorporated in the new name of Israel; and now once more at Bethel a new emphasis is placed on this name after all the years that had elapsed since Peniel.

The reason assigned for the erection of this altar is very striking: "Because there God appeared unto him when he had fled from the face of his brother." Jacob was conscious of that far-off day in the past, of which he speaks on another occasion as "the day of his distress." It is always well for us to go back to earlier experiences and refresh our memories by the recollection of some former blessing from God. This is probably one reason why thanksgiving is so strongly emphasized in the New Testament. "Lest we forget." The remembrance of past mercies in the times of trouble, distress, and danger is one of the greatest encouragements to renewed confidence in our ever-faithful, unchanging covenant God.

It was just at this time that a very precious link with the past was broken. Deborah, Rebekah's nurse, died while Jacob was at Bethel, and was buried under an oak-tree there. She very appropriately united together the two visits to Bethel, the day when he started out from home and the day of his return.

VI. *The New Revelation* (vers. 9-13).—"God appeared unto Jacob again . . . and blessed him." How striking is this word "again"! Reconciliation had been accomplished. There was now no cloud between the patriarch and his God, and the Divine appearance which was not permitted him in Shechem comes with its blessed assurance of renewed favor and sunshine after rain. This was not only a Divine command (ver. 1), but a Divine appearance, a manifestation visible as well as audible (ver. 13). The revelation of Peniel was thereupon renewed and the name Israel once more given. Not only so, but a fresh revelation of God was also granted to Jacob: "I am God Almighty." The same name of El-Shaddai which had been revealed to his grandfather (xvii. 1) was now confirmed to him as the assurance and guarantee of his fruitfulness and the marvelous increase of his family and household. It is surely not without point that from this time forward Jacob's household increased in a very remarkable way, until at length, as we know, the family became a nation in Egypt (Exod. i.).

This Divine revelation not only renewed the experience of Peniel (ver. 10), and encouraged him with assurance of power (ver. 11); it also confirmed what had already been said by God at Bethel (xxviii. 13). It linked Jacob with his father and grandfather in the Divine promise of the land to him and to his seed. Truly the sun had burst forth in glorious splendor as the wandering patriarch was once more in full fellowship with God.

VII. *The Grateful Memorial* (vers. 14, 15).—Once again Jacob sets his seal to the Divine revelation and raises his "Ebenezer." Not only did he set up a pillar of stone, but he poured a libation thereon —the first instance of drink offerings in Scripture—and then anointed it with oil. He, too, has his work of confirmation. as God had His, and once more he called the name of the place Bethel. Repentance and faith always rejoice to set up their memorials, to which they can recur in gratitude and thankfulness for all the marvelous mercies of God.

1. *God's unutterable love.*—All the time that Jacob was living away from true fellowship with God he was not forgotten. God seemed to have left him entirely alone, but in reality was working all the time in various ways to bring him back again. So is it always. While we are backsliding we are apparently left to ourselves, but it is not really so. God will not forsake His children. They may sin and wander, but He watches, waits, and endeavors to win them back. The old lessons have to be learned again and again in various

forms until His purpose is accomplished. God bears with us in tender love and over-ruling mercy, and gives us no real rest until He brings us back to a right relation to Himself. Jacob may go to Succoth and stay at Shechem, but circumstances will arise to stir up his nest till at length he is impelled—nay, almost compelled —to go to Bethel. How marvelous is the long-suffering, tender love of our God! He knows what is the right and best thing for His children. "Who teacheth like Him?"

2. *God's absolute justice.*—In bringing Jacob back to Himself God made no allowance for His servant's sin. If it be possible, God is stricter with His own children than with others. Jacob had made a solemn vow and promise that if God would be with him and bring him back to his father's home in peace, God should be his God and Bethel a Divine memorial. All, and very much more besides, had been completely fulfilled by God, and yet Jacob's part had not been performed. It was necessary therefore first and foremost that the wrong should be righted. This is always God's method of recall after spiritual declension. "Repent and do the first works" (Rev. ii. 5). When the children of Israel arrived in Canaan the very first things required of them were the renewal of the covenants of circumcision and of the Passover, in order that the people might be on the true footing of relationship and fellowship with God. And so it must ever be. Whatever can be put right must be put right, if our fellowship with God is to be renewed; and as long as we are unwilling to set right that which is wrong God will have a controversy with us, and there cannot be any spiritual rest or satisfaction of soul.

3. *God's restoring grace.*—It is truly marvelous what the grace of God can do even for a repentant believer and a returned backslider. It is perfectly true that the failure and backsliding of His children prevent them from ever being exactly what they would have been apart from these faults. At the same time it is equally true that God's overruling grace can work wonders. We think of Manasseh after his idolatry, of David after his sin, of Peter after his fall; and while we dare not say, as some would teach, "We may be all we might have been, we *can* say with absolute certainty that

"We may be something that we should never otherwise have been," because of the new elements that have entered into our life through the bitter experiences of backsliding. These things never excuse or even palliate our fall, and the repentant and restored believer will always be severe against himself by reason of his former backsliding; but we can say, and dare to say, that Divine grace takes up the threads even of our darkest experiences and weaves them into the pattern of our life from that time forward. Nature knows no forgiveness and no restoration, but grace is the mighty miracle of the universe; and if only we yield ourselves wholly and utterly to the hand of God, our lives, whatever the past may have been, shall be monuments, miracles, marvels of the grace of God.

He came to my desk with a quivering lip—
    The lesson was done.
"Dear teacher, I want a new leaf," he said—
    "I have spoiled this one "
In place of the leaf so stained and blotted
I gave him a new one all unspotted.
    And unto his sad eyes smiled—
    "Do better now, my child."

I went to the Throne with a quivering soul—
    The old year was done.
"Dear Father, hast thou a new leaf for me?
    I have spoiled this one."
He took the old leaf, stained and blotted,
And gave me a new one all unspotted,
    And into my sad heart smiled—
    "Do better now, my child."

XLVIII

THE SCHOOL OF SORROW

Gen. xxxv. 8, 16-29

8. But Deborah Rebekah's nurse died, and she was buried beneath Bethel under an oak: and the name of it was called Allon-bachuth.

16. And they journeyed from Bethel; and there was but a little way to come to Ephrath: and Rachel travailed, and she had hard labor.

17. And it came to pass, when she was in hard labor, that the midwife said unto her, Fear not; thou shalt have this son also.

18. And it came to pass, as her soul was in departing, (for she died), that she called his name Benoni: but his father called him Benjamin.

19. And Rachel died, and was buried in the way to Ephrath, which is Bethlehem.

20. And Jacob set a pillar upon her grave: that is the pillar of Rachel's grave unto this day.

21. And Israel journeyed, and spread his tent beyond the tower of Edar.

22. And it came to pass, when Israel dwelt in that land, that Reuben went and lay with Bilhah his father's concubine: and Israel heard it. Now the sons of Jacob were twelve:

23. The sons of Leah; Reuben, Jacob's firstborn, and Simeon, and Levi, and Judah, and Issachar, and Zebulun:

24. The sons of Rachel; Joseph, and Benjamin:

25. And the sons of Bilhah, Rachel's handmaid; Dan, and Naphtali:

26. And the sons of Zilpah, Leah's handmaid: Gad, and Asher: these are the sons of Jacob, which were born to him in Padan-aram.

27. And Jacob came unto Isaac his father unto Mamre, unto the city of Arbah, which is Hebron, where Abraham and Isaac sojourned.

28. And the days of Isaac were an hundred and fourscore years.

29. And Isaac gave up the ghost, and died, and was gathered unto his people, being old and full of days: and his sons Esau and Jacob buried him.

GOD has many ways of making permanent in our lives the lessons of His providence and grace, and one of these is the discipline of sorrow. "Sweet are the uses of adversity," as we are now to see in the unfolding of the story of Jacob. There is nothing in its way more striking than the fact that from the time Jacob fulfilled his vow in Bethel to the day that he learnt of Joseph's preservation in

Egypt he was scarcely ever out of "the furnace of affliction." Some of the earliest of these experiences will now come before us.

I. *The Death of an Old Servant* (ver. 8).—No sooner had Jacob reached Bethel than Deborah, the aged nurse of his mother Rebekah, died. First referred to in connection with Rebekah's coming to be the wife of Isaac (xxiv. 59), she is here mentioned again very many years after. How, why, and when she became associated with Jacob's household we know not, for there is no record. It is probable that she joined him in Mesopotamia on the death of his mother. She was a very interesting link with the past, recalling his mother and his own earliest days in the old home. What many a man owes to a faithful servant! How fine are the obituary notices from time to time of "So-and-so, for many years the faithful servant and friend of ——"! Now the link is broken, and Jacob has one connection less with the days of his youth. As time goes on, and friend after friend passes upward, we find ourselves more and more severed from the past and more and more united with the future. It is in such ways that we are led to think of the future, and to fix our hope on things to come. *"But* Deborah died." That is, notwithstanding the fact that Jacob was now at Bethel and in fellowship with God. Faithfulness to God does not exempt us from sorrow.

II. *The Death of a Beloved Wife* (vers. 16-20).—Residence at Bethel (ver 1) was, it would seem, completed with the fulfilment of his vow, and Jacob was apparently free to move southward towards Mamre, the home of his father. He and his household had not gone very far when another great sorrow came upon him, the deepest of his life. He lost his beloved wife Rachel, who died in giving birth to her second son. In her pain and anguish she was cheered by the encouraging news of the birth of another son, but the end of her earthly life was at hand. Just as she was dying she called the newly-born child Benoni ("son of my pain"), in token of the gain of a son even through sorrow. But her husband, to cheer her and himself to the end, would not allow so ill-omened a name to remain, and changed it to Benjamin ("son of the right hand"), indicative of his faith in the blessing and prosperity that

should accrue from his birth. Thus we have the first record of
death at child-birth, and the entire narrative is full of simple pathos
and exquisite beauty. Rachel's life had had its share of sorrow,
and the end itself was in no way different. Robbed at the outset of the entire love of one whose wife she was expecting to be, she
found herself the victim of jealousy in that unhappy home at
Haran. Nor did she seem to have, at any rate until late in life,
the full consolation of the worship of the true God, for she was
given to superstition (xxx. 14), and the worship of false gods (xxxi.
19). It is probable that these influences were not wholly extirpated
until the removal to Bethel (xxxv. 2, 4). She had hoped for another son in addition to Joseph (xxx. 24), but her unwise and
passionate prayer of years ago (xxx. 1) now received a very unexpected answer. She had indeed a son given to her, and died at
the time of the gift.

Once again Jacob set up a pillar, this time in memory of his love
and sorrow (verse 20), just as he had at Bethel in memory of the
Divine love and grace to him (verse 14). His love for Rachel was
remarkable in its depth and constancy. Even long years after her
death the memory was keen and poignant (xlviii. 7). It is one
of the most striking features of Jacob's character that he could love
so devotedly and tenaciously. Such a strong nature as this was
capable of great things, whatever sins and errors were on the
surface.

III. *The Sin of a Firstborn Son* (vers. 21, 22).—From the sad
scene of his great bereavement Israel journeyed on towards Mamre.
The word "Israel" is noteworthy here. It is the first occurrence of
the new name as applied to Jacob after the confirmation of it at
Bethel. Like the usage in Genesis of Jehovah and Elohim, which
are invariably employed with discrimination, the terms Israel and
Jacob are always to be carefully observed, for not seldom it is possible to see a real meaning in the particular one used. Here it seems
to suggest that he journeyed in the strength of that power with God
which was his heritage as the Prince of God, and by means of which
he faced and bore his sorrow. He spread his tent between Bethlehem and Mamre, "beyond the tower of Edar," the tower being one

of those frequently found as at once the center and safeguard of flocks and herds (2 Kings xvii. 9).

Another and terrible sorrow now falls on the patriarch in the awful sin of his eldest son Reuben. By this fearful sin (Lev. xviii. 8; 1 Cor. v. 1) he lost the birthright (Gen. xlix. 4) and incurred endless shame and infamy. Thus by a curious coincidence, and perhaps with some inner meaning, the record of the birth of Jacob's youngest son is brought into close association with the sin of the eldest son. In the light of the subsequent history of the tribes of Benjamin and Reuben we can see here another illustration of the great principle that "the last shall be first and the first last." Rachel's sons come to the front in due course. At first she, the beloved and rightful wife, was without children (xxx. 1), and every advantage seemed to be with Leah, who had been deceitfully pressed upon Jacob. But at length Rachel's turn came, and not only did she have two sons, but these sons came to their own in God's good time. Joseph in his two sons, and Benjamin also, had tribal territories allotted to them, and Ephraim was leader of Israel for centuries, while Reuben lost the birthright which would have been his as firstborn son. No one can seriously question the fact of a Divine Providence in human life, a Providence that sees justice done and wrongs righted, even though the progress may be slow and the time long.

We can easily imagine the anguish and shame that filled the patriarch's heart as he became aware of this sin of Reuben. Coming so soon after his great sorrow, it must have caused tenfold grief to a heart already wrung with pain. And yet the record simply but significantly states, "and Israel heard it." Mark the phraseology: "Israel," not "Jacob." That is to say, he heard the terrible news in the quiet strength of the new name and power implied and guaranteed by his recent revelation from God (ver. 10). This is the only real way to meet sorrow, pain and shame—"in the strength of the Lord God." Whatever the emergency, we may rest on the Divine assurance: "My grace is sufficient for thee."

How veracious is the record of Scripture! No mere human history would record the sins of notable men so fully and unflinchingly. The candour of the Bible is one of its chief claims to be Divine.

At this point we are given a full list of Jacob's children, though the names do not appear in order of birth, but according to motherhood. The children of Leah and Rachel come first, and then those of Bilhah and Zilpah. The reason for the insertion of this list here is probably because the long section of the "generations of Isaac" (xxv. 19) closes with this chapter, and new sections are about to open with the generations of Esau and Jacob (xxxvi. 1 and xxxvii. 2). The house of Isaac is therefore regarded as complete, and the subordinate position of Jacob will henceforth be changed for that of the head of the patriarchal house and line. In this connection, as we see again and again in the history, it is worth while to observe the remarkable differences between the sons of Leah and those of Rachel. They appear to be absolutely opposed in temperament and habit. Two sisters, and yet such astonishingly different children. Students of heredity will find here material worthy of their attention.

IV. *The Death of an Honored Father* (vers. 27-29).—Jacob arrives home again at last. "Jacob came unto Isaac his father unto Mamre . . . which is Hebron, where Abraham and Isaac sojourned." What memories must have been called up by that return! How he must have missed his mother as he remembered the past and all their life together there! His children, too, would be keenly interested in meeting their grandfather and the head of the family. There are few places that stir the heart more deeply than the old home of our childhood, and all the dear memories of days long gone by. Isaac, too, must have recalled the day, over thirty years before, when he spoke of himself as old and uncertain of life (xxvii. 2), and then thought of all that had happened as the result of that unhappy suggestion to Esau. But all was swallowed up in the joy of reunion, and, as we cannot doubt, in the joy of the recital of the way in which God had led both father and son all those long years of separation.

In order that the record of Isaac's life may be rounded off
mention is made at this point of his death, though as a matter of
fact he lived until Joseph was quite thirty years old, or thirteen
years after his sale in Egypt. The statement is put in here, after
the analogy of earlier accounts (xi. 32 and xxv. 8), to prepare the
way for dealing solely with the record of Jacob as the head of the
family.   Isaac was spared for over forty years beyond the time
when he expected to die (xxvii, 1, 2), and the years after Jacob's return must have been a very precious time of fellowship with God and
his son as he waited the call of God. The description of his death is
noteworthy: "he gave up the ghost," he yielded up the spirit to God
Who gave it. The phrase used of Rachel (ver. 18) is worth compar-
ing: "as her soul was in departing." The difference is suggestive of
their different ages and the circumstances of their deaths, but the idea
is essentially the same. To "depart" or to "give up the ghost" is not
to be annihilated, but to enter upon a new state, a new life in the
presence of God.   The old fathers did indeed look for more than
transitory promises.   They had respect unto the living God, and to
the city which He had prepared for them.   Isaac was also "gathered
to his people," which gives another beautiful suggestion of the
life to come—that of reunion with those whom we have loved and
lost awhile.   And so, with the spirit at rest with God and at home
with our loved ones, we learn something of what heaven is. "With
Christ" and "with *them*," all must and will be well.

At the grave of their father the two brothers, Esau and Jacob, met
again. With what thoughts they must have paid the last tribute of
filial love and borne their father's body to its restingplace! Already
reconciled (xxxiii.), this sorrow must have confirmed their friendship and made their hearts increasingly tender to each other as they
recalled the past with sins and errors on both sides.   Death is a
wonderful healer of breaches.   Happy are they who find over the
grave of a loved father or mother the opportunity of reuniting
severed ties.   Thrice happy are they who at the graveside of a loved
one have not to reunite ties, but only to deepen and confirm them
in the love and grace of God.

The life of Isaac, as we review it, is in striking contrast to those of his father and his sons. In their case we have lives full of incident; in his little but quietness and peace. Except for two occasions of sin (xxvi. and xxvii.), there is nothing in the record to disturb the impression that Isaac's life was of the pastoral, quiet, restful, contemplative type which based itself on the promises of God (xxvi. 24) and lived peacefully, waiting the development and progress of the Divine purpose. One word, used twice by Jacob, seems to give the clue to Isaac's character. Jacob speaks of God as "the *Fear* of Isaac" (xxxi. 42, 53), a striking term, especially when contrasted with the customary usage, "the God of Abraham." Isaac's nature was contemplative, quiet, reverential, full of awe. God was his "Fear," not slavish dread, but filial awe. And it was this that impressed Jacob, whose nature at its root was so like that of his father. Jacob had a profound sense of reverence for God and divine things, and it is well that he had, for with him and with us all "the fear of the Lord is the beginning of wisdom." "Holy and reverend is His Name."

The cloud of sorrow hangs heavily on these verses. There are three graves and one sin recorded, and it is in connection with the sorrow caused by these events that Jacob was taught some very precious lessons. Shall we not try to learn them for ourselves?

1. *Sorrow is not always sent as punishment.*—We often bring sorrow on ourselves through our sin, but this is not always and necessarily the case. The death of Deborah came when Jacob had put himself right with God. The death of Rachel and the sin of Reuben do not appear to be traceable to any wrong-doing of Jacob. So is it today. Sorrow is not necessarily punishment. It may be just the opposite. It all depends on the state of our spiritual life how we understand and take sorrow. If we are right with God, we shall meet sorrow as "Israel," not "Jacob," and find in it the message God intends for us. Every affliction may be viewed in two aspects; and what from one viewpoint may be thought a Benoni, may from another be seen as a Benjamin. It all depends on our faith; and if that be real and true, then "Faith can *sing* through

days of sorrow." We shall certainly "faint" if we do not "believe to see the goodness of the Lord" in the time of sorrow and pain.

2. *Sorrow is often used for spiritual training.*—Chastening is very different from punishing, and "it is for chastening ye endure" (Heb. xii. 7, R.V.) There is a very clear connection spiritually, as well as etymologically, between *discipleship* and *discipline*. We only become real disciples through discipline. The word rendered "chastening" in Heb. xii. is literally "son-making." God makes us truly His sons by subjecting us, or allowing us to be subjected, to training and discipline; and it is for this reason that we read "Whom the Lord loveth He chasteneth." When Archbishop Tait, as Dean of Carlisle, lost several children in quick succession, in the short space of a few weeks, his friend Francis Close, then at Cheltenham, wrote quoting this text to the bereaved and heartbroken father, adding, "He must love you much to chasten you so much."

3. *Sorrow is intended to yield the peaceful fruits of righteousness.* —Who shall say how much this discipline had to do with Tait's noteworthy episcopate in London and his splendid service as Archbishop of Canterbury? Many a Christian can say with David, "It is good for me that I have been afflicted; that I might *learn*" (Ps. cxix. 71). "Before I was afflicted I went astray, but *now*——" (Ps. cxix. 67). In the description of the life of the believer in Rom. v. we must not overlook the place given to "tribulation." May it not mean that one of the ways which God takes to make our experiences real is the way of suffering? As the Son of God was made "perfect through suffering," so the sons of God are brought to glory in the same way. Just as the pattern of the china vase is made permanent by being put into the fire, so the impressions of God's truth and grace become part of our character by our being passed through the furnace of affliction.

> "As gold must be tried in the fire,
> So the heart must be tried by pain."

And so, though our outward man perishes, our inward man is renewed day by day. Let us therefore yield ourselves to the Divine Potter, to be made into "vessels unto honor" and conformed to His image and likeness in order to live to His glory.

XLIX

"A PROFANE PERSON"

GEN. xxxvi. 1-8

1. Now these *are* the generations of Esau, who *is* Edom.
2. Esau took his wives of the daughters of Canaan; Adah the daughter of Elon the Hittite, and Aholibamah the daughter of Anah the daughter of Zibeon the Hivite;
3. And Bashemath Ishmael's daughter, sister of Nebajoth.
4. And Adah bare to Esau Eliphaz; and Bashemath bare Reuel;
5. And Aholibamah bare Jeush, and Jaalam, and Korah: these *are* the sons of Esau, which were born unto him in the land of Canaan.
6. And Esau took his wives, and his sons, and his daughters, and all the persons of his house, and his cattle and all his beasts, and all his substance, which he had got in the land of Canaan; and went into the country from the face of his brother Jacob.
7. For their riches were more than that they might dwell together; and the land wherein they were strangers could not bear them because of their cattle.
8. Thus dwelt Esau in mount Seir: Esau *is* Edom.

THERE is perhaps no greater contrast in Scripture than that seen in the characters of Esau and Jacob. The one on the surface was interesting and attractive, the other on the surface was unattractive and often repellent, at least for a large part of his life. And yet as we include in our view of the two men the whole Bible testimony concerning them, and study with all possible care and completeness that which lies below the surface, we cannot help coming to the very opposite of our first conclusion. We obtain the deep impression that characters are not to be judged by superficial impressions but by a careful inquiry into the right principles of life. It will be convenient at this point to gather together the various references to Esau which we find in Genesis, and then attempt to obtain a true idea of his real character.

I. *Esau's History.*—The circumstances of his birth foreshadowed a remarkable history, and whenever he appears before us we cannot help being struck with the man as he reveals himself in the record.

The first event brought before us is the sale of his birthright to Jacob (chap. xxv. 29-34). It is unnecessary in the present connection to repeat the details of the story which have already come before us, nor is it to the point to dwell upon Jacob's share in this unhappy transaction. For our present purpose it will suffice to call attention to the simple but significant comment of the writer: "So Esau despised his birthright." Whatever fault we may attribute to Jacob, and however great our contempt may be for his underhand dealing, we must not overlook the fact that in parting with his birthright Esau revealed his true character. He had already come to the conclusion, long before the time that Jacob made the offer, that his birthright was of no value to him. We must look beneath the surface from the very outset of the story of Esau, and when we do this we discover that his horizon was bounded by earth and that he had no conception whatever of the glory of the promises to Abraham and to Isaac which were associated with the birthright.

Esau comes before us next in connection with his marriage to the two Canaanitish women (chap. xxvi. 34, 35). This deliberate association with the people of the land was another significant revelation of his true nature. Not only did he introduce into his father's family the untoward and dangerous element of polygamy, but he went his way by himself without any consultation with his parents and married into the Canaanites, and thereby led to an intermixture which it had hitherto been the special endeavor of Abraham and of Isaac to avoid. No wonder that this action of their elder son caused great grief and bitterness of spirit to Isaac and Rebekah. Once again the real man showed himself in this deliberate setting at naught of some of the most cherished principles and hopes of his people.

The next time that Esau appears before us is in connection with the blessing. Having deliberately and of set purpose bartered away his birthright, it is clear that he had subsequently come to a different mind as to its importance. Consequently, when his father wished to bestow upon him the patriarchal blessing, Esau was quite ready to enter into the plot and obtain back again by craft what he had lost by a deliberate act of his own. We do not overlook the sin of Isaac, or Rebekah, or Jacob, in calling attention to the simple fact that Esau must not be absolved from a share in this blame. We can see still further what he really was, for after he had lost the blessing, he in his rage and fury determined to kill his brother when a suitable opportunity occurred. He was a man of un-governable impulse, without any fixed principle, never constant for long to any one thing.

Another event further revealed Esau's true character (chap xxviii. 8, 9). When he saw that Jacob had departed with his father's blessing to find a wife outside the land of Canaan, and from his own kith and kin, he endeavored once again to obtain an advantage at his brother's expense by taking to himself a third wife, this time a daughter of his kinsman Ishmael. Esau seems to have been fully awake at last to the importance and value of the position of the eldest son, and he sets to work to try to retrieve his position in the eyes of his parents. Even here we cannot help noticing his practical failure, for although Ishmael was the half-brother of his father, it had been made perfectly clear that there was to be no part or lot to Ishmael in the inheritance of promise and blessing to Isaac.

When Jacob returned after the years of separation in the house and country of Laban, Esau again appears as he comes with a retinue of men to meet his brother. It would seem clear that at the outset he had determined to take his revenge, but he little knew what was happening at the ford Jabbok, and how God in answer to prayer was already at work breaking down the barriers, and preparing for a full reconciliation between the brothers. Esau's hot impulses were quickly cooled at the sight of his brother, and the anger died down as they met and settled their differences in a loving reconciliation. Esau's warmheartedness shines out at this point and makes us all the more sorry that it played so small a part in the entire experiences of his life.

The brothers met again, and probably for the last time, at their father's death (chap. xxxv. 29), but they met only to separate permanently one from the other. The land was not large enough to maintain the households of both of them, and Esau therefore took all that he possessed and went into a land far away from his brother in the country afterwards known as Edom (chap. xxxvi. 1-8). Thenceforward the two tribes and afterwards the two races were kept apart not only geographically but in almost every other respect, and, as we know, Edom showed hostility to the people of Israel as the latter made their way from Egypt to Canaan.

II. *Esau's Character.*—The startling mystery of human nature is remarkably illustrated in the case of Esau. There was an undoubted attractiveness in his temperament and character. He was evidently of a happy and bright disposition. Nothing appeared to worry or trouble him. He took life easily and never seemed concerned with its shadows and difficulties. He was also of an affectionate disposition. His devotion to his father is evident in the narrative, and the fact of his father's devotion to him must be put to his credit. Even his impulsiveness had the elements of good and promise in it, for he was manifestly capable of generous and warmhearted dispositions. Not least of all there was a forgiving spirit in the man. Jacob had undoubtedly done him serious and irreparable wrong, and we should not have been surprised from the purely human standpoint if he had remained permanently embittered against the supplanter; but the opposite happened, and when they met after that long separation there was no trace of anger or revenge on the part of Esau, but every indication of forgiveness and personal reconciliation.

This attractiveness, however, was almost entirely on the surface, and when we look below we are bound to confess that there was much that was objectionable and even repulsive. The passionateness of the man is clear as we read the narrative of his attitude to Jacob. He was also in the literal meaning of the word a "sensual" man, that is, a man whose life was lived within the region of his senses and purely physical desires and tastes. He lived for personal enjoyment at the present moment, and was evidently prepared to sacrifice everything else to gratify his own desires. Whether we think of his willingness to barter his birthright for food, or contemplate his ill-advised marriage with two Canaanitish women, we see how entirely earth-bound he was, and how fully he lived for himself alone and for his own enjoyment. But all this was only indicative of what was at the root and foundation of his life. He had no true conception of the value of things spiritual. When we are told that he "despised his birthright" we are not to understand any mere impulse, or that he was merely victimized by a craftier nature; he had been leading up to this despising of the birthright by the purely secular life that he had been living. The promises of God had made no impression on him. The spiritual ideas associated with the Covenant were as nothing to him. He was in every sense earthly and earthbound. This as we have seen is the meaning of the significant judgment in the Epistle to the Hebrews (chap. xii. 16), he was "a profane person." His life was purely secular, there was no sacred enclosure in it. Everything in him was of the world and the flesh, and no part of his life was devoted to God. This was at the root of his trouble. God was not in all his thoughts.

The story of Esau and the revelation of his character, as indicated by the events, carry their own personal application, but it may be worthwhile laying special stress upon some of the outstanding messages of this sad and disappointing life.

1. *Superficial attractiveness is not enough.*—There are many natures and temperaments which are interesting and even fascinating on the surface, full of real charm of manner and disposition, and yet all the while they hide an underlying indifference to God which easily leads to a definite hostility. The young ruler who came to our Lord had the splendid advantages of age, position, wealth, opportunity, earnestness, and even moral integrity, and yet when he was put to the test he revealed his deliberate unwillingness to surrender to Christ and to allow the Lord Jesus to be the Master of his life. We must never be deceived by outward attractiveness in itself, though when such attractiveness springs from genuine spiritual relationship to God it is without question the most beautiful thing on the earth.

2. *Divine grace is absolutely essential.*—There are some natures which by environment, culture, and refinement seem to tend towards the ideal. They make people wonder whether after all true

religion is essential to real life. Experience however goes to show
in an ever-increasing way that nothing but Divine grace can guarantee a permanent character. While it is doubtless true that "character is three-fourths of conduct," it is equally true that the other
fourth represents the source, spring, and guarantee of conduct itself. "Without Me ye can do nothing" is a truth of absolutely universal application, and whatever education, circumstances, opportunity may do for us we can never dispense with Divine grace.
Esau's life was lived entirely on an earthly plane. The purely natural
elements were supreme, and when the test came he sacrificed the
spiritual opportunity that might have been his and so brought about
irrevocable disaster. Grace is as much needed for character as it is
for salvation, for the simple reason that character must necessarily
be based upon salvation, which in turn depends upon the new nature
of the divine life which is ours by faith in Christ Jesus.

3. *Opportunity comes to all.*—While it is perfectly true that God
intended Jacob to inherit the spiritual blessings of the Covenant, it
is equally certain that Esau had a sufficient opportunity of enjoy-
ing blessing at God's hands. His boyhood was spent at home under
the influence of his father and mother, and it is evident from the
sequel that he became aware when it was too late of the blessings
that he had missed. This shows that he had been trained and taught
to value those blessings, but had deliberately set them aside and
despised them. No one will be able to say in the great day of account that he had no opportunity of being good. God is righteous,
and will never allow any man to be at a disadvantage. Opportunity
comes to all, but, alas! opportunity may easily be lost through unfaithfulness. When Esau afterward desired to inherit the blessing
he was rejected, for he found no way of changing his father's mind,
though he sought a blessing earnestly with tears (Heb. xii. 17).
There is a solemn and loud warning in this word "afterward," for
it tells of an awakened conscience and blighted hopes that were
never realized. A man looking back upon his past life said that a
great deal of his time had been spent in raising tombstones over
the graves of lost opportunities. To every one of us comes the

solemn word of the Master, "How often would I . . . and ye would not."

4. *The marvel and mercy of Divine Grace.*—While we may not and must not set aside and think lightly of life's great moral responsibilities, we are encouraged by the revelation of God in Christ to believe that Divine grace can nevertheless do much to enable us to retrieve our character. While it is true that we never can be what we otherwise might have been, yet grace can do much to overrule our mistakes and even our sins. Esau always had to be content with God's second best, but even for him there was a future not unmixed with mercy and blessing. It is perfectly true that what is done cannot be undone, but it is equally true that what is done can be mended by Divine grace. Let us therefore be encouraged, in spite of our past, to put ourselves afresh into God's merciful and loving hands, feeling sure that His discipline will deal with us faithfully and lovingly, and in spite of all our sins and shortcomings bring glory to His Name out of the remnant of our life. The "afterward" of Esau's experience (Heb. xii. 17) may be met by the "afterward" of Divine mercy and grace (Heb. xii. 11), and our lives yet be used of God as we walk humbly and go softly, remembering the past, trusting for the present, and hoping in Him for the future.

L

JOSEPH'S EARLY LIFE

GEN. xxxvii

1. And Jacob dwelt in the land wherein his father was a stranger, in the land of Canaan.

2. These *are* the generations of Jacob. Joseph, *being* seventeen years old, was feeding the flock with his brethren; and the lad *was* with the sons of Bilhah, and with the sons of Zilpah, his father's wives: and Joseph brought unto his father their evil report.

3. Now Israel loved Joseph more than all his children, because he *was* the son of his old age: and he made him a coat of *many* colors.

4. And when his brethren saw that their father loved him more than all his brethren, they hated him, and could not speak peaceably unto him.

5. And Joseph dreamed a dream, and he told *it* his brethren: and they hated him yet the more.

6. And he said unto them, Hear, I pray you, this dream which I have dreamed:

7. For, behold, we *were* binding sheaves in the field, and, lo, my sheaf arose, and also stood upright; and, behold, your sheaves stood round about, and made obeisance to my sheaf.

8. And his brethren said to him, Shalt thou indeed reign over us? or shalt thou indeed have dominion over us? And they hated him yet the more for his dreams, and for his words.

9. And he dreamed yet another dream, and told it his brethren, and said, Behold, I have dreamed a dream more; and, behold, the sun and the moon and the eleven stars made obeisance to me.

10. And he told *it* to his father, and to his brethren: and his father rebuked him, and said unto him, What *is* this dream that thou hast dreamed? Shall I and thy mother and thy brethren indeed come to bow down ourselves to thee to the earth?

11. And his brethren envied him; but his father observed the saying.

12. And his brethren went to feed their father's flock in Shechem.

13. And Israel said unto Joseph, Do not thy brethren feed *the flock* in Shechem? come, and I will send thee unto them. And he said to him, Here *am I.*

14. And he said to him, Go, I pray thee, see whether it be well with thy brethren, and well with the flocks; and bring me word again. So he sent him out of the vale of Hebron, and he came to Shechem.

15. And a certain man found him, and behold, *he was* wandering in the field: and the man asked him, saying, What seekest thou?

16. And he said, I seek my brethren: tell me, I pray thee, where they feed *their flocks.*

17. And the man said, They are departed hence; for I heard them say, Let us go to Dothan. And Joseph went after his brethren, and found them in Dothan.

18. And when they saw him afar off, even before he came near unto them, they conspired against him to slay him.

19. And they said one to another, Behold, this dreamer cometh.

20. Come now therefore, and let us slay him, and cast him into some pit, and we will say, Some evil beast hath devoured him: and we shall see what will become of his dreams.

21. And Reuben heard *it,* and he delivered him out of their hands; and said, Let us not kill him.

22. And Reuben said unto them, Shed no blood, *but* cast him into this pit that *is* in the wilderness, and lay no hand upon him; that he might rid him out of their hands, to deliver him to his father again.

23. And it came to pass, when Joseph was come unto his brethren, that they stript Joseph out of his coat, *his coat* of *many* colors that *was* on him;

24. And they took him, and cast him into a pit: and the pit *was* empty, *there was* no water in it.

25. And they sat down to eat bread: and they lifted up their eyes and looked, and behold, a company of Ishmaelites came from Gilead with their camels bearing spicery and balm and myrrh, going to carry *it* down to Egypt.

26. And Judah said unto his brethren, What profit *is it* if we slay our brother, and conceal his blood?

27. Come, and let us sell him to the Ishmaelites, and let not our hand be upon him; for he *is* our brother *and* our flesh. And his brethren were content.

28. Then there passed by Midianites merchantmen; and they drew and lifted up Joseph out of the pit, and sold Joseph to the Ishmaelites for twenty *pieces* of silver: and they brought Joseph into Egypt.

29. And Reuben returned unto the pit; and, behold, Joseph *was* not in the pit; and he rent his clothes.

30. And he returned unto his brethren and said, The child *is* not; and I, whither shall I go?

31. And they took Joseph's coat, and killed a kid of the goats, and dipped the coat in the blood;

32. And they sent the coat of *many* colors, and they brought *it* to their father; and said, This have we found; know now whether it *be* thy son's coat or no.

33. And he knew it, and said, *It is* my son's coat; an evil beast hath devoured him; Joseph is without doubt rent in pieces.

34. And Jacob rent his clothes, and put sackcloth upon his loins, and mourned for his son many days.

35. And all his sons and all his daughters rose up to comfort him; but he refused to be comforted; and he said, For I will go down into the grave unto my son mourning. Thus his father wept for him.

36. And the Midianites sold him into Egypt unto Potiphar, an officer of Pharaoh's, *and* captain of the guard.

WITH the story of Joseph we come to the last division of Genesis, though the heading is "These are the generations of Jacob," since Jacob was the head of the family. The development and progress of the household of Jacob until at length it became a nation in Egypt had Joseph as a pioneer, and it is almost entirely to this development under Joseph that the reminder of Genesis is devoted. At the same time the story is not concerned with Joseph only (see xxxviii.), but with Jacob and all his sons.

The fullness of the narrative is worthy of consideration. Far more is told us of Joseph than of any of the patriarchs preceding him. There is a fourfold value and importance in the record of Joseph's life: (1) It gives the explanation of the development of the Hebrews. How was it that they who came originally from the valley of the Euphrates were found at length as a colony in Egypt? How came it to pass that they, a nomadic people, lived in possession and enjoyment of the richest province of Egypt for generations? The story of Joseph gives the answer to these questions. (2) It is a remarkable proof of the quiet operation of Divine Providence, overruling evil and leading at length to the complete victory of truth and righteousness. (3) It affords a splendid example of personal character. Joseph's life is one of the very finest recorded in Scripture. (4) It provides a striking series of typical illustrations of Christ. There are few more remarkable points of contact and coincidences with the life of our Lord than those found in the story of Joseph.

In concentrating attention on the life of Joseph it is impossible to avoid noticing the various aspects of faith represented by the leading characters in Genesis. Thus, Abel illustrates redemption through faith; Enoch stands for the walk of faith; Noah bears witness to the confession of faith: Abraham expresses the obedience of faith; Isaac is an example of the patience of faith; Jacob reveals the training of faith; while Joseph exemplifies the testing and triumph of faith.

In the chapter before us we have the commencement of the story which is so familiar and precious to all lovers of Holy Writ.

I. *Joseph's Home Life* (vers. 1-4).—Joseph was the elder son of Rachel (xxx. 24). Of his early life nothing is recorded. He could not have been more than five or six years old when his father left Mesopotamia. He was therefore the child of Jacob's later life, and escaped all the sad experiences associated with the earlier years at Haran. He comes before us in this chapter at the age of seventeen. His companions were his half-brothers, the grown-up sons of Bilhah and Zilpah. From all that we have hitherto seen of them they must have been utterly unfit companions for such a youth. Jacob's elder sons had naturally been affected by the life in Haran, by the jealousy at home, and by the scheming between Laban and Jacob. They had been brought up under the influence of the old Jacob, while Joseph had been the companion of the changed Jacob or "Israel." There are few people more unfitted for influence over younger brothers than elder brothers of bad character.

The difference between the elder brethren and Joseph was accentuated by the fact that "Joseph brought unto his father the evil report of his brethren." What precisely this meant we do not know, but from the wording in the original it was evidently something that was well known and notorious in the neighborhood. It may have been dishonesty, but most likely it was something much worse, in view of all that we know of them. It is sometimes thought that Joseph is blameworthy for telling tales; but there does not seem any warrant for regarding him as a mere spy. It is an utterly mistaken sense of honor that keeps people from giving information when wrong-doing is involved. Far from being mean and cowardly, such action is not only justifiable but necessary. Tale-bearing pure and simple is, of course, always despicable; but there is a time to speak, and on such an occasion silence is criminal. The lad had been brought up amid the more godly influences of Jacob's later years, and it is quite easy to understand the shock that would be given him at meeting with this wickedness away from home on the part of his elder brothers. So long as there was no exaggeration, no malice, and no personal ends to serve, there could be nothing blameworthy in Joseph bringing his father their evil report.

There was, however, something much more than this to account for the differences between Joseph and his brethren. Israel had a special love for this child of Rachel, and he did not hesitate to show it in a very definite way. The gift of a coat of many "pieces" (not "colors"), or rather "the tunic with sleeves," was about the most significant act that Jacob could have shown to Joseph. It was a mark of distinction that carried its own meaning, for it implied that exemption from labor which was the peculiar privilege of the heir or prince of the Eastern clan. Instead of the ordinary work-a-day vestment which had no sleeves, and which, by coming down to the knees only, enabled men to set about their work—this tunic with sleeves clearly marked out its wearer as a person of special distinction, who was not required to do ordinary work. Whether Jacob exercised sufficient prudence in showing such undisguised partiality for Joseph is an open question. It was in any case a very natural thing for him to do. He was the child of his old age, the son of his beloved wife, and without doubt a sympathetic, responsive listener to all that the patriarch had to say about the promises of God to himself and to his fathers. It was impossible after Reuben's great sin (xxxv. 22) for the transfer of the birthright from him to be disguised from the others, and it was equally natural for Jacob to appoint for Joseph the privileges of the firstborn.

And so when his brethren saw these marks of special favor "they hated him, and could not speak peaceably unto him." Although he was so young and they were grown men, their jealousy had been excited, for they readily saw all that it meant. Nor may we overlook the remarkable difference in their lives and conduct, a fact which must have rebuked the elder brothers and added fuel to the fire of their envy and jealousy. Joseph's purity of life and moral growth must have rankled in their hearts.

II. *Joseph's Dreams* (vers. 5-11).—The hatred of the brothers was soon intensified through the dreams that Joseph narrated to them. The first dream was that of the sheaves in the field. He dreamt that the sheaves of his brethren made obeisance to his own sheaf. This, in true Eastern fashion, was interpreted by the brethren to mean his dominion over them, and as a consequence "they hated him yet the more for his dreams, and for his words." Not only did they feel annoyed at his telling them his dream, but their animosity was stirred by reason of the dream itself. Again he dreamed, and this time his father and mother were included: "Behold, the sun and the moon and the eleven stars made obeisance to me." Joseph told this to his father as well as to his brethren, and Jacob at once checked him, expressing astonishment that anything of the kind could possibly come true. "Shall I and thy mother and thy brethren indeed come to bow down ourselves to thee to the earth?" The reference to the mother seems to be to Leah, who had taken the place of Rachel, and had become a mother to her sister's children. Yet, although the father rebuked the boy, he could not help being impressed. "His father observed the saying." Like Mary in after years, there was something that even Israel could not understand (Luke ii. 19, 51). The repetition of the dream seems to imply certainty of fulfilment (xli. 32), and the dreams were at once natural and supernatural. They were natural in form as distinct from any Divine vision, and yet they were clearly prophetic of Joseph's future glory.

It is sometimes thought that Joseph made a mistake in telling his brethren these dreams, or at any rate, that he was wrong in telling the second. He does not seem to have been actuated by self-consciousness or vanity, or perhaps he would not have told what he had experienced. Whether this was so or not, the effect was disastrous to him, for it only added fuel to the fire, intensifying his brothers' animosity.

How true to life are these dreams of the youth! Youth is the time for visions of the future. Young men cannot help dreaming dreams, for they would not be young men if they did not do so. A youth without ideals is a youth without inspiration; and when, as in Joseph's case, it is susceptible to spiritual intuitions, there is indeed the promise and potency of a fine manhood.

III. *Joseph's Mission* (vers. 12-17).—In the course of their work
as shepherds, Jacob's elder sons went to Shechem, about sixty miles
from Hebron; and, in view of all that had happened at Shechem
(xxxiv.), it is not surprising that Israel wished to know how it
fared with his sons and with the flocks. He thereupon commands
Joseph to take the journey of inquiry. His orders met with a ready
and full response, "Here am I." The words of Jacob should be
noted: "Go, I pray thee; see the peace of thy brethren and the
peace of the flocks." Jacob might well wish to know whether there
was *peace,* considering the danger to which the brethren and flocks
were liable in going back to the neighborhood of Shechem. Joseph,
however, has to go several miles further, for the brethren had gone
on to Dothan, which was on the southern slope of Mount Gilboa
(ver. 17). Perhaps even they felt that it was scarcely safe to remain too long in Shechem.

This promptness and thoroughness of obedience on the part of
Joseph is very characteristic of him, and should be carefully noted
all through his history. It has often and truly been pointed out
that Joseph seems to have combined all the best qualities of his
ancestors—the capacity of Abraham, the quietness of Isaac, the
ability of Jacob, and the personal beauty of his mother's family.
It is interesting to note that the same word is used of the mother
and the son (xxix. 17 and xxxix. 6).

IV. *Joseph's Brethren* (vers. 18-28).—The sight of Josph in the
distance was sufficient to stir up again all their animosity, and
"even before he came near unto them they conspired against him
to slay him." They were prepared to go the whole length of murder,
and had their answer ready for their father. "Some evil beast hath
devoured him." We can almost see the grim smile with which they
said, "We shall see what will become of his dreams." The conspiracy was all very simply but quite cleverly concocted, every point
was met, the wild beast and the ready explanation.

At this point Reuben intervened, and in view of the fact that
Joseph had superseded him in the position of firstborn, we must not
fail to observe the magnanimity of his appeal. He begged them
not to kill him but to cast him into the pit, he himself intending to

rescue him and deliver him to his father again. So far the proposal was good, but it possessed obvious elements of weakness. There was no decision about it, and no guarantee that it could be carried out. "The flighty purpose never is o'ertook, unless the deed go with it."

And then was seen another exhibition of their callousness and cruelty. They stripped the lad of that tunic which was such a bugbear to them, and cast him into one of the pits in the neighborhood, while they themselves "sat down to eat bread." Thomas Fuller quaintly remarks, "With what heart could they say grace, either before or after meat?" There within earshot was their own brother, his appeals for mercy having fallen on deaf ears. It was to this fearful hardness and cruelty that the prophet referred ages afterwards, when he spoke of those who "drink wine in bowls . . . but they are not grieved for the affliction of Joseph" (Amos vi. 6). We can also understand still more of their savagery when we remember that twenty years afterwards they recalled this moment, and said that "we saw the anguish of his soul, when he besought us, and we would not hear" (xlii. 21). Those who had butchered a whole family in Shechem were not likely to trouble themselves about the piteous cries and pleas of a mere lad whom they so cordially hated.

In the course of their meal another suggestion occurred to them. They saw in the distance a company of Ishmaelite merchants on their way to Egypt, and Judah had what must have been thought a happy idea. There was an opportunity of avoiding the sin of murder and at the same time of making a little profit by selling him to those merchants. They shrank from slaying, but not from enslaving their brother. It was something of "honor among thieves." He was not to be killed, because he was their "brother and their flesh"; but slavery did not matter in the least, even though he was their "brother and their flesh." Nor are we surprised to read that "his brethren were content" with Judah's proposal—that is to say, they "hearkened" (Heb.) with perfect acquiescence.

Circumstances sometimes seem to turn out favorably for bad men as well as good, and this shows that it is impossible to believe that circumstances alone are necessarily the voice of Providence.

They must be judged by principle; and if circumstances are wrong in themselves, no happy coincidence or association can make them right. There is a great deal of danger in interpreting circumstances, lest we should bend them to our will instead of reading them in the light of God's eternal truth.

Thus the first two proposals, to kill Joseph outright (ver. 20), and to cast him into a pit and let him die there (ver. 24), were set aside for a third, and he was sold as a slave to the Midianites (ver. 28). They therefore took him out of the pit, and in a short time he was on his way, as a slave, to Egypt, while they doubtless rejoiced in his removal and in their own possession of twenty pieces of silver (about $9.00).

V. *The Outcome* (vers. 29-36).—Reuben seems to have been away when the proposal to sell Joseph was made and carried out. People are often away when they are most needed. If he had taken the bolder course earlier in the day, the result might have been very different. He seems to have been true to his character, "unstable as water," and when he returned to his brethren he was doubtless soon made aware of what had happened, and apparently entered into the plan with the rest of them. They carried out their ideas with great thoroughness. They found it convenient that they had not sold Joseph's coat, and taking it up from where they had thrown it, they dipped it in the blood of one of the kids, ready to show their father.

When they arrived home Jacob soon recognized his son's coat, and realizing that Joseph had been devoured by an evil beast, rent his clothes and mourned many days; and though all his sons and daughters tried to comfort him their efforts proved unavailing, for he refused to be consoled. We cannot fail to note the unutterable grief of the aged patriarch. There was a time, not long before, when he met the awful sorrow and shame connected with his firstborn with dignity and trust in God (xxxv. 22), but now he seemed to be utterly overwhelmed by his sorrow. There was no expression of submission to the will of God, no testimony of faith in God, and no allusion to the new name—Israel—in the narrative. How often in the course of experience a great sorrow has so overwhelmed a soul that it has lost the peace and strength and comfort that should have been derived through faith and fellowship in God! So it was with Mary of Bethany, who sat still in the house overwhelmed with her grief when she knew that the Master was near (John xi. 20). Not only did she thus miss the glorious revelation that Martha obtained (John xi. 25, 26), but her weeping even caused trouble to our Lord. For He observed her and the Jews utterly prostrate and overwhelmed with grief in the presence of physical death, forgetful of Himself and His own power over it (John xi. 32, 33, Greek). There are few occasions on which the reality and power of Christian experience are shown more clearly than by the way we meet the shock of bereavement and death.

Meanwhile the chapter ends very significantly by telling us what happened to Joseph. The Midianites soon got rid of him, and sold him to Potiphar, a high official in Egypt.

The chapter is full of contrasts between man's sin and God's grace, and calls for special attention.

1. *The sin of man*—The root of all the trouble recorded in this chapter is envy (Acts vii. 9), a sin that has characterized human nature all through the ages. "Neither be thou envious" is the counsel of the Psalmist (Ps. xxxvii. 1); and it was the experience of an earnest man in the moment of temptation who said, "I was envious . . . when I saw" (Ps. lxxiii. 3). The crowning example of envy was that of the Pharisees against our Lord (Matt. xxvii. 18); and Christians are counselled against it in the New Testament, "Not in strife and envying" (Rom. xiii. 13). The difference between envy and covetousness is that we envy *persons* and covet *things*. We are dissatisfied with our own lot, and we are annoyed and angered that others should be superior to us in the possession of certain things. The results of envy are many and varied, and our familiar Litany rightly gives us the train of consequences: "Envy, hatred, malice, and all uncharitableness." Everything recorded here of Joseph's brethren—their anger, malice, conspiracy, cruelty, callousness, deceit—sprang originally from envy. So it is always. (Cf. Rom. i. 29; I Tim. vi. 4; Gal. v. 21.) Envy is the root of almost every sin against our brethren. And whenever it is harbored, there is

an end of all peace, rest, and satisfaction. Envy is "the rottenness of the bones" (Prov. xiv. 30), and no one can stand against it (Prov. xxvii. 4). "Where envying is, there is confusion and every evil work" (James iii. 16).

2. *The grace of God.*—If only God had been first in the lives of these men, there would have been no envy; for when He fills the soul with His love and grace, there is no room for anything unworthy and wrong (1 Cor. xiii. 4). That is why the Psalmist is not content with the negative exhortation, "Neither be thou envious," but goes on to the fourfold positive counsel, "Trust in the Lord," "Delight thyself also in the Lord," "Commit thy way unto the Lord," "Rest in the Lord" (Ps. xxxvii. 3-7). Not only are we to "lay aside all envies," but we are also to receive the Word of God into our hearts (1 Pet. ii. 1). It is by the expulsive power of this new affection that we are protected at all points from the sin of envy.

But the grace of God is also seen in this chapter in the way in which sin is defeated and the Divine purposes accomplished. Sin may hinder God's plans, but it cannot ultimately defeat His purposes. Sin is never necessary, though it may be used and overruled by God. It is absolutely impossible to bring good "out of" evil; for there never has been any good in evil, in spite of the familiar saying about "the soul of goodness in things evil." But good can be brought about in spite of evil, and so it came to pass that the very steps Joseph's brethren took to defeat God's purposes were used to fulfil those dreams. "We shall see what will become of his dreams." They were to see this to some purpose.

> For right is right, since God is God,
> And right the day shall win.
> To doubt would be disloyalty,
> To falter would be sin.

LI

A FAMILY SHAME

GEN. xxxviii

1. And it came to pass at that time, that Judah went down from his brethren, and turned in to a certain Adullamite, whose name *was* Hirah.

2. And Judah saw there a daughter of a certain Canaanite, whose name *was* Shuah; and he took her, and went in unto her.

3. And she conceived, and bare a son; and he called his name Er.

4. And she conceived again, and bare a son; and she called his name Onan.

5. And she yet again conceived, and bare a son; and called his name Shelah: and he was at Chezib, when she bare him.

6. And Judah took a wife for Er his firstborn, whose name *was* Tamar.

7. And Er, Judah's firstborn, was wicked in the sight of the Lord; and the Lord slew him.

8. And Judah said unto Onan, Go, in unto thy brother's wife, and marry her, and raise up seed to thy brother.

9. And Onan knew that the seed should not be his: and it came to pass, when he went in unto his brother's wife, that he spilled *it* on the ground, lest that he should give seed to his brother.

10. And the thing which he did displeased the Lord: wherefore he slew him also.

11. Then said Judah to Tamar his daughter-in-law, Remain a widow at thy father's house, till Shelah my son be grown: for he said, Lest peradventure he die also, as his brethren *did*. And Tamar went and dwelt in her father's house.

12. And in process of time the daughter of Shuah Judah's wife died: and Judah was comforted, and went up unto his sheep-shearers to Timnath, he and his friend Hirah the Adullamite.

13. And it was told Tamar, saying, Behold, thy father-in-law goeth up to Timnath to shear his sheep.

14. And she put her widow's garments off from her, and covered her with a vail, and wrapped herself, and sat in an open place, which *is* by the way to Timnath; for she saw that Shelah was grown, and she was not given unto him to wife.

15. When Judah saw her, he thought her *to be* an harlot; because she had covered her face.

16. And he turned unto her by the way, and said, Go to, I pray thee, let me come in unto thee (for he knew not that she *was* his daughter-in-law). And she said, What wilt thou give me, that thou mayest come in unto me?

17. And he said, I will send *thee* a kid from the flock. And she said, Wilt thou give *me* a pledge, till thou send *it?*

18. And he said, What pledge shall I give thee? And she said, Thy signet, and thy bracelets, and thy staff that *is* in thine hand. And he gave *it* her, and came in unto her, and she conceived by him.

19. And she arose, and went away, and laid by her vail from her, and put on the garments of her widowhood.

20. And Judah sent the kid by the hand of his friend the Adullamite, to receive *his* pledge from the woman's hand: but he found her not.

21. Then he asked the men of that place, saying, Where *is* the harlot, that *was* openly by the way side? And they said, There was no harlot in this *place.*

22. And he returned to Judah, and said, I cannot find her; and also the men of the place said, *that* there was no harlot in this *place.*

23. And Judah said, Let her take *it* to her, lest we be shamed: behold, I sent this kid, and thou hast not found her.

24. And it came to pass about three months after, that it was told Judah, saying, Tamar thy daughter-in-law hath played the harlot; and also, behold, she *is* with child by whoredom. And Judah said, Bring her forth, and let her be burnt.

25. When she *was* brought forth, she sent to her father-in-law, saying, By the man, whose these *are, am* I with child: and she said, Discern, I pray thee, whose *are* these, the signet, and bracelets, and staff.

26. And Judah acknowledged *them,* and said, She hath been more righteous than I; because that I gave her not to Shelah my son. And he knew her again no more.

27. And it came to pass in the time of her travail, that, behold, twins *were* in her womb.

28. And it came to pass, when she travailed, that *the one* put out *his* hand: and the midwife took and bound upon his hand a scarlet thread, saying, This came out first.

29. And it came to pass, as he drew back his hand, that, behold, his brother came out: and she said, How hast thou broken forth? *this* breach *be* upon thee: therefore his name was called Pharez.

30. And afterward came out his brother, that had the scarlet thread upon his hand; and his name was called Zarah.

WE instinctively ask why this story is found here? Why is the record of these events given, and given in such plainness by details? Why is the story of Jacob and Joseph interrupted at this point? We may be perfectly sure that in a book marked by so definite a purpose and characterized by so spiritual an aim, there must be some good reason for the inclusion of this sad and unsavoury episode. Let us see whether we cannot discover what this is. It occurs in that part of Genesis where we find recorded the steps of the Divine Providence which led to the transfer of Jacob's family into Egypt. This was to be accomplished, by Joseph as the *instrument*, through famine as the *occasion*, and through Divine power as the *cause*. And in this chapter we can see the *need* of it, the entire justification of the deportation, as we contemplate the state of the people revealed by this story of Judah. We are very sharply reminded of the grave moral dangers that surrounded the chosen family as long as they remained in Canaan; and the practical, and perhaps utter, impossibility of their being preserved pure unless removed to some shelter from such fearful contamination. We seem to have this fact suggested by the significant chronological note (ver. 1), "And it came to pass *at that time*," *i. e.* at the period of Joseph's sale into Egypt.

It is quite unnecessary and indeed impossible to dwell upon the details of the story. It carries its own meaning and message to all who read it.

The initial trouble lay in Judah going out of his way to associate himself with the people of Canaan. If he had remembered his father's and his grandfather's experiences he would have saved himself and others from these unhappy and awful ones. But up to this time there was no sign of grace in Judah's heart, and no thought of the covenant-God of his father influenced him in the slightest degree.

We are not surprised that from this wicked association wicked sons should have sprung. The first born was so wicked that he came under the Divine displeasure, "and the Lord slew him." The second son was as bad if not worse, and was guilty of that sin to which his name has ever since been given, and of which it will suffice to say that it is perhaps the very deadliest of all sins as affecting definitely body, mind and soul, and as having slain its thousands in all ages of the world's history.

The sin of Judah and of Tamar is the culminating horror of this fearful story, and the only redeeming feature about it is Judah's tardy repentance, if such it may be called, when he discovered what he had done.

1. *The awful possibilities of human sin.*—Can anything be more terrible than this record? Here is a man brought up amid opportunity of godliness, surrounded by good (if also by evil) influences, and yet sinning in these fearful ways, and becoming the occasion (and almost the cause) of the sins of others. Well for us if we realize from the narrative the plague of our own heart, and the awful extent to which sin may lead any one of us. But for the grace of God, who is there that dare say this might not be true of him?

2. *The justification of Divine Providence.*—It is abundantly clear from this story what was the moral condition of the Canaanites, and how essential it was for the family of Jacob to be safeguarded from such evil. The sale of Joseph into Egypt seemed on the face of it arbitrary and devoid of moral meaning, but God was over-ruling the evil to bring about much good to His people. And here we can see something of the Divine meaning and purpose. It was absolutely necessary for Israel to "come out and be separate," and in this story we have the proof of it vividly and awfully brought before us.

3. *The severity of Divine Righteousness.*—The absolute candour of the Bible is an almost constant marvel. And this in turn rests on the absolute justice of the God Whose book it is. Here is the sin of one of the chosen race depicted in all its hideousness. Here is the human ancestor of the Messiah revealed in all his blackness. Behold, therefore, "the severity of God." He is no respecter of persons. The sin of His sons is as faithfully dealt with as that of anyone else. There are no favorites with Him. Sin is sin at all times, and by whomsoever committed. Well for us if we learn and heed this solemn lesson.

4. *The Marvel of Divine Grace.*—It is simply astonishing that God could take up the threads of this very tangled skein, and weave them into His own pattern. First of all He dealt with Judah, and we know how great was the transformation of his character. And then, greatest marvel of all, God permitted the human descent of the Messiah to come not only from Judah, but even from Tamar. "It is evident that our Lord sprang out of Judah" (Heb. vii. 14),

and "Judah begat Pharez and Zarah of Tamar" (Matt. i. 3). Now it is clear as it can be that no *man* would have done this, even if he could. Only Divine grace could dare to take up these sorry elements of human life and use them for its own blessed purpose. There is nothing more marvelous than the power and possibilities of grace. Grace forgives, uplifts, transmutes, transforms, and then uses for its own glory. "Shall we then sin that grace may abound? God forbid." We may not, must not, dare not. And yet, "*if* any man sin we have" the blessed assurance that grace will not leave us in the mire of degradation, defeat and despair. While it is eternally true that what is done can never be undone, it is equally true that what has been broken can be mended, and the glory of grace is its power to heal broken hearts and mend broken lives. While life can never be as though sin had not been committed, yet the alchemy of grace has wonderful transforming power. Nature knows nothing of this, and can only tell of law broken and penalty exacted. But the Gospel comes to hearts broken by sin and despairing of redemption, and tells of pardon, peace and purity, in the blessed healing and transforming influences of Divine mercy, love and grace.

LII

IN EGYPT

Gen. xxxix

1. And Joseph was brought down to Egypt; and Potiphar, an officer of Pharaoh, captain of the guard, an Egyptian, bought him of the hands of the Ishmeelites, which had brought him down thither.

2. And the Lord was with Joseph, and he was a prosperous man; and he was in the house of his master the Egyptian.

3. And his master saw that the Lord *was* with him; and that the Lord made all that he did to prosper in his hand.

4. And Joseph found grace in his sight, and he served him: and he made him overseer over his house, and all *that* he had he put into his hand.

5. And it came to pass from the time *that* he had made him overseer in his house, and over all that he had, that the Lord blessed the Egyptian's house for Joseph's sake; and the blessing of the Lord was upon all that he had in the house, and in the field.

6. And he left all that he had in Joseph's hand; and he knew not aught he had, save the bread which he did eat. And Joseph was a goodly *person,* and well favored.

7. And it came to pass after these things, that his master's wife cast her eyes upon Joseph; and she said, Lie with me.

8. But he refused, and said unto his master's wife, Behold, my master wotteth not what *is* with me in the house, and he hath committed all that he hath to my hand.

9. *There is* none greater in this house than I; neither hath he kept back anything from me but thee, because thou *art* his wife: how then can I do this great wickedness and sin against God?

10. And it came to pass, as she spake to Joseph day by day, that he hearkened not unto her, to lie by her, *or* to be with her.

11. And it came to pass about this time, that *Joseph* went into the house to do his business; and *there was* none of the men of the house there within.

12. And she caught him by his garment, saying, Lie with me: and he left his garment in her hand, and fled, and got him out.

13. And it came to pass, when she saw that he had left his garment in her hand, and was fled forth,

14. Then she called unto the men of her house, and spake unto them, saying, See, he hath brought in an Hebrew unto us to mock us; he came in unto me to lie with me, and I cried with a loud voice:

15. And it came to pass, when he heard that I lifted up my voice and cried, that he left his garment with me, and fled, and got him out.

16. And she laid up his garment by her, until his lord came home.

17. And she spake unto him according to these words, saying, The Hebrew servant, which thou hast brought unto us, came in unto me to mock me:

18. And it came to pass, as I lifted up my voice and cried, that he left his garment with me, and fled out.

19. And it came to pass, when his master heard the words of his wife, which she spake unto him, saying, After this manner did thy servant to me; that his wrath was kindled.

20. And Joseph's master took him, and put him into the prison, a place where the king's prisoners *were* bound: and he was there in the prison.

21. But the Lord was with Joseph, and shewed him mercy, and gave him favor in the sight of the keeper of the prison.

22. And the keeper of the prison committed to Joseph's hand all the prisoners that *were* in the prison; and whatsoever they did there, he was the doer *of it.*

23. The keeper of the prison looked not to any thing *that was* under his hand; because the Lord was with him, and *that* which he did, the Lord made *it* to prosper.

EACH scene in the record of Joseph's life reveals some distinctive trait of character elicited by means of a crisis. We have already seen his passive submission to an awful wrong at the hands of his ruthless brothers. We naturally try to realize something of what he felt, but except for the allusion twenty years after to "the anguish of his soul" nothing is told us; no word of accusation falls from his lips, not a word of appeal or reproach finds its place in the story. This silence is surely remarkable, and tells its own tale of quiet strength and sublime power.

The record continues to reveal Joseph's character. The boy who suddenly exchanged the place of a petted and favorite son for that of a slave of foreign merchants is once again raised to high position, and as suddenly falls from honor, and is cast into prison. The revelation of his character is very striking, and deserves the closest possible study and attention.

I. *In Prosperity* (vers. 1-6).—From the hands of the Midianite traders Joseph passed into the possession of Potiphar, an officer of Pharaoh, "chief of the executioners." So from the pit into which he was cast by his brothers he passes into the pit of slavery in Egypt. It is a fine test of character for a young man when he is brought suddenly face to face with adversity, for the way in which he meets his difficulties will at once reveal and practically guarantee his future life.

The young slave filled his position to the very utmost of his powers and abilities. Instead of complaining that God was unjust to him, that his lot so far away from home was utterly hopeless, he put his whole power into the work that he had to do, and we are not surprised to read that "the Lord was with Joseph, and he was a prosperous man." Observe this use of the Divine Name, Jehovah, the God of the Covenant, Who had not left him, and Who, still more, would never forsake him. "He was a prosperous man" is a phrase that reads curiously in connection with a slave. How could he be "prosperous" in such a position? The explanation is that prosperity is not due to circumstances but to character, and character in turn depends upon faithfulness to God.

His life soon became evident, for in some way or other his master observed that God was with him and was prospering him. Not that Potiphar had any spiritual insight into the ways of Jehovah, but being in some sort a religious man, he became convinced that Joseph's powers must come from a Divine source. It is one of the finest and most glorious results of true piety when those around us who may not be of our way of thinking are enabled to see the reality of our life in our daily work and conduct.

We are therefore not at all surprised to read that Joseph "found grace" in his master's sight, and that he was made overseer over the house and over all his master's possessions. "Them that honor Me I will honor" is one of the great fundamental principles of life which find clear illustrations all through the centuries.

The crowning point of all was that "the Lord blessed the Egyptian's house for Joseph's sake; and the blessing of the Lord was upon all that he had in the house, and in the field." It is not the only time that God-fearing servants have brought spiritual blessing to the life and home of their masters. So thoroughly did Potiphar trust Joseph that "he left all that he had in Joseph's hand; and he knew not ought he had, save the bread which he did eat." This absolute confidence in Joseph's trustworthiness and capability is very striking, the one limitation being that of food, which was doubtless due to the great care of the Egyptians about ceremonial defilement (xliii. 32).

Thus Joseph lived his life in Potiphar's household, bearing testimony to God and bringing blessings to his master. "The Lord was with Joseph, and he was a prosperous man." Mr. Eugene Stock (*Lesson Studies in Genesis*, p. 119) calls attention to the rendering of "He was a prosperous man" in Wycliffe's version, "He was a luckie felowe," and makes the valuable point that a "luckie felowe" is not the rich man, but the man of character, the man of whom it can be said "The Lord is with him." Circumstances can never by themselves produce or guarantee prosperity. The "prosperous" man is the man who lives according to genuine hope, and this is only possible when our hope is based on God.

II. *In Peril* (vers. 7-12).—All was now going well with Joseph. He was trusted by his master, and blessed of his God. How things would have turned out in the usual way we know not, but an event occurred, which, however forbidding and surprising in itself, was nevertheless used as the link in the chain of that Divine providence which is so marked a feature of the story.

Joseph was young, manly and physically attractive. He had not a little of his mother's beauty (cf. xxix. 17 with xxxix. 6), and this was the occasion of fierce temptation which came from an unexpected quarter. As he was Potiphar's property why should not his master's wife do what she liked with the "living chattel"? And so the temptation came upon him in all its attractiveness and awful power. In a way it was a fine testimony to Joseph's power and influence that the wife of his master should have noticed one of her husband's slaves. Temptation is one of the great tests of life and character. It transforms innocence into virtue. Sin lies not in being tempted, but in yielding to it.

The way in which Joseph met this fierce onslaught is full of meaning. "He refused." There was his power. He met the temptation by a definite act and attitude of will. There was no dallying, no hesitation, but a "great refusal." This refusal was based on rational grounds. Behind the will were the intellect and the conscience. The first reason for his refusal was the consciousness of duty to the master who had trusted and honored him. Very plainly Joseph told the temptress that she, as his master's wife, was the one and only exception to his full sway and power in the house. The perfect faith of the master called for the perfect faithfulness of the servant. Gratitude, trust, honor, devotion to such a master demanded, and should have, the uttermost integrity of which he was capable.

But above and beyond all this, duty to God reigned supreme. He could not, and therefore would not, commit this great wickedness and sin against God. To him God was first. The lessons of the old home had not been forgotten in spite of all the treatment he had received. On the contrary the way in which the Lord God of his father had been with him and prospered him in his servitude was an additional reason for loyalty and integrity. And so on the highest ground of his relation to God, he faced this temptation and won the victory.

But sin was not to be daunted. The temptation was continued long, for "she spake to Joseph day by day." Temptation once only, and temptation continued daily, are very different experiences, and many who resist at first succumb at last. There was much more than the merely sensual in this conflict. We need not suppose that a man of Joseph's nature and circumstances was immune from the grossness of the peril; but we may be perfectly certain that this was not the deepest and strongest aspect of the foe. Dr. Marcus Dods, in one of those penetrating and searching delineations of character which make his studies of the patriarchs so valuable, very truly and acutely says:—

"It is too little observed, and especially by young men who have most need to observe it, that in such temptations it is not only the sensual that needs to be guarded against, but also two much deeper-lying tendencies—the craving for loving recognition, and the desire to respond to the feminine love for admiration and devotion . . . a large proportion of misery is due to a kind of uncontrolled and mistaken chivalry" (Dods' *Genesis*, p. 344).

At length the woman's passion overreached itself, and in the attempt to force Joseph to yield she was signally and wholly defeated.

When he was faced with this crowning attempt he did the very best —indeed, the only possible—thing, "he fled and got him out." Flight is the only safety from certain forms of temptation. Some temptations we resist by meeting them, but we can only resist others by flight. Safety is found in putting distance between us and our foe, and there is not only nothing ignoble in such flight, but on the contrary, it is the highest and truest form of virtue.

And then the woman's disappointed passion changed from love to hate. "Hell hath no fury like a woman scorned." Taking the garment that Joseph had left behind him in his flight, she used it as a proof of his guilt; and first to the servants and then to her husband she made out a case against the Hebrew slave. The way she spoke of her husband to the servants (ver. 14) shows the true character of the woman, and perhaps also the terms of her married life; while the fact that Potiphar only placed Joseph in prison instead of commanding him to be put to death is another indication of the state of affairs. For appearance' sake Potiphar must take some action, but the precise action taken tells its own tale. He evidently did not credit her story.

And thus Joseph was victorious. Her rank did not flatter him, her allurement did not entice him, in the strength of the presence of his Covenant God he was more than conqueror.

There is scarcely anything finer in Scripture than this picture of youth tested and triumphant. The simplicity, dignity and reserve of the narrative; the vividness of the portrayal of the parts played— by Potiphar, his wife, and Joseph—and the unmistakable force of the presentation of truth and righteousness, command our interest and elicit our admiration. It is the typical story for young manhood, conveying its own clear and blessed message. Young men need not sin, *can* be pure, *shall* be victorious, if only they will face their foe in the spirit and power of Joseph. Jehovah is the same today, and His covenant of grace is "ordered in all things and sure."

III. *In Prison* (vers. 13-23).—We are now to notice an instance of the victory of slander. It is often a great mystery that evil forces are allowed such freedom in a world that is controlled by a righteous and almighty God. Joseph was a victim of false accusation. There have been many such since his day. When Potiphar's wife told her story, first to the servants and then to her husband, it is possible that they may have had certain doubts of the truth of what she said, and yet were not prepared to deny altogether the likelihood of what she charged against Joseph. Perhaps those servants said among themselves, "Well, there *must* be something in it." How often people have said this on hearing a charge which they were not able to prove. Those well-known sayings, "There is no smoke without some fire," and "There *must* be some truth in it," are here absolutely disproved; and if these things were untrue of Joseph, may they not be untrue of many today? Yet insinuations continue to be made, suggestions rankle in the mind, inquiries are not made, and perhaps the trouble is never removed. How easy it is to do mischief with the tongue! And if the accused, like Joseph, keeps silence, we may easily blast a character by reason of our suspicion that "there *must* be something in it."

Joseph's silence is once again remarkable. As on the former occasion when his brothers cruelly treated him, so now he says nothing in self-defence. He will not rob his master of his wife in order to save himself. A word from him might easily have settled the matter, especially because, as we have observed, it seems pretty evident that Potiphar did not altogether believe in his wife's story. Yet to save her honor, Joseph was absolutely silent. There was no recrimination, nothing but a quiet endurance of the wrong. How he could do this is only explicable by that which is found no less than four times in this chapter—"Jehovah was with him."

In the prison his experiences soon repeated themselves, for the prisoner continued to do what the slave had been doing in the time of prosperity. He filled this post also to the utmost of his ability, and it was not long before he was exactly in the same relation to the keeper of the prison as he had been to Potiphar, for "the keeper of the prison committed to Joseph's hand all the prisoners that were in the prison; and whatsoever they did there, he was the doer of it." What magnificent rectitude and persistent faithfulness! By sheer force of character he won his way into the confidence of his keeper, and we may say that already other sheaves were "making obeisance to his sheaf." The spiritual vitality of the man is simply astonishing, and again illustrates with magnificent force the truth that God blesses and honors those who are true to Him.

Out of the wealth of material found in this chapter it may be worth while dwelling upon the element of difficulty as part of the training and discipline of human life.

1. *The Value of difficulties.*—"It is good for a young man to bear the yoke in his youth." It is easy to read this text, and not difficult to agree with it as a matter of theory; but it is quite another matter to accept it while the yoke is upon our own shoulders. And yet if only we could believe it at that time it would do incalculable service to the cause of Christian character. There were three yokes that Joseph bore: the yoke of slavery, the yoke of temptation, the yoke of suspicion and slander. Each of these by itself would have been heavy, but all three must have pressed deeply upon his soul. It is the worst possible thing for a young life to be made easy, to have everything done for it, to have a "good time." Yokes borne in youth have at least three results; they prove personal integrity, they promote spiritual maturity, and they prepare for fuller opportunity. In Nature and in human life the best things are not the easiest but the hardest to obtain. "Blessed be drudgery" is universally true.

2. *Duty in difficulties.*—How nobly Joseph comported himself amidst all these trials and hardships! He might have sulked and become embittered; but instead of this his spirit was unconquerable by reason of its trust in God. He steadfastly refused to be unfaithful to his God, whatever might be the consequences. In duty he was loyal, in temptation he was strong, and in prison he was faithful. When this spirit actuates our life, difficulties become means of grace and stepping-stones to higher things. On the other hand, if difficulties are met in a fretful, murmuring, complaining, disheartened spirit, not only do we lose the blessings that would otherwise come through them, but our spiritual life suffers untold injury, and we are weakened for the next encounter of temptation whenever it comes. There is scarcely anything in the Christian life which re-

veals more thoroughly what our Christianity is worth than the way we meet difficulties by the use of the grace of God.

3. *Assurance in difficulties.*—The secret of Joseph's power was the consciousness of the presence of God. God had not forgotten him, though it might seem to have been the case. The very incident that was apparently the most injurious was the link used by God to bring about his exaltation. One of Horace Bushnell's great sermons has for its title, "Every Man's Life a Plan of God," and to the man who is sure that he is in the pathway of God's will there will come the consciousness of the Divine presence and blessing which will be an unspeakable comfort as he "rests in the Lord and waits patiently for Him." God will bring forth his "righteousness as the light and his just dealing as the noonday." The very troubles that seem to overwhelm will prove blessings in disguise, and before long the Divine justification of His servant's faithfulness will be seen and manifested to all men. Evil may have its temporary victories, but they are only temporary. Good and right and truth must prevail, and it is for the servants of God to wait quietly, to go forward humbly, to live faithfully, and to trust boldly until God shall justify them by His Divine interposition, and glorify His grace in their lives.

> However the battle is ended,
>   Though proudly the victors came
> With fluttering flags and prancing nags
>   And echoing roll of drum,
> Still truth proclaims this motto
>   In letters of living light—
> "No question is ever settled
>   Until it is settled right."

> Though the heel of the strong oppressor
>   May grind the weak in the dust,
> And the voices of fame with one acclaim
>   May call him great and just,
> Let those who applaud take warning
>   And keep this motto in sight—
> "No question is ever settled
>   Until it is settled right."

Let those who have failed take courage,
  Though the enemy seemed to have won,
Though his ranks are strong, if he be in the wrong,
  The battle is not yet done;
For, sure as the morning follows
  The darkest hour of the night,
"No question is ever settled
  Until it is settled right."

LIII

IN PRISON

GEN. xl

1. And it came to pass after these things, *that* the butler of the king of Egypt and *his* baker had offended their lord the king of Egypt.

2. And Pharaoh was wroth against two *of* his officers, against the chief of the butlers, and against the chief of the bakers.

3. And he put them in ward in the house of the captain of the guard, into the prison, the place where Joseph *was* bound.

4. And the captain of the guard charged Joseph with them, and he served them: and they continued a season in ward.

5. And they dreamed a dream both of them, each man his dream in one night, each man according to the interpretation of his dream, the butler and the baker of the king of Egypt, which *were* bound in the prison.

6. And Joseph came in unto them in the morning, and looked upon them, and, behold, they *were* sad.

7. And he asked Pharaoh's officers that *were* with him in the ward of his lord's house, saying, Wherefore look ye *so* sadly today?

8. And they said unto him, We have dreamed a dream, and *there is* no interpreter of it. And Joseph said unto them, *Do* not interpretations *belong* to God? tell me *them,* I pray you.

9. And the chief butler told his dream to Joseph, and said to him, In my dream, behold a vine *was* before me.

10. And in the vine *were* three branches: and it *was* as though it budded, *and* her blossoms shot forth; and the clusters thereof brought forth ripe grapes;

11. And Pharaoh's cup *was* in my hand; and I took the grapes, and pressed them into Pharaoh's cup, and I gave the cup into Pharaoh's hand.

12. And Joseph said unto him, This *is* the interpretation of it: The three branches *are* three days:

13. Yet within three days shall Pharaoh lift up thine head and restore thee unto thy place: and thou shalt deliver Pharaoh's cup into his hand, after the former manner when thou wast his butler.

14. But think on me when it shall be well with thee, and shew kindness, I pray thee, unto me, and make mention of me unto Pharaoh, and bring me out of this house:

15. For indeed I **was** stolen away out of the land of the Hebrews: and here also have I done nothing that they should put me into the dungeon.

16. When the chief baker saw that the interpretation was good, he said unto Joseph, I also *was* in my dream, and, behold, *I had* three white baskets on my head:

17. And in the uppermost basket *there was* of all manner of bakemeats for Pharaoh; and the birds did eat them out of the basket upon my head.

18. And Joseph answered and said, This *is* the interpretation thereof: The three baskets *are* three days:

19. Yet within three days shall Pharaoh lift up thy head from off thee, and shall hang thee on a tree; and the birds shall eat thy flesh from off thee.

20. And it came to pass the third day, *which was* Pharaoh's birthday, that he made a feast unto all his servants: and he lifted up the head of the chief butler and of the chief baker among his servants.

21. And he restored the chief butler unto his butlership again; and he gave the cup into Pharaoh's hand:

22. But he hanged the chief baker: as Joseph had interpreted to them.

23. Yet did not the chief butler remember Joseph, but forgat him.

THE outstanding feature of Joseph's life was faithful loyalty to God under all circumstances. He carried his convictions with him and lived them out. The well-known phrase, "When in Rome do as Rome does," has brought infinite trouble upon those who have followed its guidance. Joseph never compromised his position, and as a consequence he never lost spiritual power or weakened his witness for God. Someone has said that true independence is to act in the crowd as one thinks in solitude. Joseph had already influenced the keeper of his prison, and we are now to see still more strikingly the proof that "the Lord was with him."

1. *Working* (vers. 1-4).—In the course of Joseph's incarceration two very notable people became inmates of the same prison, the chief of the butlers and the chief of the bakers of Pharaoh, King of Egypt. To these two men Joseph was appointed as servant, and in this simple fact was found one of the main links in the remarkable chain of providences associated with his life. "None of us liveth to himself," and no one could have forseen that the association of these two important servants of Pharaoh with the Hebrew slave would have brought about such far-reaching results. The smallest circumstance in life has its meaning, and it may be literally said that we do not really know the profound significance of many of the simplest details of daily life. Happy is the man whose eye is

open to see the hand of God in every-day events, for to him life
always possesses a wonderful and true joy and glory.

Again we observe the characteristic of faithfulness to duty which
actuated Joseph at all times. Although the circumstances were hard,
and his own position was the result of gross injustice, it made no
difference to the faithfulness and loyalty with which he did his duty.
The circumstances were all the harder because, as it would seem, it
was none other than Potiphar (ver. 4) who appointed Joseph to
attend to these prisoners. "A wounded spirit who can bear?" And
yet there is no trace whatever of any bitterness, but on the contrary,
a magnificent and even massive silence amid all the misunderstanding, slander, and injustice. There are times in life when silence is
indeed golden, and when to speak would be to demean one's self.
Joseph had learned the secret of suffering uncomplainingly, and in
the strength of his personal trust in God he won the victory over
self.

It is also well worth noticing that Joseph's faithful loyalty to his
religious convictions did not stand in the way of his earthly promo-
tion. The men of the world are not slow to detect real character,
and to take advantage of it. Other things being equal, a business
man, although utterly irreligious, will trust a true Christian as an
employee before one who makes no such profession. Genuine loyalty
to God will always express itself in absolute faithfulness in every-
day duty.

II. *Watching* (vers. 5-19).—Once again Joseph was to be associated with dreams, for his two prisoners, the chief butler and the
chief baker, each dreamed a dream in one night. Dreams were regarded as of great significance in Egypt, and we are therefore not
surprised to read that the men were puzzled and sad by reason of
their inability to understand the meaning of what they had dreamed.
Joseph was quick to see their sad countenances, a simple but significant testimony to his attitude of cheerfulness and the absence of
self-consciousness. He possessed that finest of all gifts, "a heart at
leisure from itself, to soothe and sympathize." Very quickly he inquired of them as to the reason of their sad looks, and he was told
the cause. Now if Joseph had been in the habit of looking on life

with the eyes of a cynic he would have had nothing more to do with dreams. He might have said that he had had personal experience of the futility of such things in the fact that his own dreams had been so entirely dissipated by his experiences. But so far from this spirit being shown, Joseph at once invited the chief butler and the chief baker to tell him their dreams, saying that interpretations belonged to God. How real God was to Joseph all this time! He never went back from his early convictions, but was true to his home-training in spite of everything that he had suffered. It takes a real man to hold fast to his integrity in the midst of suffering such as Joseph experienced, and to keep the spiritual life free from fret, strain, hardness and despair. Does not all this put us to shame as we contemplate, perhaps with astonishment, the profound reality of the consciousness of God in the life of Joseph?

Not the least remarkable point in his character was the combination of ability and agreeableness. By sheer force of personal power he raised himself, or rather was raised by God, to a position of trust, and at the same time manifested such personal amiability and attractiveness that he became acceptable to those around him. It is not often that we find so delightful a combination of personal characteristics. Sometimes we find ability without attractiveness, in which case the man is admired and even respected, but is feared, and people are apt to keep him at a distance. On the other hand we sometimes find agreeableness without ability, which gives the man an attractiveness for a while, but his superficiality at length becomes evident and his amiability counts for very little in the eyes of earnest and serious people. When, however, ability and attractiveness are combined, we have a man of real power whose influence for good can scarcely be limited.

Joseph's readiness in approaching Pharaoh's two officers is a striking illustration of the need of faithfulness in little things. He did not wait for some great occasion, but was found faithful in the pathway of everyday service. True life will always strive to be at its best, and instead of waiting for great occasions, will make every occasion great.

The combination of Joseph's testimony to God with reference to interpretation, and his invitation to them to tell him the dreams, is another interesting feature in his life. God was the Source, but His servant was the channel of the interpretation. This has always been God's method of revealing His will. The human interpreter has always been necessary and doubtless will be to the end of time.

First the chief butler's dream was told and interpreted, and after the revelation of forthcoming restoration for the butler we have an exquisite human touch which reveals the heart of Joseph. "But think on me when it shall be well with thee, and show kindness, I pray thee, unto me, and make mention of me unto Pharaoh, and bring me out of this house: for indeed I was stolen away out of the land of the Hebrews: and here also have I done nothing that they should put me into the dungeon." Joseph rightly took the opportunity of appealing to this man to use his influence to get him out of the prison. Hitherto we have been impressed with the marvelous silence and self-control of the prisoner, but these verses clearly reveal what he felt, and go to prove the truth of the Psalmist that "the iron entered into his soul."

Then came the chief baker's dream, and he, elated by the favorable interpretation of the former dream, fully expected a similar happy ending to his imprisonment. We observe here the remarkable faithfulness of Joseph, who told the baker quite frankly that a very different issue awaited him. The courage shown in this faithful revelation is noteworthy. Not even for his own advantage would Joseph swerve one hair's breadth from the pathway of truth. That which God revealed to him he passed on to the chief baker without addition or subtraction.

III. *Waiting* (vers. 20-23).—It is, perhaps, not unduly imaginative to think of the day when the prison-doors were opened and the butler was allowed to go free. We may picture him bidding farewell to Joseph with an assuring look and an encouraging word, and telling him that he would not be forgotten. And then again the doors were closed, and Joseph was still inside, wondering, doubtless, how long it would be before he would find deliverance. The story closes with the pathetic words, "Yet did not the chief butler remember Joseph, but forgat him." This must have been a terrible experience, for it was the deepest pit of his humiliation. Joseph must have been tempted to hate the world and surround himself with a wall of hardness and selfishness. Instead of this, we do not find that there was any feeling of bitterness or rebellion, or desire for revenge. Two years elapsed, and we doubt not that they had a steadying effect on Joseph's character as he waited for the fulfilment of God's purpose concerning him. He learned that there was something far more satisfying than recognition by man, the consciousness of doing the will of God. This is without exception the deepest joy in life.

These two years of waiting must also have had the effect of maturing whilst steadying Joseph's character. It is not too much to say that the self-possession and dignity which he showed when he stood before Pharaoh had their foundations laid during these two years. From time to time he would doubtless hear what was going on in Egypt, and perhaps in connection with the Court, and yet day after day passed without any remembrance from the one whose dream he had interpreted. But we are perfectly certain that he never regretted putting God first and allowing God to take care of His servant's interests. If only we take care of our character, God will take care of our interests and reputation. Daily faithfulness in ordinary duties is the very best preparation for future service. Joseph found plenty of work to do and was enabled to bear his own sorrows and troubles in ministering to the needs of others. These two years were in some respects the most vital and critical in his life. The deeper the foundation, the more durable the building; and in these two years the foundations of his future influence were laid deep and strong. Some might have thought that the forty years spent by Moses in Midian keeping sheep, were unworthy of the man's position; but the keeping of the sheep was the making of Moses. So also these two years of quiet endurance in prison went far to make Joseph the fine man he afterwards became.

The one dominant thought that runs through the chapter is the relation of God to the ordinary everyday life of His people, especially in the time of suffering, sorrow, hardship and disappointment.

1. *God's way is wisest.*—The prison was a place where Joseph was fitted for his life-work. Men of the world would have described this as "hard luck": but to Joseph it was part of the providence of God. God always sends His servants to school in order to fit them for future work, and it is necessary that they should have "a thorough education." Training, whether physical or moral, must necessarily be attended with hardship; and those whom God uses most have to be trained in the hardest schools. No chastening is pleasant at the time; but in the retrospect of experience no servant of God would ever be without the discipline which has enabled him to enter more thoroughly into the purposes of God and to help more really his fellowmen.

"Pain's furnace heat within me quivers,
  God's breath upon the flame doth blow,
And all my heart in anguish shivers
  And trembles at the fiery glow.
And yet I whisper, 'As God will!'
And in His hottest fire hold still.

He comes and lays my heart, all heated,
  On the hard anvil, minded so
Into His own fair shape to beat it
  With his great hammer, blow on blow!
And yet I whisper, 'As God will!'
And at His heaviest blows hold still.

He takes my softened heart, and beats it;
  The sparks fly off at every blow.
He turns it o'er and o'er, and heats it,
  And lets it cool, and makes it glow.
And yet I whisper, 'As God will!'
And in His mighty hand hold still.

Why should I murmur? for the sorrow
  Thus only long-lived would be;
Its end may come, and will, tomorrow,
  When God has done His work in me.
So I say, trusting, 'As God Will!'
And, trusting to the end, hold still.

He kindles for my profit purely
Affliction's fiery, glowing brand;
And all His heaviest blows are surely
Inflicted by a Master-hand.
So I say, praying, 'As God will!'
And hope in Him, and suffer still."

2. *God's time is best.*—When Joseph was taken from home and sold into slavery everything seemed to be against him. When he was cast into prison as the result of calumny, again everything seemed to combine to crush him. When the hope of deliverance through the influence of the chief butler was deferred until at length there seemed to be no hope of freedom, everything must have appeared dark and forbidding. And yet probably Joseph never forgot those early dreams at home of the sheaves making obeisance. God was working His purpose out; and though it was impossible to realize it at the time, we know that afterwards Joseph fully understood that God's time of deliverance was by far the best. God is never before His time but He is never behind. The clock of Divine providence keeps strict time, and has never been known to vary either in one direction or the other.

3. *God's grace is sufficient.*—In spite of everything that was against him, Joseph was victorious by the grace of God. Whether it was silence after calumny and injustice, whether it was cheerfulness amidst hardship, whether it was quick sympathy with the sorrows of others, whether it was patient endurance amidst hopes deferred, he was more than conqueror; and the secret of it all was, "the Lord was with him." The test of character lies in the spirit being unprovoked, though faced by constant friction and opposition; and the test of ideal service is its continuance when unrecognized. True life consists in going on, without placing any limit to goodness of character or faithfulness of service, even though neither should be acknowledged on earth; and this is only possible by the grace of God. In a certain coal-mining neighborhood, where almost everything was covered with coal-dust, there was a beautiful white flower perfectly free from dust. When someone who was strange to the place remarked that the owner must take very great care of the flower to prevent it from being covered with coal-dust, another who

was standing by threw over the flower some dust which at once fell off, leaving the whiteness and beauty as exquisite as ever. The explanation was that the flower had on it what might be called an enamel which enabled it to receive the dust and throw it off without feeling anything of the effects. So it was with Joseph. His character was covered with the enamel of Divine grace, and all these sorrows and troubles came upon him and left him untouched except for the increased strength and power that came to him from God.

And so the message to us all is that we are to wait for God. "Let patience have her perfect work that ye may be perfect and entire, wanting nothing" (James i. 4). "Ye have need of patience, that, after ye have done the will of God, ye might receive the promise" (Heb. x. 36). "In patience ye shall win your souls" (Luke xxi. 19, R.V.). And the secret of waiting for God is waiting on God. By simple trust and constant prayer, by loving fellowship and faithful obedience, we are enabled to wait for God so as to be ready when He calls. His summons to higher service comes in unexpected ways and at unexpected times, and if it does not find us ready we shall inevitably be passed by. So while we "wait patiently for Him" let us "rest in the Lord," and then, like the servants of David, we shall be able to say, "Thy servants are ready to do whatsoever my Lord the King shall appoint."

LIV

EXALTATION

GEN. xli. 1-40

1. And it came to pass at the end of two full years, that Pharaoh dreamed: and, behold, he stood by the river.

2. And, behold, there came up out of the river seven well favored kine and fatfleshed; and they fed in a meadow.

3. And, behold, seven other kine came up after them out of the river, ill favored and leanfleshed; and stood by the *other* kine upon the brink of the river.

4. And the ill favored and leanfleshed kine did eat up the seven well favored and fat kine. So Pharaoh awoke.

5. And he slept and dreamed the second time: and, behold, seven ears of corn came up upon one stalk, rank and good.

6. And, behold, seven thin ears and blasted with the east wind sprung up after them.

7. And the seven thin ears devoured the seven rank and full ears. And Pharaoh awoke, and, behold, *it was* a dream.

8. And it came to pass in the morning that his spirit was troubled; and he sent and called for all the magicians of Egypt, and all the wise men thereof: and Pharaoh told them his dream; but *there was* none that could interpret them unto Pharaoh.

9. Then spake the chief butler unto Pharaoh, saying, I do remember my faults this day:

10. Pharaoh was wroth with his servants, and put me in ward in the captain of the guard's house, *both* me and the chief baker:

11. And we dreamed a dream in one night, I and he; we dreamed each man according to the interpretation of his dream.

12. And *there was* there with us a young man, an Hebrew, servant to the captain of the guard; and we told him, and he interpreted to us our dreams; to each man according to his dream he did interpret.

13. And it came to pass, as he interpreted to us, so it was; me he restored unto mine office, and him he hanged.

14. Then Pharaoh sent and called Joseph, and they brought him hastily out of the dungeon: and he shaved *himself*, and changed his raiment, and came in unto Pharaoh.

15. And Pharaoh said unto Joseph, I have dreamed a dream, and *there is* none that can interpret it: and I have heard say of thee, *that* thou canst understand a dream to interpret it.

16. And Joseph answered Pharaoh, saying, *It is* not in me: God shall give Pharaoh an answer of peace.

17. And Pharaoh said unto Joseph, In my dream, behold, I stood upon the bank of the river:

18. And, behold, there came up out of the river seven kine, fatfleshed and well favored; and they fed in a meadow:

19. And, behold, seven other kine came up after them, poor and very ill favored and leanfleshed, such as I never saw in all the land of Egypt for badness:

20. And the lean and the ill favored kine did eat up the first seven fat kine:

21. And when they had eaten them up, it could not be known that they had eaten them; but they *were* still ill favored, as at the beginning. So I awoke.

22. And I saw in my dream, and, behold, seven ears came up in one stalk, full and good:

23. And, behold, seven ears, withered, thin, *and* blasted with the east wind, sprung up after them:

24. And the thin ears devoured the seven good ears: and I told *this* unto the magicians; but *there was* none that could declare *it* to me.

25. And Joseph said unto Pharaoh, The dream of Pharaoh *is* one: God hath showed Pharaoh what He *is* about to do.

26. The seven good kine *are* seven years; and the seven good ears *are* seven years: the dream *is* one.

27. And the seven thin and ill favored kine that came up after them *are* seven years; and the seven empty ears blasted with the east wind shall be seven years of famine.

28. This *is* the thing which I have spoken unto Pharaoh: What God *is* about to do He showeth unto Pharaoh.

29. Behold, there come seven years of great plenty throughout all the land of Egypt:

30. And there shall arise after them seven years of famine; and all the plenty shall be forgotten in the land of Egypt; and the famine shall consume the land:

31. And the plenty shall not be known in the land by reason of that famine following; for it *shall be* very grievous.

32. And for that the dream was doubled unto Pharaoh twice: *it is* because the thing *is* established by God, and God will shortly bring it to pass.

33. Now therefore let Pharaoh look out a man discreet and wise, and set him over the land of Egypt.

34. Let Pharaoh do *this,* and let him appoint officers over the land, and take up the fifth part of the land of Egypt in the seven plenteous years.

35. And let them gather all the food of those good years that come, and lay up corn under the hand of Pharaoh, and let them keep food in the cities.

36. And that food shall be for store to the land against the seven years of famine, which shall be in the land of Egypt; that the land perish not through the famine.

37. And the thing was good in the eyes of Pharaoh, and in the eyes of all his servants.

38. And Pharaoh said unto his servants, Can we find *such a one* as this *is*, a man in whom the Spirit of God *is?*

39. And Pharaoh said unto Joseph, Forasmuch as God hath shewed thee all this, *there is* none so discreet and wise as thou *art:*

40. Thou shalt be over my house, and according unto thy word shall all my people be ruled: only in the throne will I be greater than thou.

TRIALS may be viewed from two standpoints, and it will make all the difference to our spiritual life and peace which of these two points of view we take. From the human side Joseph's suffering was due to injustice on the part of Potiphar, and ingratitude on the part of the butler. From the Divine side these years were permitted for the purpose of training and preparing Joseph for the great work that lay before him. If we look only at the human side of trial we shall become discouraged, and it may be irritated and angered, but as we turn to look at it from the Divine side we shall see God in everything and all things working together for our good. How truly all this was realized in Joseph's case we are now to see.

I. *The Dreams of the King* (vers. 1-7).—The essentially Egyptian character of this section, and indeed of the entire narrative of Joseph, is worthy of constant notice, for it provides us with one of the watermarks of the Pentateuch, enabling us to perceive its historical character and its truthfulness to life. It is not too much to say that at no period after the time of Moses could anything so true to Egyptian life have been written out of Egypt by a member of the community of Israel.

Pharaoh dreamed, and his dream was associated with the River Nile, on which throughout the centuries the land of Egypt has depended for its very life. The dream was twofold: first that of the fat and lean kine, and then that of the full and thin ears of corn. In each case the dream was associated with the needs and conditions of the country.

II. *The Failure of the Magicians* (ver. 8).—The mighty monarch soon realized his limitations, for he was utterly unable to interpret his dreams. Like all Egyptians, he was profoundly impressed with the thought that the dreams had great significance, and "his spirit was troubled." He thereupon summoned to his presence all the magicians of Egypt and all his wise men, "but there was none that could interpret." In ancient days when so many natural phenomena were unknown and their true meaning not understood, there was great and constant opportunity for cleverness on the part of able and not too scrupulous men. The result was that a class sprang up which undertook to satisfy the cravings of men for knowledge; and, while there was doubtless not a little of perfectly legitimate information afforded by these magicians, in the course of time they became associated with chicanery and deceit. Here was an opportunity for them to reveal their knowledge, and inasmuch as the coloring of the dreams was essentially Egyptian it might have been thought that they would have had no real difficulty in giving some plausible interpretation; but their failure was complete, and Pharaoh was still without the relief he so earnestly desired.

III. *The Recollection of the Butler* (vers. 9-13).—The law of mental association was, however, at work in the mind of one of the monarch's attendants, and suddenly he remembered the days that were past and his own experiences in the prison. He thereupon confessed his faults and reminded Pharaoh of what had happened two years before, and then told him of the young Hebrew who had interpreted his dream which had so literally and wonderfully come to pass. How simple and yet how truly remarkable is this link in the chain of circumstances by means of which God fulfilled His purposes for Joseph! On how little does very much often depend!

IV. *The Call of the Prisoner* (vers. 14-16).—It did not take long for Pharaoh to summon the Hebrew prisoner into his presence. Joseph was brought hastily out of the prison and quickly stood before Pharaoh. What a picture it must have been—the mighty monarch and the unknown slave! It is evident that Pharaoh considered Joseph was of the same class to which his own wise men and magicians belonged; and inasmuch as such knowledge of dreams was regarded as obtainable by human powers, it seems pretty certain that Pharaoh regarded Joseph as one who was an adept in the work which his own wise men had failed to do. But the very first words of Joseph showed Pharaoh the true state of the case. "It is not in me: God shall give Pharaoh an answer of peace" (ver. 16). Mark the self-forgetfulness of these words: "Not in me: God." Utterly regardless of himself or his own fate, he had one thought only—the glory of God. Had he been a time-server or a place-seeker, or even concerned for his own personal safety, he might have fenced with the question and brought about his own deliverance. Had he been a proud man and eaten up with vanity, he might have shown eagerness to obtain personal credit. All these things were utterly alien from his mind. The supreme and overmastering thought in Joseph's life was God. His spiritual vitality was inwrought and deep-seated, and nothing could shake his integrity and fearlessness as he faced the great monarch and witnessed to his God.

V. *The Interpretation of the Dreams* (vers. 17-36).—Pharaoh thereupon told his two dreams of the kine and ears of corn, and at once the interpretation was given. The two dreams referred to one subject, the double dream merely indicating the certainty of the occurrence (ver. 32). Seven years of plenty were to be succeeded by seven years of famine, and Joseph thereupon urged Pharaoh to appoint a man who would take action to prevent the famine from causing suffering. He advised precaution being taken during the seven years of plenty: all the food of these good years that could be kept was to be stored up against the seven years of famine.

This in substance was the interpretation and the advice based upon it. Not a word was uttered about himself, nor does there seem any hint that he considered himself to be the man whom Pharaoh should appoint. Joseph does not seem to have cared about himself at all. The frankness with which he told the King the dream, the quiet dignity with which he gave his counsel, the perfect balance with which he stood before Pharaoh and his Court, are striking features of this splendid character. Six traits stand out which constitute him one of the models for all time: integrity, conscientiousness, diligence, nobility, courage, humility. He is one of the all-round, symmetrical characters of the Bible, always ready, ever conscientious, never sacrificing principle, faithful and fearless at every crisis.

IV. *The Reward of the Interpreter* (vers. 37-40).—Pharaoh and his servants quickly saw the real value of this advice and at once accepted it. Still more, the King went much further and said that

Joseph should be the one to accomplish this task. "Can we find such a one as this is, a man in whom the Spirit of God is?" Pharaoh was so deeply impressed with Joseph's wisdom that he recognized his possession of Divine powers. Whatever precisely the King understood by the "Spirit of God," it is evident he realized that Joseph was possessed of superhuman ability. The relation of the Spirit of God to certain men whose lives are recorded in the Old Testament is worthy of careful study. Joseph, Joshua, and Daniel in particular are referred to as men in whom the Spirit of God dwelt (verse 38; Numbers xxvii. 18; Daniel v. 11).

And it is particularly important to observe the connection between the Spirit of God and the gifts for practical life that are exemplified in Joseph. Thus he possessed the spirit of observation. He had not lived for thirteen years in Egypt without knowing something of its needs, and it was the spirit of wisdom that enabled him to see how those needs were to be supplied. Just as sin dulls the mental and moral faculties, so the Spirit of God cleanses and refines them. A life of faithful obedience always guarantees true insight. There is no necessary contradiction between Christianity and genuine business powers. To be clear-headed does not mean to be soft-hearted. Christianity gives clearness, far-sightedness, mental perception and balance. It is perfectly true that the Gospel cannot, or at any rate does not, make an intellectual man out of one who does not possess any powers at all; it does not give faculties to those who do not possess them; but it certainly increases the capacity and refines the faculty. It does not diminish, but on the contrary increases mental life and genuine manhood.

The gifts possessed by Joseph were not only intellectual but moral. What marvelous self-possession was his! Such a change from the prison to the Court would have killed a small nature; but Joseph's head was not turned, because of his moral rectitude. We also observe what remarkable decision of character he showed. There was no hesitation—he knew what to advise, and stated his policy with absolute clearness and frankness. Not only so, but he proved once again that he possessed the gift of management. He had been faithful in that which was little, and had thereby qualified himself to be faithful in much.

Best of all, he had spiritual gifts. What endurance was his as he had learned to obey during those thirteen years of testing! How disinterested and unselfish he was, having no personal ends to gratify, no thought of bargaining before giving his interpretation!

And thus his religion was supremely practical, and was not a hindrance to him, but a help. The Holy Spirit of God had taken full possession of every faculty of his nature, and intellectually, morally, and spiritually had been training and preparing him for this eventful moment.

The chapter speaks of life in various aspects, and carries its own messages for everyone of us.

1. *The purpose of life.*—God has some sphere for every one of us to fill. "To every man his work," and Joseph at last found his proper place. What a dignity it gives to life to realize that God has something for each one of us to do!

2. *The discipline of life.*—The most unlikely circumstances are part of our education. Joseph had spent thirteen years in Egypt, and most of those years had been spent under a cloud. What was there to show as the result of all this time? Apparently nothing, and yet really everything. All his experiences had been tending in the direction of training. Some dreams take a long time to fulfill.

3. *The duty of life.*—We cannot help wondering whether Joseph ever showed any impatience with his lot. At any rate, nothing is recorded. In spite of much to try him, much that pressed upon him again and again, he held fast his integrity. Loyalty to his master, faithfulness to his God, heartiness in his work, constituted for Joseph his duty. So it must be always. "It is required of stewards that a man be found faithful."

4. *The assurance of life.*—The secret of Joseph's loyalty was the consciousness that God was with him and was working on his behalf. He little knew how God could accomplish His will and bring about the fulfilment of the dreams; but God has marvelous facilities, and many ways of working. A monarch's dream, a butler's recollec-

tion, and everything else is brought about. How true it is that "God worketh for him that waiteth"! (Isa. lxiv. 4, R.V.).

5. *The glory of life.*—Joseph exemplified this in his constant living for others. Whether it was for Potiphar, or the jailer, or the prisoners, or Pharaoh, he laid himself out to serve others. This is the real meaning of altruism, and in it is the greatest glory of life. True influence over our fellows always comes sooner or later to the genuinely sincere man, who is devoid of all merely personal ambitions, the man who has no "axes to grind." There are men today full of shrewdness and possessing great abilities who are nevertheless not trusted and loved, but either feared or suspected or at most admired at a distance! There are others who are without great intellectual powers, but who are absolutely genuine, truly sincere, and without any *arrière pensée*, and men trust them, love them, and find themselves helped by their sympathy, sweetness, and strength.

The message for us all is to live close to God, to be ever on the watch for God's will, to find our happiness in carrying out that will, to say from the heart, "I delight to do Thy will," and then to go forth spending and being spent in the service of others. When this spirit actuates us, all difficulties, trials, and hardships will be found only the means of training, testing, and preparing us for living to the glory of God in the service of our fellows.

"What only seemed a barrier,
A stepping-stone shall be,
Our God is no long tarrier,
A present Help is He.

If all things work together
For ends so grand and blest,
What need to wonder whether
Each in itself is best?

Our plans may be disjointed,
But we may calmly rest;
What God has once appointed
Is better than our best.

What though we seem to stumble?
He will not let us fall,
And learning to be humble
Is not lost time at all."

LV

THE PRIME MINISTER

Gen. xli. 41-52

41. And Pharaoh said unto Joseph, See, I have set thee over all the land of Egypt.

42. And Pharaoh took off his ring from his hand, and put it upon Joseph's hand, and arrayed him in vestures of fine linen, and put a gold chain about his neck;

43. And he made him to ride in the second chariot which he had; and they cried before him, Bow the knee: and he made him *ruler* over all the land of Egypt.

44. And Pharaoh said unto Joseph, I *am* Pharaoh, and without thee shall no man lift up his hand or foot in all the land of Egypt.

45. And Pharaoh called Joseph's name Zaphnath-paaneah: and he gave him to wife Asenath the daughter of Poti-pherah priest of On. And Joseph went out over *all* the land of Egypt.

46. And Joseph *was* thirty years old when he stood before Pharaoh king of Egypt. And Joseph went out from the presence of Pharaoh, and went throughout all the land of Egypt.

47. And in the seven plenteous years the earth brought forth by handfuls.

48. And he gathered up all the food of the seven years, which were in the land of Egypt, and laid up the food in the cities: the food of the field, which *was* round about every city, laid he up in the same.

49. And Joseph gathered corn as the sand of the sea, very much, until he left numbering; for *it was* without number.

50. And unto Joseph were born two sons before the years of famine came, which Asenath the daughter of Poti-pherah priest of On bare unto him.

51. And Joseph called the name of the first-born Manasseh: For God, *said he,* hath made me forget all my toil, and all my father's house.

52. And the name of the second called he Ephraim: For God hath caused me to be fruitful in the land of my affliction.

ONLY thirteen years stood between the Hebrew shepherd boy and the Egyptian Prime Minister. It was a wonderful change by which, at one bound, Joseph leaped from the position of a slave in prison to that of the second ruler in the country. The story before us is the record of unchanged faithfulness amidst greatly changed surroundings. "Circumstances alter cases," and even alter persons, but there was no alteration made in Joseph's character in spite of the very great change in his circumstances.

I. *His Appointment* (xli. 37-45).—It is worth while dwelling once again on the grounds of this appointment. We naturally wonder whether Pharaoh's quickly-conceived and strong impression that Joseph was the very man for the post was warranted by the facts of the case, and the more thoroughly we seek to penetrate beneath the surface the more clearly we see the monarch's decision was justified. Joseph's ready apprehension of coming danger, together with his foresight in propounding a plan to meet it, deeply impressed Pharaoh and those with him. Not less evident were the quiet resourcefulness and genuine capacity with which the young Hebrew dealt with a gigantic matter which concerned the whole of Egypt. But beneath these marks of power lay the elements of character which were at the root of Joseph's real life. From the very first uprightness had marked all his conduct in Egypt. If he had been a schemer intent on gaining his own selfish ends he might have easily avoided the prison, but from the time he was sold into Egypt to the moment that he stood before Pharaoh he had been honest, straightforward, and true. Then again Joseph had learned the secret of patient submission. In the face of injustice and cruel wrong he accepted his lot without murmuring, and endeavored to make the best possible use of it. The way upward often lies by a downward path through the valley of humiliation. Nor may we forget the magnificently bold use of the powers that God gave him. Whether it was interpreting dreams, or showing sympathy, or organizing a national policy, he put into fine practice his divinely-given faculties, and in their exercise he found the best possible way of preparation for his life-work.

It is at once easy and profitable to dwell upon the afore-mentioned elements of Joseph's character and manhood. We must never forget, however, that they in turn need explanation, and this is to be found in what Pharaoh spoke of as the indwelling of "the Spirit of God" (ver. 38). Character is undoubtedly the secret of power, but God is the secret of character. Pharaoh was therefore perfectly correct when he said, "God hath shewed thee all this" (ver. 39).

From first to last it was the grace and power of God that made Joseph what he was.

Pharaoh very promptly gave Joseph definite proof of the appointment by putting upon him his own ring, arraying him in vestures of that characteristically Egyptian product, fine linen, putting a gold chain about his neck, making him to ride in the next chariot to his own, and calling upon the people to do him honor (vers. 42, 43). The familiar words "Bow the knee," representing the Hebrew *Abrech*, have been the cause of not a little discussion. The A.V. rendering dates as far back as the time of Jerome, but Professor Sayce is inclined to favor a Babylonian interpretation meaning "seer." It is therefore very interesting to note that some thirteen years ago a letter appeared in the *Record* mentioning that in modern Egypt *Ibrik* is in common use in the present day by camel-drivers when they want their camels to get down on their knees, and slave-mistresses in the harems say *Ibriky* when they order a slave-girl to get down on her knees and confess repentance for wrong-doing (*Expository Times*, vol. v., p. 435). It would seem therefore that there is still good reason for the old rendering.

Again, we cannot but mark the astonishing change in Joseph's circumstances, and we wonder whether he ever thought of the coat of many pieces with its significant meaning given to him by his father years before. Only once before, so we are told by the inscriptions, was a subject thus raised to a high position in Egypt.

Further assurance was given to Joseph by Pharaoh in the solemn promise that he should be kept from harm (ver. 44), and in the new name bestowed upon him, "Zaphnath-paaneah." Here again we are in the region of conjecture. By some it is thought to mean "The Revealer of Secrets," by others, "The Support of Life," and yet again modern Egyptologists are said to favor "God spoke, and he came into life" (Driver's *Genesis*, p. 344).

Joseph's wife was also given to him by the king, and in marrying Asenath, the daughter of the Egyptian priest, we see how thoroughly Pharaoh intended Joseph to become identified with Egypt and its life. He thus became naturalized in his new country; and if we are inclined to wonder whether he had any scruples in marrying into such a family we may perhaps remember that there was no such clear severance between the Hebrews and other nations at that time as there was in subsequent times.

II. *His Life* (xli. 46-52).—The new Prime Minister was not long before he took up with characteristic promptitude the work which lay before him. First of all he made a tour throughout all the land, and in the seven plenteous years he gathered up all the food and laid it up in storehouses. He carried out his policy with thoroughness and success.

Meanwhile personal and domestic happiness was coming to him. God gave to him two sons, and true to his constant recognition of the Divine blessing, he acknowledged God's mercies in the names that he gave to them. The firstborn he called Manasseh (which means "Forgetting"); "for God, said he, hath made me to forget all my toil, and all my father's house." Everything in life had a profound significance for Joseph, though we are not to take these words literally, as though all his early life had become entirely obliterated from his memory. The true meaning is that now he had a new outlook, and was able to view things from the standpoint of his own home rather than that of his father's. Hitherto his thoughts had naturally gone back with intense longing to the old home and his old father. Now, however, he had home, wife, work and interests of his own, and everything was henceforth to be judged from this new point of view. "The prosperous years were doing their office in Joseph's life. They were making changes in the man. They were working off the depression, the anxiety, the wistfulness of that sorrowful past; they were filling his soul with more ample conceptions of God's goodness; they were causing him to forget all his toil . . . His father's house, loved as it still must be, could not rise in his mind as the sole form of welfare, the sole image of good; nor could his expectations of home happiness take that form now. That, too, had gone from the present to the past . . . God had made him feel that the career of deliverance and comfort might, and did, take another shape. He filled the present for him with other scenes, and the future with other expectations; and he enriched all with a great sense of enjoyment, of peace, and welfare given and blessed by God" (Rainy, *Expositor*, series 3, vol. iv. pp. 401-411).

The name of the second son Joseph called Ephraim ("Fruitful") : "for God hath caused me to be fruitful in the land of my affliction." If the birth of the first son reminded him of the negative side of his life's experiences, enabling him to blot out the memory of the past, the birth of the second son suggested the positive side of his life in the abundant blessing that God had vouchsafed to him. How beautiful it is when life is interpreted in the light of God's dealings, and when everything, dark or light, has its own Divine significance! There was no resentment, no murmuring, no occupation with personal ills, no concern with mere second causes. Everything in Joseph's experience was illuminated by light from heaven.

Not the least important point derivable from the story at this juncture is that when Joseph became Prime Minister of Egypt he did not forget his religion, and set it aside as a thing of the past. On the contrary, he used it in the fulfilment of the duties of his important office. If Divine grace was needed in the time of his affliction, much more was it needed in the moment of prosperity. If ever Joseph needed protection, it was at this time. His self-possession and his perfect accommodation to his new surroundings could only have come through absolute dependence upon God. Prosperity therefore made no difference to him. He was the same Joseph that he had been in the days of adversity. He acknowledged God's hand and goodness, and thereby proved that he had learned some of the deepest lessons of life in the school of discipline.

The story of Joseph's life and work as Prime Minister of Egypt can, as we have seen, be regarded from the point of view of religious manhood, genuine character, and splendid work. We prefer, however, to look at it from the standpoint of the Divine purpose, and see in it lessons about God in relation to His servants.

1. *God's Providence exemplified.*—Again and again we shall find it profitable and important to recall the links in the chain which led from Canaan to Egypt, from the old home to the royal court. Jealousy by brothers, sale as a slave, faithfulness under temptation, sympathy with sadness, endurance of ills, loyalty to God, the dreams

of a monarch, the memory of past mercies—these were the slender but sufficient threads which linked the pit in Canaan with power in Egypt. Not one of these links of connection was unnecessary. Each one was essential, and formed one of the "all things" that worked together for good. How often we find this so in life! A multitude of minute events, not even one of them great or striking or marvelous, and yet at the end a truly astonishing revelation of the working of God. Let us never hesitate to believe in Him "Whose never-failing providence ordereth all things both in heaven and earth."

2. *God's Righteousness revealed.*—It was a long time from Egypt back to the youthful dreams of the boy Joseph, but now they were in a measure fulfilled and were yet to be completely realized. How true it is that "them that honor Me I will honor!" God will justify Himself at last. His providence often appears like a piece of tapestry looked at from the wrong side, but the pattern is there and only needs the true standpoint to perceive it. "Shall not the Judge of all the earth do right?" In the Great Day when everything is seen clearly it will be the testimony of every one of God's servants that "He hath done all things well." Meanwhile it is for us to "rest in the Lord and wait patiently for Him," and "He shall bring forth our righteousness as the light and our judgment as the noonday."

3. *God's Wisdom justified.*—During those years of trial, life must have been a great mystery to Joseph. The misunderstandings, misrepresentations, and persecution were unusually severe and protracted, but they brought the needed discipline for the subsequent years of exaltation. He had learned, and so could teach. Our best work is always the result of long preparation, and it is only thus that we can pass on the lessons that God teaches us. There is a plant which takes a century to develop, and flowers but for a short time. So it is with human character. The process of training is long, but the power which results is great. It took Moses eighty years to get ready for the one night of deliverance from Egypt.

4. *God's Grace manifested.*—This is the supreme lesson which meets and impresses us at every stage of Joseph's history. In adversity he trusted his God and waited God's time. In prosperity he leaned upon his God and found His grace sufficient. And thus the

balance was preserved. His heart was not tried by humiliation nor his head turned by exaltation. When the Lord exalts His servants to positions of importance it is because He has prepared them by discipline. In moments which appeal to human pride and self-sufficiency the believer needs nothing less than Divine power to keep him humble, simple, and faithful, and for all this there is no school like the grace of God.

Let us therefore make God real in our daily life, and ever put and keep Him in the foremost place in all our interests and hopes. In darkness or in daytime let us live *in* Him, and then we shall be enabled to live *for* Him. The darkness may be great and prolonged, but He is our Light. The sunshine may be fierce and dazzling, but He is sufficient. Whatever our pathway, be it shadowed or bright, He is near, He will keep, and He will make our lives strong, sweet, beautiful, fragrant and blessed.

LVI

THE AWAKENING OF CONSCIENCE

GEN. xlii

1. Now when Jacob saw that there was corn in Egypt, Jacob said unto his sons, Why do ye look one upon another?

2. And he said, Behold, I have heard that there is corn in Egypt: get you down thither, and buy for us from thence; that we may live, and not die.

3. And Joseph's ten brethren went down to buy corn in Egypt.

4. But Benjamin, Joseph's brother, Jacob sent not with his brethren; for he said, Lest peradventure mischief befall him.

5. And the sons of Israel came to buy *corn* among those that came: for the famine was in the land of Canaan.

6. And Joseph *was* the governor over the land, *and* he *it was* that sold to all the people of the land: and Joseph's brethren came, and bowed down themselves before him *with* their faces to the earth.

7. And Joseph saw his brethren, and he knew them, but made himself strange unto them, and spake roughly unto them; and he said unto them, Whence come ye? And they said, From the land of Canaan to buy food.

8. And Joseph knew his brethren, but they knew not him.

9. And Joseph remembered the dreams which he dreamed of them, and said unto them, ye *are* spies; to see the nakedness of the land ye are come.

10. And they said unto him, Nay, my lord, but to buy food are thy servants come.

11. We *are* all one man's sons; we *are* true *men*, thy servants are no spies.

12. And he said unto them, Nay, but to see the nakedness of the land ye are come.

13. And they said, Thy servants *are* twelve brethren, the sons of one man in the land of Canaan; and, behold, the youngest *is* this day with our father, and one *is* not.

14. And Joseph said unto them, That *is* it that I spake unto you, saying, Ye *are* spies:

15. Hereby ye shall be proved: By the life of Pharaoh ye shall not go forth hence, except your youngest brother come hither.

16. Send one of you, and let him fetch your brother, and ye shall be kept in prison, that your words may be proved, whether *there be any* truth in you: or else by the life of Pharaoh surely ye *are* spies.

17. And he put them all together into ward three days.

18. And Joseph said unto them the third day, this do, and live; *for* I fear God:

19. If ye *be* true *men*, let one of your brethren be bound in the house of your prison: go ye, carry corn for the famine of your houses:

20. But bring your youngest brother unto me: so shall your words be verified, and ye shall not die. And they did so.

21. And they said one to another, We *are* verily guilty concerning our brother, in that we saw the anguish of his soul, when he besought us, and we would not hear; therefore is this distress come upon us.

22. And Reuben answered them, saying, Spake I not unto you, saying, Do not sin against the child; and ye would not hear? therefore, behold, also his blood is required.

23. And they knew not that Joseph understood *them*; for he spake unto them by an interpreter.

24. And he turned himself about from them, and wept; and returned to them again, and communed with them, and took from them Simeon, and bound him before their eyes.

25. Then Joseph commanded to fill their sacks with corn, and to restore every man's money into his sack, and to give them provision for the way: and thus did he unto them.

26. And they laded their asses with the corn, and departed thence.

27. And as one of them opened his sack to give his ass provender in the inn, he espied his money; for, behold, it *was* in his sack's mouth.

28. And he said unto his brethren, My money is restored; and, lo, *it is* even in my sack: and their heart failed *them,* and they were afraid, saying one to another, What *is* this *that* God hath done unto us?

29. And they came unto Jacob their father unto the land of Canaan, and told him all that befell unto them; saying,

30. The man *who is* the lord of the land, spake roughly to us, and took us for spies of the country.

31. And we said unto him, We *are* true *men*; we are no spies:

32. We *be* twelve brethren, sons of our father; one *is* not, and the youngest *is* this day with our father in the land of Canaan.

33. And the man, the lord of the country, said unto us, Hereby shall I know that we *are true men*; leave me of your brethren *here* with me, and take *food for* the famine of your households, and be gone:

34. And bring your youngest brother unto me: then shall I know that ye *are* no spies, but *that* ye *are* true *men*; *so* will I deliver you your brother, and ye shall traffic in the land.

35. And it came to pass as they emptied their sacks, that, behold, every man's bundle of money *was* in his sack: and when *both* they and their father saw the bundles of money, they were afraid.

36. And Jacob their father said unto them, Me have ye bereaved *of my children*: Joseph *is* not, and Simeon *is* not, and ye will take Benjamin *away*: all these things are against me.

37. And Reuben spake unto his father, saying, Slay my two sons, if I bring him not to thee: deliver him into my hand, and I will bring him to thee again.

38. And he said, My son shall not go down with you; for his brother is dead, and he is left alone: if mischief befall him by the way in the which ye go, then shall ye bring down my gray hairs with sorrow to the grave.

WE now take up again the thread of God's direct purposes with Israel as exemplified in the story of Joseph in Egypt. More links in the wonderful chain of Providence come before us. The famine was affecting other lands besides Egypt, and it was the need of Jacob and his household that brought Joseph and his brethren once more together.

I. *The Journey* (vers. 1-5).—In some way or other Jacob had been informed that there was corn in Egypt, and in view of the great need of himself and his family he expostulated with his sons, and urged them to go down thither. The brethren were evidently perplexed and undecided. Their father's words, "Why do ye look one upon another?" may possibly have reference to their awakening consciousness of what Egypt might mean to them. The name clearly called up memories which they would much prefer not to have brought before them. However, the pressure of need brought their indecision and hesitation to an end, and they started from home to go down and buy corn in Egypt. Only ten of Joseph's brethren took the journey, for Jacob would not allow his youngest son Benjamin to accompany them. He was the last and only comfort of the old man's life, and it would have been the crowning disaster and sorrow if anything had happened to him. We can well imagine the feelings of the ten brethren as they journeyed to Egypt and recalled the events of twenty years before. They little knew what was in store for them, and it was well that they did not, for it might easily have led to troubles of various kinds for themselves and their father. It is a merciful Providence which hides the future from our view, and calls upon us to take one step at a time, and to learn the spiritual meaning and significance of each event in the retrospect of experience.

II. *The Meeting* (vers. 6-25).—At length the brethren came face to face with the great Governor of Egypt, and "they bowed down themselves before him with their faces to the earth." Thus all unconsciously they fulfilled his early dreams (xxxvii. 7) which had been such a cause of offence to them. It is not at all surprising that they did not recognize Joseph, for the changes in his appearance between the ages of seventeen and thirty-eight, together with his

Egyptian language, appearance and position, would effectually prevent them from associating their young brother with the great personage before whom they stood.

His hard treatment of them has been criticized as at once unnecessary and unworthy, but it still remains a question whether he did not do the very best for them under the circumstances. Joseph was undoubtedly prompted by principle in taking these steps, and it would have been weakness of the highest and most culpable kind to have revealed himself permaturely before discovering the real character of the brothers after the long lapse of time. It is an old saying that "the longest way round is the shortest way home," and we have a striking example of this in Joseph's treatment of his brethren. In view of the fact that God was so real a power in his life, there does not seem much doubt that he was divinely guided in what he did. It was essential that their character should be tested, and if there was no change in them that an endeavor should be made to bring about an improvement. Joseph thereupon charged them with being spies come to see the unfortified and unprotected position of the land. Their answer was to repel with earnestness this charge, and their language is very significant when they say, "Thy servants are twelve brethren . . . the youngest is this day with our father, and one is not." If this reference to Joseph represents their true mind, they evidently believed that he was dead, but the phrase "twelve brethren" is very suggestive, and even beautiful. Like Wordsworth's "We are Seven," they considered that the family circle was still intact, notwithstanding their brother's death. Is there not some hint here of an improvement in their spiritual condition?

Joseph lets them understand that he is not prepared to take their bare word of denial, and requires a definite proof of their sincerity and truthfulness. He makes a proposal that one of them shall return home and fetch their youngest brother, in order that it may be evident that they are speaking the truth. Thereupon he puts them in prison for three days, doubtless to give them time to consider and consult about this proposal. It is impossible to avoid associating the pit into which they thrust him with the prison into which he put them, and it would seem as though Joseph himself had this association in mind. In any case, we know that the memory of the past became acute, and their sin was brought vividly before them.

At the end of three days they had their second interview with the Governor of Egypt, and at the outset there was a note of encouragement in Joseph's assurance that he feared God. The way in which God is associated with the life of Joseph, as expressed in his words, is one of the most beautiful features of the narrative. Several instances have already come before us, and there are more to follow. Thus we remember how he said, "How can I do this . . . sin against God?" (xxxix. 9). "Do not interpretations belong unto God?" (xl. 8). "God shall give Pharaoh an answer of peace" (xli. 16). "God will shortly bring it to pass" (xli. 32). "God hath made me forget" (xli. 51). Everything in Joseph's life was guided and controlled by the thought of God. He therefore makes another proposal to the effect that one of them should be left behind and the others return home and bring their youngest brother down to Egypt.

At this point the brethren cannot refrain from connecting what they were then suffering with what they had caused Joseph to suffer over twenty years before. Conscience was now awake, and in the presence of the Governor of Egypt they admitted their guilt concerning their brother. Time does not blot out sin, nor has it any power over the conscience. Why these men should have had this sin so vividly brought to their recollection at this time is a point of very real interest. The law of association was undoubtedly at work. They were in Egypt; a simple fact that called up the memory of the Midianite merchantmen and their journey thither. They were all together in a strange land; another fact that might have had influence in calling to mind the deed which was done as the result of a former meeting together. Then again, they were in the power of a stranger whose force was infinitely stronger than their own; and this in turn may have had the effect of reminding them of the utter defencelessness of their young brother as they plotted his ruin and thrust him into the pit in spite of the anguish of soul and his cries for pity. The elements of true repentance as seen in these words of the brethren are very striking—(a) Conscience: "We are verily guilty"; (*b*) Memory: "We saw the anguish"; (*c*) Reason: "Therefore is this distress come upon us."

At this point Reuben rebuked them and reminded them of what he himself had done. It was a case of weakness reproaching badness, and was not of any great moral value. Reuben was the unstable one, and it is easy for such a character to say, "I told you so," while not having lifted a finger to remove the injustice or right the wrong. The whole tone of the brethren is, however, very striking in the change which had evidently been wrought during the twenty years in their thought of Joseph. In the old days he was scornfully stigmatized as "this dreamer," but now he is "our brother" and "the child." The mocking attitude had been changed for at least something of interest and sympathy, and they seem to be already experiencing a little of the truth that "blood is thicker than water."

All this time they were, of course, perfectly unconscious that Joseph understood every word they were saying, and we can see his real feeling towards them in the fact that he was overcome by his emotions, and had to retire to weep in silence and to avoid recognition. On his return, as they had accepted his proposal, Simeon was the one selected to be kept, and he was thereupon bound before their eyes. We do not know exactly why it was that Simeon was chosen, but from the fact that Jacob on his deathbed could say nothing of good concerning him it is very probable that he was the ringleader in the action against Joseph, as he had been in the treachery against Hamor and Shechem.

Joseph's command to restore every man's money into his sack and to give them provision for the way is another indication of his true feelings towards them. There is nothing more striking in the character of Joseph than the utter absence of revengeful feeling, whether it was against his brethren, or against Potiphar, or against the chief butler. At each step of his journey he shows the true forgiving spirit of the man to whom God is a supreme and blessed reality. There are some people who never seem to get over slight and injustice. They brood over them and take almost every opportunity of pouring out their wrongs and indulging a revengeful spirit. To such people "Revenge is sweet," and they take a pleasure in repaying people in their own coin. Not so with Joseph. To revenge may be human, but to forgive is Divine.

III. *The Return* (vers. 26-38).—The brethren had not gone far away before they discovered the money in their sacks, and when they found it "their heart failed them, and they were afraid, saying one to another, What is this that God hath done unto us?" They of course felt that they had no right to the money, and it is noteworthy that for the first time in the record God is brought into their life. Conscience was still making cowards of them, and they could not but associate the circumstance of the money in the sack with their past wrong-doing.

At length they arrived home and told their father all that had happened unto them. There were no lies this time, no deception of their aged father, and once again we are conscious of a decided improvement in the moral character of the men. Everything was told, and in particular the condition laid down by the Governor in Egypt about bringing their youngest brother with them. Their father felt the same fear that they did when he saw the money in their sacks, and the words of the old man show how keenly he took all this to heart. We wonder whether his words, "Me have ye bereaved of my children" (ver. 36), really expressed his deep conviction, in spite of what they had told him, and of the coat which they had brought home (xxxvii. 33), that *they* had really put Joseph to death? Or it may be a mere general expression that it was through their instrumentality he had lost his beloved son.

We cannot help feeling sorry for this exhibition of faithlessness on the part of Jacob. It is a case of the old Jacob once more, and not the new Israel. As he had done very often in days gone by, he was looking entirely on the human side, and never thinking of the possibility of God having some wise purpose in all these events. "All these things are against me" was his sad and really faithless outburst, when as a simple fact " all these things" were definitely and directly in his favor. Four mistakes the old man made. He said Joseph was dead, when he was not; he seems to have thought Simeon could not remain alive in Egypt, when he was perfectly

safe; he interpreted the taking of Benjamin as a loss to himself for
ever; and then, as the crowning error, said that everything was
against him.   How short-sighted it is possible for a true believer
to be!   God's "never-failing providence" was as much at work at
that moment as it had ever been in the early days of the patriarch's
chequered history.

Reuben now gets the better of his characteristic instability, and
boldly offers his two sons as hostages if Benjamin is not brought
safely back.   It was a noble and generous offer, though, of course,
it is difficult to see what power he could have to bring Benjamin
back out of Egypt, or what good it would be to his father to slay
the two sons if Benjamin did not return.   But the father would not
be persuaded, and by his refusal he not only delayed the truest
and best interests of himself and his family, but hindered the development and progress of the Divine purposes of love and grace
concerning them.

The chapter is full of varied lessons for life.   Divine mercies
and human experiences are crowded into almost every part.

1. *The persistence of the Divine purpose.*—Once again we observe
the onward sweep of God's providence concerning Joseph and Israel.
There is no halt, no resting, but a constant, steady movement. Event
after event is taken up and weaved into the plan; nothing is outside
the Divine purpose and everything is made to subserve it.   Whether
it be the lack of food to Jacob, or the power of memory in the
brethren, or the opportunity of mercy in Joseph, everything tends
to reveal the loving kindness of God and to realize His projects for
them all.   At the risk of repetition—for the subject is full of it at
every point—we must not fail to cling closely to our belief in the
constant providence of our Father in heaven.   In these days, when
law is said to reign supreme, when science can only speak of cause
and effect, or at least of continuity, and Christian people are apt
to concentrate attention on methods, principles, and laws rather
than on the Source of all these things, it is particularly necessary to
hold fast the old foundation belief that

> There is a Divinity that shapes our ends,
> Rough hew them how we will.

2. *The strength of human affection.*—Twenty and more years had elapsed since Joseph had experienced the cruelty and injustice of his brethren, and yet when he meets them again it is with feelings of deep affection. All that he says and does is really prompted by his devoted love for them and their best interests. There is nothing stronger in this world than human love. Its persistence, its forbearance, its self-sacrifice are writ large on the annals of the human race and constitute its noblest feature. And when, moreover, this human affection is inspired and prompted and controlled by love to God, it is in truth "the greatest thing in the world." Now, if human love is so great, so mighty, so enduring, what must Divine love be, of which the human is only a faint though blessed echo? If human love is the greatest thing in the world, Divine love is the greatest thing in the universe.

3. *The power of a guilty conscience.*—There are few passages more striking in the record of Holy Writ than the revelation of the power of conscience in the brethren of Joseph. The greatest punishment that a man can suffer is that which is within, and comes from a consciousness of guilt. The marvelous way in which circumstances combined to recall with intensity the events of over twenty years before is one of the most striking and significant features of the story. What a wonderful chain of simple ordinary events led to the revelation of the sin of the brethren! That they should be called to go into Egypt of all places, that they should endure hard usage at the hands of the Governor, that they should be cast into prison, and that they should be so manifestly under the absolute control of the power and mercy of the great personage, were so many links of memory that brought back to them their sin. Conscience is the "knowing" part of us, that which "knows together" with God, and agrees with the revelation of right which comes from Him (*con*-science). It is worth while observing the seven different aspects of conscience referred to in the Scriptures—a weak conscience (I Cor. viii. 7), a defiled conscience (I Cor. viii. 7), an evil conscience (Heb. x. 22), a sacred conscience (1 Tim. iv. 2), a pure conscience (2 Tim. i. 3), a good conscience (1 Peter iii. 16), a beautiful conscience (Heb. xiii. 18, Greek). The last point is of very special importance. There are consciences which, while intrinsically good, are not outwardly attractive to others, because they are full of scruples rather than

principles. The true conscience will recommend itself by its moral beauty, and this is the kind of conscience men ought to see in the children of God. This is only possible when the conscience is kept pure through the blood of Christ by the Eternal Spirit (Heb. ix. 14).

4. *The nature of true repentance.*—We see in the story the remorse and sorrow of the brethren. Why were these not sufficient? Because a consciousness and even a confession of sin is no true evidence of an altered character. Joseph saw their change of mind as to the *past,* but it was necessary for him to know it with regard to the *future* as well. To be aware of sin is not repentance, for everything proves useless if the sin should be committed again. Right views of sin are one thing, to stop sinning is quite another. Joseph could not see this until the return of the brethren to Egypt, but we can observe in the narrative (vers. 29, 37) the elements of a better life. Repentance, therefore, is a change of mind as to the past, and this we call "penitence"; it is also a change of will as to the future, and this we call "obedience." In our childhood's days many of us learned what are still the very best definitions of repentance. One is in the Church Catechism, "Repentance whereby we *forsake* sin." The other was in our hymn-book, though it is not often found in children's hymn-books today:—

> " 'Tis not enough to say,
>   'I'm sorry and repent,'
> And then go on from day to day
>   Just as we always went.
>
> Repentance is to leave
>   The sins we loved before,
> And show that we in earnest grieve
>   By doing them no more."

5. *The short-sightedness of human reason.*—At the end of the story we see this in the experience of Jacob. The old man made a list of his troubles, and, on the face of it, all that he said was in a sense verbally true; and yet he made deplorable mistakes by drawing wrong deductions. We may put our own record of life in one column and argue accordingly, but we do not know all and we ought therefore to wait until we can put God's record in the op-

posite column. Through judging by appearances Jacob proved himself to be utterly wrong; and while we dare not blame him—for we
ourselves do the same so often—faithfulness compels us to observe
that his earlier experiences might well have taught him to believe
more truly in the unwearied faithfulness of God. He said "All these
things are against me," and that is what we say as we continue to be
occupied solely with circumstances. If, however, we would but look
up above circumstances, we should see things as they really are, and
thus be able to cry out with the Apostle, "All things work together
for good." And we should say this because of our strong confidence
that "all things are yours." The message is therefore clear. We
must look up to God through and beyond circumstances. It was
when Peter took his eyes off Christ and occupied his attention with
the waves that he lost his faith and began to sink. Circumstances
are only things that "stand round" us, and they can never do more
than this. They do not shut out the sky or "stand over" us; and if
only our gaze is ever fixed on God, and we believe to see the goodness
of the Lord in spite of circumstances, we shall never be put to confusion.

> "Rest in the Lord, my soul;
> Commit to Him thy way.
> What to thy sight seems dark as night,
> To Him is bright as day.
>
> Rest in the Lord, my soul;
> He planned for thee thy life,
> Brings fruit from rain, brings good from pain,
> And peace and joy from strife.
>
> Rest in the Lord, my soul;
> This fretting weakens thee.
> Why not be still? Accept His will;
> Thou shalt His glory see."

LVII

DIVINE DISCIPLINE

GEN. xliii.—xliv.

1. And the famine *was* sore in the land.

2. And it came to pass, when they had eaten up the corn which they had brought out of Egypt, their father said unto them, Go again, buy us a little food.

3. And Judah spake unto him, saying, The man did solemnly protest unto us, saying, Ye shall not see my face, except your brother *be* with you.

4. If thou wilt send our brother with us, we will go down and buy thee food:

5. But if thou wilt not send *him*, we will not go down: for the man said unto us, Ye shall not see my face, except your brother *be* with you.

6. And Israel said, Wherefore dealt ye *so* ill with me, *as* to tell the man whether ye had yet a brother?

7. And they said, The man asked us straitly of our state, and of our kindred, saying, *Is* you father yet alive? have ye *another* brother? and we told him according to the tenor of these words: could we certainly know that he would say, Bring your brother down?

8. And Judah said unto Israel his father, Send the lad with me, and we will arise and go; that we may live, and not die, both we, and thou, *and* also our little ones.

9. I will be surety for him; of my hand shalt thou require him: if I bring him not unto thee. and set him before thee, then let me bear the blame forever:

10. For except we had lingered, surely now we had returned this second time.

11. And their father Israel said unto them, *If it must be so* now, do this; take of the best fruits in the land in your vessels, and carry down the man a present, a little balm, and a little honey, spices, and myrrh, nuts, and almonds.

12. And take double money in your hand: and the money that was brought again in the mouth of your sacks, carry *it* again in your hand; peradventure it *was* an oversight:

13. Take also your brother, and arise, go again unto the man:

14. And God Almighty give you mercy before the man, that he may send away your other brother, and Benjamin. If I be bereaved *of my children,* I am bereaved.

413

15. And the men took that present, and they took double money in their hand, and Benjamin; and rose up, and went down to Egypt, and stood before Joseph.

16. And when Joseph saw Benjamin with them, he said to the ruler of his house, Bring *these* men home, and slay, and make ready; for *these* men shall dine with me at noon.

17. And the man did as Joseph bade; and the man brought the men into Joseph's house.

18. And the men were afraid, because they were brought into Joseph's house; and they said, Because of the money that was returned in our sacks the first time are we brought in; that he may seek occasion against us, and fall upon us, and take us for bondmen, and our asses.

19. And they came near to the steward of Joseph's house, and they communed with him at the door of the house,

20. And said, O sir, we came indeed down at the first time to buy food:

21. And it came to pass, when we came to the inn, that we opened our sacks, and, behold, *every* man's money *was* in the mouth of his sack, our money in full weight: and we have brought it again in our hand.

22. And other money have we brought down in our hands to buy food: we cannot tell who put our money in our sacks.

23. And he said, Peace *be* to you, fear not: your God, and the God of your father, hath given you treasure in your sacks: I had your money. And he brought Simeon out unto them.

24. And the man brought the men into Joseph's house, and gave *them* water, and they washed their feet; and he gave their asses provender.

25. And they made ready the present against Joseph came at noon: for they heard that they should eat bread there.

26. And when Joseph came home, they brought him the present which *was* in their hand unto the house, and bowed themselves to him to the earth.

27. And he asked them of *their* welfare, and said, *Is* your father well, the old man of whom ye spake? *Is* he yet alive?

28. And they answered, Thy servant our father *is* in good health, he *is* yet alive. And they bowed down their heads, and made obeisance.

29. And he lifted up his eyes, and saw his brother Benjamin, his mother's son, and said, *Is* this your younger brother, of whom ye spake unto me? And he said, God be gracious unto thee, my son.

30. And Joseph made haste: for his bowels did yearn upon his brother: and he sought *where* to weep; and he entered into *his* chamber, and wept there.

31. And he washed his face, and went out, and refrained himself, and said, Set on bread.

32. And they set on for him by himself, and for them by themselves, and for the Egyptians, which did eat with him, by themselves: because the Egyptians might not eat bread with the Hebrews; for that *is* an abomination unto the Egyptians.

33. And they sat before him, the firstborn according to his birthright, and the youngest according to his youth: and the men marveled one at another.

34. And he took *and sent* messes unto them from before him: but Benjamin's mess was five times so much as any of theirs. And they drank, and were merry with him.

1. And he commanded the steward of his house, saying, Fill the men's sacks *with* food, as much as they can carry, and put every man's money in his sack's mouth.

2. And put my cup, the silver cup, in the sack's mouth of the youngest, and his corn money. And he did according to the word that Joseph had spoken.

3. As soon as the morning was light, the man were sent away, they and their asses.

4. *And* when they were gone out of the city, *and* not *yet* far off, Joseph said unto his steward, Up, fcllow after the men; and when thou dost overtake them, say unto them, Wherefore have ye rewarded evil for good?

5. *Is* not this *it* in which my lord drinketh, and whereby indeed he divineth? Ye have done evil in so doing.

6. And he overtook them, and he spake unto them these same words.

7. And they said unto him, Wherefore saith my lord these words? God forbid that thy servants should do according to this thing.

8. Behold, the money, which we found in our sacks' mouths, we brought again unto thee out of the land of Canaan: how then should we steal out of thy lord's house silver or gold?

9. With whomsoever of thy servants it be found, both let him die, and we also will be my lord's bondmen.

10. And he said, Now also *let* it *be* according unto your words: he with whom it is found shall be my servant; and ye shall be blameless.

11. Then they speedily took down ever man his sack to the ground, and opened every man his sack

12. And he searched, *and* began at the eldest, and left at the youngest: and the cup was found in Benjamin's sack.

13. Then they rent their clothes, and laded every man his ass, and returned to the city.

14. And Judah and his brethren came to Joseph's house; for he *was* yet there: and they fell before him on the ground.

15. And Joseph said unto them, What deed *is* this that ye have done? wot ye not that such a man as I can certainly divine?

16. And Judah said, What shall we say unto my lord? what shall we speak? or how shall we clear ourselves? God hath found out the iniquity of thy servants: behold, we *are* my lord's servants, both we, and *he* also with whom the cup is found.

17. And he said, God forbid that I should do so: *but* the man in whose hand the cup is found, he shall be my servant: and as for you, get up in peace unto your father.

18. Then Judah came near unto him, and said, Oh my lord, let thy servant, I pray thee, speak a word in my lord's ears, and let not thine anger burn against thy servant: for thou *art* even as Pharaoh.

19. My lord asked his servants, saying, Have ye a father, or a brother?

20. And we said unto my lord, We have a father, an old man, and a child of his old age, a little one; and his brother is dead, and he alone is left of his mother, and his father loveth him.

21. And thou saidst unto thy servants, Bring him down unto me, that I may set mine eyes upon him.

22. And we said unto my lord, The lad cannot leave his father: for *if* he should leave his father, *his father* would die.

23. And thou saidst unto thy servants, Except your youngest brother come down with you, ye shall see my face no more.

24. And it came to pass, when we came up unto thy servant my father, we told him the words of my lord.

25. And our father said, Go again, *and* buy us a little food.

26. And we said, We cannot go down: if our youngest brother be with us, then will we go down: for we may not see the man's face, except our youngest brother *be* with us.

27. And thy servant my father said unto us, Ye know that my wife bare me two *sons*:

28. And the one went out from me, and I said, Surely he is torn in pieces; and I saw him not since:

29. And if ye take this also from me, and mischief befall him, ye shall bring down my gray hairs with sorrow to the grave.

30. Now, therefore, when I come to thy servant my father, and the lad *be* not with us; seeing that his life is bound up in the lad's life;

31. It shall come to pass, when he seeth that the lad *is* not *with us,* that he will die: and thy servants shall bring down the gray hairs of thy servant our father with sorrow to the grave.

32. For thy servant became surety for the lad unto my father, saying, If I bring him not unto thee, then I shall bear the blame to my father for ever.

33. Now therefore, I pray thee, let thy servant abide instead of the lad a bondman to my lord; and let the lad go up with his brethren.

34. For how shall I go up to my father, and the lad *be* not with me? lest peradventure I see the evil that shall come on my father.

THE great detail of the story of Joseph's relations to his brethren is a noteworthy feature, and sheds not a little light on the fundamental purpose of this section and of the Book of Genesis as a whole. It is history written from a religious standpoint, and in these chapters now to be considered everything seems to be subservient to the Divine testing, revelation, and development of the character of the brothers under the stress of the discipline administered to them. In view of the great particularity of the story it is impossible to do more than touch upon its salient features; but it will repay the closest attention as a striking manifestation of Divine action and of human character.

I. *The Dire Need* (xliii. 1-14).—It was not very long before the need of food was as great as ever in Jacob's family at Hebron. The famine continued, and Jacob thereupon urged his sons to go again to Egypt to buy food. Judah at once represented to his father the utter impossibility of going without taking Benjamin with them, because of the definite and solemn words of the Governor of Egypt. With perfect plainness he told Jacob that they would not go down unless he was prepared to send Benjamin.

One significant and suggestive touch of the old native shrewdness seems to come out in the reply of Jacob: "Wherefore dealt ye so ill with me, as to tell the man whether ye had yet a brother?" (ver. 6). That is, "Why did you need to say anything about it; why not have kept silent?" His sons told him that this was an utter impossibility, for the man asked pointed questions which admitted only of equally pointed answers.

Once again Judah appealed to his father and urged him to yield the point. He promised to be surety for Benjamin, and expressed his willingness to bear the blame for ever if he did not return with him in safety. At length Jacob recovered his spiritual equilibrium, and consented to let Benjamin go. He also told them to take a gift to the great man in Egypt. In the old days he had tried to appease his brother Esau, and here again he adopted the same policy. Not only so, they were to take double money in their hand, and the money that was brought again in their sacks. He also commended them to the God of Power (El-Shaddai), praying that the Mighty God would give them mercy before the man and send back Simeon and Benjamin. The old man's closing words indicate a fine spirit of acceptance of the Divine will: "If I be bereaved of my children, I am bereaved."

II. *The Notable Reception* (xliii. 15-34).—The men soon arrived in Egypt and stood before Joseph, and the sight of Benjamin was more than enough to make Joseph decide to receive them and show them hospitality in his own house. The fear of the brethren immediately on their arrival is very striking, and they at once told the steward of Joseph's house what had happened about the money found in their sacks. The answer of the man is deeply interesting: "Peace be to you, fear not: your God, and the God of your father hath given you treasure in your sacks: I had your money." Simeon was thereupon restored to them, and we can well imagine the feelings with which they waited for the appearance of their host.

On Joseph's arrival they once again fulfilled his early dreams as they "bowed themselves to him to the earth." His keen inquiries after their father was yet another opportunity for them to acknowledge his supremacy, "and they bowed down their heads, and made obeisance." How simple is the narration, and yet how remarkable is the way in which God's providence had brought about the fulfilment of the dreams!

The sight of Benjamin was too much for Joseph, and the narrative gives a beautiful touch in describing Benjamin as "his mother's son." Joseph's feelings compelled him to turn aside and weep in private; but recovering himself, he went back to his brethren and at once the feast commenced. He had not overlooked the order of their seniority, and as they sat, placed according to age, we are not surprised to read that "the men marveled one at another." It was also a very significant act that Benjamin's mess was five times so much as any of the others, for it gave Joseph an opportunity of discovering their feelings towards Benjamin, and whether there was anything like the same jealousy towards him as there had been towards the brother with the coat of many colors. The time passed with hilarity and satisfaction, their fears proving groundless, and everything promised well for their journey home as one united company to greet again their aged father.

III. *The Significant Plan* (xliv. 1-17).—Joseph's orders were to provide the men with as much corn as they could carry, to put every man's money into the mouth of his sack, and to put the silver divining-cup in the mouth of the sack belonging to Benjamin. It is not certain what the process was in which divining-cups were used. Some think that small pieces of gold were thrown in the cup and demons invoked. Others think that the cup full of water was taken out into the sun, and that as the sun played upon the water the figures made were interpreted as omens, good or bad. It would seem clear from the narrative that Joseph was in the habit of using the art of divination.

They started at the break of day; but before they had gone very far they were overtaken by the steward and rebuked for taking away the silver divining-cup that did not belong to them. We can picture the scene. They were returning happy, if not exultant, with Simeon free and Benjamin safe. Suddenly, however, their elation was destroyed, and fear once again possessed them. They protested with all earnestness that they were innocent, and urged in proof of it that they brought again the money which had been found in their sacks' mouths on the former journey. They were also perfectly ready—so conscious were they of innocence—that the one with whom the cup was found should die, and the rest would be slaves to the great Egyptian Governor. The steward would not allow this for a moment, only claiming that he with whom the cup should be found must become a slave, the others being free to return home. We can well imagine the consternation when, after examining into every sack, it was found in the last of all, Benjamin's. Instead of allowing Benjamin to go while they returned to their father, they determined to cast in their lot with him, and so they all returned to Egypt. Once again they found themselves in the house of Joseph, and "fell before him on the ground." Joseph asked them solemnly and severely what they had done, and whether they did not know that such a man as he could certainly divine. Judah's words are very striking: "What shall we say unto my lord? . . . God hath found out the iniquity of thy servants: behold, we are my lord's servants, both we and he also with whom the cup is found." If these words refer to Judah's belief in the guilt of Benjamin, it is very striking that he speaks of "the iniquity of thy servants," as though they were all included in his sin. But it may not be without some allusion to the iniquity of the old days, which they now at length confess that "God hath found out."

Joseph, however, would not permit of Judah's proposal that they should become his slaves. All that he required was that the man in whose sack the cup had been found should be his slave: the rest of them could go up in peace to their father. It would seem as though Joseph's purpose in this stratagem was to test the brethren in relation to Benjamin, and to see whether they would be prepared to sacrifice him to their own safety. It may also be that he wished to retain Benjamin alone, at least for a time, to gratify his own intense love by having him in Egypt as a companion. But the outcome was soon to prove very different.

IV. *The Earnest Intercession* (xliv. 18-34).—Then Judah drew near and interceded on behalf of his brethren, and in the course of these verses we have one of the most exquisite pieces of literature in the whole world. We observe in the first place the defence and humility with which Judah approaches Joseph—another striking fact, in view of those early dreams. We also observe the beautiful simplicity with which he tells the story of his father and the child of his old age—his youngest one who alone is left of his mother, his brother being dead. The pathos of the recital is also deeply touching and almost perfect as he goes on to show how the old man, bereaved of his two favorite sons, will be brought down to his grave in sorrow. Then the appeal closes with the heroic offer to become a bondman in the place of Benjamin, to sacrifice himself on behalf of his brother. "For how shall I go up to my father, and the lad be not with me? lest peradventure I see the evil that shall come on my father."

No further words are necessary in connection with this touching and beautiful story except to call attention to the way in which it reveals the changed character of Judah and the brethren. Assuming that Benjamin was guilty, his act had brought disgrace upon them all, and if the men had been as they were of old it would have been perfectly easy to settle the question by killing Benjamin on the spot and thereby clearing themselves of all complicity. But this was exactly what they did not and would not do. At once they returned to Egypt, and more marvelous still, there was actually no reproach of Benjamin. They were doubtless conscious of their own greater guilt, and so they returned to suffer together. At last they were a united family; and Judah's pathetic appeal was the crowning proof that they were now docile and disciplined, and ready for God's further and higher purposes concerning them.

The entire section is filled with striking and suggestive illustrations of human life under the training of Divine discipline.

1. *The recovery and victory of faith.*—The way in which Jacob recovers himself is deeply interesting. At first he would not hear of Benjamin going down. Reuben's appeal (xlii. 37, 38) was utterly powerless, and was doubtless due, in some measure at least, to Jacob's knowledge of his instability of character; but Judah proves more successful, and at last the old man gives his consent. Now, indeed, he is Israel, and not Jacob. Faith is sometimes checked and even defeated as we look on the dark side of things; but as we continue to face the facts, and realize that after all God is Almighty, faith regains strength, courage is restored, and victory becomes ours. Like Jacob, we face the contingency of sorrow, not with mere passive resignation, but with the consciousness that everything that comes is included in the Divine will, and must be among the "all things" that work together for our good. "This is the victory that overcometh . . . even our faith."

2. *The moral power of fear.*—There is scarcely anything more interesting and striking in the story of Joseph's brethren than the way in which they were impressed and actuated by fear from first to last. Fear possessed them on their first journey; fear actuated them when they found the money in their sacks (xlii. 28); fear continued to affect them as they once again appeared before Joseph (xliii. 18); and the crowning fear was seen when the discovery was made of the cup. God uses fear to recall the heart to Himself. Fear probes, searches, warns, purifies, and keeps the heart tender and true, sensitive to God's will, and ever shrinking from sin, and an intense desire to be true to God—and it is because of these things that it is "The beginning of wisdom." There are few subjects more worthy of careful and prolonged attention and practical meditation than the fear of the Lord as it is revealed in Holy Scripture.

3. *The necessity of prolonged discipline.*—As we read the story of the length of time, from the moment the brethren were first tested to the time when Joseph revealed himself to them, we cannot but be struck with the almost continuous discipline which they experienced, and we naturally ask why it was necessary that so thorough, persistent, and deep a work was attempted. The answer is probably to be found in the need of thoroughness of moral and spiritual training.

When a large building is to be erected, it is important that there should be not merely a wide, but also a deep foundation; and it is the same with spiritual building.   There are old corruptions to be swept away, there is the power of habit to be removed; and not the least result of God's work in the sanctification and purification of the soul is to deepen the consciousness of our own nothingness, to arouse and maintain in our souls an increasing sense of His all-sufficiency.   This is doubtless the reason why God deals with believers by bringing to their memory old sins and causing them to learn the same painful lessons over and over again.   God's work must be thoroughly done, and it is for us to bow before Him and become malleable to His will.

4. *The naturalness and unconsciousness of moral testing.*—The brethren little knew that all these ordinary events in their life were proving the occasion of the most searching and thorough examination of their character.   It was the most natural thing in the world for them to go down into Egypt to buy corn and to return; and yet all the while, and quite unconsciously to themselves, they were being subjected to the severest scrutiny on the part of Joseph.   How true this is to daily experience!   We think of the way in which Gideon's men were tested by the simple way in which they drank from the river.   This ordinary act was made use of by God to separate the three hundred from the rest.   In like manner the ordinary insignificant events of daily life are the very best test of a man's true character.   It is comparatively easy to shine on great occasions when we are conscious that the eyes of others are upon us; it is not by any means so easy to shine when we are free from the constraint of other people, when we are alone in our room doing the duty of the moment with equal need of faithfulness to God.   Still more, we are being tested most thoroughly by those around us in our ordinary life when we are absolutely unconscious of anything of the kind. Some years ago a gentleman expressed his deep indebtedness to the silent influence of another gentleman whom he did not know, but who, lunching each day at the same restaurant, quietly bowed his head to say grace before meat.   Miss Havergal, in one of her books, prays that her "unconscious influence" might be all for Christ. One

of Bushnell's sermons is on the deeply interesting subject of "Unconscious Influence." What a glory all this gives to every-day life! There is nothing trivial—nothing which cannot, and perhaps does not, test and reveal character. The Christian is always on duty.

5. *The danger of misinterpretation.*—We see how true this is as we think of Jacob's first impression that everything was against him, and that nothing but sorrow and trouble could come of Benjamin's being allowed to go into Egypt. We see it also in the utter unconsciousness of the brethren that all that was done to them by Joseph was actuated, not by severity, but by sympathy. We are not blaming them for this lack of knowledge, but only calling attention to the simple fact that the same action may be quite easily interpreted from two points of view. This is the case in daily life. God's providence in our every-day affairs may easily be misinterpreted. What we think is actuated by severity may really be prompted by the truest loving kindness. The believer often mistakes chastisement for punishment, and there is perhaps no lesson that is harder to learn than the fact that our Heavenly Father deals with us, not punitively, but in discipline. How often we are tempted to misinterpret the ways of God with us! "Thou thoughtest that I was altogether such an one as thyself"; and yet, if only we could and would see things in their proper light, we should understand that "whom the Lord loveth He chasteneth," and that this is done "that we might be partakers of His holiness." Let us not misunderstand and misinterpret God's attitude to us, but let us seek in fellowship with him to understand his ways; for we shall find that "the secret of the Lord is with them that fear Him, and He will show them His covenant."

6. *The necessary condition of spiritual blessing.*—The one requirement in the case of Joseph's brethren was the proof of their repentance. It was necessary for Joseph to see the reality of their changed life. The long period between the first and second visits might well have been regarded by him as suspicious, and it was therefore essential that they should be subjected to a proper test upon their return to Egypt. Everything was thus leading up to repentance and to the proof of it. Consciousness of sin must always issue in conversion from sin. God cannot act without our repentance.

There will always be a barrier to His blessing unless we are prepared to turn from sin with a hearty and true repentance. It is perhaps specially essential to emphasize this need of repentance today, for we are naturally too apt to lay stress on "believe" without preparing for faith by insisting upon repentance. It is not too much to say that no blessing can come unless there is that change of mind which issues in a change of will, and enables us to forsake sin and renounce our evil ways.

7. *The marks of deepening character.*—While the proofs of great moral change are found connected with all the brethren, they are especially visible in the case of Judah. His name had been given to him at his birth amid circumstances of hope on the part of his mother, for Judah means "Praise" (xxix 35). His early youth did not, however, afford any proof whatever that he was living up to his splendid name. On the contrary, the part that he played in the sale of Joseph (xxxvii. 26) and the choice of his wife among the Canaanites (xxxviii. 2), together with the subsequent sad events following his association with the Canaanites (xxxviii.), show that his life was altogether different from what it ought to have been as the son of his father and the bearer of such a name. But when he appears before us in these later chapters it is evident that there had been a remarkable change. He comes to the front in these emergencies with great force of character, and the whole tone of his exquisite appeal on behalf of Benjamin shows that he is now living up to his name. We are not at all surprised to read later on that its meaning is once more emphasized and acknowledged as true to life (xlix. 8). There is something very striking in the study of Judah as he appears in the Book of Genesis, and in particular in the revelation of his character in the chapters now being considered. God's Spirit was at work, testing, training, transforming him. There is nothing like the discipline of life to elicit and to deepen character. The pressure of poverty, the stings of conscience, the deepening of family love, the shaking of self-confidence, are a few of the ways in which Judah was brought into the line of true life and enabled to take the lead in these family troubles and sorrows. Let us therefore never shrink from any discipline that God may put upon us, only seeking for

grace and wisdom to learn every lesson, to make permanent every impression, and then to manifest His grace in our lives as we endeavor to live to His praise. "No chastening for the present seemeth to be joyous but grievous: nevertheless afterward it yieldeth the peaceable fruit of righteousness to them which are exercised thereby. Wherefore lift up the hands which hang down and the feeble knees; and make straight paths for your feet, lest that which is lame be turned out of the way; but let it rather be healed."

LVIII

RECONCILIATION

GEN. xlv

1. Then Joseph could not refrain himself before all them that stood by him; and he cried, Cause every man to go out from me. And there stood no man with him, while Joseph made himself known unto his brethren.

2. And he wept aloud: and the Egyptians and the house of Pharaoh heard.

3. And Joseph said unto his brethren, I *am* Joseph: doth my father yet live? And his brethren could not answer him; for they were troubled at his presence.

4. And Joseph said unto his brethren, Come near to me, I pray you. And they came near. And he said, I *am* Joseph your brother, whom ye sold into Egypt.

5. Now therefore be not grieved, nor angry with yourselves, that ye sold me hither: for God did send me before you to preserve life.

6. For these two years *hath* the famine *been* in the land: and yet *there are* five years, in the which *here shall* neither *be* earing nor harvest.

7. And God sent me before you to preserve you a posterity in the earth, and to save your lives by a great deliverance.

8. So now *it was* not you *that* sent me hither but God: and he hath made me a father to Pharaoh, and lord of all his house, and a ruler throughout all the land of Egypt.

9. Haste ye, and go up to my father, and say unto him, Thus saith thy son Joseph, God hath made me lord of all Egypt: come down unto me, tarry not:

10. And thou shalt dwell in the land of Goshen, and thou shalt be near unto me, thou, and thy children, and thy children's children, and thy flocks, and thy herds, and all that thou hast:

11. And there will I nourish thee; for yet *there are* five years of famine; lest thou, and thy household, and all that thou hast, come to poverty.

12. And, behold, your eyes see, and the eyes of my brother Benjamin, that *it is* my mouth that speaketh unto you.

13. And ye shall tell my father of all my glory in Egypt, and of all that ye have seen; and ye shall haste and bring down my father hither.

14. And he fell upon his brother Benjamin's neck, and wept; and Benjamin wept upon his neck.

15. Moreover he kissed all his brethren, and wept upon them: and after that his brethren talked with him.

16. And the fame thereof was heard in Pharaoh's house, saying, Joseph's brethren are come: and it pleased Pharaoh well, and his servants.

17. And Pharaoh said unto Joseph, Say unto thy brethren, This do ye; lade your beasts, and go, get you unto the land of Canaan;

18. And take your father and your households, and come unto me: and I will give you the good of the land of Egypt, and ye shall eat the fat of the land.

19. Now thou art commanded, this do ye; take your wagons out of the land of Egypt for your little ones, and for your wives, and bring your father, and come.

20. Also regard not your stuff; for the good of all the land of Egypt *is* yours.

21. And the children of Israel did so: and Joseph gave them wagons, according to the commandment of Pharaoh, and gave them provision for the way.

22. To all of them he gave each man changes of raiment; but to Benjamin he gave three hundred *pieces* of silver, and five changes of raiment.

23. And to his father he sent after this *manner*; ten asses laden with the good things of Egypt, and ten she asses laden with corn and bread and meat for his father by the way.

24. So he sent his brethren away, and they departed: and he said unto them, See that ye fall not out by the way.

25. And they went up out of Egypt, and came into the land of Canaan unto Jacob their father.

26. And told him, saying, Joseph *is* yet alive, and he *is* governor over all the land of Egypt. And Jacob's heart fainted, for he believed them not.

27. And they told him all the words of Joseph, which he had said unto them: and when he saw the wagons which Joseph had sent to carry him, the spirit of Jacob their father revived:

28. And Israel said, *It is* enough; Joseph my son *is* yet alive: I will go and see him before I die.

THERE was no need of further delay on the part of Joseph in making himself known to his brethren. Judah's touching appeal had shown conclusively that the character of the brethren was entirely altered. The prolonged tests had proved satisfactory and the moment had come for the surprising manifestation.

It is scarcely possible to comment on this passage without robbing it of its charm and power.

"If the writer of this inimitable scene of Joseph's reconciliation with his brethren was not simply an historian, he was one of the great dramatic geniuses of the world, master of a vivid minuteness like Defoe's, and able to touch the springs of tears by a pathetic simplicity like his who painted the death of Lear. Surely theories of legend and of mosaic work fail here" (Maclaren's *Genesis*, p. 261).

I. *The Revelation* (vers. 1-8).—The intensity of his feelings over-came Joseph as he listened to the earnest pleading of Judah, and he ordered all the Egyptians to go out, leaving him alone with his brethren. It was impossible for him to reveal himself before others. He needed the sacredness of privacy for so special and noteworthy an occasion. It is not difficult to understand Joseph's tears as "he wept aloud." He had been for years accustomed to the solitary life of Egypt, and now his pent-up feelings burst forth and the true man revealed himself. Overcome and vanquished by his own love, he was unable to control himself any longer. Then he cried: "I am Joseph: doth my father yet live?" Brevity, force, and pathos are here strikingly combined. His first thought is about the aged parent who had loved him, and whose love he had never forgotten.

The brethren met this disclosure with silence and fear. "His brethren could not answer him; for they were troubled at his presence." We are not surprised at this, for it must have been an astounding revelation to hear the words "I am Joseph" spoken by the great ruler before whom they had bowed themselves, and in whose hands their lives had been.

Joseph at once recognized this hesitation and fear, and said to his brethren: "Come near to me . . . I am Joseph your brother, whom ye sold into Egypt." He did not hesitate to acknowledge his relation-ship even while he was compelled to remind them of what they had done against him. "I am Joseph your brother." Yes; the same, and yet not the same. He was a very different Joseph from the lad whom they had cast into the pit. Twenty years of varied experience had made their mark on him, and into the old nature had come all the enlargement of capacity and depth of experience consequent up-on his prolonged trials and altered circumstances.

It is beautiful to notice that there was not the slightest word of reproach uttered as he revealed himself to the brethren. On the contrary, he urged them not to be grieved or angry with themselves, telling them that in spite of everything God had overruled their sin to bring about a blessing. "God sent me before you to preserve you a posterity in the earth, and to save your lives by a great deliver-ance." How characteristically Joseph bore his testimony to God, as

he had done so often before! To his brethren he said: "Not you
. . . but God;" just as years before he had said to Pharaoh: "It
is not in me; God shall give." He also called their attention to his
own position in Egypt as "a father to Pharaoh, and lord of all his
house, and a ruler throughout all the land of Egypt."

II. *The Commission* (vers. 9-13).—Based upon this manifestation of himself and the statement of his authoritative position in
Egypt, he urged them to hurry back home and tell his father what
had happened. "Thus saith thy son Joseph" was what they were to
say. He is not ashamed of his aged father, notwithstanding his
exalted position in Egypt. There is perhaps nothing more pitiable
than to see a son who has attained to a high position ashamed of his
father who has remained in a humble walk in life. At all points
Joseph stands out as the true man, because he was a man of God.
They were also commanded to bring their father down to Egypt, with
the promise of a safe and sheltered home and the assurance that he
should be near his son. The special reason alleged for this command
was that there were still five years of famine, and it was therefore
essential that they should be protected against poverty and want.
Even Joseph did not realize the full meaning of the contemplated
journey into Egypt. He thought of it quite naturally, as simply a
preservative against famine; but God knew that it was the way in
which the promise to Abraham was to be fulfilled and the family
transformed into a great nation. How significant it is that our
actions are left perfectly free, and yet all the while we may be
unconsciously accomplishing the great and far-reaching purposes
of Divine wisdom! It gives a dignity to life to realize that nothing
is trivial and without meaning.

Joseph added some strong encouragement that they were to convey to their father. They were assured by the sight of their own
eyes that it was their brother who was speaking to them; but not
only so, they were to tell their father of all Joseph's glory in Egypt.
Joseph evidently knew that his father would be impressed by these
outward and visible marks of power, for not once or twice had Jacob
been impressed and influenced by the tangible and visible, as distinct from the purely spiritual and non-material elements of life.

III. *The Reconciliation* (vers. 14, 15).—With these words of encouragement and command Joseph "fell upon his brother Benjamin's neck and wept, and Benjamin wept upon his neck." The tears of joy on both sides were the only and fitting expression of the meeting after all those years of severance. Moreover, we read with profound suggestion that "he kissed all his brethren and wept upon them." Mark the phrase, *"all* his brethren"; Simeon, Reuben, Judah, and the rest who were responsible for his being cast into the pit and sold into Egypt were all kissed and wept over by the forgiving brother against whom they had done what might have seemed irreparable injury. Nor are we surprised to read that: *"After that* his brethren talked with him." They could hardly have done otherwise, for he surely gave abundant proof, not only of his identity, but of his entire good-will to them.

IV. *The Departure* (vers. 16-24).—The news of all that was going on soon came to Pharaoh's ears, and "it pleased Pharaoh well and all his servants. There was something very fine about the character of the king. From the moment that he came into contact with Joseph we observe truly admirable points in him, and at this juncture we find him urging Joseph to send a hearty invitation to his father and family to come into Egypt, and to be assured of the royal protection and favor. They were not to "regard their stuff"; that is, they were not to have any anxiety about the property they were leaving behind, since everything in Egypt would be at their disposal.

Then Joseph gave them wagons and provision for the way, according to Pharaoh's command; and it is noteworthy that while he gave each man changes of raiment, to Benjamin were given 300 pieces of silver and five changes of raiment: no doubt in order to make some reparation for the period of anxiety that Benjamin had recently passed through in connection with the supposed theft of the cup. It is also interesting to observe the generous present sent to his father. This was according to the usual marks of courtesy of that day, though at the same time it would help to assure his father of the reality of the messages sent by the brethren.

We may not overlook his parting counsels to the brethren: "See that ye fall not out by the way." We might at first suppose that there was some irony in these words, as though Joseph, knowing of old the quarrelsomeness of his brothers, gave them these counsels as a parting shot; but it is much more likely that he had a genuine fear that they might not readily accommodate themselves to the new experiences when they had left him and were once more by themselves. It might easily have been that their former dispositions would have reasserted themselves and caused trouble. We shall have occasion to see later on in the story that they were by no means so thoroughly conformed to the new state of affairs as to make such a counsel altogether unnecessary. It was all so strange and unlike their former days. A new and wonderful vista had opened out before them.

V. *The Result* (vers. 25-28).—Their safe arrival home was, we doubt not, a great satisfaction to their aged father, more particularly as he caught sight of Simeon and of his beloved Benjamin. The circle was complete. The brethren had brought back a plentiful supply of provisions, and there seemed to be nothing more needed by Jacob. What then must have been his surprise when he was told that "Joseph is yet alive, and he is governor over all the land of Egypt." No wonder "Jacob's heart fainted and he believed them not." The news was far too good to be true, and Jacob, who had never been particularly strong in believing without seeing, was not prepared to accept so astonishing a piece of information when they told him Joseph's words; but "when he saw the wagons which Joseph had sent to carry him, the spirit of Jacob their father revived."

What a remarkable touch this is, "When he saw the wagons." Their word without the wagons does not seem to have been sufficient. Jacob was always a strong believer in the truth expressed by the well-known cynical phrase, "Seeing is believing." All through his career it was the actual, tangible, material, and visible that impressed him, and "the infection thereof remained even in the regenerate." Why was it that the wagons had this impression on him? It is more than probable that in the quiet ordinary pastoral life of Jacob wagons were unknown, and it may also be that they formed part of the royal equipage of Pharaoh, and thus their very strangeness impressed the patriarch with the assurance that something out of the

ordinary must have happened to bring these wagons to his home.
It is also deeply interesting to observe the exact words of the text.
"The spirit of *Jacob* revived; and *Israel* said." Jacob thus once
again becomes Israel, and it is the Prince of God who makes this
resolve to go down to see his son Joseph. He had had his doubts,
but these had been removed, and with belief had come prompt decision. "It is enough; Joseph my son is yet alive; I will go and
see him before I die."

It is impossible to read this story without associating with it the
spiritual ideas connected with Him of Whom Joseph was a type.
Later on we shall have occasion to consider this typical aspect of
Joseph's life in its entirety; but meanwhile, as we consider the disclosure made by Joseph to his brethren we may see in it some of the
most precious truths concerning the revelation of Christ to the soul.

1. *The fulness of the revelation.*—Joseph's manifestation to his
brethren was the disclosure of one whom they had rejected; but
one also whose love had remained all through the years and had
now conquered. It was love stooping, love conquering, love blessing.
The condescension of love for the purpose of uplifting the lives of
others is one of the most beautiful features in human life, and much
more it is the case when we think of the Divine love. The highest
serves the lowest, and God's love expresses itself in self-sacrifice on
behalf of mankind.

2. *The method of the revelation.*—We observe the privacy with
which Joseph disclosed himself to his brethren. This is also true in
the spiritual realm. The revelation of Christ to the soul is one of
the most private of experiences. There are things far too sacred
at such a time for any eye-witness or any record. At the first thought
we naturally desire to know what happened between our Lord and
Peter on the morning of the Resurrection; but second thoughts are
best, and we are glad that "something sealed the lips of the Evangel-
ist."

Not only was it private, it was personal. "I am Joseph." So is it
always; the revelation is not of a truth, or an institution, or a
philosophy, or a code of ethics; but of a Divine, living, loving Per-

son. Christianity has well been defined as devotion to a Person, and it is so because of that personal revelation of Christ to the soul.

This revelation is not only private and personal, but affectionate. Joseph kissed his brethren and thereby proved beyond the shadow of a doubt the reality and intensity of his feelings towards them, and the Divine disclosure to the soul is, above all things, a proof of God's persistent, everlasting love; the "Love that will not let us go."

3. *The power of the revelation.*—We cannot but be impressed with the splendid magnanimity of Joseph notwithstanding all that they had done. There is no word of reproach or rebuke, but only of encouragement and cheer. How like this is to God's method of manifesting Himself to the sinner. There is no reproach on the part of God; but it is the sinner who learns to reproach himself as he becomes conscious of the love of God towards him. We are not surprised that Joseph's brethren were full of fear, for the revelation was too much for them. It is often the case that the consciousness of sin becomes more acute after the revelation of God's mercy in Christ than it ever did before. The consciousness of God's long-suffering love breaks down the soul, deepens our penitence, and enables the heart to see things as it could not see them before conversion. Not only so, but in this revelation of Joseph to his brethren they found their true life. Up to that time they had been haunted with the ghost of their former sin. They had tried to leave it behind them; their characters were manifestly improved, and yet the sin clung to them and at almost every turn they were reminded of what they had done. But after the revelation of Joseph and their reconciliation to him, new hopes, new ideas sprung up in their lives, and they were enabled to see things in their proper light and find peace in regard to their former wrongdoing. Joseph did not reproach them, but they reproached themselves, and in that self-reproach was one of the guarantees of avoidance of sin in future.

4. *The outcome of the revelation.*—We cannot fail to observe that the immediate results of Joseph's disclosure of himself were threefold: (*a*) It brought *peace* to the brethren; peace between Joseph and them; peace among themselves; and peace with their aged father. (*b*) It also assured them of *protection*. They were to be

safe from that time forward under the guardianship of their brother.
(c) It also guaranteed to them *plenty*, for everything in the land of
Egypt was to be placed at their disposal. How true this is to New
Testament teaching needs hardly more than suggesting. Reconciliation with God brings peace—peace between God and the soul, peace
in the soul itself, peace between the soul and others. And not only
so, but there is also the guarantee of protection and provision for
all emergencies. When the prodigal returned to the father's house
he received the kiss of reconciliation, followed by the robe and all the
other proofs of reinstatement in the old home. Those who have
been reconciled by the death of God's Son are certain to be kept
safe in His life. (Cf. Rom. v. 10.)

5. *The responsibility of the revelation.*—Joseph laid one burden
upon his brethren. They were given a commission. They were
not to keep the news to themselves but to go back at once and tell
their father three great facts: (a) that Joseph was *alive;* (b) that
he was in an *exalted* position; (c) that he was willing to *receive* his
father and all of them. This commission was faithfully carried out,
and thus they fulfilled their brother's will. In the same way the
reconciliation of the soul with God involves obedience to what we
speak of in the New Testament as the Great Commission. It is for
us to go far and near with the same message, that our Lord is indeed
alive and risen from the dead; that He is *exalted* to be a Prince
and a Saviour; and that He is willing to *receive* all that come unto
God by Him. This is our bounden duty, and if we have been reconciled to God it will be for us to carry out this commission and fulfil
our responsibility.

And so we praise God for His great revelation of Himself in
Christ. All of Christ's is ours, and all of ours ought to be Christ's.
Nothing must, and nothing need, come between us and our Saviour.
We may draw from his fulness and use it, we must assimilate His
image and reflect it, and then show day by day by a humble, loving,
lowly, earnest life that we love much because we have been much
forgiven.

LIX

INTO EGYPT

GEN. xlvi. 1-30

1. And Israel took his journey with all that he had, and came to Beer-sheba, and offered sacrifices unto the God of his father Isaac.
2. And God spake unto Israel in the visions of the night, and said, Jacob, Jacob. And he said, Here *am* I.
3. And he said, I *am* God, the God of thy father: fear not to go down into Egypt; for I will there make of thee a great nation:
4. I will go down with thee in Egypt; and I will also surely bring thee up *again*: and Joseph shall put his hand upon thine eyes.
5. And Jacob rose up from Beer-sheba: and the sons of Israel carried Jacob their father, and their little ones, and their wives, in the wagons which Pharaoh had sent to carry him.
6. And they took their cattle, and their goods, which they had gotten in the land of Canaan, and came into Egypt, Jacob, and all his seed with him:
7. His sons, and his sons' sons with him, his daughters, and his sons' daughters, and all his seed brought he with him into Egypt.
8. And these *are* the names of the children of Israel, which came into Egypt, Jacob and his sons: Reuben, Jacob's first-born.
9. And the sons of Reuben; Hanoch, and Phallu, and Hezron, and Carmi.
10. And the sons of Simeon; Jemuel, and Jamin, and Ohad, and Jachin, and Zohar, and Shaul the son of a Canaanitish woman.
11. And the sons of Levi; Gershon, Kohath, and Merari.
12. And the sons of Judah; Er, and Onan, and Shelah, and Pharez, and Zarah; but Er and Onan died in the land of Canaan. And the sons of Pharez were Hezron and Hamul.
13. And the sons of Issachar; Tola, and Phuvah, and Job, and Shimron.
14. And the sons of Zebulun; Sered, and Elon, and Jahleel.
15. These *be* the sons of Leah, which she bare unto Jacob in Padan-aram, with his daughter Dinah: all the souls of his sons and his daughters *were* thirty and three.
16. And the sons of Gad; Ziphion, and Haggi, Shuni, and Ezbon, Eri, and Arodi, and Areli.
17. And the sons of Asher; Jimnah, and Ishuah, and Isui, and Beriah, and Serah their sister: and the sons of Beriah; Heber, and Malchiel.
18. These *are* the sons of Zilpah, whom Laban gave to Leah his daughter, and these she bare unto Jacob, *even* sixteen souls.
19. The sons of Rachel, Jacob's wife; Joseph, and Benjamin.

20. And unto Joseph in the land of Egypt were born Manasseh and Ephraim, which Asenath the daughter of Potipherah priest of On bare unto him.

21. And the sons of Benjamin *were* Belah, and Becher, and Ashbel, Gera, and Naaman, Ehi, and Rosh, Muppim and Huppim and Ard.

22. These *are* the sons of Rachel, which were born to Jacob: all the souls *were* fourteen.

23. And the sons of Dan; Hushim

24. And the sons of Naphtali; Jahzeel, and Guni, and Jezer, and Shillem.

25. These *are* the sons of Bilhah, which Laban gave unto Rachel his daughter, and she bare these unto Jacob: all the souls *were* seven.

26. All the souls that came with Jacob into Egypt, which came out of his loins, besides Jacob's sons' wives, all the souls *were* threescore and six;

27. And the sons of Joseph, which were born him in Egypt, *were* two souls: all the souls of the house of Jacob, which came into Egypt, *were* threescore and ten.

28. And he sent Judah before him unto Joseph, to direct his face unto Goshen; and they came into the land of Goshen.

29. And Joseph made ready his chariot, and went up to meet Israel his father, to Goshen, and presented himself unto him; and he fell on his neck, and wept on his neck a good while.

30. And Israel said unto Joseph, Now let me die, since I have seen thy face, because thou *art* yet alive.

ALTHOUGH hitherto the story of Joseph has been full of great detail we are now reminded that Jacob is still the head of the family, and that everything in the record is to be regarded as subservient to the development of the promises of God concerning him and his house. The message from Joseph, as we have seen, proved successful, and Jacob decided to go down into Egypt.

I. *The Journey* (vers. 1-7).—We are not surprised to find in this later period increasing references to the name of Israel rather than to that of Jacob, though the latter is not altogether displaced. "Israel took his journey with all that he had." It was a very definite change and transplantation. He had been many years in Canaan, with all that it meant of settlement and stability. Besides this, the grave of his beloved wife was not far away from his home, and it must have meant a real uprooting to leave the land. Above all, it was the Land of Promise which God had assured to him and to his father and grandfather before him. We can well understand therefore the mixed feelings with which he left a country so full of blessed memories and strong ties.

On his way he halted at Beersheba, and it would seem as though the memory of the place impelled him to offer sacrifices and worship to the God of his father. It was in Beersheba that Abraham had had a special revelation of God (xxi. 33), and where he lived after the offering of Isaac (xxii. 19). It was there also that Isaac his father lived, and where he too received a manifestation of the Divine presence (xxvi. 24). It was also the place of Jacob's own home in those early days before he set out to Haran (xxviii. 10). We can therefore fully appreciate the reasons which prompted him to approach God on this occasion.

The Divine revelation was quickly given in response to his worship. "God spake unto Israel in the visions of the night, and said, Jacob, Jacob." Observe how God uses the old name of Jacob, and calls him twice, just as He had called His grandfather before him (xxii. 11). The prompt answer of Jacob is also noteworthy, "Here am I." It was a phrase that sprang spontaneously to the lips of those who were in true and full fellowship with God (Gen. xxii. 11; Exod. iii. 4).

God revealed Himself by a twofold name. "I am El" (the Mighty One), and "I am the God of thy father." Thus was Jacob encouraged by a revelation of the Divine character and attitude, and this encouragement was further emphasized by the words, "Fear not to go down into Egypt," followed by a fourfold promise of what should happen there: (a) "I will there make of thee a great nation." (b) "I will go down with thee." (c) "I will also surely bring thee up again." (d) "Joseph shall put his hand upon thine eyes." This fourfold promise is very striking, and, as we shall see, extends far beyond the temporary circumstances connected with the famine and the need of going into Egypt for food. The real object of Israel going down into Egypt was much more than temporary and accidental; it was a definite and very significant step by which the family became transformed into a nation. For many years the chosen race had been a mere handful of people. Abraham had long to wait before Isaac was born, and Isaac had only two sons. One of these was still only the father of a comparatively small number, and if the promise to Abraham about being "as the stars of heaven for multitude" was to be fulfilled, something very special and definite must take place. Although many years had elapsed since the promise of the land and the seed had been given to Abraham, there was as yet no sign of the one, and not much of the other. Added to this there was the constant danger of attack from the Canaanites, and the possibility of the comparatively small number of the chosen seed being entirely destroyed. To obviate all these difficulties, and at the same time to allow the family to grow in safety, events were overruled to bring about the journey into Egypt, where they would have all possible safety and all necessary separation from others. Not only this, but these plain, simple, pastoral men would in Egypt come in contact with civilization, established government, and the administration of law. Every advantage of training and discipline would be theirs, and we cannot help observing in the light of the subsequent history how true were the words of God, "I will *there* make of thee a great nation." It was to be done there, or, humanly speaking, it would not have been done at all. (Cf. Dods' *Genesis*, pp. 321 ff.)

With these promises ringing in his ears, Jacob rose up, and all his family with him, and journeyed towards Egypt.

II. *The Family* (vers. 8-27.)—At this juncture the compiler of Genesis felt that it would be appropriate to give a list of "the names of the children of Israel which came into Egypt." The enumeration includes some who were doubtless born in Egypt. The number is seventy, and we cannot help observing the symbolism of this figure when we recall the seventy nations into which the earth was divided according to the Jewish view, the seventy Elders of Israel, and the seventy Disciples of our Lord. The number seventy seems to suggest a completed development, and it is probably for this reason that the complete list of Jacob's descendants is given in this section.

"It is clear that our list contains not only Jacob's sons and grandsons already born at the time of the emigration, but, besides this, all the sons that formed the ground of the twelve-tribed nation—or, in general, all the grand and great-grandchildren that became founders of *mischpa-hoth*, or independent, self-governing families. Thus only can the fact be explained—the fact otherwise inexplicable—that in the days of Moses, with the exception of the double tribe of Joseph, there were, in none of the tribes, descendants from any grandson or great grandsons of Jacob that are not mentioned in this list" (Kiel).

According to the Septuagint the number of those who came with Jacob into Egypt was seventy-five, and this number was used by Stephen (Acts vii. 14). The additional five seem to be the grandsons of Joseph, who are mentioned in the Septuagint version from which he quoted.

III. *The Meeting* (vers. 28-30).—We can well imagine the feelings both of Jacob and of Joseph as the time drew near for the meeting. Jacob sent Judah before him to direct his face to Goshen. Judah was once again honored. He had proved his worth in his attitude to Joseph in the matter of Benjamin, and his father was now able to trust him and lean upon him as the firstborn.

And then Joseph came to meet Israel his father, "and presented himself unto him, and he fell on his neck, and wept on his neck a good while." This loving reunion after all the years that had elapsed, and in view of all the circumstances of Joseph's life, is one of the most beautiful episodes recorded in Holy Scripture. No wonder that Israel said unto Joseph, "Now let me die, since I have seen thy face, because thou art yet alive." How much there is summed up in these touching words! They show, among other things, that the general idea of death ushering the soul into the gloom of the unseen world was not the sole conception of the patriarchs. Jacob clearly implies by these words that there was nothing further to live for, and that he was perfectly ready to depart, having once again seen his beloved son.

As we review the entire circumstances of Jacob's life from the moment that Joseph was taken away from him and sold into Egypt we cannot but be impressed with the wonderful revelation of God's providence, grace, and truth to his servants.

1. *The greatness of God's purpose.*—When Jacob was told in Beersheba that God would make of him a great nation in Egypt he was also given the Divine promise, "I will also surely bring thee up again, and Joseph shall put his hand upon thine eyes." We cannot help wondering whether Jacob fully understood these words.

We feel that he naturally expected soon to return out of Egypt when the famine was over; and yet his family was there for at least two, if not for four, centuries. "I will also surely bring thee up again." God did so, but it was his dead body that was brought up, and the promise about Joseph "putting his hand" on his father's eyes doubtless refers to his closing the eyes in death. We clearly see from this the importance of taking large views of God's purpose. While Jacob and Joseph naturally thought that the family was in Egypt as a protection against famine, God was using these temporary circumstances to bring about His own wonderful purposes concerning Israel. "The love of God is broader than the measures of man's mind." "Thy judgments are a great deep," and yet the obscurity is not in God but in ourselves. As we contemplate the stretch of God's providence and the width of His wonderful purpose, shall we not continually pray, "Open Thou mine eyes"?

2. *The reality of God's guidance.*—Whether we think of Joseph or of Jacob, God was leading them step by step, sometimes by outward circumstances, sometimes by special visions. The guidance was the same all through, and as real as it was precious and blessed. When Jacob put himself into God's hands at Beersheba, the assuring vision came that God would be with him, guide him to Egypt, and bless him there; and Jacob, as we know, realized at every step of his journey that it was not man but God Who was guiding. The guidance of God is as real, as certain, and as precious today as ever. "Thine ears shall hear a word behind thee saying, This is the way, walk ye in it." It is for us to remember that the Word is "behind" us, and that we are therefore not to go on too far, or too fast, lest we should fail to hear the Divine Voice. "When He putteth forth His own sheep He goeth before them." As someone has well said, "You can always tell the way by the fact that the path is smoothed." "I will guide thee with Mine eye" is the promise for every believer; and if he will abide closely with God, "the meek will He guide in judgment, the meek will he teach His way."

3. *The wisdom of God's love.*—Mark carefully this thought. Sometimes we are tempted to think that God's love is not wise. Circumstances happen to us which we find very difficult to reconcile

with the love of God. Jacob had had the promise of the land of Canaan, and yet he was called upon to depart into Egypt. Not only so, but his family were out of that land for centuries; and as the days and years went on, it must have been a problem how to reconcile their continuance in Egypt with the assurance of Canaan for a possession. But they did not see 'the end of the Lord." There was nothing arbitrary in God's dealings. Jacob yielded up his possessions in Canaan temporarily, to receive them permanently a hundredfold. Before he could inherit the land he and his must be trained and disciplined to enjoy it. They were called upon to forego a partial possession in order afterwards to value a complete possession, and in all this we see the wisdom of God's love. The Divine promises were unchangeable, the Divine love to Abraham and his seed was unalterable, and yet the Divine wisdom knew how best to fulfil those promises and to manifest that love. What a call this is for unbroken and enthusiastic faith! Let us trust where we cannot trace. Let us rest our hearts upon the wisdom of God's love. The pathway may sometimes be hard, but God still lives and loves. Experiences may often be trying and testing, but God abides faithful. Our life may be shadowed by sorrow and suffering, but the cloud will always have a silver lining, since God will never leave nor forsake His own.

> "One hope supports me in the storm,
>   When flesh and spirit quail:
> My Father holds me with His arm,
>   His promise cannot fail.
>
> The ocean of His grace transcends
>   My small horizon's rim,
> And where my feeble vision ends
>   My heart can rest in Him.
>
> In confidence I bide the tryst:
>   His promise is for aye.
> He guides me still, through cloud and mist,
>   Unto the perfect day."

LX

THE NEW HOME

GEN. xlvi. 31—xlvii. 12

31. And Joseph said unto his brethren, and unto his father's house, I will go up, and shew Pharaoh, and say unto him, My brethren, and my father's house which *were* in the land of Canaan, are come unto me;

32. And the men *are* shepherds, for their trade hath been to feed cattle; and they have brought their flocks, and their herds, and all that they have.

33. And it shall come to pass, when Pharaoh shall call you, and shall say, What *is* your occupation?

34. That ye shall say, Thy servants' trade hath been about cattle from our youth even until now, both we, *and* also our fathers: that ye may dwell in the land of Goshen; for every shepherd *is* an abomination unto the Egyptians.

1. Then Joseph came and told Pharaoh, and said, My father and my brethren, and their flocks, and their herds, and all that they have, are come out of the land of Canaan; and, behold, they *are* in the land of Goshen.

2. And he took some of his brethren, *even* five men, and presented them unto Pharaoh.

3. And Pharaoh said unto his brethren, What *is* your occupation? And they said unto Pharaoh, Thy servants *are* shepherds, both we, *and* also our fathers.

4. They said moreover unto Pharaoh, For to sojourn in the land are we come; for thy servants have no pasture for their flocks; for the famine *is* sore in the land of Canaan: now therefore, we pray thee, let thy servants dwell in the land of Goshen.

5. And Pharaoh spake unto Joseph, saying, Thy father and thy brethren are come unto thee:

6. The land of Egypt *is* before thee; in the best of the land make thy father and brethren to dwell; in the land of Goshen let them dwell: and if thou knowest *any* men of activity among them, then make them rulers over my cattle.

7. And Joseph brought in Jacob his father, and set him before Pharaoh: and Jacob blessed Pharaoh.

8. And Pharaoh said unto Jacob, How old *art* thou?

9. And Jacob said unto Pharaoh, The days of the years of my pilgrimage *are* an hundred and thirty years: few and evil have the days of the years of my life been, and have not attained unto the days of the years of the life of my fathers in the days of their pilgrimage.

10. And Jacob blessed Pharaoh, and went out from before Pharaoh,

11. And Joseph placed his father and his brethren, and gave them a possession in the land of Egypt, in the best of the land, in the land of Rameses, as Pharaoh had commanded.

12. And Joseph nourished his father, and his brethren, and all his father's household, with bread, according to *their* families.

THE arrival of Jacob and his household in Egypt meant a very great deal both to him and to Joseph, and many things had to be arranged before they could be perfectly settled in the new surroundings. There were still five years of famine, and for that time at least proper accommodation had to be found for the household of the patriarch. In all the details Jacob still appears as the head. even though most of the work had necessarily to be done by Joseph.

I. *The Necessary Arrangement* (xlvi. 31-34).—It was impossible for Jacob's household to settle in Egypt, even with Joseph's approval, without the matter being referred to Pharaoh for his royal sanction. Joseph thereupon told his brethren that he would interview Pharaoh and explain the whole case to him. Joseph's words are an interesting combination of principle and prudence. On the one hand it was essential to Israel that the family should have room to grow, and, at the same time, be separated from the Egyptians; on the other hand, the feelings of the Egyptians towards shepherds necessitated the two peoples being kept apart. Joseph's frankness in telling Pharaoh how matters stood was the only way of solving the problem. It is not yet known why "every shepherd was an abomination unto the Egyptians." The words are clearly those of the historian, not of Joseph, and there is independent testimony to their truth in Herodotus—so far, at least, as swineherds are concerned. It is also interesting to observe proofs in history that those who kept cattle were greatly despised in Egypt, Egyptian artists showing their contempt by depicting them as either lame, or dirty, or in some other forbidding way. It is sometimes thought that the explanation of this feeling was due to the resentment again the rule of the shepherd kings, but on the whole there does not seem sufficient warrant for accepting this explanation. Probably it was due to some feeling on the part of the Egyptians that the keepers of sheep were of an impure caste. (See, more fully, *Pulpit Commentary*, p. 504.)

II. *The Complete Provision* (xlvii. 1-6).—Joseph at once carried
out his project of telling Pharaoh, and took with him five of his
brethren. Why five out of the eleven should have been taken is not
at all clear, except that the number five seems to have had some
significance among the Egyptians (xliii. 34; xlv. 22). As Joseph
had anticipated, Pharaoh asked the brethren as to their occupation,
and they replied, according to Joseph's directions, that they were
shepherds, and requested to be allowed to dwell in the land of Goshen
owing to the famine in the land of Canaan. Pharaoh at once granted
their request, telling Joseph that the land of Egypt was at his disposal, and that he was to arrange for his father and brethren to dwell
in the best of it. Not only so, but if there were any of his family
suitable for the posts, Joseph was to make them rulers over the
King's cattle. It is very interesting to observe the various occasions on which Pharaoh comes before us in this narrative, from
the moment that Joseph was taken out of prison to interpret the
King's dream. There is a real and attractive graciousness about
the man, and it is hardly too much to say that some of it may have
been due to the influence of Joseph. The large-heartedness, sympathy,
and liberality of the King towards Joseph and his family reveal a
nobleness of nature that must have sprung from some Divine influence, however indirect and unconscious.

III. *The Notable Interview* (xlvii. 7-10).—Joseph then brought
in his aged father and placed him before Pharaoh, and immediately
on his entrance "Jacob blessed Pharaoh." As Pharaoh had asked
the sons as to their occupation, so naturally he enquired of the father
as to his age. "How old art thou?" Jacob's answer was very touching. "The days of the years of my pilgrimage are an hundred and
thirty years; few and evil have the days of the years of my life
been, and have not attained unto the days of the years of the life of
my fathers in the days of their pilgrimage." In comparison with
the hundred and seventy-five years of Abraham and the hundred
and eighty years of Isaac, Jacob's days seemed few, though "few"
and "many" are relative terms in more senses than one. That his
days had been "evil" was mainly due to the fact of the almost cease-
less disquiet, sorrow, and discipline of his life. It is a striking picture

that is called up before the imagination—the aged and feeble patriarch standing before the mighty monarch and blessing him. Old age affords a natural opportunity for bestowing benediction, but added to this, Jacob was the representative of his God, the Covenant God of his fathers, as he stood and blessed Pharaoh.

IV. *The Special Care* (xlvii. 11, 12).—Joseph at once did as Pharaoh had commanded, and placed his father and his brethren "in the best of the land." After the King's word no one could charge him with "nepotism." From henceforth Jacob and his household were the special care and thought of Joseph, who nourished them with bread "according to their families." The Hebrew of this phrase is very beautiful in its literalness, "according to the little ones." In the same way Joseph promised later on to nourish his brethren and "their little ones." The children were not to be forgotten. Thus everything turned out exactly as Joseph had anticipated, and Jacob and his house were ensured protection all through those five years of famine.

1. *The simplicity of Divine providence.*—As we read this story and concentrate attention first of all on the narrative as ordinary history, we see nothing whatever but the obvious, the natural, the simple and the straightforward. A famine caused a family to leave home and sojourn in a strange land. They came there under perfectly usual circumstances, and never expected to remain longer than the years of special need. Everything is quite clear and straightforward, with no circumstances left unexplained; and yet with it all we can see, as we review the story, that God in His providence was taking hold of these everyday events, and weaving them into His own Divine pattern for Israel. How true this is to life is at once clear to us all. The smallest experiences of our every-day life may form part of a mighty and far-reaching Providence. We pay a visit, intending to stay a week, and then we are led to take up our abode in that place, with all the course of our life entirely altered from that day forward. Or it may be that into the even tenor of our life comes a letter with a simple request which has very far-reaching effects, changing not one life, but several. It is all perfectly simple and yet perfectly Divine; and though, as we review our pathway

in the retrospect, we can see nothing in detail that has been marvelous or out of the way, yet the sum-total of everything stands out as an astonishing example of the providence of God. Let us cultivate the habit of investing every detail of life with significance, and try to learn the precise lessons that God desires to teach us. Let us refuse to limit God and His providence to the great occasions of life, and let us believe that nothing can come across our pathway unless it is in some way or other part of His loving and wise will concerning us.

2. *The splendour of honest toil.*—The sons of Jacob were shepherds, ordinary working men, who earned their living by manual labor. There was nothing unworthy in the precise trade to which they devoted themselves, but on the contrary, there was a true honor and glory in their toil. This is one of the essential privileges and glories of life, the capacity and opportunity for work. Whether the toil is manual or mental, it is that for which we have been placed in the world, and no one whose occupation is chiefly manual should for a moment think that there is anything unworthy of the noblest nature in devoting itself to its daily calling. If only we realize that work is part of God's will for us, then whatever precise work we may be called upon to do, we shall do as "under the great Taskmaster's eye," and

> A servant with this clause
> Makes drudgery Divine.
> Who sweeps a room as for Thy laws,
> Makes that and the action fine.

3. *The sacredness of family life.*—The relations of Joseph with his father and brethren once more bring before us the beauty and glory of family life, and we are reminded of the oft-quoted saying that "Blood is thicker than water." It is hardly too much to imagine the Egyptian courtiers as tempted to sneer at the great ruler when they found out the very ordinary circumstances of his family life, more particularly as his brethren were of a trade that was an abomination to the Egyptians. We can picture, without any great difficulty or injustice, these Egyptian magnates remarking with surprise that the one who had done so great a work for Egypt, and

was occupying so exalted a position, should have had so humble an origin. We can also fully enter into Joseph's feelings, as he told Pharaoh with perfect frankness of his brethren's occupation, hateful though that was to the Egyptians. In all this, Joseph never faltered or hesitated. His love for his father and brethren was pure and strong, and nothing was allowed to affect it in the very least. So it should always be. Whatever differences of position may take place between members of the same family, the strength of family love should remain unimpaired, and every rightful opportunity taken of expressing it. God has placed the solitary in families, and in the maintenance and furtherance of family life and love will be found one of the channels of blessing to the world.

4. *The significance of ordinary life.*—We notice that twice over Jacob uses the word "pilgrimage" to express his idea of his own life and the life of his fathers. "The days of the years of my pilgrimage." To him life had been a journey, with a starting point and a goal, and it is this aspect of life as a pilgrimage which enabled Jacob to invest it with a sacred and special significance. The same idea of life as a pilgrimage is found all through the Bible. Holy Scripture represents life as a sojourning, a temporary residence in a land which is not one's own. Even Canaan, to the patriarchs, was regarded as the land of their pilgrimage, and in due time this idea was heightened and transformed into the thought of a heavenly Canaan (Gen. xvii. 18; xxviii. 4; Lev. xvii. 12; Deut. xxiv. 14; 1 Chron. xxix. 15; Psalm xxxix. 13). The same idea is taken up in the New Testament, and the patriarchs are said to have longed for a better country, confessing themselves to be "strangers and sojourners upon earth" (Heb. ix. 13, Greek). This thought of life as a sojourning away from our true home does not obtain the prominence now that it did of old. This is due in great measure to the sneer of George Eliot about "other-worldliness." Nevertheless it is as true today as ever that "this is not our rest," and that "here we have no continuing city, but we seek one to come." This is the true perspective for every believer. He should regard the present life as a pilgrimage, not as a place in which he is to live permanently, but one through which he is to hasten, looking off from self and circumstances to

Him who has gone before us as the Captain of our Salvation to bring many sons to glory. The thought of life as a pilgrimage will inspire and cheer the heart under the storm and stress of earthly discipline, for amidst all troubles and trials, shadows and sorrows, the heart will ever be darting forward in hope and expectation of "the rest that remaineth to the people of God."

"O pilgrim, as you journey, do you ever gladly say,
In spite of heavy burdens and the roughness of the way,
That it does not surely matter—all the strange and bitter stress,
Heat and cold, and toil and sorrow—'twill be healed with blessedness,
    For the road leads home?

Home! the safe and blissful shelter where is glad and full content,
And companionship of kindred; and the treasures early rent
From your holding shall be given back more precious than before.
Oh, you will not mind the journey with such blessedness in store,
    When the road leads home.

Oh, you will not mind the roughness or the steepness of the way,
Nor the chill, unrested morning, nor the dreariness of the day;
And you will not take a turning to the left or to the right,
But go straight ahead, nor tremble at the coming of the night,
    For the road leads home.

And often for your comfort you will read the guide and chart;
It has wisdom for the mind and sweet solace for the heart;
It will serve you as a mentor, it will guide you sure and straight
All the time that you will journey, be the ending soon or late—
    And the road leads home."

LXI

A WISE RULER

GEN. xlvii. 13-26

13. And *there was* no bread in all the land; for the famine *was* very sore, so that the land of Egypt and *all* the land of Canaan fainted by reason of the famine.

14. And Joseph gathered up all the money that was found in the land of Egypt, and in the land of Canaan, for the corn which they bought: and Joseph brought the money into Pharaoh's house.

15. And when money failed in the land of Egypt, and in the land of Canaan, all the Egyptians came unto Joseph, and said, Give us bread: for why should be die in thy presence? for the money faileth.

16. And Joseph said, Give your cattle; and I will give you for your cattle, if money fail.

17. And they brought their cattle unto Joseph: and Joseph gave them bread *in exchange* for horses, and for the flocks, and for cattle of the herds, and for the asses: and he fed them with bread for all their cattle for that year.

18. When that year was ended, they came unto him the second year, and said unto him, We will not hide *it* from my lord, how that our money is spent: my lord also hath our herds of cattle; there is not aught left in the sight of my lord, but our bodies, and our lands:

19. Wherefore shall we die before thine eyes, both we and our land? buy us and our land for bread, and we and our land will be servants unto Pharaoh: and give *us* seed, that we may live, and not die, that the land be not desolate.

20. And Joseph bought all the land of Egypt for Pharaoh; for the Egyptians sold every man his field, because the famine prevailed over them: so the land became Pharaoh's.

21. And as for the people, he removed them to cities from *one* end of the borders of Egypt even to the *other* end thereof.

22. Only the land of the priests bought he not; for the priests had a portion *assigned them* of Pharaoh, and did eat their portion which Pharaoh gave them: wherefore they sold not their lands.

23. Then Joseph said unto the people, Behold, I have bought you this day and your land for Pharaoh: lo, *here is* seed for you, and ye shall sow the land.

24. And it shall come to pass in the increase, that ye shall give the fifth *part* unto Pharaoh, and four parts shall be your own, for seed of the field, and for your food, and for them of your households, and for food for your little ones.

25. And they said, Thou hast saved our lives: let us find grace in the sight of my lord, and we will be Pharaoh's servants.

26. And Joseph made it a law over the land of Egypt unto this day, *that* Pharaoh should have the fifth *part*: except the land of the priests only, *which* became not Pharaoh's.

IT is always interesting to study great men from different points of view. Joseph lived a many-sided life, and we are enabled to see him in his personal and domestic, and also in his public and official relations. Hitherto we have observed him mainly in regard to his personal life to God and to his family. In the present section he comes before us as a statesman wielding a mighty influence by his national policy.

It is important, however, to notice why this section describing his policy during the famine appears at this place in the story. A summary of the fourteen years has already been given in xli. 53-57, but the narrative at that point was interrupted in order to account for the coming of Joseph's brethren into Egypt and all that arose out of it. This occupied the long section from xlii. 1—xlvii. 12, and even now the Egyptian policy seems to be introduced almost entirely from Israel's point of view, for it is embedded between one small section (vers. 11, 12,) and another (ver. 27) which describe Israel's position and progress in Egypt. We shall see as we proceed how definite a bearing Joseph's policy had on the life and future of his father's family. The famine is shown to account quite definitely for the need of urgency in the care of his father's household.

We will, however, take a general look at Joseph's administration during these years. Whatsoever has been written has been written "for our learning," and there are very definite and valuable lessons derivable from Joseph's statesmanship.

I. *The Plan.*—The main idea of Joseph's policy was to take necessary steps during the years of plenty in order to economize for the years of famine. Overseers were appointed over the land, and a tax of one-fifth part was made during the seven plenteous years. Then the food of those good years was stored up against the years of famine. When the famine came and there was no bread in the land, the people came to Joseph according to Pharaoh's orders (xli. 55) and bought corn with their money. When the money was all spent and they still needed food during the famine, they bought food with their cattle. Last of all, when there were no more cattle to bring, they offered themselves and their lands for bread. Joseph thus bought up the land of Egypt for Pharaoh, with the exception of the portion that belonged to the priests, and the people entered into a sort of feudal service to the King.

II. *The Wisdom of the Plan.*—Joseph's policy has been questioned from time to time on several grounds. In the first place, it is charged against him that he showed undue partiality to his own kindred in providing them with bread when everybody else had to pay for their own. But it should be pointed out that the people of Israel were in Egypt as the guests of Pharaoh; they were not beggars, but on an entirely different footing. Besides, there was no possibility of their purchasing food in view of the fact that they had left all their possessions behind them. They had been told by Pharaoh not to be anxious about what they possessed in Canaan, and he promised that all the good of Egypt should be theirs (xlv. 20). Joseph did nothing that was not clearly sanctioned and indeed ordered by Pharaoh, and he cannot be blamed for the kindness he showed to his father and brethren. Their temporary sojourn in Egypt as visitors placed them in an entirely different category from the inhabitants of the land. Pharaoh's care of them was a matter of philanthropy, while a free gift of corn to the people would probably have resulted in pauperisation.

It is also charged against Joseph that he did the people an injustice by leading them into servitude and putting them altogether at the mercy of the Crown, but it is not correct or fair to speak of it as servitude in the strict sense of the word. They were Crown tenants rather than slaves, and the tax that he imposed was a very moderate one in view of the great productiveness of the Nile Valley. The true interpretation of verse 21 seems to be that Joseph "removed" them from place to place for the purpose of guaranteeing to them an efficient supply of food as needed (xli. 35). Nor is it correct to speak of the money as an exaction, for 20 per cent would not have been an exorbitant tax. They were free laborers or tenants of the Crown, instead of being independent landlords. Knobel (quoted in Driver's *Genesis*, p. 374 says:—

"In view of the fertility of Egypt the proportion does not seem excessive. In the time of the Maccabees the Jews, until Demetrius freed them, paid the Syrian Government one-third of the seed and one-half of the fruit (1 Macc. x. 30). Under Turkish rule the proportion is sometimes one-half of the produce, and Arab exactions from the *fellahin* are similar. In Syria cases occur where it is two-thirds; and about Ispahan, in Persia, the peasants, who receive land and seed from the Government, pay even three-fourths of their harvest."

It is also very probable that some such naturalization of the land was necessary. As Sayce says: "The power of the old aristocracy was broken as completely as it has been in Japan in our own day."

But the main proof of the wisdom of Joseph's plan is the simple fact that those who were chiefly affected by it accepted it with readiness and thankfulness. They were only too conscious of the benefits that accrued to them in those terrible years of famine. It is surely impossible to conceive of the entire absence of complaint, opposition or rebellion on the part of such people as the Egyptians if the policy was one that did not meet with their entire acquiescence and approval.

In view of all the foregoing considerations it does not seem difficult to justify Joseph's policy. At the same time we ought to bear in mind that the fact of certain actions by one of God's servants being recorded in Scripture is no necessary proof of any Divine vindication of it. We are not called upon to justify everything that Joseph did, simply because the story of his life is found in Genesis; but bearing in mind that he is described as "a man in whom the Spirit of God is" (xli. 38), we have no hesitation in believing most thoroughly in the Divine guidance, and therefore in the perfect justification, of his actions during the years of famine.

It is impossible to pass by the recent reference to a discovery by one of the foremost of modern Egyptologists, Brugsch Bey, of a hieroglyphic record of the failure of the Nile to rise for seven consecutive years, which resulted in a terrible famine. Even as an illustration and natural explanation of the famine recorded in Genesis the discovery would be of intense interest, but according to the discoverer the date of the failure of the Nile to rise was B.C. 1700, and this corresponds exactly to that which has been recognized by students of chronology as the date of the story of this chapter. The subject will doubtless be further considered by those who are qualified to discuss it. Meanwhile it is at least an interesting coincidence.

III. *The Results of the Plan.*—The immediate outcome of Joseph's policy was the salvation and protection of the entire country of Egypt. The people's lives were saved, and as we have seen, they frankly and fully acknowledged what Joseph had done. Then again, the influence of Egypt was undoubtedly extended by the policy. It is not without point to read that "all countries came into Egypt to Joseph to buy corn." In view of the constant action of nation against nation, and the wars that were from time to time waged against Egypt, we can easily understand the real value and importance to the country of the action of Joseph during these years.

Not only so, but the protection of Israel was assured by this policy. By putting all the power into Pharaoh's hands Joseph prevented any of the aristocracy or chiefs of the people from thwarting the government. It made Joseph's action much easier in providing for his father and brethren during these years. The people of Egypt might easily have been jealous of this special attention, but inasmuch as Pharaoh became the owner of the lands and all the produce, the people of Israel were safe during their sojourn in Egypt. Israel needed safety in order to develop, and for this a stable government was required. Herein undoubtedly is the real significance of this section coming in between verses 12 and 27, for it shows that Joseph's policy was part of the Divine providential care of Israel. At the same time we must not forget that this policy led eventually to the affliction of Israel under a new Pharaoh. With all the power in the hands of the King it was at once easy for the Pharaoh of Joseph's time to protect Israel, and for the new Pharaoh to afflict Israel when Joseph and his work were forgotten (Exod. i. 8). Meanwhile, however, God's purposes were being accomplished in Egypt, and Israel was becoming transformed from a family into a nation.

As we ponder the public life of Joseph we see plainly the qualities which characterized him and enabled him to do the great work that he accomplished.

1. *Three essential qualities of true life.*

a. *His discretion.*—We cannot help observing the wisdom which actuated Joseph from first to last. Before the years of famine came he was enabled to look ahead, and with rare foresight take all possible precautions. This is one of the essential characteristics of true life; thought, discretion, foresight, wisdom. If a man does not exercise his reasoning faculties and think out the matters with which he is concerned, he will fail at a vital point. The absence of thought is always the presence of weakness, while the presence of thought is always one guarantee of real manhood.

b. *His promptitude.*—Joseph acted at once the moment he obtained Pharaoh's permission: and all through those years, as he journeyed from place to place, promptitude and energy characterized his actions. There was no hesitation, no vacillation, no weakness; a genuine decision of character stamped everything that he did. This again, is one of the essential features of a true life. The man who is always "letting I dare not wait upon I would" will never accomplish anything. Even the man who makes mistakes is not always and necessarily blameworthy for acting, for he shows his readiness to do something. On the other hand, the man who is cautious, slow to move, and constantly fearing consequences is only too likely to end by doing nothing at all. There is no reason why mistakes should be made by a prompt, energetic, decided nature, if only with his promptitude he has the quality of discretion. The two together go far to make the real man.

c. *His thoroughness.*—He not only thought, but thought to some purpose, and took every factor into consideration. He not only acted promptly but he acted with thoroughness, doing everything that he had to do with all his heart. The policy of thoroughness, when it is based on genuine principle, is the only policy that ministers to true life and service. Half-heartedness in any work is useless and hopeless, and can only bring trouble in its train.

These three qualities should be carefully noted separately and together. They constitute three of the most important requirements for every true man; the exercise of his mind, the energy of his heart, and the action of his will.

2. *The source of these qualities.*—We are accustomed to speak of discretion, promptitude, and thoroughness as purely natural characteristics capable of almost infinite development by use and habit. This is undoubtedly true, so far as it goes, but it leaves quite unexplained the source whence these natural characteristics come, and Joseph is a striking illustration of the fact that all these elements of true nature come from God. "If any man lack wisdom let him ask of God" (James i. 5). All that Joseph did in this emergency sprang from his relation to God. "A man in whom the Spirit of God is." We must not narrow down the operations of the Spirit of God to those things which are purely spiritual and redemptive in the New Testament sense of the word. The presence and work of the Spirit of God are the source of all that is good and true in life and human nature. There is nothing outside His power. Joseph was as much influenced by the Spirit of God in selling corn as he was in bearing witness to Pharaoh and interpreting his dream. True religion touches life at every point, and nothing can be considered outside its scope. This ought to be an encouragement to us all to refer everything in our daily life to God, and to seek the wisdom that cometh from above. There can be no doubt that the presence of the Holy Spirit does affect with vivifying power the faculties of mind, emotion, and will; and the Christian man, other things being equal, ought to show in his life, in all the natural events and actions of his daily career, the power and value of the possession of the Holy Spirit.

It is also a point to be pressed home that a Christian can succeed in business and yet be a Christian, though we must not for an instant make worldly success the measure and proof of our Christianity. It is essential that we should keep in mind the simple fact that Christianity is no bar to success. There is no incompatibility between goodness and brains. On the contrary, we believe it to be a simple fact of Nature as well as of history that only in the sanctions and supports of true religion can our intellectual faculties find their fullest and completest exercise and justification. Joseph's life is a testimony to the simple but significant fact that a man can serve God and be successful, that a man can occupy the highest position and glorify his Maker, that a man can be a statesman, propounding policies affecting nations, and yet all the while be a humble-minded, true-hearted child of God.

Thus we may speak of Joseph quite literally as "diligent in business, fervent in spirit, serving the Lord." To use a colloquial but very expressive American phrase, he was a man of "grace, grit, and gumption," the three essential features of all true life and manhood. He was not afraid of work, and he did that work to the utmost of his power and ability. That was a fine testimony to real character suggested by a notice in a shop window, "Difficult work invited." It was the measure of the man inside the shop, and showed he did not fear to face difficult problems in his business. So it was with Joseph; he was a man of principle. His religion affected every part of his life, and the result was that he glorified God, and, we doubt not, was the means of extending the influence of true religion wherever he went. Let us therefore remember the well-known words of Archbishop Benson, "To the Christian there is nothing secular but what is sinful." Religion is to be applied to every department of human life, and whatever we have to do we must do it to the fullest possible extent of all the powers we possess. *"Whatsoever ye do,* do it heartily as to the Lord" (Col. iii. 23). *"Whatsoever ye do,* in word or deed, do all in the Name of the Lord Jesus" (Col. iii. 17), *"Whatsoever ye do,* do all to the glory of God" (1 Cor. x. 31). With these three principles ever actuating us we come to learn, and others come to learn through us, the real meaning of life.

> "So he died for his faith. That is fine—
> More than most of us do.
> But, say, can you add to that line
> That he lived for it too?
>
> In his death he bore witness at last
> As a martyr to truth.
> Did his life do the same in the past
> From the days of his youth?

It is easy to die. Men have died
  For a wish or a whim—
From bravado, or passion, or pride—
  Was it harder for him?

But to live—every day to live out
  All the truth that he dreamt,
While his friends met his conduct with doubt,
  And the world with contempt;

Was it thus that he plodded ahead,
  Never turning aside?
Then we'll talk of the life that he led—
  Never mind how he died."

ERNEST ABBOTT.

LXII

A LIFE'S SUNSET

GEN. xlvii. 27—xlviii. 22

27. And Israel dwelt in the land of Egypt, in the country of Goshen; and they had possessions therein, and grew, and multiplied exceedingly.

28. And Jacob lived in the land of Egypt seventeen years: so the whole age of Jacob was an hundred forty and seven years.

29. And the time drew nigh that Israel must die: and he called his son Joseph, and said unto him, If now I have found grace in thy sight, put, I pray thee, thy hand under my thigh, and deal kindly and truly with me; bury me not, I pray thee, in Egypt:

30. But I will lie with my fathers, and thou shalt carry me out of Egypt, and bury me in their buryingplace. And he said, I will do as thou hast said.

31. And he said, Swear unto me. And he sware unto him. And Israel bowed himself upon the bed's head.

1. And it came to pass after these things, that *one* told Joseph, Behold, thy father *is* sick: and he took with him his two sons, Manasseh and Ephraim.

2. And *one* told Jacob, and said, Behold, thy son Joseph cometh unto thee: and Israel strengthened himself, and sat upon the bed.

3. And Jacob said unto Joseph, God Almighty appeared unto me at Luz in the land of Canaan, and blessed me.

4. And said unto me, Behold, I will make thee fruitful, and multiply thee, and I will make of thee a multitude of people; and will give this land to thy seed after thee *for* an everlasting possession.

5. And now thy two sons, Ephraim and Manasseh, which were born unto thee in the land of Egypt before I came unto thee in Egypt, *are* mine; as Reuben and Simeon, they shall be mine.

6. And thy issue, which thou begettest after them, shall be thine, *and* shall be called after the name of their brethren in their inheritance.

7. And as for me, when I came from Padan, Rachel died by me in the land of Canaan in the way, where yet *there was* but a little way to come unto Ephrath: and I buried her there in the way of Ephrath; the same *is* Bethlehem.

8. And Israel beheld Joseph's sons, and said, Who *are* these?

9. And Joseph said unto his father, They *are* my sons, whom God hath given me in this *place*. And he said, Bring them, I pray thee, unto me, and I will bless them.

10. Now the eyes of Israel were dim for age, *so that* he could not see. And he brought them near unto him; and he kissed them, and embraced them.

11. And Israel said unto Joseph, I had not thought to see thy face: and lo, God hath shewed me also thy seed.

12. And Joseph brought them out from between his knees, and he bowed himself with his face to the earth

13. And Joseph took them both, Ephraim in his right hand toward Israel's left hand, and Manasseh in his left hand toward Israel's right hand, and brought *them* near unto him.

14. And Israel stretched out his right hand, and laid *it* upon Ephraim's head, who *was* the younger, and his left hand upon Manasseh's head, guiding his hands wittingly; for Manasseh *was* the firstborn.

15. And he blessed Joseph, and said, God, before whom my fathers Abraham and Isaac did walk, the God which fed me all my life long unto this day,

16. The Angel which redeemed me from all evil, bless the lads; and let my name be named on them, and the name of my fathers Abraham and Isaac; and let them grow into a multitude in the midst of the earth.

17. And when Joseph saw that his father laid his right hand upon the head of Ephraim, it displeased him: and he held up his father's hand, to remove it from Ephraim's head, unto Manasseh's head.

18. And Joseph said unto his father, Not so, my father: for this *is* the firstborn; put thy right hand up his head.

19. And his father refused, and said, I know *it*, my son, I know *it*: he also shall become a people, and he also shall be great: but truly his younger brother shall be greater than he, and his seed shall become a multitude of nations.

20. And he blessed them that day, saying, In thee shall Israel bless, saying, God make thee as Ephraim and as Manasseh: and he set Ephraim before Manasseh.

21. And Israel said unto Joseph, Behold, I die: but God shall be with you, and bring you again unto the land of your fathers.

22. Moreover I have given to thee one portion above thy brethren, which I took out of the hand of the Amorite with my sword and with my bow.

AS the record of Genesis approaches the death of Jacob it is noteworthy how full of detail it becomes. This clearly shows the importance of the events in the eyes of the author. Joseph recedes into the background, or at any rate takes a very secondary position. The prominent figure is the great patriarch as head of the chosen family. When the seven years of famine came to an end we wonder, from the human standpoint, why Jacob and his family did not return to Canaan. We may be perfectly sure that some indication of the will of God was given enjoining them to stay where they were. At length, twelve years afterwards, Jacob drew near to the end of his life, quite conscious that he would die in Egypt and not in Canaan. This and the succeeding section are therefore filled with the events of the last days of the patriarch, and are fraught with the deepest spiritual meaning in relation to him and to Israel.

I. *The Solemn Requirement* (xlvii. 27-31).—"The time drew near that Israel must die," the inevitable event was now near at hand. Even Israel must go the way of his fathers. He therefore called his son Joseph, and begged him not to bury him in Egypt, but to take him back to the land of promise. "When I sleep with my fathers thou shalt carry me out of Egypt and bury me in their burying-place." These words are full of the deepest meaning. The way in which sleeping with the fathers is distinguished from the act of burial clearly shows that Jacob had a very definite conception of a future life as "with his fathers." But more than this, the desire to return to Canaan seems to be associated with a belief in God's promises, which could only be realized by the resurrection from the dead. To Jacob it was perfectly certain that God would fulfil His ancient word, and give that land to him and to his seed. It was thus no mere sentiment, but a very definite religious faith that led to his making this request of Joseph. Joseph, of course, at once promised to do what his father wished, and gave a solemn oath to carry out his word. The matter thus satisfactorily settled, "Israel bowed himself upon the bed's head." If we are to read the Hebrew, it means that he turned himself over in the bed and knelt upon it in the attitude of prayer. If, however, we follow the Septuagint, which only differs from the Hebrew in the matter of vowel punctuation, we shall read that Israel "worshipped leaning upon the top of his staff." The latter rendering, which is favored by many authorities, has the great advantage of being in close agreement with Egyptian custom at that time. In either case, worship closes the life of the patriarch, who is now indeed "Israel," not "Jacob." Here, as elsewhere, the usage of these two names should be carefully considered.

II. *The Striking Decision* (xlviii. 1-7).—It was not long after this that Joseph heard of his father's illness, and, knowing that the end could not be far off, went to see him, taking with him his two sons Manasseh and Ephraim. Jacob roused himself to greet his son, and when they were together the old man naturally recalled the past, and told Joseph of what God had done from that day when He appeared to him in the vision at Bethel. This reminder of the Divine promise about Canaan was then followed by the surprising and even startling announcement that Joseph's two sons were to be regarded as no longer their father's children, but as their grandfather's, taking the place of Reuben and Simeon among the twelve sons and twelve tribes. Any other sons that Joseph might have were to remain their father's, but Ephraim and Manasseh were to be separated from Joseph and to belong in name and fact to Jacob.

This adoption of Ephraim and Manasseh was a very remarkable occurrence. We naturally ask ourselves first of all how Joseph regarded it, and though the narrative is quite silent we can readily see by his perfect acquiescence that he was prepared to allow his sons to cast in their lot with the people of God rather than to continue in Egypt with all the possibilities and opportunities that might be before them. Joseph in this as in every other case, never forgot that he belonged to a chosen race, to the people of God. "By faith" everything became possible and even easy since God was so real to him.

But what are we to think of the decision in relation to Manasseh and Ephraim? They were at this time twenty years of age at the least, and their position must have been to all intents and purposes settled for them by their father's position in the land of Egypt. Their prospects were obviously bright and even glorious, and making every allowance for the authority of Joseph over them, we are surely right in assuming that the decision to separate them from Egypt and to include them in the shepherds of Israel must have meant a real test to them as well as to their father. May we not assume that they had been taught by Joseph the real meaning of the position of Jacob and his family in relation to God and His promise? And if this was so, these young men were prepared to abjure all the hopes of high estate and great power in Egypt in order to cast in their lot with the people of God.

The touching reference to Rachel (ver. 7) with which Jacob closed his words to Joseph is very striking. The presence of Rachel's elder son recalled the past with intensity and vividness, and the circumstances of his beloved wife's death came home to him keenly at the moment. "As for me, when I came from Padan, Rachel died, to my sorrow" (R.V. margin) "in the land of Canaan." The memory of that day lived with the aged patriarch. And yet we believe that there was something more than the memory of a sorrow in his reference to Rachel. He wished to honor the memory of his beloved wife by giving her three tribes among the twelve—Benjamin, Ephraim, and Manasseh.

III. *The Special Blessing* (xlviii. 8-16).—The dimness of Jacob's sight prevented him from recognizing those whom Joseph had brought with him, but when told who they were, he asked that they might be brought near that he might bless them. How beautiful are those words of his, "I had not thought to see thy face; and lo, God hath showed me also thy seed." God is ever surprising His people with added blessing beyond our expectations, because "He is able to do exceeding abundantly above all that we ask or think." Joseph thereupon placed one son at one side and the other at the other side of the patriarch, so that the elder son Manasseh might have the blessing from Israel's right hand, and the younger son Ephraim the blessing from the left hand. But this was not to be. Israel deliberately stretched forth his hands and crossed them, so that the firstborn received the blessing from the left hand. Then the father and the two sons were blessed by the patriarch in words that live in the memory as we read them. The threefold testimony to God as the God of his fathers, the God of his own life, and the God who had preserved him, is very striking. While we may not read into it the full New Testament doctrine of the Trinity, it is impossible to overlook the threefoldness of the reference. We may also associate with this a similar threefoldness found elsewhere in the Old Testament (Num. vi. 24-26; Isa. vi. 3). God was asked to bless the lads, and the blessing was to take two forms—spiritual and temporal. They were to be incorporated into the family of Israel, and also to grow into a multitude in the midst of the earth. How truly all this was fulfilled in the subsequent history of Ephraim and Manasseh is evident from the record of Holy Scripture.

IV. *The Significant Action* (xlviii. 17-22).—In accordance with the general feeling about the firstborn, Joseph was displeased that his father should have laid his right hand upon the head of Ephraim, and he thereupon attempted to remove it, telling Jacob that Manasseh was the firstborn. The father, however, was equal to the occasion, and doubtless to the surprise of his son said, "I know it, my son, I know it." It had been done wittingly and deliberately, for the younger son was to be the greater even though Manasseh himself was to be great. This passing over the firstborn is one of the most striking features of the book of Genesis. So it was with Seth instead of Cain: Shem instead of Japheth; Abraham instead of Haran; Isaac instead of Ishmael; Jacob instead of Esau. And now it was Ephraim instead of Manasseh. Thus did God display His sovereignty and prevent anyone imagining that His blessings necessarily follow the line of natural privilege. God has again and again chosen the weak things of the earth, and even those that are despised, to set at nought those that are mighty. Grace is sovereign, and by no means follows, but rather opposes the course of nature.

Thus the patriarch had his way, and Joseph promptly and fully accepted the situation. Is it not remarkable, in spite of all Joseph had been, that his name was not to appear in the list of his father's sons, but that instead of his own his two sons were to take his place? We do not know whether Jacob intended the birthright to pass thereby from Judah to Joseph and to be realized in his two sons, though it is clear afterwards (1 Chron. v. 1, 2) that the birthright was regarded as belonging to Joseph. Joseph's self-abnegation and faith are once again evident.

The closing word of assurance and promise was given to Joseph himself. Israel assured him that though he himself was about to die, God would be with them and bring them again to the land of their fathers. Not only so, but Joseph was granted "one portion above" his brethren, the portion which his father had taken out of the hand of the Amorite. It is sometimes thought that this reference is to Shechem, as the word "portion" in the Hebrew is identical with the name Shechem, and that it is to be interpreted of the episode in xxxiii. 19. If this be the case, it must mean that, while Jacob had originally deprecated and condemned the treachery of his sons, nevertheless, the deed being done, the property belonged to him as the head of the house and of the family. He therefore bestows it, not upon those who had treacherously taken it, but on Joseph, as a special mark of privilege and as a guarantee of future inheritance. Others, however, think that the reference is prophetic, and looks forward to the time when Canaan shall be taken out of the hand of the Amorite by the seed of Jacob. It is perhaps best of all to regard it as referring altogether to an episode which is not otherwise recorded in the history of Jacob.

This picture of the sunset of Israel's life is one of extreme beauty and suggestiveness, and may well be taken as a type and model for old age today.

1. *Faith, looking upward.*—The one thing that seems to stand out pre-eminently in this narrative is the reality to Jacob of God's presence and promise. All through the story the one theme is God (xlvii. 3, 11, 15, 20, 21). The troubled waters of Jacob's life had now settled and cleared, and were flowing placidly in a quiet stream of fellowship with God. He rested his heart upon what God had done for him, and on what God had promised to him and to his seed. Faith is always occupied with the Word of God, and finds in that Word its nutriment, encouragement, inspiration, and power. Trust in man answers to truth in God. The Divine faithfulness is met by human faith, for faith is the only, as it is the adequate, response to a Divine revelation. Happy are they to whom God is equally real, whose hearts rest upon His Word, and who are able to say, "I believe God that it shall be even as it was told me."

2. *Gratitude, looking backward.*—It is very helpful to contrast the two outlooks of life associated with Jacob. When he was before Pharaoh (xlvii. 9) he spoke of his days as "few and evil," but in his words to Joseph (xlviii. 16) he speaks of One who had "redeemed him from all evil." These two aspects of life seem to represent two moods of the ancient patriarch. In the former he himself was everything and God practically nothing, except in so far as life was thought of as a "pilgrimage." In the latter God was everything, and he himself nothing. It has been suggested that in taking

such a gloomy view of his life when he stood before Pharaoh he missed a splendid opportunity of witnessing for God. This may be so, but there can be no doubt of the definite testimony before Joseph and his sons. God was everything to him in that threefold description. (*a*) "The God before Whom my fathers did walk." (*b*) "The God Who hath shepherded me all my life long unto this day." (*c*) "The Angel which hath redeemed me from all evil." Nothing could well be finer or more appropriate than this description of God, and, whatever we may say of the former testimony, this one is full of genuine gratitude as he recalls his life from that memorable night at Bethel, when God blessed him and gave him such wonderful promises (xlviii. 3, 4). As we are passing through trials and troubles, it is not always easy though it ought to be possible for us to see the hand of God; but as we review the past and look over life's journey we are enabled to see the way in which God has led us, and our grateful adoring testimony in the retrospect of life will undoubtedly be, "He hath done all things well."

3. *Love, looking outward.*—The aged patriarch not only thought of God and of his own past, but also of Joseph and his two sons, and with hands outstretched he called down the Divine benediction upon his grandsons, praying that God would "bless the lads." His affection for Joseph and his sons prompted this outpouring of loving prayer and blessing, that the same God Who had been with him would continue to be with his dear ones. Happy are those young men who can enjoy the privilege of the benediction of a father or grandfather; happy, too, are those who can give this blessing, for in it without a doubt is the assurance of Divine as well as of human love.

4. *Hope, looking onward.*—Israel's faith was not only occupied with God as a present reality, but expressed itself in hope and expectation as he looked forward to the glorious future assured by God to him and to his seed. "I die; but God shall be with you, and bring you again unto the land of your fathers." Hope is an integral part of the Christian life, and must never be severed from faith and love. Just as St. Paul kept these three graces in close proximity (1 Thess. i. 3), so must it be in every true, full, and well-balanced

Christian experience.   Faith looks upward, Hope looks onward.
Faith accepts, Hope expects.   Faith is concerned with the present
promising, Hope is concerned with the thing promised.   Faith appropriates, Hope anticipates.   Faith is always occupied with the
past and present, Hope lives entirely in the future.   Our life will be
weakened, narrowed, and even maimed, if hope does not occupy
a very definite place in our life.

And thus we see what the true ending of life should be—a blending
of faith, gratitude, love, and hope; a consciousness of the presence
and peace of God; an assurance of the mercy and blessing of God;
a confidence in the promise and assurance of God; an expectation
that what God hath promised He is both able and willing to perform.   When life is lived on this plane of experience it fulfils completely the Divine ideal by manifesting itself in true character, proving a blessing to those around, and bringing ever-increasing glory
to God.   Then indeed, God is its "all in all."

LXIII

FATHER AND SONS

GEN. xlix. 1-27

1. And Jacob called unto his sons, and said, Gather yourselves together, that I may tell you *that* which shall befall you in the last days.

2. Gather yourselves together, and hear, ye sons of Jacob: and hearken unto Israel your father.

3. Reuben, thou *art* my firstborn, my might, and the beginning of my strength, the excellency of dignity, and the excellency of power:

4. Unstable as water, thou shall not excel; because thou wentest up to thy father's bed; then defilest thou *it*: he went up to my couch.

5. Simeon and Levi *are* brethren; instruments of cruelty *are in* their habitations.

6. O my soul, come not thou into their secret; unto their assembly, mine honor, be not thou united: for in their anger they slew a man, and in their selfwill they digged down a wall.

7. Cursed *be* their anger, for *it was* fierce; and their wrath, for it was cruel: I will divide them in Jacob, and scatter them in Israel.

8. Judah, thou *art he* whom thy brethren shall praise: thy hand *shall be* in the neck of thine enemies; thy father's children shall bow down before thee.

9. Judah *is* a lion's whelp: from the prey, my son, thou art gone up: he stooped down, he couched as a lion, and as an old lion; who shall rouse him up?

10. The sceptre shall not depart from Judah, nor a lawgiver from between his feet, until Shiloh come; and unto him *shall* the gathering of the people *be*.

11. Binding his foal unto the vine, and his ass's colt unto the choice vine; he washed his garments in wine, and his clothes in the blood of grapes:

12. His eyes *shall be* red with wine, and his teeth white with milk.

13. Zebulun shall dwell at the haven of the sea; and he *shall be* for an haven of ships; and his border *shall be* unto Zidon.

14. Issachar *is* a strong ass couching down between two burdens:

15. And he saw that rest *was* good, and the land that *it was* pleasant; and bowed his shoulder to bear, and became a servant unto tribute.

16. Dan shall judge his people, as one of the tribes of Israel.

17. Dan shall be a serpent by the way, an adder in the path, that biteth the horse heels, so that his rider shall fall backward.

18. I have waited for thy salvation, O Lord.

19. Gad, a troop shall overcome him: but he shall overcome at the last.

20. Out of Asher his bread *shall be fat*, and he shall yield royal dainties,

21. Naphtali *is* a hind let loose: he giveth goodly words.

22. Joseph *is* a fruitful bough, *even* a fruitful bough by a well; *whose* branches run over the wall;

23. The archers have sorely grieved him, and shot *at him,* and hated him:

24. But his bow abode in strength, and the arms of his hands were made strong by the hands of the mighty *God* of Jacob; (from thence *is* the shepherd, the stone of Israel;)

25. *Even* by the God of thy father, who shall help thee; and by the Almighty, who shall bless thee with blessings of heaven above, blessings of the deep that lieth under, blessings of the breasts, and the womb:

26. The blessings of thy father have prevailed above the blessings of my progenitors unto the utmost bound of the everlasting hills; they shall be on the head of Joseph, and on the crown of the head of him that was separate from his brethren.

27. Benjamin shall ravin *as* a wolf; in the morning he shall devour the prey, and at night he shall divide the spoil.

THE dying words of Jacob to his twelve sons mark the close of the patriarchal dispensation. The family was already commencing its development into the nation, and it is in every way appropriate that the aged patriarch should foresee and foretell the general course of events which was to happen to his sons in the far-off future. The fact that he called his sons unto him in order to tell them what should befall them in the latter days shows the importance of the occasion, and its real bearing on the subsequent history of the twelve tribes in the light of God's great purpose for the patriarchs and their seed.

The chapter is usually described as the Blessing of Jacob, but it is obviously quite inaccurate to describe it in this way, since the predictions about several of the sons are characterized by the very reverse of blessing. The chapter is rather to be understood as a prediction of the results of character. It consists at once of a review of the past and a foresight of the future in the light of that past.

1. *The Certainty of the Fulfilment.*—The opening verses of the chapter clearly imply and assume the prophetic character of Jacob's words. Solemnly he called together his sons in order that they might hear "Israel" their father (vers. 1, 2). The words of the patriarch fitly come at this point, and mark a stage in the development of the Divine promise, which was first given in Eden concerning the seed of the woman, and then repeated and developed in the

blessings to Abraham and Isaac. Looking back over the record in Genesis, and looking forward to the time of Moses, these words of Jacob come midway between the earlier and later stages of the development of the Divine purpose.

It is impossible to overlook the great problem raised by modern writers in regard to this chapter. Are we to understand it as a genuine prediction of Jacob? Or is it to be interpreted as the utterance of a later writer some ages after the time of Jacob, who used this form for the purpose of conveying the lessons he wished to teach Israel?

On the one hand we have the very definite words of Dr. Driver, who says that "it is not to be supposed that the blessing was actually pronounced by Jacob . . . . The present with which the blessings contained in Genesis xlix, are connected is not the age of Jacob, but the age of the Judges, or a little later; and this accordingly is the period in which they must be supposed to have originated. . . . From the terms in which Judah is eulogized it may be inferred with tolerable certainty that the author was a poet belonging to that tribe" (*Genesis*, pp. 380, 381).

On the other hand Dr. Green is equally definite, saying that "the structure and contents of this blessing make it impossible to explain it as a *vaticinium post eventum*," and after arguing the matter in detail he concludes by saying that "All this points to the genuineness of this blessing as really the utterance of Jacob, which it claims to be, and is declared to be" (*Unity of Genesis*, pp. 522-524). It certainly seems difficult to understand how a later writer, in the time of the Judges or later, could have set down calmly what is here said of Levi, whose tribe at that time had the place of honor as the priestly tribe. Nor does it seem easy to understand how anyone writing as late as the Judges could have reflected so severely on the ancestors of the tribes of Reuben and Simeon. It is to be feared that most of the objections to this chapter as a genuine utterance of Jacob arise out of a too circumscribed and almost preconceived idea of what line prophecy should take, or else proceed on the assumption that prediction is impossible. Reviewing all the circumstances and the varieties of conclusions arrived at by critics of the passage (see

Green *in loc.*), it does not seem too much to say, with the editor of Lange's *Commentary*, that "There is but one part of the Scripture to which this blessing of Jacob can be assigned without making it a sheer forgery, and that, too, a most absurd and inconsistent one. It is the very place in which it appears. Here it fits perfectly. It is in harmony with all its surroundings; while its subjective truthfulness—to say nothing now of its inspiration or its veritable phophetic character—gives it the strongest claim to our credence" (Lange, *Genesis*, p. 651). Is there really any middle course? The chapter is either Jacob's, or is a forgery; and if it be the latter we naturally ask, What is its value, whether historical or spiritual?

II. *The Variety of the Fulfilment.*—Into the details of Jacob's predictions of his sons it is impossible now to enter. It would seem as though the announcements are grouped round two of the sons, Judah (vers. 3-18) and Joseph (vers. 19-27); six sons being associated with Judah and four with Joseph. So far as the character of each individual man is known, the patriach's words seem based upon his knowledge of what they were, and he predicts their future history in accordance with their individualities.

It would be profitable to ponder carefully what is said of each man individually under the guidance of a commentary like Driver's or Lange's, to discover first what is the true interpretation of each word and phrase, and then to read what is said in the light of the subsequent history of the tribes so far as it is known to us.

III. *The Accuracy of the Fulfilment.*—There can be very little doubt of the general, and in many respects exact agreement of what is here said with what actually happened in the subsequent history of the tribes. Thus Reuben is predicted as not able to excel (as he should have done being the firstborn) by reason of his instability, and this came literally to pass. "No judge, no prophet, not one of the tribe of Reuben is mentioned" (Smith's *Dictionary of the Bible*, article "Reuben," quoted in Dods' *Genesis*, p. 428). Again, Simeon and Levi are foretold as divided and scattered, which came literally true, for Simeon was absorbed in the South of Palestine, while Levi had no part in the land owing to his being appointed as the tribe from which the Jewish priesthood was taken.

The fulness of reference to Judah is another case in point, for we have only to remember that David came out of this tribe, to see that during the period of the monarchy these words were abundantly fulfilled. Not least of all is the accuracy with which the tribes of Ephraim and Manasseh realized the blessings here predicted for Joseph. Ephraim was the leading tribe for at least three centuries, and his land afterwards became the scene and centre of the Northern Kingdom of Israel.

All this goes to prove the essential truthfulness of the record of this chapter as a veritable utterance of the patriarch. Unless it is a true prediction, it is difficult to account for several features which are perfectly intelligible on the assumption of genuineness. Thus, if this chapter really dates from the time of the Judges, as is suggested by Dr. Driver, it is difficult to understand why there is so much of Judah in Genesis, while he is not mentioned in Deborah's song (Judges v.). The differences of reference to Issachar as compared with Deborah's song, and to Levi as compared with the blessing of Moses (Deut. xxxiii.) should also be observed. Surely this independence implies originality, or else a very definite attempt at forgery. As Dr. Redpath truly says, if there is any inspiration at all, insight into the future, based on a knowledge of personal characteristics, may well be included in it (Redpath, *Modern Criticism and Genesis*, p. 81). Prophecy has been defined (not quite fully perhaps) as "moral prescience," and it is suggested that we have in the present chapter one of its best illustrations. "This is no fancy painting. It is the power of the soul in its last efforts to see what crops will come out of this seed and of that; it is a man standing upon fields charged with seed, the quality of which he well knows, forecasting the harvest. Moral prophecy is vindicated by moral law" ("People's Bible," *Genesis*, p. 350). Add to this the supernatural action of the Spirit of God, and we may well rest our faith in the accuracy, and therefore in the moral value, of this chapter.

IV. *The Spirituality of the Fulfilment.*—The references to Jacob's sons go far beyond the merely temporal history of the Jewish nation. There are in it some of those very definite Messianic elements in which that history found its spiritual culmination. Thus, we find in the allusion to "Shiloh" a very true prediction of the Messiah as the "Rest-Giver" (ver. 10). Notwithstanding all that has been written on this verse during recent years, there is still good reason to interpret Shiloh as a personal name, as in the R.V. The alternative to this rendering seems very trite and altogether inappropriate to the detailed description of future power and glory associated with Judah. Even those who do not interpret the word "Shiloh" as personal say that the verse is undoubtedly Messianic in the broader sense of the term by reason of its anticipation of an ideal future for Judah (Driver, *Genesis*, p. 414). Those who still maintain the personal interpretation have a great deal to say for themselves after everything else has been considered on the other side.

Another element of the spiritual interpretation is seen in the exclamation, "I have waited for Thy salvation, O Lord" (ver. 18). This puzzles many commentators, and yet perhaps the true interpretation is not far to seek. In the preceding verse a reference had been made to an adder in the path that bites the horse's heels and causes the rider to fall backward. Is it not at least possible, not to say likely, that this allusion to a serpent recalled to the aged patriarch the primeval promise of the seed of the serpent bruising the heel of the seed of the woman? Then at once he burst out in earnest appeal to God for that salvation which had been promised as the result of the enmity between the two seeds.

The blessing of Joseph can hardly be limited to the subsequent history of Ephraim and Manasseh, but must include some of those spiritual elements which were evident and prominent throughout the subsequent history of Israel. It seems in every way best to regard the phrases in verses 24, 25, as a series of descriptions of God as "The Mighty One of Jacob," "the Shepherd," "the Stone of Israel," "the God of thy father," "the Almighty." In this full revelation of God lay the secret of Israel's uniqueness, and a guarantee of Israel's blessing (Maclaren, *Genesis*, pp. 295-304).

The chapter is so full of material that it is quite impossible to do more than suggest in the briefest way some aspects of teaching with special reference to daily, practical life. Taking the chapter as a revelation of personal character, we may regard the sons of Jacob as among those beacons of the Bible which are set before us, "written for our learning." Beacons are at once guides and warnings, and the delineation of his sons' characters by the aged patriach affords to us inspiration for imitation, and warning for avoidance.

1. *The danger of instability.*—We see this in Reuben. Of him it was true, "To one thing constant never," and what is especially sad is that the instability was due to sin. It is always so. Morality and character go together. To commit sin is to render ourselves unable to act aright because we become morally unstable.

2. *The disgrace of treachery.*—The description of Simeon and Levi is very terrible. Their father never forgot their treachery and violence to peaceful and harmless neighbors. There is scarcely anything more awful in life than treachery, more particularly when, as in the case of Simeon and Levi, it was associated with apparently religious motives and phraseology. We dare not do evil in the name of good.

3. *The blessing of sovereignty.*—Judah had fully redeemed his character, and the future depicted for him is one of glory and blessing. From him was to come the Messiah, and thence would issue blessing to the world. The life of power when exercised rightly will always be fraught with blessing to others. To serve is to reign, and to reign is to bless.

4. *The responsibility of opportunity.*—Zebulun is described as dwelling near the sea with the opportunity of providing a haven for ships. The Jews were never particularly enamoured of seafaring life, but this reference to Zebulun clearly shows the possibility of this method of living if they had been willing to seize upon it. It is worthy of notice that at the present day the only natural harbor in Palestine is that of Haifa, and the Hebrew word for "haven" (ver. 13) is thought to be the original from which the modern word Haifa comes. This would be interesting if true, especially as Haifa is not otherwise mentioned in the Old Testament. Opportunity ample and free comes in one way or another to us all. It is for us to seize it, and to be the means of blessing to others, or else by missing it to lose every chance of real life.

5. *The weakness of timidity.*—Issachar is described as occupying a very delightful position, and succumbing to the temptation of an easy life and of yielding to the slavery of others. He was content to bear burdens rather than to exert himself courageously on behalf of his own position and rights. How easy it is to let ourselves remain content with quiet life instead of exerting ourselves strenuously on behalf of what is right and good and true!

6. *The peril of subtilty.*—Dan is described as a serpent, biting and causing trouble. The subtilty of the serpent has become proverbial; and whilst the Apostle advises us to be "wise as serpents," the wisdom does not mean cunning, but that spiritual shrewdness which is essential to all true life. There is nothing more contemptible than cunning, and when cunning and deceit are used in connection with religion men sound almost the lowest deeps of infamy.

7. *The glory of victory.*—Gad is described as being overcome by a troop, but as overcoming at the last and pressing upon the heels of his enemies. Life is often associated with pressure and hardship, but victory is promised to the faithful soldier, and "to him that overcometh" there are blessings untold and everlasting.

8. *The privilege of felicity.*—Asher means "Blessed," and the promise to him is marked by fulness and real plenty. Blessedness is one of the marks of the true life. "Blessed is the man" (same root in Hebrew, Psa. i. 1). So long as we always remember that every aspect and element of blessedness is intended for use and service, and not for mere luxury, we may enjoy to the full all the blessedness and wealth of grace provided for us in the Gospel. The keynote of the New Testament, as of the Old, is "Blessed be the man" because God is a God of blessing. "The blessing of the Lord maketh rich."

9. *The need of activity.*—It is a little difficult to understand what is meant precisely by the reference to Naphtali, but it seems to refer generally to activity, vigor, and movement. The active life is always the happy life, and the easy-going is always the dangerous life. Activity is necessitated not only by our personal safety, but by the interests of the Kingdom of God. "Zealous of good works."

10. *The joy of prosperity.*—The blessing of Joseph may be summed up in the one word "fruitfulness," than which there is nothing more glorious in life. Fruit is the natural and necessary expression of the spiritual life, and the way in which our Lord emphasizes fruit (John xv.) shows the importance assigned to it in the Gospel. The man who, like Joseph, is true to God will ever bring forth fruit, and his life will abound in the "fruits of righteousness which are by Jesus Christ to the glory and praise of God."

11. *The value of ability.*—Benjamin is compared to a wolf, and in speaking of him as ready both morning and evening to go after his prey it would seem as though the idea were that "he is at all times equally ready for fighting, and equally successful in the wars which he undertakes" (Driver, *Genesis*, p. 394). Benjamin was the smallest of the tribes, and yet was one of the most martial. From this came Ehud and Saul, and in many other ways this very insignificant tribe became prominent for its courage, fierceness, and power. We may perhaps spiritualize and say that we must ever be ready with spiritual ability and agility to attack any task that may be placed before us, and carry it forward to a successful issue.

Reviewing all these various elements of character as suggested for us by these men, we may well ask ourselves, with the Apostle, "Who is sufficient for these things?" Character undoubtedly makes the greatest demands upon us. Other elements of natural power and ability may come easy to men, but moral and spiritual character requires much care and effort for its proper and full manifestation. Like the Apostle, we may, however, answer our own question, "Our sufficiency is of God." It is true that Character makes the Man; it is equally true that Christ makes the Character.

LXIIV

LIGHT AT EVENTIDE

GEN. xlix. 28—1. 14

28. All these *are* the twelve tribes of Israel: and this *is it* that their father spake unto them, and blessed them; every one according to his blessing he blessed them.

29. And he charged them, and said, unto them, I am to be gathered unto my people: bury me with my fathers in the cave that *is* in the field of Ephron the Hittite.

30. In the cave that *is* in the field of Machpelah which *is* before Mamre, in the land of Canaan, which Abraham bought with the field of Ephron the Hittite for the possession of a burying-place.

31. There they buried Abraham and Sarah his wife; there they buried Isaac and Rebekah his wife; and there I buried Leah.

32. The purchase of the field and the cave that *is* therein *was* from the children of Heth.

33. And when Jacob had made an end of commanding his sons, he gathered up his feet into the bed, and yielded up the ghost, and was gathered unto his people.

1. And Joseph fell upon his father's face, and wept upon him, and kissed him.

2. And Joseph commanded his servants the physicians to embalm his father: and the physicians embalmed Israel.

3. And forty days were fulfilled for him: for so are fulfilled the days of those which are embalmed: and the Egyptians mourned for him threescore and ten days.

4. And when the days of his mourning were past, Joseph spake unto the house of Pharaoh, saying, If now I have found grace in your eyes, speak, I pray you, in the ears of Pharaoh, saying.

5. My father made me swear, saying, Lo, I die: in my grave which I have digged for me in the land of Canaan, there shalt thou bury me. Now therefore let me go up, I pray thee, and bury my father, and I will come again.

6. And Pharaoh said, Go up, and bury thy father, according as he made thee swear.

7. And Joseph went up to bury his father: and with him went up all the servants of Pharaoh, the elders of his house, and all the elders of the land or Egypt.

8. And all the house of Joseph, and his brethren, and his father's house: only their little ones, and their flocks, and their herds, they left in the land of Goshen.

9. And there went up with him both chariots and horsemen: and it was a very great company.

10. And they came to the threshingfloor of Atad, which *is* beyond Jordan, and there they mourned with a great and very sore lamentation: and he made a mourning for his father seven days.

11. And when the inhabitants of the land, the Canaanites, saw the mourning in the floor of Atad, they said, This *is* a grievous mourning to the Egyptians: wherefore the name of it was called Abel-mizraim, which *is* beyond Jordan.

12. And his sons did unto him according as he commanded them.

13. For his sons carried him unto the land of Canaan, and buried him in the cave of the field of Machpelah, which Abraham bought with the field for a possession of a buryingplace of Ephron the Hittite, before Mamre.

14. And Joseph returned into Egypt, he, and his brethren, and all that went up with him to bury his father, after he had buried his father.

FEW of the deaths recorded in Scripture are more beautiful in their simplicity than that of Jacob. His departure from earth was not only the quiet, peaceful close of a chequered life; it also signalized the close of a very definite stage in the development of the Divine purpose concerning his seed.

I. *The Last Words* (xlix. 28-32). The words of Jacob concerning his twelve sons and their future came to a close with the reference to Benjamin, and as the end of the patriarch's life was at hand, he gave his sons his final Benediction: "Everyone according to his blessing he blessed them." Not one was overlooked, even though he had had to speak so faithfully about the temporal results of the sin of some of them. Each one was blessed with his own special blessing, and a legacy of benediction was left to them all. The retrospect, as he went over name after name, must have been as sad to him as it was to his sons; but at length all this was over, and only the Divine benediction was in the mind of their father. His affection for them was unshaken by anything that he had said, and he called down upon them each and all the blessing of the Lord his God.

With the blessing came a solemn charge. His mind was full of the promise made to Abraham and Isaac, and what he had said to Joseph (xlvii.) he pressed upon them all, charging them to bury him in Canaan in the field that Abraham purchased as a buryingplace. Egypt was no place for him; and although the fulfilment of God's promises was not to be realized during his life-time, he had no sort of doubt that a fulfilment would take place, and for this reason he wished to be buried in the Land of Promise. We can well believe, although it is not actually recorded, that his sons were just as ready as Joseph had shown himself to do according to their father's will.

II. *The Closing Scene* (xlix. 33).—At length everything was accomplished. The last counsel had been given, the last blessing bestowed, the last charge laid upon his sons, and then the aged patriarch "yielded up the ghost, and was gathered unto his people." In these two phrases we have a simple but very significant idea of what death meant to the patriarch. To God he yielded up his spirit, and with his people he was reunited. A careful study of the various references to the close of life in Genesis reveals more about the early ideas of death than we are accustomed to credit to the patriarchs.

III. *The Filial Love* (l. 1-6).—The loss to Joseph was necessarily great. He had lived, we may almost say, for his father, and as we review all the circumstances from the earliest days of his life we fully realize the closeness of the tie between them. "Joseph fell upon his father's face, and wept upon him, and kissed him." It is, perhaps, worth while observing that during those years of stress and hardship, with cruelty, disappointment and misunderstanding as his portion, we do not read of Joseph giving way to tears. We read of his tender feelings when he met his brothers after the lapse of years; but, so far as personal sorrow is concerned, this seems to be the first record of his feelings. There was nothing unmanly in these tears as he gazed upon the beloved form of the father who had been as devoted to him as he had been to his father. Henceforth life could not but be very different for Joseph. A blank had been made which could never be filled, and we cannot wonder at his sorrow.

In view of Egyptian custom, and also because of the dying charge of Jacob, the body was embalmed. Embalming was something of a testimony to a belief in the resurrection. "It was believed that the soul would in time return to its body after death, and pains were therefore taken to preserve the body from dissolution in the grave" (Driver, *Genesis*, p. 395). It is true that the idea was associated with metempsychosis, but even so it is one of those "broken lights" which bear their witness to the full Biblical truth of resurrection.

Seventy days altogether were devoted to mourning for Jacob; and as the usual time for mourning for a king was seventy-two days, we can readily see the respect that was shown to Joseph in this almost royal mourning for his father.

When the days of mourning were over Joseph approached Pharaoh through members of the royal household, asking permission to take the body of his father up to Canaan in order to fulfil the patriarch's dying charge. It is not quite clear why he did not go direct to Pharaoh. Probably it was because he was still in the habiliments of mourning with hair and beard uncut, or it may have been that he wished to associate himself for the moment with his brethren as the head of the family, rather than approach Pharaoh in his position as Prime Minister of Egypt. Pharaoh at once gave consent, and Joseph was free to carry out his solemn promise to his father.

IV. *The Complete Obedience* (l. 7-14).—The funeral cortège must have been a striking sight, for with Joseph "went up all the servants of Pharaoh, the elders of his house, and all the elders of the land of Egypt," besides the members of Jacob's family. Pharaoh clearly desired to pay the highest possible tokens of respect to Jacob in sending such a cavalcade with Joseph and his brethren.

When they arrived at the threshing-floor of Atad which is beyond Jordan, they remained seven days, according to the Hebrew time of mourning, and mourned "with a great and very sore lamentation." Even the Canaanites were impressed by this great sorrow and regarded it as of special import (ver. 11). Then "his sons did unto him according as he commanded them." The oath of Joseph (xlvii. 29, 30) was fulfilled, and Jacob was buried in the cave of the field of Machpelah. Just as Abraham had charged his servant not to obtain a wife for Isaac in the land of Canaan (xxiv. 2), so Jacob had charged his sons that they should not bury him out of the land of Canaan. This emphasis on Canaan shows beyond all question the deep impression made by the Divine promises, and the way in which those promises were cherished by succeeding generations.

Then came the sad return to Egypt. Joseph and his brethren and all that went up with him turned their faces from the Land of Promise to go back to the land of their adoption. We may perhaps imagine their questioning among themselves why they were not to stay in Canaan; why, after God's promise, they were not to abide in the land that had been assured to them. But the time was not yet. There was much to be accomplished before they would be ready for the land or the land ready for them. We may also think of them turning round as they finally left Canaan, to take a last look at some familiar scenes, perhaps with the thought that it was the last time they would ever have the opportunity of seeing the Land of Promise. Soon Joseph was engaged once more in his ordinary occupation in Egypt, with all its responsibilities; and though his father would never be forgotten, yet time and work would, as always, lay their healing balm upon his heart and life.

Leaving for further and fuller consideration the story of Jacob's life as a whole, it may be worth while looking at this story as revealing to us some of the aspects of a believer's death. "Let me die the death of the righteous, and let my last end be like his." What marks the death of the righteous as suggested by the close of Jacob's life?

1. *The power of faith.*—We observe Jacob's mind and heart occupied with God, His promises, and His grace. The blessing that he bestowed upon his sons showed that he was concerned with very much more than temporal blessings. "By faith Jacob, when he was a-dying, blessed each of the sons of Joseph, and worshipped, leaning upon the top of his staff." Happy, thrice happy, is that deathbed where God is a reality, and where faith in God is the strength and support of the passing soul.

2. *The glory of love.*—Death is the great reconciler.—There had been many a difficulty, many a conflict, many a sorrow in the relations of Jacob and his sons; and even on his deathbed it was essential that the patriarch, with prophetic insight and foresight, should speak quite plainly of some of the past events in their connection with the future. But even this did not affect his personal feeling for them, for he blessed them every one; and as they gathered round his deathbed the spirit of love possessed him, and as we may

believe possessed them all. Happy, thrice happy, is that deathbed where all alienations are at an end, and everything is peace and love.

3. *The expectation of reunion.*—The emphasis placed several times upon being "gathered unto his people" clearly shows that Jacob expected to be reunited with his loved ones. It is impossible to interpret a phrase like this to mean nothing more than being buried with them. It must mean that he looked forward to reunion and recognition as he and they were gathered together once again. This thought of a reunion thus hinted at, and more than hinted at, in the early pages of the Old Testament becomes fuller and clearer in the course of Divine revelation, until at length in the full revelation of the New Covenant it becomes one of the inspirations of life.

"Our own are our own for ever, God taketh not back His gift;
They may pass beyond our vision, but our souls shall find them out,
When the waiting is all accomplished, and the deathly shadows lift,
And glory is given for grieving, and the surety of God for doubt."

4. *The inspiration of hope.*—Jacob while on his deathbed not only looked up to a present God of grace and blessing; he looked forward also to a time when the promises of God to his forefathers would be fulfilled. The intense concern about being buried in Canaan was associated with the fulfilment of those promises. That cave in the field of Machpelah, with the precious bodies of his loved ones, was as it were an outpost, a guarantee, and a pledge of the complete fulfilment of God's promises. Like Abraham and Isaac before him, Jacob looked for a city which had foundations whose maker and builder was God. The fathers did not look only for transitory promises, for they were occupied with the thought of Resurrection. God is not the God of the dead, but of the living. All this is a thousand-fold clearer and more certain today. The Christian is inspired with the hope of the Resurrection. It is this that fills the horizon with light and joy. "The sky, not the grave, is our goal," and this hope of Resurrection transforms and transfigures death, and enables us to realize that it is only the gateway to the fuller life which is ours in Christ.

This is true dying. If God should call us through death to be with Him, happy will it be if we have the same faith, the same love,

the same hope, the same expectation, for then will the words find
their very literal fulfilment: "Blessed are the dead which die in the
Lord."

"How beautiful to be with God,
When earth is fading like a dream.
And from this mist-encircled shore
We launch upon the unknown stream!
No doubt, no fear, no anxious care,
But, comforted by staff and rod,
In the faith-brightened hour of death
How beautiful to be with God!

How sweet to lay the burden by,
The task inwrought with toil and prayer,
Assured that He Who calls will send
One better still the yoke to bear!
What peace, when we have done our best.
To leave the pilgrim path, long trod,
And in yon fields of asphodel
Snow-white, be evermore with God!

Beyond the partings and the pains,
Beyond the sighing and the tears,
Oh, beautiful to be with God
Through all the endless, blessed years;
To see His Face, to hear His Voice,
To know Him better day by day,
And love Him as the flow'rs love light,
And serve Him as immortals may.

Then let it fade, this dream of earth
When I have done by life-work here,
Or long, or short, as seemeth best—
What matters, so God's will appear?
I will not fear to launch my bark
Upon the darkly rolling flood;
'Tis but to pierce the mist—and then
How beautiful to be with God!"

LXV

JOSEPH'S LATER LIFE

GEN. l. 15-26

15. And when Joseph's brethren saw that their father was dead, they said, Joseph will peradventure hate us, and will certainly requite us all the evil which we did unto him.
16. And they sent a messenger unto Joseph, saying, Thy father did command before he died, saying,
17. So shall ye say unto Joseph, Forgive, I pray thee now, the trespass of thy brethren, and their sin; for they did unto thee evil: and now, we pray thee, forgive the trespass of the servants of the God of thy father. And Joseph wept when they spake unto him.
18. And his brethren also went and fell down before his face; and they said, Behold, we *be* thy servants.
19. And Joseph said unto them, Fear not: for *am* I in the place of God?
20. But as for you, ye thought evil against me; *but* God meant it unto good, to bring it to pass, as *it is* this day, to save much people alive.
21. Now therefore fear ye not: I will nourish you, and your little ones. And he comforted them, and spake kindly unto them.
22. And Joseph dwelt in Egypt, he, and his father's house: and Joseph lived an hundred and ten years.
23. And Joseph saw Ephraim's children of the third *generation*: the children also of Machir the son of Manasseh were brought up upon Joseph's knees.
24. And Joseph said unto his brethren, I die: and God will surely visit you, and bring you out of his land unto the land which he sware to Abraham, to Isaac, and to Jacob.
25. And Joseph took an oath of the children of Israel, saying, God will surely visit you, and ye shall carry up my bones from hence.
26. So Joseph died, *being* an hundred and ten years old: and they embalmed him, and he was put in a coffin in Egypt.

IT is inevitable that life should take on a different aspect after the death of one's parents. Even a middle-aged man cannot help realizing that he is only a son while his father is alive, but when his father has passed away there comes the full consciousness that henceforward he must stand in the front rank and take the lead. As long as Jacob was alive he was the head of the family, and everything connected with his household was necessarily influenced by his position, notwithstanding the fact of Joseph's high standing in the land of Egypt. It was only after Jacob's death that Joseph could really take the lead in matters affecting the life and welfare of his brethren. In the passage before us there are two distinct subjects connected with the people of Israel, in both of which Joseph is the central figure.

I. *Fear* (vers. 15-18).—It is with surprise that we find the old trouble between Joseph and his brethren brought up once more. It might have been thought at an end with the full reconciliation years before. But under the new conditions consequent upon the death of their father, Joseph's brethren conceived the idea that he would fully requite them all the evil they had done. This sense of guilt after so long a time is very striking. The men were now getting on in years, and yet remained fully conscious of those early sins and were in dread of their consequences. "It may be that Joseph will hate us, and will fully requite us all the evil which we did unto him." It is a characteristic of weak, base natures to find it difficult to believe in the nobility of others. They measured Joseph by themselves, and thought that he was harboring resentment and only biding his time. What a revelation of their own nature they thus gave! In our suspicions of other people we often reveal ourselves. It is so different to credit others with magnanimity and the spirit of forgiveness.

They thereupon sent a message to Joseph, probably (so we may imagine) by Benjamin, saying that their father commanded them before he died to ask Joseph's forgiveness. It is thought by some that this use of their father's name was unwarranted, and was only for the purpose of gaining favor with Joseph. On the other hand, it seems quite likely that Jacob said this when he observed their fears that after his death a very great change would occur. May it not also show that some barrier was felt by them, and perhaps even by Jacob also, during those years in Egypt, in spite of all that Joseph had done for them?

Their two-fold plea in sending this message is worthy of note. They based it first on this appeal to their father's memory, and then they spoke of themselves as the "servants of the God of thy father." Following this message they went themselves and made full submission to their brother, saying, "Behold, we be thy servants."

II. *Forgiveness* (vers. 19-21).—No wonder that "Joseph wept when they spake unto him." It was not the first time they had misunderstood and mistrusted him, and he doubtless felt the deepest pity for them as well as sorrow that they should have thought him capable of such unworthy feelings and intentions after all the years that had elapsed since his restoration to them. There is scarcely anything more trying and searching in life than the experience of being misunderstood, with motives misconstrued and intentions distorted. Joseph was, however, utterly unspoiled and unsoured by the various experiences of misunderstanding which fell to his lot throughout his life. He bade them not to fear, and reminded them that he was not in the place of God, that it belonged to God, not to him, to deal with their sin. At the same time he took the opportunity of speaking to them quite plainly about what they had done and what God had done in overruling their sin. "As for you, ye meant evil against me, but God meant it for good." We cannot fail to see the true reserve and the equally true frankness which characterize these utterances. What a comparison and contrast are here made! "Ye meant evil . . . but God meant it for good." And then he assured them once again: "Fear ye not: I will nourish you, and your little ones. And he comforted them, and spake kindly unto them." Distrust and misunderstanding are only too apt to embitter and deaden the nature. There are few things in life more hard to bear than ungrounded suspicion, but Joseph was superior to all these feelings, and instead of altering his attitude to them, he only assured them once again of his willingness to nourish them and their families, and to do all that he could for them. This is the true attitude to take up. When our good is evil spoken of, our best intentions misinterpreted, our loving actions suspected and even reviled, then is the opportunity for showing the true spirit of Christ and proving the reality of our profession. It is easy to write this, it is easy to conceive of it being done, but it is not by any means so easy to put it into practice. Yet God's grace is sufficient even for this, and it is in such ways that the genuineness of our religious profession is best proved.

III. *Faith* (vers. 22-26).—This last paragraph of Genesis refers to events fifty-four years after the preceding verse. Joseph's life in Egypt was doubtless lived in the ordinary routine of daily responsibilities and duties, and although he was necessarily engrossed with the demands of his important post we can see from the sequel that his heart was still true to the faith of his fathers. That faith enabled him to do his work loyally day by day, while at the same time it prevented him from being so entirely immersed in it as to forget the calls of his father's house.

Earthly joys were equally unable to remove him from the steadfastness of his faith. He saw the great-grandchildren of his son Ephraim and the grandchildren of his son Manasseh, and although he was surrunded with everything that was happy, bright and joyous in his home, and although every personal and family interest seemed to be inextricably bound up with Egypt, his faith enabled him to cling to God and never to forget the supremacy of the covenant with his fathers.

And the faith which enabled him to do his duty and to keep true amidst all the attractions of earthly happiness did not fail him when he came to die. He summoned his brethren, and in view of his approaching death gave them a solemn charge. "I die: but God will surely visit you, and bring you out of this land unto the land which He sware to Abraham, to Isaac, and to Jacob." The faith of his childhood was still working powerfully in his life, and his dying words clearly show where his heart had been all through the years in Egypt. He was the simple, God-fearing Hebrew to the very end of his days, and was not affected in the least by his high position, great responsibilities, and the fascination of life in Egypt. Once again we can see how possible it is for a man to serve God humbly and faithfully in the highest walks of life. God was first, and everything else was dominated by that simple but all-embracing principle.

Like his father before him, he took an oath of the children of Israel. "God will surely visit you, and ye shall carry up my bones from hence." Like Jacob, he was determined that Egypt should not be the final resting-place of his body. His heart was already in Canaan, and his body was to be there also. So at length he died, "and they emblamed him, and he was put in a coffin in Egypt." That coffin would be a constant reminder to the people of Israel of God's promise to their fathers. Joseph being dead would yet speak, and in the days that were not far ahead of them the coffin would remind them of the glorious future and inspire them with hope and courage amidst present difficulties.

"So Joseph died." Like the rest of us, even this noble man was called hence, withdrawn from the scene of his earthly labors, where his presence was so important and his life a constant benediction— a reminder that not even the best man on earth is indispensable. God will take care of His own work.

It is interesting and significant that the one event in Joseph's life seized upon by the writer of the Epistle to the Hebrews was that which was associated with his closing days. "By faith Joseph, when his end was nigh, made mention of the departure of the children of Israel, and gave commandment concerning his bones" (Heb. xi. 22). It was also an act of Jacob just as he was dying that is mentioned as the proof of his faith, in the same chapter (ver. 21). The comparisons and contrasts between the closing days of Jacob and Joseph give much food for thought.

I. *The faith of Jacob and Joseph.*—Jacob as he was dying thought chiefly of the past in desiring to be buried in the cave of Machpelah. He had been in Canaan a long time, and it was only natural that he should wish to be taken back there on his death. On the other hand, Joseph's thought was concerned with the future. "He made mention of the departure of the children of Israel," though that departure was not to take place for many a day. Joseph had grown up in Egypt, and to him Canaan was little more than a memory, so far as personal experience was concerned, but to him as well as to Jacob the place was the Promised Land; and thus Jacob's faith looked back as though to say, Do not forget the Canaan from which you have come, while Joseph's faith looked forward and said, Do not forget the Canaan to which you are going.

2. *The oath of Jacob and Joseph.*—It has been very helpfully suggested (Candlish, *Genesis*, pp. 338 ff.) that Jacob took the oath from his sons when they were in the midst of Egyptian plenty, peace, and happiness, and that Joseph took the oath from the brethren when the time of the bondage was not far distant. The one oath meant, "Rest not in Egyptian prosperity"; the other meant, "Faint not in Egyptian adversity." (See also Stock, *Lesson Studies in Genesis.*) The solemn promise elicited by Joseph that he should not be buried permanently in Egypt is a striking testimony to the power of his faith. It was a triumph over that sentiment which naturally thinks of resting in a hallowed burial-place. It was a triumph over the inevitable temptation to have that fine and magnificent funeral which was his due, and which would have been doubtless accorded him by the people of Egypt. Above all, it was a constant testimony to the supreme conviction which actuated him, and which he wished to perpetuate among his brethren, that God would surely visit them. While he was living his voice could speak, but afterwards that un-buried body would make its silent yet all-powered appeal. It kept before them the story of God's faithfulness, and was intended to inspire their hearts with undying hope as they waited for the day of deliverance.

3. *The first and last verses of the Book of Genesis.*—The contrast between i. and l. 26 is surely more than an ordinary coincidence. The book opens with life, it ends with death—"a coffin in Egypt," because in between had come sin which brings forth death. And yet that coffin spoke of life as well as of death. It was a symbol of hope, a message of patience, a guarantee of life everlasting. Joseph may not have known very much of the future life, but the fact that he pledged them to carry his body is a proof that in some measure at least he believed in immortality. Genesis, with its coffin in Egypt, was followed by Exodus, which means departure, deliverance; and Joseph spake of that exodus which they were to accomplish in God's time. After nearly 200 years of watching and waiting that coffin was carried up out of Egypt: "And Moses took the bones of Joseph with him: for he had straitly sworn the children of Israel, saying, God will surely visit you; and ye shall carry up my bones away

hence with you" (Exod. xiii. 19). Then for forty years it accompanied the people of Israel wherever they went, and at length came the fulfilment of Joseph's hopes and of the solemn promise of his brethren. In the days of Joshua "the bones of Joseph which the children brought up out of Egypt buried they in Shechem" (Josh. xxiv. 32). At Shechem they now show the tomb of Joseph. Travelers are interested in a little enclosure wherein is a small mound by the side of which grows a vine. Not very far away is another spot equally associated with the story of Joseph, for it was there that the brethren cast their brother into the pit and plotted against his life. He little thought when suffering at the hands of his brethren that a larger number of mourning descendants would accompany his body 200 years afterwards to its burial at Shechem.

4. *The perpetual presence and persistent purpose of God.*—One lesson above all others is writ large in the story of Jacob and Joseph, as it is indeed in the entire narrative of Genesis. "I die: but God shall be with you" (xlviii. 21). "I die: but God will surely visit you" (l. 24). One Name abides all through these centuries, the Name of the everlasting God. Adam, Noah, Abraham come and go; Isaac, Jacob, and Joseph live their lives and pass away; but God remains, the Dwellingplace of His people in all generations, "God from everlasting to everlasting." "God buries his workmen and carries on His work." Well for us if we realize this simple but all-embracing truth. Amid all the changes and chances of this mortal life God abides, God reigns, God rules. His kingdom will be set up, His purposes shall be realized, His will must be done. Let us take heart of grace as servant after servant of God passes into the unseen. Let us take large views of the future, and not be tempted to concentrate attention solely upon our own narrow little life in the present. "I die: but God will surely visit you." It is this assurance of God's unchanging presence and undeviating purpose that alone can keep the heart peaceful, restful, trustful, and hopeful amid all the vicissitudes of life. "Thou wilt keep him in perfect peace, whose mind is stayed on Thee: because he trusteth in Thee. Trust ye in the Lord for ever: for in the Lord Jehovah is an everlasting rock."

"Why do we worry about the nest?
    We only stay for a day,
Or a month, or a year, at the Lord's behest,
    In this habitat of clay.

Why do we worry about the road,
    With its hill or deep ravine?
In a dismal path or a heavy load
    We are helped by hands unseen.

Why do we worry about the years
    That our feet have not yet trod?
Who labors with courage and trust, nor fears,
    Has fellowship with God.

The best will come in the great "To be,"
    It is ours to serve and wait;
And the wonderful future we soon shall see.
    For death is but the gate."

LXVI

"THOU WORM JACOB"

THERE is perhaps no character recorded in Scripture about which there has been more controversy than that of Jacob. His very weaknesses seem to attract us because they make him more human, and bring him into closer contact with our own lives. There is an intense reality about the man from the first that impresses every reader, and gives rise to constant discussion as to his merits and demerits. In all ages of the Church people have been attracted and even fascinated with his history, and his individuality will doubtless continue to make him a prominent figure for ages to come.

I. *Jacob's History.*—We need not do more than call attention to the seven periods of his life, during each of which he was being trained and disciplined. He is first seen at home under the influence of his strong-minded and strong-willed mother Rebekah. Then comes the crisis at Bethel, when he came into personal contact with God, perhaps for the first time in his life. This notable event was followed by the years in the service of Laban, that time of intense and prolonged discipline which had so much to do with his later life. Then came Peniel, another turning point in his career, when he became conscious not only of the House of God (Beth-el), but also of the Face of God (El-beth-el), and surrendered to God the control of his life. Peniel was, however, followed by a period of backsliding at Shechem, with all that resulted of trial and sorrow to himself and his household. At length came the return to Bethel, and with it the restoration to Divine favor and fellowship, and an upward advance in the spiritual life from which he never afterward receded. Last of all came those quiet, restful, fruitful years in Egypt, when, restored to his beloved son, he lived in happiness and at length died in peace.

In all this history we must not fail to see the importance of the first vision at Bethel, the mysterious struggle at Peniel, and the return to Bethel once more. At this last visit things took a permanent turn for the best. We see this in the usage of the two names, Jacob and Israel. From the moment of the restoration at Bethel (ch. xxxv.) it is deeply interesting to study carefully and closely the occurrence of these two names. In almost every case "Israel" is used in connection with his spiritual life and experience as the Prince of God.

II. *Jacob's Character.*—What puzzles most readers is the striking contrasts in this remarkable man. Almost all through his life there was a blend of two different and in themselves divergent qualities. There are men brought before us in Scripture like Moses, David, Isaiah, St. Paul and St. John, who were by no means without their faults and sins, but all these are almost entirely forgotten in the glory of their character and devotion to Christ. It is somehow different with Jacob. There was on the one hand a remarkable quietness and gentleness of disposition, and on the other an intense ambition to be the head of the family and the inheritor of the promises. On the one hand there was a genuine devoutness, a clear perception and full appreciation of the Divine covenant with his fathers, while on the other hand there was an utter self-seeking disposition which stopped at nothing to gain its ends. On the one hand there was a love which centered itself first upon his mother, then upon his wife, and then upon his two boys, while on the other hand there was a caution, a hesitation, a suspiciousness that seemed to distrust everybody but himself. On the one hand he was a man of high aims working for high ends, while on the other he stooped to the meanest methods and the most contemptible ways of accomplishing his purposes. He was indeed a mixture, a glaring contrast of opposite qualities.

The slow development and progress of his character is also very noteworthy. It would have been far happier for him and for everybody connected with him if the transformation of Jacob into Israel had been made more quickly and more thoroughly, but the old nature was not only never wiped out, it seemed to be strong and

vigorous almost to the last. Jacob was still there even though Israel
was making his way. The ultimate victory of the Israel nature is
very clearly seen. There was a gradual victory of the higher over
the lower in him. We cannot help noticing his steadfastness of purpose amidst all difficulties, trials, and opposition, his prudence and
forethought as he faced the problems of his life, and, above all, a
genuine appreciation of Divine realities and of everything that was
best and truest in human life. Whatever appears on the surface,
there can be very little doubt that from his earliest days Jacob had
set his heart upon the possession of all that was possible in the
Covenant of God with his fathers, and as he draws near to the end
of his life we can see quite clearly the results of the discipline in the
strength and even glory of his character and life.

III. *Jacob's Training.*—The one thing of importance in life is the
power of making permanent our passing ideas and impressions.
Character is only built up gradually as our experiences become part
of ourselves. Jacob was brought back to fellowship with God, and
enabled to abide in fellowship by training in three schools.

The School of Personal Sorrow. Colors are painted upon earthen-
ware, and then burnt in, in order to be made permanent. So it was
with Jacob. Sorrow made and left its permanent mark upon him.
The discipline in Haran, his disappointment over Rachel, Rachel's
death, Reuben's sin, the hatred and loss of Joseph, the famine, the
demand for Simeon and Benjamin, are some of the ways in which
sorrow dealt with him and trained him for God.

The School of Divine Providence. In his youth he was evidently
full of indomitable hardness and self-reliance, and all through his
career we find proof after proof of the native force and vigor of
his character. He was ever a man of quick initiative, ready resource,
and dauntless courage. Up to the end of his life he took the lead,
and not even Joseph superseded him in the patriarchal position. It
was therefore all the more necessary that he should be dealt with by
the discipline of life. God's providence is man's inheritance, and it
was the very best thing that could have happened to Jacob that the

roughnesses of his nature were made smooth, and his weaknesses taken away in the hard, stern school of Providence. There is nothing like it to develop character. No chastening seems profitable at the time, but in the retrospect we see and acknowledge that it yields the peaceable fruits of righteousness.

The School of Divine Grace. This was the greatest and best training-ground of Jacob's life, and it enables us to understand the prolonged nature and even the severity of the discipline in the other two schools. From the vision at Bethel to the closing days in Egypt, God's presence was with Jacob whether he knew it or not. That presence was assured to him, and he never really forgot the wonderful promise, "I am with thee, and I will not leave thee," which he received at Bethel. Thence-forward the promises of God were his strength and stay. He pleaded them, depended on them, and believed to see their fulfilment. Meanwhile God's power was at work in his soul, dealing with him now in severity, now in goodness, until at length he could say, "I have waited for Thy salvation O Lord."

IV. *The God of Jacob.*—There is scarcely anything more striking in the whole of the Old Testament than the frequency of the title, "the God of Jacob," in the Psalms and in Isaiah. We could well understand God being the God of Israel, but to be called the God of Jacob is surely the crowning proof of Divine mercy and grace. What a remarkable point there is in the well-known words, "The Lord of Hosts is with us; the God of Jacob is our refuge" (Ps. xlvi. 7). "The Lord of Hosts" is the God of Providence, protecting against foes, overcoming difficulties, and providing for all emergencies, but "the God of Jacob is our refuge" is very much more than this. It tells of His mercy and grace. The God of Jacob is a God of unwearying love, of unerring wisdom, of unfailing grace. He is our Refuge in spite of our sins, in the face of our failures, in view of our fears. And because He is all this He asks for our unreserved surrender, our unquestioning faith, our unflinching loyalty, our unfailing hope, and whispers in our hearts, "Fear not thou worm Jacob . . . I will help thee, saith the Lord, and thy Redeemer is the Holy One of Israel." It is because God is the God of Jacob that we have such unbounded confidence in His mercy and grace, in His love and longsuffering. It tells us what grace can do for even the very worst of us. As a man said to a clergyman not long ago, "I am cheered when I read the life of Jacob; for if the grace of Almighty God was able to straighten up that man, there must be some hope for me" (see a fine Sermon on Jacob, by the late Ian Maclaren. *Homiletic Review*, vol. liv. p. 49).

LXVII

"A FRUITFUL BOUGH"

THE character of Joseph is one of the choicest and most striking of all those in Holy Scripture. The fulness of detail which characterizes the record of his life from beginning to end clearly shows the importance attached to him by the writer, both personally and as an instrument for the fulfilment of the Divine purposes concerning Israel. Not only in Genesis, but in other books of the Old Testament, Joseph is brought before us as a man upon whom the Divine blessing signally rested, and in whom God's grace was very definitely manifested (Deut. xxxiii. 13-16; Ps. cv. 17-19; Acts vii. 9, 10).

I. *His History.*—The story of his life falls quite naturally into eight periods, each of which has its special interest and its direct bearing upon his life and character. He is seen first of all at home in the days of his youth as the companion of his father, and it is evident that he was a fit and willing pupil of the aged patriarch as he was told of God's covenant with his fathers. Then the hatred and jealousy of his brethren had no effect in spoiling the beauty of that early promise. We find him next in slavery, and now the promise of the early days begins to be fulfilled. Integrity, purity, honor, and faithfulness characterize him and make him steadfast and true to his God. In prison, too, he maintains his position, and in faithful obedience to his daily round and common task, he glorifies God and is made a blessing to those around him. At Pharaoh's court he next appears revealing the secrets of the monarch's dream and declaring God's will concerning Egypt. This led at once, as we have seen, to the remarkable transformation of the prison slave to the Prime Minister. His home and work in Egypt next come before us, and in spite of the remarkable change in his circumstances he is the same simple and true-hearted man as ever. His relations with his brethren serve to reveal other aspects of his life, while the meeting with his father was the crowning point after years of trial, sorrow and discipline. The last fifty years of his life in Egypt reveal him as still the same in his nobleness of mind and heart, and in his genuine confidence in and obedience to the Lord God of his fathers. Whether then we think of him as a youth, a young man, a middle-aged man, or an old man, there is a continuity in his life, amid all circumstances, which stands out as one of the noblest and most striking features of a remarkable career.

II. *His Character.*—We must however go further into detail, and seek to delineate more thoroughly the various points in his character that stand out from the narrative. He seems to have belonged to God from the very first. His father doubtless gave him his first impressions and ideas of the glories of their Covenant God, and the seed fell upon good ground, and led from the very outset to a life of true-hearted devotion. But what in particular are the points of his character that were evidently seen and written for our learning? They can only be mentioned, but it will be well worth while to turn to the particular parts of his life, where these features appear, and ponder them again in the light of his history. Here are some of those qualities that make up the truest, noblest, and best types of manhood: (1) Guilelessness, (2) frankness, (3) tactfulness, (4) sensitiveness to evil, (5) purity of heart and life, (6) humility of word and deed, (7) wisdom, (8) executive ability, (9) filial affection, (10) manly energy, (11) resolute adherence to duty, (12) prudence, (13) self-control, (14) sympathy, (15) hopefulness, (16) considerateness, (17) equanimity, (18) courage, (19) patience, (20) large-hearted generosity. These are perhaps the most important features, though there are doubtless others that can be found. Joseph was good without ever being "goody-goody." He was great and yet simple, true to God and yet attractive to man. He is a signal instance of the possibility of combining piety with success, manliness with true religion, intellectual force with spiritual fragrance. There are few men whose lives are more full-orbed and complete in moral beauty and glory.

III. *His Secret.*—What was the secret of all this power? The answer is that God was an ever-present reality. "I fear God." This was the keynote of his life. The name of God was often on his lips, but still better, the presence of God and the fear of God were always in his heart. It was as natural to him to refer everything to God as it was to breathe or to speak, and whether he thought of the danger of sinning against God (ch. xxxix. 9), or the blessing of God upon his own life (ch. xli. 51, 52), or the providence of God in allowing him to go into Egypt (ch. xlv. 5-9), or the assurance that God would not leave his brethren (ch. l. 24), God dominated Joseph's life, and this was the secret of all that he was and did.

How did he learn this secret? We cannot but believe that it began in those early days at home with his father. His devotion to his father was, we may well believe, not merely due to the human relationship, it was based upon spiritual kinship as well. It is hard to say which is the more beautiful, Jacob's devotion to his son or Joseph's devotion to his father. It is a testimony to both that God was so real in their lives. It is always well if the consciousness of God can come early in life. There is no need for a period of wandering, and of sowing wild oats to be a strong, vigorous, noble, manly Christian. They are the strongest and best who find God early, who live from the very first days in His presence, surrounded by a parental life and love which breathes the atmosphere of devotion and fellowship.

How was this secret developed? By simple loyalty and obedience to every day duty. Joseph always did his best. Faithfulness characterized everything about him, and God was the source, center, and spring of every word and action of his life. This must ever be the supreme method of deepening religious impressions, and of realizing in daily experience the lessons we have learned from our earliest days.

How was this secret proved? By its results. God justified His servant's trust and confidence by honoring him in slavery, in prison, at court, and in his home. No life lived for God is ever without its vindication. "Them that honor Me I will honor," and the man who sets out, as Joseph did, to put God first and make God real in life will always find it true that God sets His seal of favor and blessing upon him.

How was this secret continually made effectual? The answer is in the simple but significant words of the Epistle to the Hebrews, "By faith, Joseph." It was simple trust in God that enabled him to be what he was and to do what he did. What is it in faith that makes it so powerful? What is there in trust which brings about such results? Faith *realizes* God's presence and lives in it moment by moment. Faith *relies* on God's Word and believes that what He says shall be done. Faith *responds* to God's call, and obeys with readiness and loyalty. Faith *receives* God's grace, and finds it all-sufficient for daily needs. Faith *rests* in God's will, and believes to see the goodness of the Lord in the land of the living. Faith *rejoices* in God's protection, and knows that it shall not be put to shame. Thus faith is man's complete response to God's revelation. It links man's life to God, and provides him with the simple yet all-powerful secret of a life of power, purity and progress. Well may the Word of God lay stress upon faith. "Without faith it is impossible to please him." "This is the victory that overcometh, even our faith."

LXVIII

A TYPE OF CHRIST

IN addition to the lessons from Joseph as a historical person which are so clear that he who runs may read, there are other points of profound interest and importance in which his life has some very striking and remarkable points of comparison and contrast with that of our Lord. It is perhaps too much to say that we have in this the element of prediction, because there does not seem to be a single reference in the New Testament to the typical nature of Joseph's life, and yet it is impossible to avoid seeing the close, prolonged, and striking resemblances between Joseph and Christ. It is not mere ingenuity that endeavors to see in the story of the one some of the outstanding events in the life of the Other. While we are careful not to proceed to fanciful extremes, it is not only legitimate, but in every way spiritually profitable to ponder the life of Joseph in the light of the history of our blessed Lord (see Candlish, *Genesis*, vol. ii. 138-146).

I. *Joseph and His Father.*—Joseph was the beloved son of his aged father Jacob, and those early dreams clearly indicate that he was the subject of high destinies. There was to be in some way or other a remarkable future for this beloved son. In like manner our Lord Jesus Christ was the Only Begotten of the Father. "Thou art my Beloved Son in Whom I am well pleased." He too was appointed heir of all things, and the destinies of the world were linked with Him.

II. *Joseph and His Brethren.*—We notice three points in the story in this connection. (1) He was sent to inquire after his brethren's well-being. (2) His brethren were envious of him, being altogether out of sympathy with their father's love and purposes concerning him. (3) Joseph, however, maintained his faithfulness, not abating his testimony, but speaking frankly and fully that which he believed to be right. He might have been spared the pit had he been willing to yield to his brothers' wishes. In all this we cannot help seeing the Lord Jesus and His brethren. (1) Was He not sent by His Father? (2) Were not His brethren envious of Him, being altogether opposed to the Divine purpose as expressed in Jesus Christ? (3) Did He not, however, abide faithful, bearing testimony with dauntless courage, telling both high and low of their sin in the sight of God? He might have spared Himself the Cross had He been willing to abate His testimony and keep silence in the face of opposition.

III. *Joseph's Rejection.*—Once again we notice the story for its typical lessons. (1) His brethren conspired against him, "Come let us kill him." (2) He was betrayed by his brethren. (3) He was sold by his brethren for money. When we turn to the pages of the New Testament we are struck with the almost literal agreement with these events in the life of our Lord. "When they saw him, they said, This is the heir, let us kill him." "He came unto His own and His own received Him not." Our Lord, too, was betrayed and sold by His brethren into the hands of the Gentiles. Just as the sight of Joseph brought out all that was latent in the anger and animosity of the brethren, so Christ by His life and teaching brought out all that was evil in the human heart, so that they no longer had any cloak for their sins (John xv. 22).

IV. *Joseph's Humiliation.*—Once again let us trace the story of the Hebrew lad. (1) He became a servant and entered into the degradation of slavery. (2) He was sorely tempted and yet sinned not. (3) He was alone in the dungeon through no fault or sin of his own. (4) He won the respect of his jailer and was entrusted with responsible service. (5) He was the means of blessing to the butler and the messenger of judgment to the baker. Again we are impressed and even awed by the striking agreement point by point with our Lord's earthly history. He took upon Him the form of a servant. He was tempted in all points like as we are, without sin. He was alone, forsaken of God and man, and yet on the Cross He called forth the admiration of the centurion, was the means of blessing to the penitent robber, and the occasion of judgment to the impenitent one. Surely in all this we may find food for prayerful meditation and whole-hearted adoration.

V. *Joseph's Exaltation.*—As Joseph stood before Pharaoh we notice that his exaltation accomplished three ends. (1) It revealed God's purposes for Egypt. (2) It manifested God's righteousness in bringing him out of prison. (3) It established Joseph's position as next to Pharaoh. When our Lord was raised from the dead He was exalted to be a Prince and a Saviour. God raised Him and gave Him glory. He was declared to be the Son of God with power. God set Him at His own right hand, exalted Him, and put all things under His feet until that day when the Son shall have delivered up the Kingdom to God the Father and God shall be all in all.

VI. *Joseph's Marriage.*—We notice that this marriage was appointed by Pharaoh, and in the New Testament we read of a certain King that made a marriage for His Son. We are also told of the Church which is at once the Body and the Bride of Christ, the figure of the Body suggesting the union of life, the figure of the Bride the union of love. In the case of Joseph the bride was a stranger to him, and the Bride of Christ consists of those who were once estranged and alienated by wicked works, and are now reconciled to God by the death of His Son. Joseph's bride shared his glory; all the nearness and intimacy of true wedded life belonged to her. His position gave her her position; she was what she was because she was his wife. So is it with the Bride of Christ. As He is so are we in this world. The Church is to share His glory. Not only are we crucified together, we are raised together, and even now seated together, and by and by shall reign together with Him in glory.

VII. *Joseph's Office.*—Why was Joseph exalted? What was the purpose of it? It was not for his own sake, but that he might become the channel of blessing to the whole world. So also our Lord was exalted to be a Prince and a Saviour to give repentance and remission of sins (Acts v. 31).

The work of Joseph's life was to provide food for the people. During the famine it was to him that they turned, and from him they received all that they needed. By some authorities his Egyptian name Zaphnath-paaneah is interpreted to mean the "bread of life," but whether this be the case or not he certainly was the bread of life to the people. Our Lord came as the Bread of Life. "I am come that they might have life." There is, however, one significant difference between the type and the ante-type. The people came to Joseph to buy bread, but we come to Christ "without money and without price" (Isa. lv. 1).

The order of Joseph's work is very striking. He provided first for the Gentiles as represented by Egypt, then he provided for his brethren, and subsequently all nations came to Egypt to buy corn. May we not see in this some slight adumbration of the order of our Lord's spiritual work in the accomplishment of God's purposes? His Church today is mainly composed of Gentiles, those who are willing to receive Him, but the day is coming when He will reveal Himself to His brethren the Jews, and they will look upon Him Whom they pierced, and be reconciled to Him with tears of repentance. Then will come, and only then, the blessing to the whole world, and the reign and rule of Christ as King of Kings and Lord of Lords.

(For the typical meaning of Joseph's revelation to, and reconciliation with his brethren, see page 116.)

There was one sole condition of blessing during the years of famine. That was unconditional submission to Joseph. He was their saviour because he was their master. They trusted him wholly, and their trust was justified by the marvelous and perfect provision that he made for all their needs. This is the one and only requirement in things spiritual. Unconditional surrender, unquestioning submission, unwavering trust. When this attitude is taken up and maintained our spiritual needs are all provided for, our wants met, our desires satisfied, our lives protected, our hopes realized. Christ is only truly our Saviour in proportion as He is our Lord. Whenever people came to Pharaoh he had one word and one word only for them: "Go unto Joseph, and what he saith to you, do." So is it today. In view of all our needs, sins, sorrows, weaknesses, failures, fears, one word suffices for them all: "Whatever He saith unto you, do it."

LXIX

REVIEW

IN the light of all the details which have come before us in our meditations on the Book of Genesis it may be well worth while to review the entire book, and endeavor to gain an idea of its general purpose, plan, and meaning. In our first chapter we considered several points by way of introduction, and we may now add to these some further suggestions for general study. We must ever strive to obtain and keep a true idea of the book as a whole.

The literary structure of Genesis is, as we have seen, clear and simple. It consists of an introduction and ten sections, each with a virtually identical heading. But there is a religious unity in the book as well as a literary oneness, and for this reason it should be studied as a whole, and an impression formed of its general character. All authorities, whatever their critical views, agree in regarding the book in its present form as characterized by unity. The genealogies form a regular series, and even the apparent digressions are strictly in accordance with the fundamental principle of the book as a book of beginnings. Still more, the religious aim is ever kept in view, showing how under the guidance of Divine providence the purpose of redemption was accomplished by separating a chosen man and a chosen race from all others.

The early chapters (i—xi.) show the descent of Abraham from Adam, and explain why a new commencement was necessary. They also reveal God's principle of selection in the choice of Seth, Noah, Shem and Abraham. The law of selection governs the entire narrative, and is a special sign of unity. First of all there is the selection of a special people as represented by Abraham, then the selection of a special land, then the preparation of the patriarchs by Divine discipline, and all this arising out of the prediction concerning the seed of the woman.

We see therefore in these chapters the continuous development of the Divine purpose as it adjusts itself to the circumstances brought about by the sin of man. Everything in human life and civilization, human sin, and human worship is made to subserve the Divine will and contribute to the accomplishment of the Divine purpose. Starting with the great fact and feature of the unity of all mankind as represented first by Adam, and then by Noah and his descendants, we are led on step by step until attention is concentrated on one branch of the human race as the special medium of the Divine revelation.

Then comes the great section (chs. xii.—l.), in which we have the record of the providential training of the patriarchs for their part in the fulfilment of the Divine will. There is no hiatus or dislocation after the early chapters (i.—xi.), but a very distinct order and progress. After three failures in the persons of Cain and Abel, the races of the Sethites and Canaanites, and the family of Noah, a new commencement was necessary, and instead of a covenant of works with the entire human race a covenant of grace is instituted with one individual. With Abraham's call a special series of Divine manifestations is brought before us which were evidently intended to teach him by delivering him from his own errors, revealing to him the one true God, and leading up to fellowship with God.

The patriarchal narratives are the story of the way in which God trained and disciplined Abraham, Isaac, Jacob, and Joseph to fulfil His purposes. The narrative is brought before us in three different sections or cycles associated with the names of Isaac, Jacob and Joseph. God's covenant with Abraham is prepared for, made, and fully realized (ch. vi. 27—xxv. 18); then that covenant is maintained by means of the Divine revelation to Isaac as the head of the family after Abraham's death (ch. xxv. 19—xxxvii. 1); and finally the chosen family develops into a nation by the providential preparation for its departure into Egypt, the providential removal into Egypt, and the providential protection in Egypt (ch. xxxvii. 2—l. 26).

The Divine promise was continually confirmed during the course of the history, and a gradually-developing idea of God's character and relation to the people was being formed. As we read the story we are conscious of growth, progress, consolidation, and an ever-widening movement until at length both Jacob and Joseph have the future clearly and steadily in view, and look forward with certainty to deliverance from Egypt and a settlement in Canaan. "God will surely visit you," is the last keynote of this memorable book as Genesis closes and leads on to the next stage of the development of the Divine purpose in Exodus.

The value of this book is therefore evident. It is in some respects the foundation of the Biblical revelation of God. It is the germ and explanation of everything that follows in the history of Divine redemption through the seed of the woman. It may almost be said that there is no truth of the Bible that is not found here in germ. Thus the seven great doctrines which form the warp and woof of the Bible are all in this book. (1) The Doctrine of God as Creator, Preserver, Law-Giver, Judge, Redeemer. (2) The Doctrine of Creation as the act and process of the Divine will, wisdom, and power. (3) The Doctrine of Man in his contact both with earth and heaven, a union of flesh and spirit in a twofold nature. (4) The Doctrine of the World as the sphere of the human race in its unity, variety, and divisions. (5) The Doctrine of Human Life, first as individual, then as social and in the family, then as tribal, and at length gradually developing into national life. (6) The Doctrine of Sin as the assertion of man's independence of God, his unwillingness to remain loyal to the Divine will, with the results of evil both negative and positive in the loss of holiness and fellowship with God, and the impossibility of rendering to God the obedience and glory due to His Name. (7) The Doctrine of Redemption, with the universe as its sphere, man as its subject, Divine grace as its source, the Covenant as its method, and the people of Israel as its repository and instrument. Redemption is found in promise and in symbol, and is prepared for by the onward march of Divine providence. When Genesis is carefully studied along these lines we readily see that it contains the promise and potency of that varied, prolonged, and complete development which we find elsewhere in the Bible.

We must therefore take care to study Genesis not merely as a book of history, or even as a record of human character, human sin, human discipline. It is much more than all these, for it is a record in some of the stages in God's gracious endeavor to lead man back to Himself. It is only in the light of its specific religious purpose that we can understand both what it omits and what it contains.

It is evident, therefore, that Genesis will never yield its true meaning unless it is considered in constant view of the presence of a supernatural element in it from first to last. God and Redemption are its keynotes, and in these are found the essential features of the book and the true explanation of its difference from all others, and its infinite superiority over all other works dealing with the early days of the human race.

Above all, Genesis must ever be studied as the first book of a volume which is called the Word of God. Its presence in this volume is the simple fact that gives it whatever authority it possesses. Unless we ever keep in mind its place as an integral part of a volume which we believe to be in some sense divinely inspired, we shall never enter into its meaning or really profit by its lessons.

If therefore the book is studied and pondered in the light of its clearly arranged contents, its varied lines of teaching, its definite religious purpose, its manifest principle of unity, and its evident marks of progress, it will be found to be one of absorbing interest, profound spiritual value, and perennial importance for mind and heart and life.

THE END